Developments in American Politics 7

Edited by
Gillian Peele
Christopher J. Bailey
Bruce E. Cain
and
B. Guy Peters

Editorial matter, selection and Chapter 1 © Gillian Peele, Christopher J. Bailey, Bruce E. Cain and B. Guy Peters 2014

Individual chapters (in order) © Gillian Peele, Jon Cohen, Bruce E. Cain and Peter J. Ryan, Lee Drutman, Philip J. Davies, Jon Herbert, Aaron Ray and James A. Thurber, Cornell W. Clayton and Lucas K. McMillan, Paul L. Posner, Christopher J. Bailey, Richard C. Fording, B. Guy Peters, John Dumbrell, Desmond King.

First published 2014 by
PALGRAVE MACMILLAN

Palgrave Macmillan in the UK is an imprint of Macmillan Publishers Limited, registered in England, company number 785998, of Houndmills, Basingstoke, Hampshire RG21 6XS.

Palgrave Macmillan in the US is a division of St Martin's Press LLC, 175 Fifth Avenue, New York, NY 10010.

Palgrave Macmillan is the global academic imprint of the above companies and has companies and representatives throughout the world.

Palgrave® and Macmillan® are registered trademarks in the United States, the United Kingdom, Europe and other countries

ISBN 978-1-137-28922-3   hardback
ISBN 978-1-137-28921-6   paperback

This book is printed on paper suitable for recycling and made from fully managed and sustained forest sources. Logging, pulping and manufacturing processes are expected to conform to the environmental regulations of the country of origin.

A catalogue record for this book is available from the British Library.

A catalog record for this book is available from the Library of Congress.

Printed in China

Contents

List of Tables, Figures and Maps

Tables

Figures

Map

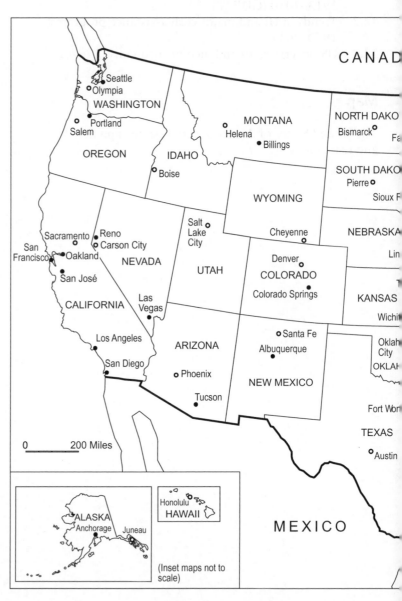

The United States of America: states, state capitals, and main cities

Key:
● Major cities/conurbations
○ State capitals

Preface

This is the seventh volume of *Developments in American Politics*. It addresses a number of themes in American politics at a time when the capacity of the governmental system is increasingly questioned and politics and society appear divided over a wide range of issues. These divisions were seen in the elections of 2012 which returned President Obama to office but which also left Republicans with a majority in the House of Representatives and failed to give Democrats a commanding majority in the Senate. This outcome posed a number of severe problems for governance in America and generated questions about politics and policy in the country. Individual chapters in this book explore the political landscape that followed the 2012 elections and the policy dilemmas facing the second Obama administration. As with previous volumes our aim is to provide a timely and stimulating account of key aspects of contemporary American politics and an understanding of the institutions of American government. Although our primary focus is on recent developments, we recognize the importance of providing sufficient historical context to allow a full appreciation of the current controversies and debates.

Once again we have been privileged to have secured an outstanding team of contributors from both sides of the Atlantic. By tradition the book uses American spelling in order to convey the color and idioms of American political life. Major references are collected at the end of the book and there is also a short guide to further reading for each of the chapters.

The editors would like to thank our publisher Steven Kennedy and his team at Palgrave Macmillan (Helen Caunce and Stephen Wenham) for their support and encouragement. Thanks are also due to our colleagues at the universities of Oxford, Keele, Stanford and Pittsburgh. We are also immensely grateful to Graeme Wallace, Meryl Nolan and Emma Alexander for research assistance and to Janet Wardell and Glynis Beckett for secretarial help and support.

GILLIAN PEELE
CHRISTOPHER J. BAILEY
BRUCE E. CAIN
B. GUY PETERS

Acknowledgements: We are grateful to *The Washington Post* and the Kaizer Family Foundation for permission to reproduce the material in Table 3.3, and Figures 3.1 and 3.2; to Keith T. Poole and Howard Rosenthal for permission to cite material from vote-view.com contained in Figures 4.1 and 4.2 and in Figures 8.4 and 8.5; and to Kay Schlozman for permission to use data in Figure 5.1.

Notes on the Contributors

Christopher J. Bailey is Professor of American Politics at Keele University, UK.

Bruce E. Cain is Professor of Political Science at Stanford University, USA, and Director of the Bill Lane Center for the American West.

Cornell W. Clayton is Director of the Thomas S. Foley Institute for Public Policy and Public Service, and the Cornell Johnson Distinguished Professor of Political Science at Washington State University, USA.

Jon Cohen is Vice-President of Research at the Pew Research Center. He was formerly Director of Polling at *The Washington Post*.

Philip J. Davies is Director of the Eccles Centre for American Studies at the British Library and Professor Emeritus of American Studies at De Montfort University, Leicester, UK.

Lee Drutman is a senior fellow at the Sunlight Foundation and an adjunct professor at the University of California and Johns Hopkins University, Baltimore, USA.

John Dumbrell is Professor of Government at Durham University, UK.

Richard C. Fording is Professor of Political Science at the University of Alabama, USA.

Jon Herbert is Senior Lecturer in American Politics at Keele University, UK.

Desmond King is the Andrew W. Mellon Professor of American Government at the University of Oxford, UK.

Lucas K. McMillan is a doctoral student in Political Science at Washington State University, USA and Editorial Assistant at the *Political Research Quarterly*.

Gillian Peele is Fellow and Tutor in Politics at Lady Margaret Hall, Oxford, UK.

B. Guy Peters is Maurice Falk Professor of American Government at the University of Pittsburgh, USA.

Paul L. Posner is Professor and Director of the Centers on the Public Service at George Mason University, USA.

Aaron Ray is a doctoral student in Political Science at American University, Washington, DC, USA.

Peter J. Ryan is Visiting Ptofessor at the University of California, Washington Center, USA.

James A. Thurber is Distinguished Professor of Government at American University, Washington, DC, USA, and Director of the Center for Presidential and Congressional Studies.

List of Abbreviations and Acronyms

AARP	American Association of Retired Persons
ACA	Affordable Care Act 2010
ACLU	American Civil Liberties Union
ACOs	Accountable Care Organizations
AFDC	Aid to Families with Dependent Children Program
ANES	American National Election Studies
APSA	American Political Science Association
ARRA	American Recovery and Reinvestment Act 2009
BCRA	Bipartisan Campaign Reform Act 2002
BLS	Bureau of Labor Statistics
BRIC	Brazil, Russia, India, and China
CMF	Congressional Management Foundation
CPS	Current Population Service
CRS	Congressional Research Service
DCCC	Democratic Congressional Campaign Committee
DNC	Democratic National Committee
DOJ	Department of Justice
DOL	Department of Labor
DREAM Act	Development, Relief, and Education for Minors Act
DSCC	Democratic Senatorial Campaign Committee
DW-NOMINATE	Dynamic, Weighted, Nominal Three-Step Estimation
EEOC	Equal Employment Opportunity Commission
EITC	Earned Income Tax Credit
EPI	Economic Policy Institute
FCCP	Office of Federal Contract Compliance Programs
FEC	Federal Election Commission
FECA	Federal Election Campaign Act 1971
FHA	Federal Housing Authority
FIRE sector	Finance, Insurance and Real Estate
FNC	Fox News Channel
GA	General Assistance
GAO	Government Accountability Office
GDP	Gross Domestic Product
GOP	Grand Old Party (Republican Party)

HLOGA	Honest Leadership and Open Government Act 2007
HMOs	Health Maintenance Organizations
LDA	Legislative Disclosure Act 1995
NATO	North Atlantic Treaty Organisation
NFIB	National Federation of Independent Business
NGA	National Governors Association
NRA	National Rifle Association
NRCC	National Republican Congressional Committee
NRSC	National Republican Senatorial Committee
PAC	Political Action Committee
PPACA	Patient Protection and Affordable Care Act 2010
PPIP	Public Private Investment Program
RNC	Republican National Committee
SCHIP	State Children's Health Insurance Program
SNAP	Supplemental Nutritional Assistance Program
SSA	Social Security Act 1935
SSI	Supplemental Security Income
TANF	Temporary Assistance for Needy Families
TARP	Troubled Assets Relief Program
UI	Unemployment Insurance
UMRA	Unfunded Mandates Reform Act 1995

Chapter 1

Introduction: Obama's Second Term

Gillian Peele, Christopher J. Bailey, Bruce E. Cain, and B. Guy Peters

The contrast between the optimism which surrounded Barack Obama's first election victory and the weary relief which greeted his second win was stark. The electoral mood of the United States in 2012 had often seemed as negative as had been the campaign. No sooner was victory in the bag than the media turned their attention to the multiple problems facing the President in his second term, most notably the budgetary conflict that was a legacy of the 112th Congress. The challenge of working with a continuing, albeit smaller, Republican majority in the House, and a Senate where the Republican minority could use the filibuster and other procedural devices to obstruct business, also loomed large on the horizon. The legislative gridlock which had marked the last two years of Obama's first term, concerning raising the debt ceiling and budgetary issues, quickly reappeared in his second term. Although going over the so-called 'fiscal cliff' was avoided at the last minute, Senate Republicans seemed poised to block Obama's new cabinet and sub-cabinet nominees, underlining the antagonistic relationship between the legislative and executive branches and the intensely partisan atmosphere in Washington. A few months into the new Obama Administration a significant number of important executive positions remained unfilled.

Tensions in the American polity

The tensions at the outset of Obama's second term of office reflect both long term changes in American society, in the economy and the political system as well as shorter term shifts in tactics and strategy on the part of key political actors. Census and other data continue to confirm a series of profound demographic shifts which promise to transform the face of the United States and have challenging implications for the political system. Foremost among these changes is the country's ethnic mix. Pew Center Reports commenting on the Census Bureau's analysis of the 2012 presidential election noted that the non-white percentage of voters was 26.3 percent, although the non-white population was 33.9 percent. (A significant part of the non-white population was either ineligible to vote or did not participate in 2012. However, it should be noted that in this year black turnout exceeded that of white Americans for the first time.) By 2020 the non-white population was projected to grow to 37.2 percent and by 2060 it would be 54.8 percent (US Census Bureau, 2012, 2013; Taylor and Lopez, 2013). An earlier (2008) analysis had suggested that between 2005 and 2050 the population would rise from 296 million to 438 million with 82 percent of that increase coming from new immigrants and their descendants (Passell and Cohn, 2008). Put starkly, the white population of the United States would become a minority by 2060, outnumbered by the combination of a fast growing Hispanic community, African Americans and Asians. Within the US population there has been a major growth of the Hispanic/Latino minority. Already a majority in some states, by 2050 this will be the largest ethnic group, and one in three Americans will be Latinos. Traditionally Hispanic Americans 'punch below their weight', and in 2012 their turnout at 48 percent was lower than that of both the black (66.2 percent) and the white groups (64.1 percent). But as the Pew Center and others have frequently pointed out, Hispanics have a high share of the under 18 population (24 percent) compared with their presence in the population as a whole (17 percent). Time and generational replacement will naturally enhance their clout in the electorate, especially as these younger Hispanics are mainly American citizens and thus eligible to vote; they are also socialized within the country and so are more likely to participate in elections. These demographic shifts pose a challenge especially for the Republican Party whose limited appeal to ethnic America was underlined by Mitt Romney's inability to attract more than 17 percent of the non-white vote in 2012 (Taylor and Lopez, 2013).

The United States has always been a diverse society which has been made and remade by immigration. The sources of new immigration changed radically after 1965 when the abolition of national origin quotas opened the way for more immigration from Latin America, Africa and Asia. The country is also a fast-growing society. In 2010 the population stood at 308.7 million which was a major increase of nearly 10 percent on the previous census figure recorded in 2000. The proportion of the population which was foreign born was high – around 12 percent in 2010, although this figure may be an underestimate. On one level this might seem to promise political gains for the Democrats in the longer term. On another level it could produce a bitter renewal of ethnic hostilities in the nation's politics.

Certainly these demographic shifts have not been universally wel-comed across the United States, making the discussion of both legal and illegal immigration policy contentious. By the time of the George W. Bush presidency (2001–09) there was a stiffening of attitudes towards illegal immigration and much discussion of initiatives to make entry into the country harder, including the building of a projected wall along the Mexican border. State-level initiatives to deal harshly with illegal immigrants included a 2010 Arizona statute which strengthened police powers to check the status of anyone they had reasonable cause to suspect was in the country illegally. Although parts of that law were struck down by the Supreme Court in 2012 (in *Arizona et al. v. US*) the hostility and mindset endured.

President Obama himself had come to office committed to promoting legislation that would aid the path to citizenship especially for young illegal immigrants of good character. However, a Congressional initia-tive to achieve this (known as the DREAM Act) failed and immigration reform seemingly dropped down Obama's list of legislative priorities, although he did use his executive power to try to achieve some modifi-cation of the treatment of immigrants. Notwithstanding that disap-pointment, the Latino community (which had at various points over previous decades been courted by the Republicans) gave him strong support in 2008 and 2012. Solidifying the fast growing Latino vote is extremely important for the Democratic Party and its chances of rebuilding its majority status in the electorate at large. Immigration reform remains contentious, however, and a bill drafted by a bipartisan group of senators had by 2013 run into stiff opposition, although it had also divided Republicans.

Apart from the changes in ethnic composition mentioned earlier, there were other demographic shifts of importance to the character of American society and politics. Complex changes in the age structure of the United States also seem likely to produce political tensions. Growth in the numbers of the aging population has long been seen as a problem for the funding of many government services. To some extent the growth in the younger age groups may compensate for the enhanced numbers of seniors. On another level it may signal the possi-bility of conflict between the generations over scarce resources as well as of strain on the social programs – Social Security and Medicare – on which the elderly rely.

There is also some evidence that the number of female headed households has grown in recent years. This demographic shift also seemed problematic for the Republican Party. Certainly in the recent elections the Republicans have experienced difficulty attracting the votes of women who, in addition to concern about such issues as reproductive freedom, have been increasingly concerned about eco-nomic fairness.

These demographic projections have had implications beyond the two parties and they may have contributed to a hardening of Republican tactics in relation to the electoral system. They raised questions about the country's identity and created a sense of uncertainty that was reinforced by economic and international challenges. Here, the rise of China and other BRIC economies threaten American economic pre-eminence and arguably contribute to a sense of unease about America's place in the world. Taken together these developments have undermined faith in the United States as a country where progress was assured and where the standard of living would inevitably rise from generation to generation.

The challenges to American identity and fears about the country's future prosperity have fed into the politics of America in the early 21st century. A resurgent right-wing populism exemplified by the Tea Party movement gained traction in and from the 2010 mid-term elections by highlighting concerns about taxation, about the size and role of government, and about social and cultural values, echoing the impact of the religious right of earlier years. This movement, which brought many new activists into politics, in turn influenced the Republican Party, constraining its leadership who feared retribution in the polls if they departed from the conservative orthodoxy by compromising with the President. This intractable style of politics, which was evident in Obama's first term, continued unabated in Washington, DC, after 2012, frustrating efforts to address major policy issues and creating an atmosphere in which a series of short-term fixes had to be adopted in the absence of executive-legislative agreement. Obama's second term seems likely to be marked by bitter partisan conflict, and his prospects for any policy achievement appear dependent on his skill in circumventing Congress.

The challenges for the Obama Presidency

The increasingly polarized party system presented a difficult context for Obama even from the moment of his first victory in 2008. Obama had entered office in 2009 making a tactical peace with his primary opponent Hillary Clinton and holding out the promise of a bipartisan approach to governing. But even the first term had seen him struggling to find agreement with an ideologically inflexible Republican Party which after the 2010 mid-terms had a majority in the House and which was highly sensitive to its own right-wing fiscal hawks and its Tea Party activists. Securing economic recovery still posed the major challenge, although by April 2013 there was a glimmer of recovery evidenced by a fall in the unemployment rate to 7.5 percent, its lowest since December 2008. In addition to continuing nervousness about the

American economy, however, there were a host of foreign policy problems and domestic issues on the national agenda, including immigration and gun control. The issue of gun control had become especially pressing as a result of the massacre of school children and teachers in Connecticut.

The gun control question illustrates the difficulty of addressing contentious policy issues in the United States. It is not merely that America's divided political institutions and ideologically antagonistic political elites take radically different sides on such questions as whether gun ownership should be regulated. It is also that some of the key players in the debate – the wealthy and well-organized single issue groups such as the National Rifle Association (NRA) – have the capacity to influence politicians and the public through their strategic use of extensive campaign contributions and publicity.

Understanding the Obama Presidency

Whether Obama can navigate the political and constitutional obstacles to governing effectively and provide the strong leadership necessary for America to tackle its multiple domestic problems, let alone provide secure guidance in the international arena, is a key question. The likelihood of Obama delivering a successful second term of his presidency depends on a number of factors, including his character and strategic sense, the institutional context, and what some scholars of the presidency now refer to as 'presidential time' (Skowroneck, 1993). None of these factors seemed clear cut in 2008, and they remain uncertain today. Part of the puzzle reflects continuing uncertainty about the skills, priorities and capacity of the president himself.

The Obama enigma

The American presidency is a highly personalized institution. The public and the media as well as other political actors naturally focus on the personality of the incumbent and his leadership style. Presidents themselves encourage voters to believe that a change in who occupies the White House can have a major impact on public policy and improve social and economic conditions for America's citizens. The rhetoric of promise, however frequently dashed in practice, remains a constant feature of political discourse. Obama's call for 'change we can believe in' was simply the most recent of a series of appeals to the electorate to invest in the better future on offer from a presidential aspirant. The reality of the American political system is a limiting constitutional system designed to check and balance executive power. It is also one which provides multiple veto points which can be exploited by America's multiple and frequently wealthy interest groups. American pluralism has always been skewed towards established well-financed groups but that bias has become more evident, especially as a result of the Supreme Court's dismantling of legal constraints on campaign expenditure. However much successive presidents have bridled at the constraints of their office and sought to overcome them, they have found their opportunities to implement their agenda restricted by the constitutional design of the Founders, by the tangle of interests able to frustrate policy initiatives and by the contingencies of political life.

Few recent presidents can have brought to the office such symbolism through their election as did Barack Obama in 2008. The victory held not just the promise of an end to racial injustice but of a more ideologically liberal and progressive steer to public policy. As will become apparent in these chapters, however, the extent to which either racial or more general social and economic equality have been fully achieved is open to doubt. The interesting question, for those who seek to understand Obama's style of leadership, is the extent to which, underneath all the rhetoric of change, he really embraced a radical agenda on entering office. How far were his initial policy choices driven by core ideals and deep-seated values? Put slightly differently, did Obama bring to the presidency an outlook that was ideologically coherent and, if so, what had shaped that ideology? Or was the reality a shrewd, pragmatic and detached politician whose approach to governing was driven by tactical concerns rather than principled considerations? And crucially we need to ask how far his understanding of the presidency has changed with the experience of government.

Part of the difficulty in answering these questions stems from the relative obscurity from which Obama had risen to be a presidential candidate in the first place. But part of it also reflects Obama's adaptation to a changing political situation and the emerging new strategy for dealing with Congressional opposition which faced him after the 2010 mid-term election defeat.

Efforts to understand the mind set of Barack Obama and his place in the Democratic tradition have already generated a raft of writing, some of it highly polemical. Much of it has focused on the unusual background of Obama and his family influences, especially on an alleged hatred of colonialism (d'Souza, 2010; Remnick, 2010; Marannis, 2012). One of the intriguing features of the Obama presidency has indeed been the extent to which he has occasioned criticism both from the right (which has generally portrayed him as undermining American values and corroborating in America's global decline) and from the center left which has deplored his unwillingness to be more radical. For those opposed to him on the right there have been a range of criticisms which suggest he is un-American, even alien. For those who have opposed him from the left he has seemed too cautious in his approach to the economy, unwilling to spend political capital and put his presidency on the line behind reforms, and more dedicated to continuity with his predecessor in foreign policy than his campaign rhetoric suggested. And, despite the symbolism of being the first black president, there has been some disillusion both among black Americans, who have felt him unsympathetic to their social and economic plight and not 'black enough', and among other groups looking for substantive policy reform especially on immigration.

The separation of powers

Presidents know that they have to manage a complex system of shared powers and that the constitutional framework may frustrate their agendas. Even without the opposition which comes from having a different party control Congress, the separation of the executive and the legislative branch can constrain a president as it did in the cases both of President Carter (1977–81) and President Clinton (1993–2001). When in the first two years of his presidency (2009–10) Obama had a formal majority in both chambers it was clear that his party troops under Nancy Pelosi's leadership in the House and Harry Reid's in the Senate would not allow their support to be taken for granted (Grunwald, 2012).

Obama came to power in 2009 with an overwhelmingly Democratic House and a Senate just short of the 60 votes needed to overcome a filibuster. With the switch of Arlen Spectre to the Democrats that strength became a nominal 60, although control was tenuous because of the veteran Senator Ted Kennedy's terminal illness. When Kennedy died, the loss of his Massachusetts seat to a Republican in 2009 prefigured the heavy Democrat losses in 2010. These losses were fueled in part by the sudden rise of intense opposition to Obama and the mobilization of the anti-government Tea Party movement. Power in the House changed hands, although the Democrats kept their majority in the Senate.

The 2010 mid-terms dealt the Democrats a bitter defeat and pitted Obama against a Republican majority whose leadership was itself nervous of pressure from Tea Party and other right of center activists and which, as a result, was less open to the possibility of bargaining. By contrast with the 111th Congress, in which the President had scored some notable legislative victories including the passage of the momentous health care reform, the 112th Congress was marked and marred by a series of procedural wrangles and nail-biting negotiations over the economy. There was little legislative achievement.

In addition to the constraints imposed by a House in Republican hands after the 2010 mid-terms, Obama faced a Supreme Court which had been shaped by his Republican predecessors and had a conservative majority. While Obama could expect to make at least one or two appointments to the Court, and did nominate two new justices (Sonia Sotomayor and Elena Kagan) in his first term, the timing of the vacancies meant that he was reshaping the personnel, but not the ideological balance, of the Court. And that will almost certainly be true of any second term judicial selections to the Court unless Anthony Kennedy, frequently the swing vote on the Court, were to retire. The character of the Court matters to a president, not just because it has the capacity to cut down legislation central to his agenda, but also because it can change the context of the political competition and affect the situation of different groups within America's diverse society. Since the Reagan Presidency the Court has been reshaped with a conservative majority whose jurisprudence is sharply at odds with that of liberals. President Obama's health care legislation was vulnerable to constitutional challenge; and although in the end the Court upheld it in *National Federation of Independent Business* v. *Sibelius*, the prospect of a constitutional overthrow was a real one notwithstanding the implications of such an outcome. The Court's conservative disposition has the potential for fundamental and traumatic conflict with the elected branches, and such a stand off may yet occur. But even without a replay of the constitutional battles of the New Deal, the Court has had a major political impact, even in the period since 2008, especially on the electoral process itself as the Court handed down a series of decisions affecting campaign spending. The Court's agenda as Obama entered his second term of office underlined its importance for American society. Not merely was the divisive issue of gay marriage on the agenda but so too was affirmative action which had been a central but highly contested strategy in liberal efforts to promote equality for racial and other disadvantaged groups.

The American constitutional framework has been made the more difficult to operate by its contemporary political dynamics, especially the intense partisanship and 'asymmetrical polarization' which have marked the parties since the 1980s (Abramowitz, 2010; Mann and Ornstein, 2012). The explanations of why this polarization has occurred are varied and range from the impact of primaries to the consequences of partisan reapportionment. Yet whatever the explanation, there is little doubt that an intense partisanship has affected the way key national institutions work and has had a profound impact on politics at every level of the political system. Congress has clearly been affected by this development but so too have other aspects of the political system, including at the state level where questions of party advantage have set an aggressive new agenda for the approach to electoral rules, for example. As a result, partisanship and its consequences are major themes in this book and run through many, if not most, of the individual chapters.

The political order

The question of partisanship leads to the issue of where Obama stands in relationship to the wider political order or regime, the cycle of forces which constitute the context in which a president must operate (Skowroneck, 1993). The period from Reagan's election victory in 1980 can generally be seen as one in which conservative ideas and Republican politics were dominant. The last years of the George W. Bush presidency saw the conservative coalition splitting apart over foreign and domestic policy disputes (Aberbach and Peele, 2011). The important issue here is whether the election of Obama in 2008 was a sign that the conservative era had passed, to be replaced by a more liberal one. Or was the election victory the product of more short-term factors, most notably an unpopular president in the person of George W. Bush and an economic downturn which was generally deemed the worst since the Great Depression of the 1930s?

Defining the character of a presidency in terms of its relation to the political order is probably easier in retrospect than simultaneously. However, the Democratic mid-term defeat of 2010, the eruption of the Tea Party movement, the continuing conservative tilt of public opinion and the outcome of the 2012 Congressional elections suggests at least that caution is necessary in proclaiming the end of the conservative movement and the dawn of a new progressive liberal era. Although it is not entirely clear how Obama himself interpreted his 2008 victory, his second inaugural address offers a much stronger statement of his commitments and values and especially of his concern to promote the goal of equality. It was commitment to the idea of equality, he argued, that had made America exceptional (Obama, 2013). Obama forcefully made the point that the country could not succeed 'when a shrinking few do very well and a growing many barely make it'. Nor would the journey be complete until the country's wives, mothers and daughters could earn a living 'equal to their efforts' and its 'gay brothers and sisters' were equal under the law.

The reason for probing the meaning of an election victory and analyzing the interpretation given to it by a president is of course that it will shape his understanding of his priorities and how much freedom he has to define his agenda. It may also be an indication of how he should mobilize support for that agenda. An uncertain meaning is likely to focus presidential attention on the practical matter of day to day governing in a system which is more effective at blocking initiatives than facilitating them. The obstacles and constraints erected by the constitutional system and the United States institutional arrangements are not insurmountable: a president with the appropriate skill set and personality to identify and exploit the opportunities for brokerage and to forge consensus from antagonism may flourish (Edwards, 2012). It is, however, very likely that his will be a series of small and incremental victories rather than the transformative achievements so often promised on the campaign trail.

Learning to govern

Learning to govern and how to exploit the authority of the office tend to grow with time but this learning curve will usually involve some false steps along the way. It is a paradox of the American system that competence and confidence in managing the process of governance tends to be in inverse proportion to the ability to make use of those qualities. Presidents see things more clearly as their time is running out. But the second term of a presidency has its own negative features. The individuals whose support and advice may provide strength for the chief executive at the beginning of an administration are unlikely to last the course, so that a president in his second term may find himself with a ticking clock and the need to reconstruct and rejuvenate his administration. Certainly Obama's second term has seen a series of major changes to the inner team including the replacement of Hillary Clinton at State by Senator John Kerry and of Timothy Geithner at Treasury by former Chief of Staff Jack Lew. Obama also selected Republican Chuck Hagel as Secretary of Defense to replace Leon Panetta, an appointment which initially occasioned considerable opposition from former Republican colleagues. Observers noted that Obama's second-term team reflected a certain preference for insiders and known allies and was also less ethnically diverse and had fewer women than his first-term team.

The public policy agenda

Presidential prospects are also deeply affected by the issue agendas they face as well as by the unpredictable events which erupt during their time in office. For Obama the major factor shaping his presidency was the economy and the legacy of the Great Recession of 2007–09. Although he inherited continuing wars in Iraq and Afghanistan, it was the impact of the economic environment that was the most baleful inheritance from Bush. Unemployment when Obama took office in

January 2009 was 7.6 percent and in December 2012 it was 7.8 percent. Although, as noted earlier, the jobless total has since improved, two important factors give cause for continuing concern. First, the American unemployment figures almost certainly conceal a much higher level of joblessness because some long-term unemployed do not register. Second, the distribution of unemployment is not spread evenly across the country: economic distress is felt especially keenly by America's ethnic minorities. In particular America's black and Latino minorities were hit harder than white Americans. By the time of Obama's re-election in 2012 African American and Latino unemployment rates were 13.4 and 11 percent respectively, compared with a national average of 7.8 percent. Behind these stark unemployment statistics was an even harsher picture of differential suffering in relation to education, health status, housing and life expectancy. Poverty again displayed a sharp ethnic dimension.

The United States is no stranger to inequality despite the mythology of unbounded opportunity and the efforts to extend that opportunity equally in the period after 1945. The heightened inequality of the early 21st century – greater concentration of wealth which allowed some critics to refer to a new 'gilded age' and a more intense and recalcitrant poverty – is a complex phenomenon which pervades much of the discussion in this book. Whose fault this sharpening of inequality is, and what if anything can be done about it, remain key questions permeating the specific issues on the American political agenda. Obama and the Democrats had won in part as a result of class-based concerns. In more favorable economic and political conditions they might have been expected to address the problem of poverty with substantive legislative initiatives. In the constrained political and economic circumstances in which Obama took his oath of office for the second time, it was not clear what room he or his party had for maneuver.

The United States in 2013 was thus a society deeply divided by inequality and opportunity differentials; but it was also one where some of the long-standing optimism about the future had been eroded, not least because of the apparent impotence of government to change material conditions.

The structure of the book

The chapters that follow all touch in various ways on these themes. Gillian Peele (Chapter 2) asks the question of whether the American political system is broken. She looks at the apparently dysfunctional effect of the traditional Madisonian model and notes how some commentators have begun to suggest the incompatibility of this model with the partisanship of recent years (Mann and Ornstein, 2012). She looks not only at the extent to which aspects of the American constitutional framework as a whole have has ceased to work well in relation to its key governing institutions including the Supreme Court, but also suggests that there has been a growing dissatisfaction with the quality of American democracy as a result especially of the growing power of wealthy interests in electoral politics and an undermining of faith in the fairness of the electoral system. However, the difficulty of formal constitutional amendment in the United States makes it unclear how these weaknesses can be resolved. Such fundamental questioning of the American constitutional design and about the quality of American democracy does however make it likely that the political agenda will be concerned with issues of political reform for some time to come (Levinson, 1988, 2006; Lessig, 2011; Cain, forthcoming).

Clearly ethnic and other divisions feed back into the voting behavior and beliefs of the different groups in the electorate. In Chapter 3 Jon Cohen revisits the 2012 elections and traces the electoral changes underpinning Obama's successful quest for a second term. As he notes, many of these changes have been long in the making and many of the demographic changes are troubling for the Republican Party.

Bruce Cain and Peter Ryan (Chapter 4) analyze the meaning of electoral change for the parties and especially in the changed circumstance of a world where restrictions on campaign finance are fewer. Their discussion of the new partisanship – its roots and likely endurance – provides essential clues to the operation of the political system as a whole. Lee Drutman (Chapter 5) looks at the mobilization of special interest in politics and at the changes in the world of lobbying, changes which have occasioned a good deal of critical comment among observers. Philip Davies (Chapter 6) explores the developments in the traditional media and in newer social media, assessing their impact on the electoral system and on the terms in which politics are discussed in the United States.

All of these changes in the political mood of the United States and in its political dynamics feed into the operation of its key institutions which seem to many observers to be functioning imperfectly. Jon Herbert (Chapter 7) takes as his starting point the tension between Obama's recognition of the highly partisan environment in which the presidency now operates and the need to transcend that partisanship. And he, like Gillian Peele, suggests that in his second term Obama is likely to embrace a stronger conception of executive power in order to govern. Similarly Aaron Ray and James Thurber (Chapter 8) show how Congress has been affected by intense partisan loyalties and the erosion of a willingness to seek consensus. They highlight a series of problems with Congress and its inability to function and suggest some possible remedies. Cornell Clayton and Lucas McMillan (Chapter 9) show how the ideological agenda of successive Republican presidents has affected the jurisprudence of the Supreme Court and reshaped its own institutional identity.

In Chapter 10 the theme of institutional dysfunction arises again in Paul Posner's discussion on federalism. The American states in their governance arrangements and in their financial viability have suffered in recent years despite the promises of many Republican presidents to restore their political position. The states are also key agents in the crafting and delivery of so many of the services required by ordinary American citizens and, if they are debilitated, the policy process in many areas will also be undermined. Chris Bailey (Chapter 11) in his discussion of American economic policy looks at the central questions of policy-making and at the massive disagreement between Republicans and Democrats over the right approach to getting the economy on track. Richard Fording (Chapter 12) looks at social policy and especially at the financial problems facing some of the key social programs on which Americans rely. Guy Peters (Chapter 13) focuses on the design of the most controversial of Obama's first-term legislation, the Patient Protection and Affordable Care Act, which promises to transform health care.

Foreign policy is covered by John Dumbrell in Chapter 14. He, like Chris Bailey, notes the concern with America's declining competitiveness on the global stage and looks at the points of continuity and departure from the policies pursued by George W. Bush. In addition to the unfinished business of the wars inherited from his predecessor, Dumbrell analyzes the situation generated by the Arab spring as well as the continuing dilemma of how to cope with the problem of Iran.

Finally Desmond King (Chapter 15) revisits the issue of equality for black Americans and the extent to which what he calls the 'civil rights state' has failed in its promise to African Americans. King shows how, on a number of points at which America's fragmented state interacts with its African American citizens (including such key points as housing), it has fallen short of delivering equal treatment. What the outcome of this failure will be is uncertain, but it is not a happy scenario for a polity dedicated to equality.

These themes and issues will undoubtedly continue to absorb the attention of the American political system well beyond the Obama Presidency. We hope that the treatment given them here will stimulate interest in the distinctive features of government and politics in the United States and will encourage both students and general readers to learn more about its history, public policy-making and culture.

Chapter 2

An Emerging Constitutional Debate

Gillian Peele

The United States on one level is a powerful nation, still in many ways the most powerful player in the international arena. Its system of democratic government is long standing and its values remain much admired throughout the world. Indeed America's constitutional arrangements have provided an inspiration, if not an institutional template, for many other countries. Within the United States itself the written Constitution has long been at the core of a small number of symbols that are crucial to national identity (Kammen, 1986; Amar, 2012). Popular veneration of the Constitution is not, of course, entirely replicated in the scholarly community where there has recently emerged a vigorous debate about the health of the constitutional system. As James E. Fleming put it, there is 'considerable talk of failure in the air these days – including constitutional failure, moral failure, and institutional failure' (Fleming, 2009). Sanford Levinson, one of the major scholars who has attempted to bring an unblinkered eye to the Constitution, has noted that the constitutional system has become a central, if sometimes challenged, element of the American political tradition and of the American civil religion (Levinson, 2011). Levinson's analysis questions the Constitution on normative as well as practical grounds, asking whether it is sufficiently democratic or majoritarian (Levinson, 2006). Although for some critics the problems with the United States' governmental system are that it has too much democracy rather than too little, Levinson now perhaps has more company than before. There is an increasingly rich vein of scholarship which suggests looking at America's Constitution anew and raises the question of whether the design made in 18th-century Philadelphia may be in need of revision. (See for example LaFountain and Shea (2011) on whether the constitutional order is broken.)

Much of the contemporary constitutional debate has been focused on values and on the tension between the ideals of American democracy, including the notions of equality and justice, and the reality of

14

American political practice as expressed, for example, in its electoral system (see for examples Ackerman, 2010; Balkin, 2011; Levinson, 2011; Amar, 2012). I will address some of these normative issues below when I look at the quality of American democracy. Here a number of questions have surfaced, ranging from the role of money and the power of interest groups in the American polity to the fairness of the system of representation and the integrity of electoral laws (Clawson et al., 1998; Fiorona and Abrams, 2009; Kaiser, 2009; Hacker and Pierson, 2010; Lessig, 2011; Levinson, 2011). Concerns about the quality of American democracy are, of course, not new. However, some commentators, such as Lawrence Lessig, have seen a qualitative change occurring around 1995 – the year Newt Gingrich became Speaker of the House of Representatives – when the legislature became dominated by the imperative of fund-raising (Lessig, 2011). And new controversy has come to swirl around the meaning of some of the rights guaranteed under the Constitution as the Supreme Court has given effect to a distinctive conservative jurisprudence sharply at odds with the political perspective taken by many liberals. But in some areas such as gay marriage the courts have taken a more permissive approach and themselves been met with opposition expressed through state legislatures and referenda. Such clashes have embroiled the courts in an unstable series of campaign and counter-campaign (Klarman, 2013).

Much of the immediate debate about constitutional capacity, by contrast, is more practical and focuses on a cluster of problems in American government and the institutional and political impediments to its effective functioning. Thus the inability to reach agreement on key policy issues, such as raising the debt ceiling, has brought the United States to the brink of default and budgetary conflict has occasioned shutdowns of government, an outcome which, although not unprecedented in the United States, is highly unlikely in most other advanced democracies.

In addition to the debates about the overall functioning of the American constitutional system, confidence has been eroded many of the most distinctive institutions. Congress as a whole has come in for a good deal of criticism, with the Senate receiving a particularly negative evaluation because of the ability of minorities to block legislation and nominations by using or threatening to use filibusters (Binder and Smith, 1997; Mann and Ornstein, 2006; Koger, 2010; Ackerman, 2010; Packer, 2010; Bruhl, 2011; Kaiser, 2013). Other institutions have also been the object of critical concern in recent years. Thus the Supreme Court has been attacked for its apparent partisanship and its 'triumphalism' (Ackerman, 2010); and it has also been attacked for the pursuit of a jurisprudence calculated not merely to reverse decades of reform efforts in such areas as campaign finance regulation and voting equality but to bring it into headlong conflict with the elected branches.

The identification of institutional weakness is of more than academic interest. The failure to frame and implement policy effectively obviously has a major impact on governance so that, for example, the Senate's inability to pass legislation that had succeeded in the House because of the lack of a supermajority threatens policy areas ranging from immigration to election regulation. The Senate's power to stymie nominations to executive positions and indeed to judicial posts undermines the capacity of government to function at an even more basic level.

Taken together these debates raise important questions about the constitutional underpinnings of the American body politic and a rich, if somewhat gloomy, agenda of concerns about both its constitutional architecture and its governance. Although I cannot examine all of these concerns in depth, I will highlight some of them. I start by looking at the impact of ideological polarization on American politics and its implications for the Madisonian system before moving on to look at weaknesses which have emerged in specific institutions. I then examine concerns about the quality of democracy, especially in relation to the electoral system and the role of money. I will discuss the arguments about rights within the American polity and finally ask what, if anything, can be done about these weaknesses in the context of a constitutional system where formal amendment was always difficult but which has arguably now become virtually impossible. The process of formal constitutional amendment, it should be noted, has always been awkward to achieve and is arguably even more so now that the mobilization of opposition to any proposal is relatively easy when backed with new technology, social media and money.

Polarized politics and constitutional gridlock

One fashionable explanation of the gridlock which has occurred in Washington, DC, is the toxic combination of the Madisonian system of separation of powers, divided government and intense partisan conflict between the parties (Mann and Ornstein, 2012). A variety of explanations have been given for that polarization, including primaries and reapportionment, while some critics suggest that there is a divergence between a deeply divided political elite and the electorate where the polarization is much less acute (Fiorina and Abrams, 2009). But there is little doubt that there has been an ideological polarization between the parties which has narrowed the scope for compromise and policy brokering (see Nivola and Brady, 2006–08; Abramowitz, 2010). In this context many commentators attribute responsibility primarily to the Republican Party where fierce anti-government sentiments expressed most recently in the Tea Party movement have changed the style of party competition, creating an intransigent populism of the right, both in Congress and in the country as a whole (Mann and Ornstein, 2012).

The changed style of political conflict, however, has a deeper significance than the clash of parties and gridlock in governance, important though they are. As E. J. Dionne has recently suggested, these new activists of the right have become the 'most energetic force in the Conservative movement and the Republican Party' and the gulf between them and their opponents reflects profound differences in the understanding of American history, values and ideals (Dionne, 2013). Not surprisingly, perhaps, given the iconic status accorded to the American Constitution in their arguments, these activists of the right pronounce themselves as loyal to the Founders' Constitution rather than the Constitution which has been adapted to 21st-century imperatives. They inevitably draw a sharp distinction between today's flawed and imperfect federal government in Washington, DC, and the constitutional framework established in Philadelphia in 1787. The right's invocation of the Constitution as a political symbol may be seen from the way that Jeffrey Duncan (R: South Carolina), one of the newly elected Republican members of the 112th Congress after the 2010 midterms and a member of the Tea Party Caucus, publicized the fact that he had always kept a copy of the Constitution in his pocket on the campaign trail; and he reiterated on his website his belief in it, noting that it was a constitution that contained the Second Amendment (Draper, 2012). Thus part of the problem of governance in the contemporary United States is that for many Republicans the modern structures of public power and authority are illegitimate departures from the purity of the Framers' original design. Whatever the consequences, they feel justified in trying to block what they see as further illegitimate moves away from that original vision. The common ground between such insurgent politicians and their opponents is narrow and their own party leaders are likely to be attacked if seen to compromise. Although the Tea Party Caucus had apparently lost some of its organizational momentum in Congress by early 2013, there remained a significant pool of Congressmen and Senators who shared its ideas and were ready to mobilize behind them.

The dimension of hostility to an expansive federal government is not entirely new in American history. Looking back over the 20th century, one can find points at which political forces on the right wished to turn the clock back and reverse developments which had occurred since the New Deal. What makes this early 21st-century expression of radical conservative nostalgia somewhat different from its predecessors is that it is no longer a marginal element of American party politics which can be dismissed as irrelevant and impotent to the rational politics of the mainstream. Rather the mobilization of the populist right takes place against the background of a conservative movement which has grown infinitely more sophisticated since the 1960s and a Republican Party which has become used to being a realistic contender for power (Aberbach and Peele, 2011). And even if the demographics of the United States seem to be moving towards the Democratic Party and away from the Republicans at the presidential level, this does not preclude Republican victories, especially at mid-term elections. Congressional and state-level victories can give both parties enormous opportunity to exercise power over both the content of legislation and the structures of political competition through apportionment and other aspects of the electoral process. It is worth noting here that as of 2013 Republicans controlled a plurality of the state governments as opposed to states in Democrat hands or in split control.

The divisions between liberals and conservatives and between Democrats and Republicans has found its most obvious expression in sharply divergent views between the parties about the role of the federal government. Gallup, in its annual governance survey in September 2012, found that two-thirds of Democrats thought that government should do more, while an even larger proportion of Republicans thought that government was doing too much of what should be left to business or to individuals (Gallup, 2012a). But perhaps the more interesting finding was that, of those who defined themselves as 'independents', an increasingly significant group, six out of ten, thought that government was doing too much. As was noted in the poll, the number of those urging further governmental intervention has rarely exceeded those who wish to curb it. Indeed a predominance of pro-government sentiment had been found only twice in Gallup's history of asking the question – once in the early years of the Clinton presidency and once in the immediate aftermath of 9/11. An activist Democratic president such as Obama is thus likely to find himself having to mobilize support in unpromising territory.

Yet, although a very large part of the contemporary governance problems are the product of profound changes in the style of party politics and profound disagreements about values including the role of government, part of the explanation of America's governance problems is attributable to the Madisonian system itself which divides executive and legislative power. It is worth noting here that the federal level of government is not alone in its vulnerability to constitutional constraints of a paralyzing kind. While the difficulties of governance have gained most attention at the federal level, the state level of government has experienced parallel problems. In Minnesota, for example, the state government was forced to close for three weeks in 2012 as a result of partisan conflict between the legislature and the Governor over budgetary policy. More generally, increased demands on state budgets combined with inflexible revenues have exacerbated the financial pressures on state governments and in some cases, such as California, highlighted fragilities in their constitutional arrangements and governmental infrastructure. Indeed, in contrast to the federal level where constitutional amendment is difficult, many state governments have sought and achieved substantial changes to their constitutions, and proposals for further reform are a staple item of debate.

The Founders' design

The Madisonian system of checks and balances is a highly distinctive one. Few polities have successfully emulated the United States in its construction or in operating a presidential system that separates legislative and executive power. The alternative model of parliamentary government and the more recent hybrid of semi-presidentialism in its various forms have generally proved better able to combine democratic ideals and effective governance. Indeed, one of the interesting intellectual questions for students of comparative government and of American politics is why the United States has been able to work its Madisonian system of checks and balances and thus far survive the gridlock and conflict which it so often entails.

The United States' system of separated powers was, of course, designed in a period when relatively little was expected of the federal government domestically; and in the field of foreign policy the expectation was that the country as a peaceful trading nation would have little need for the prerogative powers that executives enjoyed elsewhere. It might have been expected, therefore, that the rise of mass democracy, the intense pressures on government to provide services and regulate society, and the demands of world power status would have overwhelmed the 18th-century structures erected by the Founding Fathers. That they did not reflects three important aspects of American historical development.

The first is that ad hoc adjustments could be made in times of crisis. The most notable example of such adjustment occurred in the New Deal period when there was a multifaceted rebalancing of the Constitution: what Ackerman (2010) has referred to as a decisive moment or break in constitutional continuity. The presidency of Franklin D. Roosevelt (1933–45) saw not merely a transformation of the presidential office but also a major expansion of the federal government and a reconsideration by the Supreme Court of its role in the wider polity following intense conflict with Congress and the President over the constitutionality of many of the New Deal's novel legislative measures. Ironically that deference to Congress and the President about the power to regulate is apparently under threat as the Court now flexes its muscles over the scope of government authority and the Commerce Clause.

The second reason the 18th-century constitutional architecture has been able to survive into the 21st century is that American society has traditionally been able to rely on a variety of alternative structures to deliver services and compensate for a fragmented state. Thus a richly textured network of voluntary sector actors have provided support which the State did not, and those voluntary organizations, together with the state and local governments, have filled a gap in federal governmental provision.

The third aspect of American political development which is relevant is the difficulty of mobilizing and sustaining opposition to the status quo in the political system. In a fragmented and geographically diverse polity it has always been hard to organize support for causes or movements for radical change. Of course there have been important social and political movements across the panorama of American history. However, their impact, when successful, has not usually been to disrupt but rather to allow the political process to adapt to reform.

The fact that America's constitutional architecture has survived does not mean that it has not at times been seen to creak even before the current expressions of unease. Concern about the problem of divided government emerged as a topic of sustained political debate in the 1970s and 1980s. The approach of the celebration of the Constitution's bicentenary in 1987 took place against the background of the Carter Administration's (1977–81) problems of governing with an assertive Congress, an assertiveness which itself formed an important part of the Republican's critique of Carter's weakness in government. The immediate aftermath of the Vietnam and Watergate era saw a strengthening of congressional prerogatives which were then judged by some critics to be undermining America's capacity to act on the world stage. Although the Reagan Administration (1981–89) saw a determination to reassert the powers of the presidency, its own experience of divided government prompted both scholarly examination of the logic of the Madisonian system and some pressure for substantive constitutional reform.

A constitutional commission set up under the co-chairmanship of Lloyd Cutler, a Washington lawyer who served as Legal Counsel both to the Carter and the Clinton administrations, was concerned primarily with the governance problems facing the American executive branch. Cutler was explicit in his analysis of the flaws of the constitutional design: 'a particular shortcoming is the inability of our government to propose, legislate and administer a balanced program for governing ... The separation of powers between the legislative and executive branch, whatever its merits in 1793, has become a structure that almost guarantees stalemate today' (Cutler, 1980). Cutler had been especially dismayed by the failure of the Carter Administration to secure a coherent foreign and defense policy in the face of congressional opposition. The remedies advocated by the Commission in particular were an adjustment to the electoral timetable so that House members would serve a four-year term. Other strategies to overcome the effects of division and to strengthen the executive included allowing members of Congress to serve in the Cabinet and replacing the treaty confirmation requirement of a two-thirds majority with a simple majority.

Behind the thinking of the Cutler Commission and others was the sense that the analysis put forward in the 1950 APSA report, 'Toward a More Responsible Party System', had been accurate and that a more cohesive party system like the British would aid accountability and governance (APSA, 1950; Ranney, 1954). Ironically, greater partisanship has indeed occurred since the 1990s but, as critics have underlined forcefully, the constitutional effects have been rather different from what Cutler and others envisaged. Enhanced partisanship, far from making the system work better, has eroded the room for compromise and made the Madisonian system more vulnerable to gridlock (Mann and Ornstein, 2012).

The Constitutional Commission's proposed remedies met with a mixed reception from both academics and politicians. For some, the executive bias of the Commission was out of keeping with the Founders' intent and their own suspicion of strong presidential power. For others, the problems were overstated.

Since the 1980s the constitutional issue has not disappeared but arguably become more intractable. The character of divided government has changed, too, so that recent Democratic presidents have faced Republican legislature. Until 1980 divided government was relatively rare, but since 1981 periods of unified government were the exception. From 1981 there have been three periods of unified government: during Clinton's first two years (1993–95), from 2003 to 2007 when Republicans controlled the presidency and both houses of Congress, and during Obama's first two years (2009–11). There are of course scholars who argue that divided government does not necessarily impede the governing process even in the most recent period of partisan division. Thus Gerhard Casper (1985) argued that the problem was more the proliferation of checks and balances than a design flaw. David Mayhew, on the basis of long-term examination of the effect of divided government, rejected the notion that Congress has become a 'broken branch' (in Mann and Ornstein's phrase). He rebutted the need to fix the constitution by pointing to the legislative achievements in periods of divided government, including the 112th Congress (Mayhew, 2005, 2009).

The 104th Congress was in many ways a turning point in the evolution of the debate about whether the Constitution was in fact functioning well. The first Republican controlled House for 40 years, the ambitions of Gingrich himself, the antagonism to President Clinton and the impact of the Contract with America lent the period a confrontational quality which provided a foretaste of what has happened since. The more recent 112th Congress, however, has been compared very unfavorably, even with the 104th Congress, for its inability to address major policy problems or pass legislation.

At the heart of the conflict is the management of taxing and spending. The Republicans wanted drastic cuts, especially to welfare benefits, and an automatic sequester was put in place in the Budget Control Act of 2011 to cut federal spending if the special congressional committee (the Super-committee) could not reach agreement on the totals. Although an agreement was not forthcoming when the original date for agreement occurred, the deadline for automatic sequester was extended until March 1, 2013. Both the executive and the legislative branch warned of the implications of this automatic process, especially for areas of public policy such as border security. Individual states have been alerted to the impact on their revenues and services. But in the absence of agreement Obama had little option but to sign the order putting what he saw as deeply destructive cuts in place.

There are three important points here. First, few executives outside the United States have so little control of their budget. Second, recourse to such insensitive mechanisms for cutting programs indicates a failure of government, a retreat from the sophisticated tools available for decision-making. Third, the whole process of government at all levels is inevitably placed in a position of uncertainty and paralysis to an extent which faces few other advanced democracies.

Presidential power and the Constitution

Debate about whether the Constitution afforded enough space for the president to exercise executive leadership has been an on-going one since the Constitutional Convention itself. The period of Vietnam and Watergate saw massive controversy about both the proper sphere of the executive branch and the proper role of the legislature. As Rudalevige (2005) has noted, that era shaped the current one in numerous tangible ways, both as a reaction and a counter-reaction. And it had, he wrote, established a framework of presidential–congressional relations that was critically important for understanding a wide range of current issues, from war powers to budgeting, government ethics, and executive secrecy.

One of the features of the Cutler Commission recommendations which rendered it unpalatable to many observers, as previously mentioned, was its effort to strengthen the executive. Although the governance problem was acknowledged, many critics were inherently suspicious of any proposals to reinforce presidential power. That suspicion was massively exacerbated by George W. Bush's efforts to strengthen presidential authority unilaterally during his controversial and polarizing two-term presidency.

The ferocious debate about presidential power surrounding Bush's use of such tactics as signing statements, surveillance, habeas corpus suspension and torture (Rudalevige, 2005; Pfiffner, 2009; Fisher, 2008) assumed a new urgency in the early 21st century with the 9/11 attack and the subsequent 'war on terrorism'. What Blumenthal has called the 'radical' presidency of George W. Bush (2001–09) indeed seemed to mark a turning point in the debate in three ways: the claims made about the role of the presidency; the actual exercise of presidential power, especially its impact on civil liberties; and the constitutional controversy surrounding the Bush Administration's understanding of the office (Blumenthal, 2006). However, the important point to note is that the operation of the separation of powers system is a powerful factor encouraging presidents to push at the boundaries of their authority. To quote Rudalevige (2005) again: 'when George W. Bush took the oath of office for the second time in January 2005, he presided over a presidency much stronger in absolute and relative terms than the framers had conceived it. Increased partisan polarization and the structural divide between executive and legislature enhanced the incentives for the president, whoever the incumbent, to claim unilateral authority and to try to make it stick'.

In other words, one important aspect of contemporary constitutional politics in the United States is the effect the separation of powers will have on a president's approach to the office, encouraging him to maximize his use of the powers of his office, even at the expense of being labeled 'imperial'. That incentive is bound to be the greater when there is partisan confrontation. Reaction to George Bush's unilateral theory of presidential power was intense and there was a fierce backlash against what was seen as a distortion of the proper understanding of the Constitution, including within sections of the Republican Party (Fisher, 2008; Aberbach and Peele, 2011).

Obama himself campaigned in 2008 as an upholder of the Constitution and against the novel plebiscitary approach of Bush and Cheney and its encroachment on civil liberties, its secrecy and its assertion of inherent presidential authority. However, as has become apparent, Obama's handling of the presidency, while it does not reflect the same theoretical claims as his predecessor, is not hyper-sensitive or squeamish about the use of presidential power. Thus Obama deeply disappointed those who thought he should condemn the Bush Administration for its abuses, including torture, and make a conscious effort to restore the rule of law in relation to the handling of suspects and detainees. Instead he has appeared pragmatic in his use of presidential power and initiated military engagement without congressional authorization in Libya. Despite receiving the Nobel peace prize early in his period of office, Obama has earned sharp criticism for his use of drones, his kill-list and his failure to close the Guantanamo Bay detention center which remains at the top of ACLU's 'to do' list. He has reversed George W. Bush's effort to impose secrecy on presidential records but has maintained state secrecy on a number of other fronts. Equally importantly, while he initially made relatively modest use numerically of executive orders, it seems that in some key policy areas he will be relying increasingly on his own executive powers to secure policy change during his second administration. Thus, he announced that he intended to use executive orders in the effort to control firearms in the wake of the Sandy Hook massacre. This initiative occasioned an intense reaction both from Congress and from assorted groups on the right who nominated February 23 as a 'national day of resistance'.

What emerges from Obama's approach to the presidency points up the constraints on a president who needs to drive the system of government. Although he takes a rather different view of the constitutional powers of his office than did George W. Bush, Obama has already encountered a situation in relation to Congress where he will have to rely on such devices as executive orders and bypass the legislature. That strategy in turn is likely to provoke a very different response from his partisan opponents than did Bush's resort to executive orders, signing statements and the 'inherent powers' of his office.

The Electoral College

The presidency of George W. Bush also ignited a renewed debate about the method of electing the country's chief executive and about the Electoral College. The 2000 presidential election exposed a number of flaws in America's electoral systems (effectively a series of different systems across the several states) and it especially focused attention on the Electoral College and its ability to make president someone who had not secured a majority of the popular vote. Reform of what Levinson has called an 'iron cage' of the Electoral College is now very much discussed, although in a manner which is shot through with partisan concerns. The key objection to the Electoral College is that it can deliver a winner without a popular majority. It is also arguably flawed because it gives disproportionate weight to small states and encourages presidential candidates to campaign in swing states rather than across the nation as a whole. Its supporters argue that the College remains appropriate in a system that is federal, that it prevents over-concentration on large states in campaigns and that it has broadly worked over its history.

There are a range of alternatives to the Electoral College as currently constituted, with four broad approaches. First would be the direct popular vote: a nationwide tally. This is a plan advocated by Fair Vote, an organization which has promoted a campaign in the states to pass a National Popular Vote Plan to replace the Electoral College. Second, a somewhat modified version of this would be to require the electors to vote in favor of the candidate who won the popular vote. A third option would be to move from a winner-takes-all allocation of votes to a proportionate one. Finally there is an option which might allocate the votes through congressional districts.

This last option is in some ways the most intriguing since it would translate into the presidential system any biases and distortions which have occurred in the apportionment process. Not surprisingly perhaps, Republicans (who are now in favor of Electoral College reform, though their immediate post-*Bush v Gore* stance saw them defending the existing system) have attempted to promote proposals which would change the electoral system using their control of the state legislatures to try to advance initiatives. Thus in Virginia a bill to reform the Electoral College introduced by state Senator Carrico failed, while one in Pennsylvania promoted by state Senator Pileggi seemed unlikely to be taken further. How much traction there is in reform proposals is unclear but certainly enough to concern organizations such as Fair Vote.

Dysfunctional institutions?

Beyond the debate about presidential power, the last few years have seen a surge of concern about the working of particular American institutions. Congress has frequently suffered from a low public evaluation of its competence (Hibbing and Larrimer, 2008). In April 2013 the polling organization Rasmussen reported that the Congressional approval rating of 8 percent meant that it had been in single digit figures for two months in a row. Public approval of the job the Senate was doing stood at 12 percent, while the House notched up a 19 percent approval rating.

Congressional performance attracted scholarly criticism under George W. Bush (Mann and Ornstein, 2006). Mann and Ornstein directed their fire against congressional failure to fulfill its proper role, especially in relation to scrutiny. Under Obama, Congress has been criticized for its failure to address public policy problems.

One reason of course why Bush for much of his presidency encountered little opposition in Congress was that for six of the eight years

Congress was in Republican hands. During that period, according to some scholars, the quiescence of the Republican Party not only allowed the adoption of policies which were out of keeping with Republican values but undermined the ability of Congress to perform its traditional roles, especially that of scrutiny. Rudalevige (2005) noted the extent to which the congressional Republican majority gave the President a blank check in relation to Iraq in a move that was eerily reminiscent of the Gulf of Tonkin Resolution on Vietnam. A general discussion of Congress is given in Chapter 8, but here three aspects of Congress and its role in recent history which appear problematic should be underlined. The first is the role of special interests and the susceptibility of Congress, if not to corruption, to a distortion of its priorities. The second is the difficulty of reforming Congress because of the inbuilt investment which Senators and Congressmen have in maintaining the status quo. The third is the extent to which the hardball tactics of party leaders combined with the exploitation of dilatory procedures in the Senate have recently transformed the atmosphere of the legislature, making it much more antagonistic than would be the norm in a parliamentary system like the United Kingdom's.

Special interests have always played a role in Congress. What some commentators argue has changed is the role of money in the life of Congress which makes fundraising a much more prominent concern. This argument is not about direct quid pro quo for cash but a much broader culture in which influence is obtained as a result of a complex series of gifts and donations which generate obligations and dependency on the part of Congressmen (Lessig, 2012). In that elaborate environment, lobbyists (who have themselves grown in number over the period since 1990) act as the middle men, the brokers of influence. Obama, as Lessig noted, promised to change the way Washington works but, faced with a choice between working the system and attacking it, he pragmatically chose the former.

The difficulty of reforming Congress remains immense despite the idealistic, almost innocent, determination of some of those newly elected to Congress in 2010 (Draper, 2012). The transformation of the atmosphere of Congress and the decline of parliamentary norms of procedural fairness and agreement seem difficult to reverse. The debate about the role of the filibuster in the Senate underlines how difficult it is to move Congressmen from settled ways, although as the recent very moderate reform suggests, small incremental changes may be possible.

The Senate has come in for special criticism. There are of course important theoretical objections to the design of the Senate, not least its lack of proportionality and the use which Senators can make of their voting power to distort public policy. The more immediate objections to its role revolve around the use of the filibuster and ability of a small minority to block appointments (including judicial ones) and to delay legislation.

The Court and rights

Constitutional doubt has not merely swirled around the essential elements of the Constitution – the separation of powers and federalism – it has also addressed the jurisprudence of the Court and the understanding of rights. Here polls reveal that, although not perhaps as marked as in relation to Congress, public approval of the Court has declined in recent years. Indeed a Pew Research poll in March 2013 found that public evaluation of the Court had sunk to a new low with only 52 percent viewing it favorably. Intriguingly, although conservatives have a majority on the Court, conservative voters became critical of it for being insufficiently conservative after the decision on Obama's health care reforms.

The Court's upholding of the Patient Protection and Affordable Care Act was on one level a relief to the President and to those who feared the constitutional challenge might succeed. On another level, however, the judgment of the Chief Justice (whose vote, though unexpected, was crucial) sounded a warning note of the Court's determination to limit the scope of congressional authority to what could be seen as consonant with the Founders' intention. Thus commenting on whether the individual mandate would be covered by the Commerce Clause, the Chief Justice noted 'the Framers knew the difference between doing something and doing nothing. They gave Congress the power to *regulate* commerce, not to *compel* it. Ignoring that distinction would undermine the principle that the federal government is a government of limited and enumerated powers. The individual mandate thus cannot be sustained under Congress's power to regulate commerce' (*National Federation of Independent Businesses v Sibelius*). Thus the Court reaffirmed its determination to be the arbiter of constitutional acceptability even in relation to Congressional legislation passed by a popularly elected president who had made that legislation a major personal commitment.

The potential for a clash between the Supreme Court and the political branches has become greater as the conservative movement and Republican presidents have clarified their approach to constitutional interpretation in the period since Reagan. This is a story which is further developed in Chapter 9. The important point here is that the Supreme Court in the United States has the crucial power to shape the policy choices of society and the options available to government. It can do this as a result of a doctrinal imperative which is, to say the least, contested. The impact of this institutional power can be seen in the series of cases since *Buckley v Valeo* which have increasingly dismantled efforts to regulate campaign finance.

It is perhaps not surprising in a society as diverse as the United States that some rights will be highly controversial. There is little common ground between those who see abortion as a woman's right to choose and those who see it as murder. The challenge to rights such as abortion, which had been thought secure, and the confusing and costly battles amongst state legislatures, courts and pressure groups (often using the tools of direct democracy) over such issues as gay marriage creates not merely uncertainty around a series of delicate policy areas but makes rights the subject of political factors and not solemn constitutional agreement (Klarman, 2012). Thus the 40th anniversary of *Roe v. Wade* in 2013 prompted reflection on the extent to which this issue divided America's political elites and remained a symbol of the secular/religious divide within the country, as well as testimony to the fluidity of constitutional 'rights'. As many commentators noted, the Supreme Court's grounds for upholding a woman's right to an abortion had changed in the years since 1973, most notably in the landmark case of *Casey*. In addition the Republican Party's shift to the right on social issues had made an anti-abortion stance a litmus test for candidates, a development which caused Romney in 2012 to do a volte-face on the issue. The other significant change however has been the surge of state initiatives to try to constrain the exercise of the abortion right as well as the withdrawal of many abortion facilities.

Other contested rights have generated conflict and confusion. Gay marriage has become legal in some states but it has also been the target of opposition groups trying to secure its prohibition. Even if, as Klarman suggests, opinion on this issue appears to be shifting, the series of cases and challenges, campaigns and protests, underlines a deeply divided society and one where the prospect of consensus in the short term at any rate is remote.

The important point for the American system however is that the courts and judges shape the agenda both positively and negatively to an extent which is not seen in other societies. That judicialization of the political agenda not merely has a substantive effect on policy but ultimately may have an impact on the legitimacy accorded to America's key institutions, including the Court itself.

Addressing public policy concerns

The conflicts which have occurred between the executive and Congress have been seen as a large part of the explanation for the failure to reach agreements on key policy problems, ranging from the environment to immigration and of course the economy. Critics have also pointed to the way in which Congress sometimes passes poorly drafted legislation even when it does manage to legislate on a major measure. But critics have also suggested that there is a deeper problem with governance more generally. Jeffrey Sachs (2009), for example, in a wide-ranging article in *Scientific American* in 2009 pointed to extensive failures in American government, ranging from Iraq and the attacks of 9/11 to the financial crisis and Hurricane Katrina, as evidence of systemic governance flaws. Sachs argued that such factors as privatization, the collapse of planning and underfunding were all factors in the weakness of American government and noted that such failures were not found to that extent in other governmental systems.

The quality of American democracy

Alongside these concerns about governance there are a cluster of issues related to the quality of democracy in America. To some extent there have always been tensions with American democracy about the relationship between majoritarian opinion and minority rights, the meaning of equality, representative versus direct democracy, and the role of government. What seems to have changed is the tone of much of the debate which has, in Dionne's (2013) words, become 'ugly', indicating the extremism of some of the tactics and the number of bitterly fought issues on the American agenda.

One major problem as far as the quality of representative democracy is concerned has been growing unease about the fairness of the electoral system. Despite the efforts to reform the machinery of voting after the experiences of the 2000 presidential election, 2012 still saw a system that gave grave cause for concern. The most obvious manifestation of breakdown were long queues at the polling stations. In addition, the efforts of some states to tighten their electoral laws by introducing strict individual voter identification procedures has caused widespread disquiet about the partisan nature of these initiatives and their impact on minorities, the poor and the elderly. In theory, the states which had undertaken such reforms were doing so to reduce voter fraud. But the new requirements placed a heavy burden on groups who found producing photographic identification difficult. That the states who seemed most enthusiastic for these drives were Republican reinforced the view that these initiatives were far from neutral (Mayer, 2012).

Money remains one of the perennial concerns about the quality of American democracy. Here the wheel seems to have gone full circle. The Watergate era led to an attempt through the FECA of 1971, and amended in 1974, to control the role of money in elections through the setting of limits on both campaign contributions and spending by candidates. As noted earlier, since 1974 successive Supreme Court judgments have eroded the original legislation and the Federal Election Commission, the body put in place to administer the regulatory system, has been dismissed by some observers as 'comatose'. The Supreme Court's decisions in *Wisconsin Right to Life*, *Speechnow* and *Citizens United* ushered in a new era of free spending prior to the 2012 election. If the Court's decision to review limits on contributions to parties in *McCutcheon v Federal Election Commission* (2013) results in the striking down of contribution limits to parties, there will be virtually nothing left of the system established in the early 1970s and there will be an open season for financial interest to shape campaigns and American politics more broadly.

Conclusions

E.J. Dionne, in his 2013 book on American divisions, argues that the contemporary United States has seen the collapse of what he calls the 'long consensus'. Reform was an important part of that consensus. In the late 19th and early 20th centuries the Progressive Movement inspired substantive reforms to both the institutions of American democracy and thinking about the role of government. The direct election of Senators, the enfranchisement of women and the spread of direct democracy brought extensive change to the operation of American government. Over the 20th century the scope of government also expanded to allow it to regulate the economy to provide social security and increasingly after the World War II to promote racial justice and equality. This liberal reform tradition affected both parties, although after the New Deal it was most clearly associated with the Democratic Party. Certainly from the 1970s those who sought to use government to promote reforms would have looked to the Democratic Party, supported by a host of liberal pressure and advocacy groups and think tanks, rather than the Republicans.

From the 1970s, however, the growth of a powerful conservative movement in sometimes uneasy alliance with the Republican Party began to offer an alternative to the hitherto intellectually and politically dominant Democratic liberal consensus. This story has been told many times and there is not space to repeat it here. What is important to emphasize however is that, over successive waves of conservative resurgence, there is a new agenda which rejects the narrative of reform and progress and wishes to return to a different political era. Many of the activists recruited to the conservative cause were motivated by opposition to government initiatives on such issues as abortion, affirmative action and busing; but there was also a strong almost visceral hostility to federal authority and taxation. Individualism and anti-government sentiments became a hallmark of the right. The association with religion and conservative social values often gave campaigns the character of a crusade which, to its opponents, combined anti-intellectual and extremist elements with conviction and certainty. Finally the organization of the right was transformed by the shrewd activity of a new breed of political entrepreneur and the strategic deployment of money to build an infrastructure of the right.

These developments have shaped the current constitutional and political climate, altering the language of political and constitutional discourse and setting new agendas for different political camps. In this atmosphere of ideological and partisan conflict efforts to identify, let alone achieve, reforms based on common notions of good government or fair politics have proved impossible. The conflict has also fed into and onto more mundane concerns about the operation of American government, creating a vicious circle of a weakened public authority which further alienates those already inclined to wish to reduce the role of government. It remains to be seen what if anything can be done to ameliorate the situation. There is certain to be any simple fix or magic bullet, and rebuilding consensus is likely to be a long and arduous process. The difficulty of amending the Constitution has already been mentioned but should be reiterated. There is of course the possibility of change as a result of Supreme Court rulings, although here the ideological battle for control of the court makes it unlikely that the production of decisions will come to command widespread legitimacy. State-initiated reforms are possible, but such initiatives are necessarily open to partisan manipulation. In these circumstances the process of governing the United States will continue to generate problems, both of policy failure and public alienation, and once revered institutions will be vulnerable to a decline in public esteem – at least until a new consensus about governing and the rules of the game can be created.

Chapter 3

The 2012 Elections

Jon Cohen

Elections are the product of both short-term forces and deeper under-lying political or demographic trends. But in some instances, economic conditions, an unpopular war or a really weak candidate primarily tip the scale. Such was the case in 2010 when a bad economy and strong anti-government sentiment, fueled in part by negative reaction to President Obama's Affordable Care Act, led to big congressional losses for the Democrats. The outcome of the midterms contrasted with 2008, where, by comparison, the short and long-term forces were better aligned, resulting in decisive Democratic presidential and con-gressional victories. The central question leading up to the 2012 elec-tions was whether deep economic problems or steadily accumulating shifts in the composition of the electorate would prevail.

The 2012 presidential campaign was a turbulent, unpredictable series of events that, over the course of two years, exposed rifts in the elec-toral coalitions of both major American political parties. Republicans were divided over social issues, their own leaders' Medicare reform plans, and even the very basic question of whether it was acceptable to make compromises to get things done. Democrats were split over the legalization of gay marriage, immigration reform and tax policy, among other issues. These divisions made for difficult decisions for each party's leaders – and their core supporters – explaining much of what unfolded throughout the campaign. The divisions, along with the growing power – and threat – of independent voters, suggest that future elections will be even more volatile and hard-fought, with voters in the two major parties increasingly hostile toward one another.

In the wake of 2012, it is the Republican Party that appears to face the bigger challenges, both because of its deep internal divisions as well as profound demographic changes in the country. The major electoral change shaping the Party's fortunes in recent decades had been the large-scale abandonment of the Democratic Party by white working-class voters and white southerners. Such defections picked up steam in the 1960s, marking the commencement of an era of Republican domi-nance (Beck, 1977; Abramowitz, 1994; Bullock III et al., 2005). The

Republicans won five of six presidential contests starting in 1968, eventually ending a 40-year span of Democratic control of the House of Representatives. But more recently immigration, especially after 1965, the increasing numbers of highly educated women in the workforce and persistent problems in appealing to young voters have all eroded the Republicans' long-term electoral advantages (Abramowitz, 1994; Coffin, 2003; Keeter et al., 2008). Indeed, the Republicans appear to be facing an uphill battle in the years ahead.

After the November 2012 election, it seemed obvious – inevitable, even – to some that Obama should have prevailed in his bid for re-election. He was, after all, a relatively popular sitting president with clear personal appeal. He was matched against a demonstrably weak challenger, former Massachusetts Governor Mitt Romney. Romney was the first Mormon nominated to a major party ticket. He had emerged bruised from a long primary battle against a slew of other Republicans to mount what some critics decried as a campaign that could only sing one note: criticizing Obama on the economy.

Still, there were ample reasons for Obama's campaign to worry about the outcome. His party had lost control of the House of Representatives in 2010, a stinging defeat the President dubbed 'a shellacking'. It was a loss that suggested that his historic 2008 triumph might not have been the start of an irreversible Democratic trend, as supporters had hoped and researchers had speculated (Hopkins, 2009; Caraley, 2009). There were signs that independent voters – who make up more than one-third of the electorate – were swinging more wildly than ever between the two parties. And Democrats were extremely uneasy about Obama's leadership style (Westen, 2011). Above all, the economy was still weak – with particularly high levels of unemployment, as Romney's campaign noted gleefully at every turn. Obama's ratings on handling the economy were exceptionally poor, leading some prognosticators to declare that he would succumb to history (recall: 'it's the economy, stupid') and lose (Barbaro et al., 2011; Goldfarb and Wallsten, 2011; Pethokoukis, 2012a).

Despite their concerns, Obama's top aides always believed that his superior ground operation – fueled by far better technology – and important demographic changes in the country, would give him an advantage in 2012. After the election, Jim Messina, the winning campaign manager, extolled his campaign's technological superiority that facilitated personalized appeals to voters in key swing states: 'we ran county commission campaigns in each of these places', he reportedly said at a post-election conference, referring to the retail style of his campaign structure (Slack, 2012).

The dim view of Romney's severe trouble with demographics – and being the standard bearer of a party almost exclusively dependent on white voters – was best expressed by a senior strategist for John S.

Table 3.1   *Presidential election results, 2012*

	Barack Obama	Mitt Romney	Other	Total
Popular vote	65,899,660	60,932,152	2,235,850	129,067,662
Popular vote (%)	51	47	2	
Electoral college	332	206		

Source: Federal Election Commission (FEC)
http://www.fec.gov/pubrec\fe2012/2012presgeresults.pdf; Archives.gov
http//www.archives.gov/federal-register/electoral-college/map/historic.html.

McCain, the previous GOP nominee. Bemoaning Romney's approach to winning the primaries by playing to staunch conservatives – most notably on immigration – John Weaver said 'he's now trapped demographically and doesn't seem to understand it' (Brownstein, 2012).

In the end, the thesis driving the Obama campaign proved correct. Obama won the election, winning with a slim, but firm, majority. The final tally was 51 percent for Obama to 47 percent for Romney, with the Republican challenger finishing at the '47 percent' level that would become infamous after the publicity around his disparaging remarks about Obama supporters at a private fundraiser.

There was ultimately less competitiveness when it came to the all-important Electoral College. Obama won with 332 Electoral College votes to Romney's 206, a big margin that cemented the idea that the Obama campaign's tight focus on state-level results proved the superior strategy (see Table 3.1). Yet there were signs of dissent in Obama's victory. Voters were more skeptical of big government than they had been just four years earlier when he took office. Even on the economy, people in 2012 reported wishing that the government would do less, not more, leaving important recovery work to individuals and businesses (Feldman and Zaino, 2012). Obama also failed to score a clear win among political independents, as he had done four years earlier (see Table 3.3).

But there were even more troublesome signs for Republicans. By the time the 2012 campaign was over, people held more negative than positive views of the GOP. The momentum that had swept the Republicans into the majority in the House of Representatives in 2010 had stalled everywhere else, and barely kept apace even in Congress.

The Democrats had been widely seen to be on the defensive in the Senate before the 2012 elections, with 23 Democratic or Democratic-leaning seats up for election, compared with only ten for the GOP (Kraushaar, 2010; Trygstad et al., 2011). But the Democrats held their

Table 3.2   *Presidential votes 1982–2012, by race (percent)*

	Democratic candidates		Republic candidates	
	White	Non-white	White	Non-white
1972	77	23	96	4
1976	84	16	96	4
1980	77	23	96	4
1984	76	24	96	4
1988	74	26	95	5
1992	79	21	94	6
1996	73	27	93	7
2000	70	30	91	9
2004	66	34	88	12
2008	61	39	90	10
2012	56	44	89	11

Source: National election polls.

narrow majority in the chamber, notching a nearly 40-year best by winning 22 of the 23 seats they were defending; Republicans held seven of their ten (Giroux, 2012).

Even in the House of Representatives, the Republican majority was diminished, although not over-turned. Moreover, Republican voters were starting to change their minds on core party issues such as taxes, with voters largely siding with Democrats on the need to raise them, while the GOP was also increasingly out of step with majority opinion on social issues, including the legalization of gay marriage and immigration.

The Republican Party proved out-of-step with most Americans on immigration reform, and, perhaps more importantly, its image as anti-immigration hurt it among an increasingly diverse electorate. The GOP's stance on the matter deepened over the course of Romney's presidential campaign as he took and held onto conservative immigration positions in order to win his party's base, and ran smack into demographic changes in the country, particular the rapid growth of numbers of Latino voters nationally and in key states alike. Without a move to appeal to more Latinos, Republicans appear poised to face even harder elections in 2016 and beyond, making 2012 an important case study. Consider this: in 2012, only 27 percent of Hispanics voted for the Republican presidential nominee. That put the GOP Hispanic vote – the vote, in other words, of the country's fastest-growing minority group – lower than in the previous three presidential elections.

For some time, the major parties' internal conflicts were masked by unity against external threats: divided and unwieldy coalitions coming together in the hopes of defeating the other side. Partisanship is increasingly the common bond within each party, as the two sides have grown more hostile to one another. Yet the threat of victory by the other side is no longer sufficient for Republicans. By Election Day, 2012, Republicans were as motivated as they had ever been to defeat the Democratic president, overcoming their earlier skepticism about Romney to support firmly his candidacy. There just were not enough of them. By the time the electoral dust settled, it appeared that the Republicans would need to expand their horizons, not only over-coming internal divisions but also expanding into new terrain.

The background to the 2012 presidential election

Mitt Romney's performance in the 2012 campaign will be the subject of much scrutiny for years to come, in part because his campaign lasted so long and started with so many advantages. He had been widely considered the certain Republican nominee for years, and remained the widely assumed front-runner even as he faced a growing number of competitors. He was heavily funded, and sitting on a per-sonal fortune of hundreds of millions of dollars to back up a bevy of well-heeled donors freed by more open campaign finance rules and reg-ulations. Romney eventually spent nearly $80 million in the primaries, more than the next four challengers combined (Riley, 2012). He was also the choice of many in the Republican establishment, in a party that tends to reward candidates who have waited their turn. He had also been running a shadow campaign ever since his defeat in the 2008 primaries, putting him organizationally well ahead of his rivals. He had the advantage on hiring key staffers and building a campaign infrastructure. By mid-January 2012, more than three months before he officially secured enough delegates to be the party's nominee, 74 percent of Republican voters expected him to prevail in the nominating contest.

Once Romney did secure the nomination, he had other apparent advantages. Voters had deep uncertainty about the trajectory of the American economy, something his campaign saw as crippling for Obama. In official statistics, the economic recession that started in late 2007 formally ended in June 2009, but more than three years later, few voters noticed. In November 2012, 77 percent of presidential voters said the economy was in bad shape, according to the national exit poll sponsored by the television networks and the Associated Press – even as the economy was actually on the upswing (Cohen et al., 2012). And Romney could count on their focus: voters all year overwhelmingly said they were focused on the economy; in the same exit poll, 59 percent of all voters called it issue No. 1, by far their top concern.

Despite the evident economic funk, Romney lost the election. It was immediately fashionable to highlight the short-term factors – a blundering campaign team, his stilted performance on the campaign trail or his numerous verbal gaffes. Most distressing of all to Republicans was that their party had seemed to be on the ascendant just two years earlier, and they appeared to have the economic winds at their backs. How, analysts wondered, was Romney unable to translate those factors into victory over Obama?

A big part of the answer, in retrospect, lay in the demographic shifts in the electorate and in much longer-term historical trends. While the Republicans held onto the assumption that the electorate in 2012 would look as it had before, the Obama campaign was working hard to make sure it reflected the changing demography. Romney's advisors anticipated an electorate that was 'a blend of 2004 and 2008'.

Even so, it was not at all inevitable, as many now think, that Romney would lose (a subject that will also be explored later on in this chapter) given the state of the economy. To be sure, the Republican base did not enthusiastically embrace the former Massachusetts governor during the nomination process. Early polls in the GOP contest showed surprising strength for Minnesota Representative Michele Bachmann, Texas Governor Rick Perry and a wild-card candidate, businessman Herman Cain. Later, once the actual primary voting began, Romney had to weather strong showings by former House Speaker Newt Gingrich, who had led the Republican revolution and its 1994 takeover of Congress, and former Pennsylvania senator Rick Santorum, a favorite of religious conservatives. Each of these competitors excelled against Romney among the most staunchly conservative Republican voters, many of whom had adopted the mantle of the Tea Party political movement. Very conservative voters are the mainstay of GOP primary voters, so Romney's inability to attract significant support from that group kept the nomination contest going in earnest all the way through April 2012.

The Tea Party challenge to the Republican establishment started in 2009, with conservative backlash to the bailout of major financial institutions and the nearly $800 billion economic stimulus package that was the marque legislation of Obama's early months in office (Herszenhorn, 2010; Zernike, 2010). The movement's leaders preached orthodoxy on tax cuts and budgeting that proved difficult for even sympathetic office holders used to securing government services for their constituents. Romney's position as presumptive-nominee made it particularly challenging to navigate the rhetoric of the movement and the repositioning that would be inevitable in a general election contest (West and Mehta, 2011).

But despite Romney's weaknesses in appealing to a strident GOP base – and the middle of the electorate – Obama had serious liabilities of his own, weaknesses that were reflected in the public polling up until the very end. The President's single biggest challenge was that Romney consistently tied or beat him when it came to voters' trust on their top issue, the economy. And Obama's own ratings on the issue had languished ever since optimism faded early in his first year in office. More broadly, most polls showed Obama and Romney neck-and-neck at the national level up until the final weekend before Election Day. While the President held a consistent edge in many key swing states – including Colorado, Florida, Ohio and Virginia – his leads often hovered in 'margin of error' territory, making a win hardly a sure thing, certainly not until very late. Even after the fact, exit polling showed that people still had reservations about the man they had just re-elected, some of them deeper than in 2008: most 2012 voters saw the federal government doing too much to intrude on individuals and private businesses, a reversal from 2008. And voters also returned the Republicans to the majority in the House of Representatives, guaranteeing that Obama would have resistance to carrying out his agenda.

What, then, were the overarching forces at play – forces so strong that seeming advantages for Mitt Romney were fully drowned out on Election Day? One factor was simply the dwindling number of Americans seeing themselves as Republicans. The number identifying with the GOP was shrinking, a trend that seemed cemented when Obama was first elected in 2008 and showed no reversal even with GOP wins in 2009 and 2010. In 2012, fewer than one in four Americans described themselves as Republicans, according to data assembled by the Pew Research Center. Part of the problem for the Republican Party is that it has had little success appealing to non-white voters. As the Democratic Party has become increasingly a coalition of Latinos, Asians and African Americans, together with liberal whites, the Republican Party has remained an overwhelmingly white party. Hard-line positions on immigration, affirmative action and the recent enactment of stricter voter participation laws (requirements of official photo identification in order to vote, limitations on early voting and registration drives) have reinforced the white–non-white partisan divide. Florida, Ohio and Pennsylvania – all key battleground states – had intense battles over voting procedures in 2012, with Pennsylvania ultimately becoming a major turning point in the debate over voter suppression and voting rights. Earlier in the year, the majority leader of the Pennsylvania State House, Republican Mike Turzai, bragged that 'voter ID ... [requiring voters to bring state-issued photo identification to their voting precincts] ... is gonna allow Governor Romney to win the state' (Barnes, 2012). State records showed more than 700,000 registered voters in

Pennsylvania lacked photo identification from the Transportation Department, with most studies estimating a disproportionate impact on non-white voters (Warner, 2012; Associated Press, 2012).

In the end, African Americans and Hispanics waited significantly longer to vote than did white people in 2012 (Peters, 2013), a discrepancy that lines up with a broader complaint about Republican machinations (Williams, 2012; Yeomans, 2013). At the same time, political independents were turning decisively toward Democrats on policy, just as they had in the previous presidential election. Republican intransigence in Congress had effectively stymied Democratic efforts to pursue economic recovery through stimulus measures and to tackle global warming, but these legislative victories came at a cost. Most people perceived the Republicans as excessively partisan.

Although the country appears evenly divided on issues, there is no such parity on political partisanship. The Democrats' ranks have solidified, as the Republicans' shrunk. Across poll after poll, more Americans these days think of themselves as Democrats than as Republicans. Democrats have had a consistent advantage over Republicans for years, although the gap has shifted over time.

Democrats outnumbered Republicans by 13 percentage points on average in 1981, the year *The Washington Post* and ABC News started polling jointly. (The Democrats' long-standing advantage was one reason Reagan needed 'Reagan Democrats' to win.) Over time the tide turned; by 2003 Republicans had advanced to precise parity with Democrats as a consequence of the Reagan Revolution against the big government programs of the 1960s and then later amplified by the patriotic reaction to the September 11th terrorist attacks.

But as soon as the GOP managed to neutralize the historic Democratic edge, it again slipped away. George W. Bush spearheaded another invasion of Iraq, the war turned deeply unpopular and a new trend away from the GOP began, disrupting the gradual pattern of the previous two decades. Republican allegiance quickly faded. Democrats advanced, peaking in 2008, just in time for Barack Obama. When the struggling economy flattened the Democrats' trend line, the ranks of independents – not Republicans – ticked higher.

The downturn in Republican Party identification also paralleled a large demographic shift in the American electorate. Once almost uniformly white, the electorate by 2008 was about one-quarter non-white. The number of non-whites would reach another record high, 28 percent, in the 2012 election, despite what many Republican pollsters, punsters and political operatives on the right had wishfully forecast. African Americans again turned out in record numbers to vote to re-elect the country's first black President, as did Hispanics, who for the first time made up 10 percent of all voters, according to the national exit poll (see Table 3.3).

Table 3.3 *Presidential votes, 2012, by voter group*

	% of voters	Obama	Romney	D-R
Age				
18–29	19	60	37	23
30–44	27	52	45	7
45–64	38	47	51	−4
65+	16	44	56	−12
Race				
White	72	39	59	−20
Black	13	93	6	86
Asian	3	73	26	47
Hispanic	10	71	27	43
Sex				
Female	53	55	44	11
Male	47	45	52	−7
Party identification				
Democrat	38	92	7	86
Republican	32	6	93	−87
Independent/Other	29	45	50	−5
Family income				
Under $50,000	41	60	38	21
$50,000 to under $100,000	31	46	52	−7
$100,00 or more	28	44	54	−10
College degree				
No college degree	53	51	47	3
College graduate	47	50	48	2
Religion				
Protestant or other Christian	53	42	57	−15
Catholic	25	50	48	2
Jewish	2	69	30	39
Other	7	74	23	51
No religion	12	70	26	44
Sex by marital status				
Married men	29	38	60	−22
Married women	31	46	53	−7
Non-married men	18	56	40	17
Non-married women	23	67	31	35

Source: Exit poll conducted by Edison Media Research for the National Election Pool, *The Washington Post* and other media organizations. Typical characteristics have a margin of sampling error of plus or minus four percentage points.

As more and more non-whites entered the electorate, however, the Republican Party remained almost completely dependent on white voters. In 2008, fully 90 percent of those who voted for Republican John S. McCain over Obama were white. Romney would do no better: 89 percent of his voters were white. At the same time, independent voters were moving away from the Republicans on a variety of issues, including on immigration and on reforming the country's Medicare and Social Security systems. Obama had already demonstrated cross-over appeal to the middle of the political spectrum: he had won independent voters in 2008 by 8 percentage points, far outpacing his recent predecessors. Perhaps the question, then, should be not how Romney lost but instead how, with so many long-term forces undercutting him, did he get so close?

An opportunity created by the economy and Obamacare

The key to Romney's lost opportunity lay in the economy. That opening was immediately apparent after Obama was elected in 2008. For all the problems the Republicans faced at the outset of the Obama administration, there were even stronger short-term forces buffeting the country's new Democratic president: an economy in the midst of a major, historic downturn.

Obama was also pulled down by a relentless focus on congressional machinations around his signature health care law. There has not been a single time in the history of the Gallup poll where the public's ratings of the US Congress have outpaced a president's. Obama could only be hurt by public attention to legislative wheeling and dealing, which endured for much of 2009 and deep into 2010 before Congress voted to approve a version of what would become known as 'Obamacare'.

But it was the economy that proved the biggest challenge for the Democratic incumbent and provided the most spark for the opposition, including the newly formed Tea Party movement. Before Obama's first year was out, most Americans, 52 percent, said they disapproved of the way he was handling the economy. And intensity ran clearly against him: nearly twice as many said they 'strongly disapproved' than 'strongly approved'. Majorities would hold negative views of his performance on this – the clear top issue – all the way through his bid for re-election.

The effects of the economic downturn were widely felt. About two-thirds of Americans said they were worried about maintaining their standard of living. Just before the 2010 congressional elections, more than half said they were concerned about paying their rent or mortgage, up sharply from before Obama took office (Cha and Cohen, 2010).

There were direct political consequences from this as well. Most importantly, the emergence of the Tea Party. The Tea Party movement capitalized on widespread anti-government sentiment, which was higher in 2010 than it had been at any point since just after the government shutdown ended in early 1996. Made up largely of conservatives identifying with the Republican Party, the Tea Party helped the GOP by providing an energetic base. Some of that energy centered on opposition to Obama. Asked what motivated their movement, big majorities of Tea Party supporters highlighted three things: concern about the economy, distrust of government and dislike of Obama's policies. The stiff concern on these points put a drag on Obama's approval ratings, which dipped into the low 40s as Election Day 2010 approached.

It is worth noting that the economy persisted as the chief electoral concern all the way through Obama's re-election. In the spring of 2012, 76 percent of all Americans said they felt the country was still in a recession. In the fall, a nearly identical percentage of presidential voters said the economy was in bad shape, even though by then a recovery was well underway. A relentless focus on the struggling economy kept Romney competitive with Obama throughout the campaign, as negative assessments of the President's performance on the matter framed his re-election effort. Even when voters acknowledged that Obama had inherited a sluggish economy from his predecessor, George W. Bush, they expressed opposition to many of Obama's remedies. Consistent majorities, in fact, disapproved of the way Obama was dealing with the economy for most of his term. Even greater majorities gave negative ratings to his handling of the burgeoning federal budget deficit.

But the sputtering economy was on the upswing in 2012, dampening some of the criticism of the President, particularly as unemployment began to drop over the course of the year. A favorite Romney attack line in the fall campaign was to recite the long stretch of time that the country's unemployment rate had topped 8 percent. The record streak of 43 straight months above that threshold was broken only in October 2012, taking the steam out of Romney's specific line of criticism.

In terms of getting his message across on the economy, it was not simply that the Republican Party proved a drag on Romney, but that he was also perhaps uniquely hampered in changing its image in key areas. Romney had a deficit on empathy, battled a perception that he had not paid his fair share of taxes and, most fundamentally, had to contend with a widespread sense that he would favor the wealthy over the ordinary American. As a consequence, throughout the campaign, Obama led Romney on the question of which of the two better understood the economic problems people were having. A similar advantage over McCain had helped to boost Obama in 2008, after the economy went into free-fall after a crash in the financial markets. In 2012, Obama beat Romney by 10 percentage points, 53 to 43 percent, as the one 'more in touch with people like you', according to the exit poll. Empathy matters to American voters, not just management or policy judgment.

Romney had previously failed for similar reasons to differentiate himself from his competitors in the primaries on this score: even when he had a sizable lead in the contest, about as many people said Gingrich, Santorum and Ron Paul were the closest to understanding their problems. In his effort to connect with average Americans, Romney had to contend with personal tax issues. Throughout the campaign there were demands that he release his tax returns, potentially detailing how he made and invested money. When he did release his 2010 tax return during the GOP primaries, they showed that he had paid about a 14 percent federal tax rate on income of about $22 million, far below the rate paid by most American taxpayers. Although perfectly legal, since his investment income is taxed at a lower rate than wage earnings, in February, two-thirds of all Americans said Romney was not paying his 'fair share'. In the fall, Republicans rallied around Romney on the tax issue, just as they had on nearly every other, yet still about half of Americans said he had not paid enough tax after he released his 2011 returns.

A broader challenge for Romney was that about six in ten Americans saw inequity in the economic system, favoring the wealthy, to be a bigger problem than government overreach, siding with Obama's basic view. Anti-government sentiment ran high in 2012, but even so, throughout the spring and summer, barely more than a third of Americans said 'over-regulation of the free market that interferes with growth and prosperity' was a larger concern than rich people benefiting unfairly. This vantage point hurt Romney, whom a clear majority of voters anticipated would favor the wealthy over those with middle incomes, were he to win the presidency. By contrast two-thirds of voters consistently said that Obama's policies favored those with middle incomes, not those on the top end of the scale.

Obama held another advantage on the economy: nearly four years after George W. Bush had handed over the reins of the national economy to Obama, more people continued to blame the former president, rather than Obama, for the ongoing economic problems. In the end, the economy was bad enough to make the election close and good enough to allow Obama to win. Political science forecasting models, based heavily on economic conditions, were divided, offering no consensus on the ultimate outcome. Out of 13 projections published in the October issue of *Political Science*, eight forecast that Obama would win the popular vote; five said Romney would prevail on that score (Balz, 2013).

With the economy in the gray zone, other factors could tip the balance, such as the Obama campaign's effective targeting of the growing ranks of younger and non-white voters. Had the economy completely recovered, the election might have been over from day one. Had the economy been substantially worse, the Republicans could have won even as their mainly white base was losing its long-term edge.

The confusing message of the 2010 election and internal Republican divisions

Republicans had a big victory in 2010, winning over 63 seats in the House of Representatives, enough to reclaim the majority in the chamber. The GOP also narrowed the Democratic advantage in the Senate, as voters were simply too frustrated with a sputtering economy to give fresh support to a president who had promised change.

The results underscored the economic distress that defined the 2010 elections. In that year's exit poll, nearly nine in ten said the national economy was in bad shape. A scant 14 percent said their own family's financial situation had improved over the previous two years – the lowest recording in exit polls since 1984. Overall, 41 percent of voters described themselves as supporters of the Tea Party (21 percent supported it strongly) and an overwhelming proportion of them – around nine in ten – voted for Republican House candidates.

But were the Republican victories in 2010 a repudiation of Obama's historic win just two years before, with a newfound congressional mandate? Or was it something simpler: a characteristic midterm defeat for a president whose tenure had been buffeted by a continuing series of financial crises? There were certainly enough favorable indications heading into 2012 to embolden Republican leaders. The Party had won back governorships in New Jersey and Virginia in 2009, and scored a surprise senatorial victory in heavily Democratic Massachusetts to start 2010. But the 2010 midterms provided the biggest boost. That year, female voters split their ballots evenly between Democratic and Republican House candidates. It appeared to some that the gender gap – which had given Democrats an advantage for years, as women heavily split in their favor – had slipped away.

Moreover, political independents sided with the GOP by a gaping 19 percentage point margin in 2010. Just four years before, independents had voted for a Democratic House by a similarly wide margin. The turnaround was unprecedented and confounding for many political analysts. But the volatility among independents – crucial swing voters – was unsettling for partisans on both sides. It was also disconcerting that 2006, 2008 and 2010 were all broadly classified as 'wave' elections, ones where at least 20 House seats switched from one party's control to the other's. Such a swing had happened only once in the ten elections before 2006.

In fact, as the 2012 primaries would make clear, the Republican wins of 2010 did little to reconcile the party's internal divide that had been so apparent years earlier. Short-term forces had lulled the Republicans into complacency about their long-term prospects. Michael Barone, the conservative commentator, summed up a core GOP interpretation of the midterm elections from the 2010 midterm elections: 'it's a landslide'. According to Barone, 'the depth and the breadth of Republican victories ... shows that the Tea Party movement was a genuine popular upheaval of vast dimensions' (Barone, 2010).

The Republican bravado was apparent in their presidential nomination fight in which the candidates fought to capture the conservative base and made little effort to appeal to moderates – independents, highly educated women and non-white voters. The premise of the Romney campaign was to overcome the tensions by a strategically calculated contradiction: move to the right to capture the base during the primary and then move back to the center for the November election.

With his candidate still mired in a tough fight for the Republican nomination, Eric Fehrnstrom, a senior Romney advisor, brushed off a reporter's question about potentially negative effects of a long primary: 'well, I think you hit a reset button for the fall campaign. Everything changes. It's almost like an Etch A Sketch. You can kind of shake it up and we start all over again' (Kamen, 2012).

The flippant answer reverberated widely, resonating with voters already wary of Romney's consistency and how closely he would adhere to conservative causes. More than half of all Republicans surveyed later that week by the Pew Research Center said they had heard about Fehrnstrom's remark. As a consequence, even when Romney enjoyed a sizable, 14-point advantage in the race for the GOP nomination in early February, he barely edged out the competition when it came to being the most 'honest and trustworthy' contender, according to polling by *The Washington Post* and ABC News.

Ultimately, of course, not moving more quickly toward the center proved a problem for Romney in the general election. But from the perspective of his nomination bid there may have been few options. First with Bachmann and Cain, then Perry and finally with Gingrich and Santorum, Romney faced a seemingly unending series of competitors pushing him rightward. Not only did the Republican campaign last longer than his campaign had hoped for – with new, emergent challengers by the month – but Romney also had 20 debates where he took positions geared to a very conservative, and white, GOP electorate.

A key moment in the debates – which stretched from May 2011 to February 2012 – may have been when Romney said he favored 'self-deportation' for illegal immigrants currently in the country. The logistics of such a policy were never clear, but the conclusion for supporters of legal immigration was obvious: that a Romney administration would never support any 'path to citizenship' for the nearly 12 million undocumented immigrants in the country. The phrase represented a harsh approach to a sensitive issue, and one clearly at odds with the views of a majority of American voters, most of whom support a path to citizenship, with conditions, for undocumented immigrants. At the time, Romney was struggling to reassert himself after a devastating loss in the South Carolina primary. He followed that loss by staging a comeback in the crucial Florida primary, sharply attacking former House Speaker Newt Gingrich, who had dislodged the frontrunner just ten days beforehand.

Nothing proved easy for Romney, however, and on the morning after regaining his footing in Florida, he blunted his own momentum by declaring, 'I'm not concerned about the very poor'. That proved a preview for the secretly recorded '47 percent' comments (in which Romney said that the 47 percent of voters who supported the President were doing so because they were dependent on government), which marked a critical point in the fall campaign. Romney consistently struggled to win the most conservative Republicans throughout the primaries and caucuses. Former Pennsylvania senator Rick Santorum won more of these voters in the first test (Iowa) and again in Romney's home state of Michigan. Gingrich prevailed among these voters in South Carolina and in Florida. The battle for these voters, though, locked Romney into conservative positions that proved costly in the long run. He prevailed because his rivals demonstrated even less ability to straddle the party's ideological spectrum.

On a pair of key questions, Romney proved a steady winner throughout the primaries, according to exit polls. He regularly won among voters prioritizing electability, a candidate's perceived ability to beat Obama. Romney also almost always topped the competition on voter trust to handle the country's flagging economy, the overwhelming top issue in the primary campaign as well as the general election.

Of course, big majorities of Republican voters across the 2012 nominating contests were conservative, and almost all were white, so even in victory Romney was unable to hone the broader pitch that his advisors envisioned. He failed to win any GOP caucus or primary where evangelical Christians made up a majority of voters, but his unrelenting pursuit of these voters may have hampered his ability to expand his appeal to less religious voters in the general election.

Against Obama, Romney won white evangelicals by the same margin as had George W. Bush in his bid for re-election eight years earlier. But Romney lost the rest of the voting population by a wide margin, 60 to 37 percent, far worse than Bush had done. By the time Romney accepted the nomination at the party's convention in Tampa, Florida, he had achieved one unenviable milestone: at the time he had the lowest personal popularity of any major-party nominee in polls dating back to the 1980s.

The Republican coalition

Why was it so hard for Romney to bridge the divide and develop a broad appeal? Republicans ostensibly were united in their conservative fiscal orientation and opposition to big government. They had strong support in the majority racial group, i.e. non-Hispanic whites. At least that was the case on the surface. But deep fault lines lay beneath, revealed in the primary election battles between Tea Party conservatives and more establishment politicians and tensions that pitted economic conservatives against religious and social conservatives.

A detailed analysis of the party conducted in August 2012 by *The Washington Post* and the Kaiser Family Foundation yielded five distinct types of Republicans (Balz and Cohen, 2012). Four had become familiar elements of the GOP coalition: Tea Party Movement Republicans, Old-School Republicans, Religious Values Voters and Pro-Government Republicans. The fifth, a group labeled Window Shoppers, were self-identified Republicans who in many respects seemed out of place in an increasingly conservative party; before the election, more than a third in this group said they would vote for Obama (see Figure 3.1).

Big majorities of the Pro-Government, Tea Party Movement and Values Voters groups said they attended religious services weekly; few Window Shoppers and Old-School Republicans went to church that regularly. There also were stark differences in their attitudes about the role that religion should play in public life. (Tea Party and Old-School Republicans are the two biggest groups, together accounting for half of all self-identified Republicans.)

Underlying demographic and behavioral differences led to conflicting attitudes and values on many issues. Most, 53 percent, of Old-School Republicans supported gay marriage, for instance; just 6 percent of Tea Party Republicans agreed. Most Republican groups favored confrontation over cooperation and compromise, but Old-School Republicans and Window Shopper tended to favor negotiation with the Democrats. Almost all Tea Party Movement and Old-School Republicans said people should take care of themselves and not look to government for

Figure 3.1   *Republican divisions*

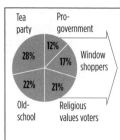

TEA PARTY MOVEMENT 28%

Most conservative of the GOP groups, with most identifying as tea party supporters. Almost all in this group are married and white. They have a uniform desire for smaller government with less regulation of business. Thay think gay marriage and abortion should be illegal. They say the GOP leadership is taking the party in the right direction.

OLD-SCHOOL REPUBLICANS 22%

More male, white, educated and wealthy, with moderate views on social issues but conservative views on fiscal issues. They are the least religious of Republicans groups. They oppose raising taxes on the rich and are fearful of increases to the budget deficit.

RELIGIOUS VALUES VOTERS 21%

More female, focused on religious heritage and conservative on social and fiscal issues. They take a more or less moderate view on issues of equality. Although they prioritize the role of religion in public life, they are not as religious on a personal level as Tea Party Movement Republicans.

WINDOW SHOPPERS 17%

Young Republicans with more progressive views on many social and fiscal issues. They are more female, less white and less religious than other groups. A majority prefer a larger government with more services, see regulation of business as necessary and want government to improve the standard of living.

PRO-GOVERNMENT 12%

Working-class Republicans who are highly religious and very conservative on social issues. But they are more open to the idea of a larger government. The smallest Republican group, with lower income and less educated, they want to see an active government improve the standard of living for people.

Source: *The Washington Post*, 18 August 2012.

help, a sentiment that dropped sharply among Pro-Government conservatives.

On Medicare, an issue that proved central to the presidential campaign, the Republican coalition was divided. The Washington Post-Kaiser survey asked everyone whether they preferred changing Medicare to a premium-support program for younger workers, in which people would have the option to purchase their own health-care plans after retiring, an idea Vice-Presidential nominee Paul Ryan outlined and Romney embraced. Or, they were asked, would they prefer to keep the government health program largely as it was? Tea Party Movement Republicans were the only one of the five GOP groups in which a majority favored the premium-support approach advocated by Ryan. About four in ten Old-School Republicans said they supported such a change. But more than 60 percent of those in each of the other groups said they opposed the idea. Even had he prevailed, Romney would have been faced with harnessing a party that in a variety of ways was pulling in different directions, substantively and stylistically.

At bottom, the Grand Old Party has an image problem, with negative views of the Party regularly outnumbering positive ones for the past six years. However, it is not simply a matter of branding. On specific policies, Republicans seem to be on the wrong side. On taxing the rich, most voters side with Obama and the Democrats. Majorities also recoil at large scale cuts to entitlements like Medicare and Social Security, which has basically been Obama's position. Even with deficits spiraling and a 'fiscal cliff' defining the end of the election year, voters were as apt to say government should spend more than pare back, which again was Obama's argument.

More problematic for the GOP is that it appears to be holding losing cards in other areas as well. There is a clear trend toward public acceptance of gay marriage, most voters see climate change as real, and a sizable majority advocates giving undocumented immigrants a path to citizenship. Public support for immigration reform such as the Dream Act also highlights the Republican challenge with Hispanic voters. Many Republicans remain adamantly opposed to providing pathways to citizenship for undocumented immigrants and favor strict attempts to control the country's borders, including mass deportations. Just 27 percent of Hispanics supported Romney in November; 71 percent backed Obama's re-election. Hispanics made up 10 percent of voters nationally, according to exit polls, up from just 2 percent in 1992.

Given that around nine in ten of all Romney voters were white, Republicans are stubbornly relying on a shrinking part of the American electorate. White voters continue to make up a sizable majority of all voters, but their share has been steadily declining. In 2012, 70 percent of all voters were white, according to the exit poll. Twenty years before, 87 percent of voters were white. While the country's demographics have changed dramatically, the GOP remains almost as reliant as ever on white voters. The vote among Hispanics – the country's fastest growing minority group – was more lopsided than at any point since the 1990s. Among Asians, Obama won by a lopsided 73 to 26 percent, continuing a trend for the increasingly Democratic Asian electorate. The GOP's challenge with non-white voters frames the party's problems moving forward, even as it may be winning a broader ideological argument about the role of government.

The Democratic coalition and potential future fissures

While the tensions within the Republican Party coalition are more obvious in the wake of losing the popular vote in five of the past six

Figure 3.2   *Democratic divisions*

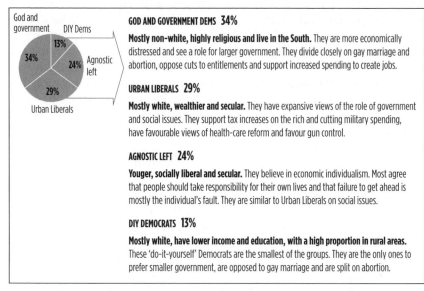

God and government

DIY Dems

Agnostic left

Urban Liberals

GOD AND GOVERNMENT DEMS 34%

Mostly non-white, highly religious and live in the South. They are more economically distressed and see a role for larger government. They divide closely on gay marriage and abortion, oppose cuts to entitlements and support increased spending to create jobs.

URBAN LIBERALS 29%

Mostly white, wealthier and secular. They have expansive views of the role of government and social issues. They support tax increases on the rich and cutting military spending, have favourable views of health-care reform and favour gun control.

AGNOSTIC LEFT 24%

Youger, socially liberal and secular. They believe in economic individualism. Most agree that people should take responsibility for their own lives and that failure to get ahead is mostly the individual's fault. They are similar to Urban Liberals on social issues.

DIY DEMOCRATS 13%

Mostly white, have lower income and education, with a high proportion in rural areas. These 'do-it-yourself' Democrats are the smallest of the groups. They are the only ones to prefer smaller government, are opposed to gay marriage and are split on abortion.

Source: *The Washington Post*, 18 August 2012.

presidential elections, the Democratic Party too has a diverse coalition that may not be as unified in 2016 when Obama is not on the ballot.

In 2012, Obama had his own struggles with his party's coalition. His election-year announcements on gay marriage and a naturalization policy for undocumented immigrants seemed to play to a Democratic base, one largely supportive of his moves. But Democrats too were divided – particularly on gay marriage (see Figure 3.2).

Fully 85 percent of those labeled 'Urban Liberals' – one of the biggest of the Democratic groups – said they felt strongly that gay marriage should be legal, according to the Post-Kaiser survey from August 2012. But that dropped to 26 percent among 'God and Government' Democrats, the largest group, and just 13 percent among the smallest cadre, the do-it-yourself (DIY) Democrats.

Religion, social issues and the size and scope of government were the main pivots dividing the Democratic coalition, but demographic differences also contributed to the fissures. Urban Liberals – the most traditionally liberal of the groups – were nearly three-quarters white and by far the most educated and highest income earners among Democrats. The God and Government contingent was two-thirds non-white and far more apt than even two of the five Republican groups to go to religious services at least once a week.

Urban Liberals and the 'Agnostic Left', another group of liberals who seldom go to church, overwhelmingly said there should be a high degree of separation between church and state, while sizable majorities of the other two groups of Democrats said the government should take special steps to protect America's religious heritage. About a third of DIY Democrats advocated a larger federal government, offering more in services, a position backed by most of those in other groups, peaking at 85 percent among Urban Liberals. DIY Democrats were by far the least likely of any of the four groups to support new spending at the cost of deficit reduction. But they also represented only about one in eight Democrats – only about a third of the size of the God and Government group. The Agnostic Left, about two-thirds of whose members were under 50 years old, nearly matched the DIY group in its overall espousal of economic individualism but differed sharply when it came to issues around religion's role in public life.

Obama was able to stitch together a unique coalition, still reliant on a non-white base but reaching into some segments of voters previously resistant to Democratic presidential candidates. But the near universal support from Democrats in the election masks deep disagreements that could color his effectiveness during the rest of his presidency. Still, the internal differences within the Democratic ranks do not appear to be severe enough to tear the coalition apart or even endanger the party's future electoral prospects.

While Obama ultimately notched a convincing re-election win over Republican standard-bearer Mitt Romney, there was support for the broad-based Republican aversion to big government on Election Day 2012. In this sense, the 2012 election affirmed some contradictory lessons about what American voters want, enough to nourish the toxic clash between the country's two major political parties over the role of government. Even as Obama raked up 332 Electoral College votes, a slim majority of voters in the presidential election said Washington is doing too much that is better left to businesses and individuals, a reversal from four years earlier when the former Illinois Senator rode into the White House on a wave of sentiment for more expansive government action.

In 2008, amidst the major financial crisis, 51 percent of voters said the government should be doing more, not less, to solve problems; 43 percent said Washington should pare back its activity. Four years later, those numbers were exactly flipped, according to the exit poll. Of course, the 2012 election followed a series of government attempts to stimulate economic growth, an historic bailout of the American automobile industry and the quick rise and sudden success of the anti-government Tea Party political movement. So-called Tea Party Republicans swept the party into the majority in the House of Representatives in the 2010 midterm elections. The reaction against the Affordable Care Act serves as a vivid reminder that the Democrats can over-reach their mandate and lose despite the structural advantages that recent trends have afforded the party.

Prospects for the future

The prolonged nominating fights in the last two presidential elections (it took Obama until nearly summertime 2008 to defeat then-senator Hillary Clinton), with the party's candidates competing for the base vote, have spotlighted the widening gap between the two major parties. This has repelled moderate voters, feeding the trend toward a greater number of independent voters. In a 1998 *Washington Post* poll conducted with the Kaiser Family Foundation and Harvard University, 41 percent of Republicans and 45 percent of Democrats said they considered themselves 'strong' partisans. By 2012, those numbers had shot up to 65 and 62 percent, respectively.

Over this time period, the gap between Democrats and Republicans widened, particularly when it comes to attitudes about the federal government. A clear majority of Republicans score highly on a series of questions about limited government, which was not the case 14 years before, even amidst the partisan rancor of Bill Clinton's second term in office.

One set of answers in the *Washington Post*–Kaiser Family Foundation poll was particularly revealing: the number of Republicans who said they felt strongly that the government controls too much of daily life jumped 24 percentage points since the 1998 survey to 63 percent. The number of Democrats strongly disagreeing with the assertion doubled.

The debates during Obama's presidency over health care, economic stimulus and financial regulatory reform underscore how far apart the parties are on economic issues and on attitudes about the government's role. For example, more than twice as many Democrats as Republicans say regulation of business is necessary to protect the public interest. Most Republicans say regulation does more harm than good. Republicans see deficit reduction as more important than spending money in an effort to create jobs. Democrats believe the opposite.

Divisions over religious and social issues are equally stark. As a whole, the two parties are mirror images of each other on whether organized religious groups should stay out of politics or stand up for their beliefs in the political arena. They are similarly at odds over whether there should be a high wall of separation between church and state and whether government should more actively protect religious heritage. Both parties contain deeply observant people as well as many who seldom go to a church, synagogue, or mosque. But in general, a higher percentage of Republicans, by far, are frequent churchgoers.

One of the fastest growing segments of the Democratic Party in recent years has been non-believers or infrequent churchgoers.

Big majorities in both parties see tolerance of others' lifestyles as important, but Republicans and Democrats take opposite positions on whether changing mores should affect personal convictions. A majority of Democrats agree with the proposition that as the world changes, people should adjust their morals and values. An even bigger majority of Republicans disagree with that statement, with most saying so strongly. Far more Republicans than Democrats see Americans in general as too tolerant of behavior that was once considered wrong or immoral.

On abortion and gay marriage, the divide between the parties is wide. Twice as many Democrats as Republicans say abortion should be legal in all or most cases. The margin between the parties is similarly gaping when it comes to same-sex marriage. Another key area where Republicans and Democrats see the world the same way, though from totally different perspectives, is a shared sense of being at risk of losing what they have. Almost identical percentages – around six in ten in each party – say groups and people who hold values similar to theirs are losing influence in American life.

All of this makes for strategic complexity for both parties. Their activist bases demand loyalty to basic principles but a growing number of independents want less partisan acrimony and more practical problem solving. The prevailing wisdom of American elections used to be that the party that moves to the middle and captures the independent vote wins the election and control of government. George W. Bush turned that logic on its head in 2004, when his campaign concentrated on turning out the base as opposed to wooing the independent voters. Sometimes a successful strategy is misleading. Relying on the base works as long as that party's base is bigger than the other's. It is a recipe for defeat otherwise. Political parties can sometimes win elections even when they are divided or when their base is dwindling because short-term circumstances favor them. Hence the Democrats could win presidential elections in 1976, 1992 and 1996 even when conservative ideology and white voters were in their ascendancy. Adjusting to long-term coalitional change is the most difficult challenge any political party must face. The next few elections will reveal which American party is better suited to the task.

Chapter 4

Political Parties

Bruce E. Cain and Peter J. Ryan

American political parties have been traditionally characterized as organizationally weak and ideologically incoherent. European parliamentary parties, with their card-carrying members and centralized control over resources and candidate selection, were often thought to be efficiently modern while their American counterparts seemed to be mired in a state of arrested political development (Duverger, 1951). Organizationally weak parties in America were also accompanied by an incumbent-centered and interest-group-driven politics. Party-line voting in Congress was traditionally far lower than the discipline common in parliamentary systems, and the political opinions of elected party officials were more ideologically incoherent (Converse, 1994). Consequently, American parties apparently did not stand for any firm principles (e.g. Finer, 1949). As Lord Bryce observed, they were like two bottles, each with different labels and both empty (Bryce, 1910: 699).

Some American political scientists lamented the debilitated state of American political parties. Shortly after World War II, APSA issued a famous report entitled 'Toward a More Responsible Two Party System', arguing that the failure of the two parties to provide clear choices undercut political accountability. They recommended stronger national party organizations and more coherent party platforms. The party renewal movement continued to press for stronger parties throughout the post-war period, hoping to counteract the power of incumbency and interest groups on American policy (Pomper, 2003).

Fast-forward to the present day and American attitudes toward political parties have shifted dramatically. Many Americans now believe that there is *too much* partisanship and that the choices between the two parties have become too stark. Led by cable TV and talk radio, the media have become more politicized. Congressional voting measures reveal a widening gap between Democratic and Republican members of Congress. Critics argue that Congress has become dysfunctional and stalemated, with Democrats and Republicans trying incongruously to operate like disciplined parliamentary parties in a Congressional government system (Mann and Ornstein, 2006).

Partisanship is clearly on the rise, but curiously the official American political party organizations have not become any stronger or more disciplined. The proliferation of party primaries ensures that party 'machines' play little role in the selection of candidates, while recent court decisions have strengthened the role of outside groups in campaign finance. Instead, Americans have managed to achieve higher partisanship without the centralized, strong, political parties that Europeans are familiar with. The country's unique path to greater political partisanship owes more to an increasing alignment between party identification and ideology, a phenomenon often called 'polarization'. The rise of ideological, party affiliated groups, an increasingly politicized media, and changes in congressional rules and culture have all contributed to polarization. So too have socio-political shifts, such as rising income inequality and the realignment of Southern states away from the Democratic Party.

Although there is still significant debate over which factor has had the biggest impact on these increased levels of polarization, its effects are indisputable. American government at the federal, and increasingly the state, level finds itself stalemated over fiscal choices, social issues and environmental policies. Previously routine matters like authorizing the debt-limit ceiling increases or approving the nominations of lower Federal court judges today incite pitched battles that often end in bitter stalemates. As a result, instead of strong parties and responsible government, many Americans feel they have stronger partisanship and more irresponsible governance.

The party as an organization

The distinctive institutional features of US government shape American political party organizations in various ways. The separation of executive and legislative powers often creates electoral tensions between congressional leaders and the president from the same party, a fact that has contributed to organizational fragmentation. Fragmentation is also a function of the federal system; state parties often have very different electoral needs from the national party organizations, and as a result often act quite independently of them. American courts treat political parties more like regulated public utilities than private organizations, upholding regulations that limit donations to party campaign committees and allowing the state effectively to run the party's candidate nomination process in the form of primaries. Organizational fragmentation, restrictions on party funds and the inability to control the candidate nomination process have contributed to weak formal party structures and left a vacuum that well-funded and often ideologically extreme party affiliated groups have filled.

The formal party committees

The United States has several formal national party organizations. In contrast to their European counterparts, however, their role is almost exclusively in assisting candidates in elections by providing campaign support and services to them (Epstein, 1986; Herrnson, 1988) rather than dictating party policy or in helping to select candidates. In total, there are six federal party committees: the Democratic National Committee (DNC) and Republican National Committee (RNC), which focus mainly, though not exclusively, on presidential elections; the Democratic Congressional Campaign Committee (DCCC) and the National Republican Congressional Committee (NRCC), which are dedicated to electing members of their respective parties to the House of Representatives; the Democratic Senatorial Campaign Committee (DSCC) and the National Republican Senatorial Committee (NRSC) are focused on electing their party's nominees for Senate seats.

These contemporary national party organizations, which have become increasingly professionalized and well-funded since the 1970s (Herrnson, 1988), provide a range of services to party nominated candidates such as voter contact lists, research, advertising production facilities and advice, and access to donors to help fund their campaigns (Jacobson, 1985; Herrnson, 2008). At the House and Senate levels, the party committees are also active in helping to recruit candidates, while at the presidential level the DNC and RNC still play a role in determining the rules governing presidential primaries. The national committees also raise and spend money on behalf of candidates, though campaign finance laws impose strict limits on the amount that can be spent in 'coordination' with candidates (Herrnson, 2009: 1210). Moreover, such money is generally only spent to help candidates that have already won their party's nomination. Nevertheless, given that the maximum contribution that can be given to party organizations is far higher than those that can be made to individual candidates (the figures were $30,800 versus $2,500 respectively during the 2011–12 electoral cycle), the national party committees are still valuable sources of finance for candidates in the general election.

State party committees perform similar service-oriented functions to candidates for statewide and local office, though the degree of their professionalization and the permanence of their structures do vary significantly from state to state (Roscoe and Jenkins, 2010). Local party organizations often play a more important role in candidate selection compared to their national and state counterparts. With fewer groups competing to provide campaign services and candidates that often have much less well-developed networks of their own, local party organization often become the critical 'brokers' that provide access to the money, expertise and volunteers needed to win elections (Frendreis and Gitelson, 1999).

Despite this, however, both federal and state party organizations still play a much smaller role in American elections than in other advanced democracies. Instead, a more loosely aligned network of party-linked outside groups tends to provide most of the resources – money, expertise and volunteers – needed by candidates to win their party's primary elections and, to a lesser extent, the general election. Therefore, these groups – many of which are ideologically extreme – have a far greater influence over the selection of the party's candidates, a fact that, as we shall see later, has contributed to heightened polarization. This imbalance in influence between the formal 'establishment' party and the ideological interest groups that comprise the 'shadow party' has been exacerbated by campaign finance decisions that have successively weakened the fundraising capacity of the formal party organizations and has given outside groups a disproportionate influence, particularly in the nominating (primary election) process.

Campaign finance and the rise of the shadow party

The modern US campaign finance regulation era really begins with the passage of the post-Watergate Federal Election Campaign Act (FECA) in 1973 and the ensuing landmark case, *Buckley v Valeo* (1976), that set the constitutional parameters for contemporary reform measures. The original FECA legislation was quite comprehensive, enacting extensive new contribution and expenditure limits, disclosure rules and public financing. The *Buckley* decision threw out the expenditure limits entirely as an infringement of first amendment free speech and association rights and mandated that public financing schemes could be voluntary only. It left in place only contribution limits and disclosure requirements on individuals, groups and political parties. Importantly, the FECA regulated not only the amount of money that individuals and groups could give to party committees, but the amount of money that the parties could contribute to their own candidates.

Few objected to these political party restrictions at the time, but the logic seems contorted upon reflection. The Court had held that preventing quid pro quo corruption was the only legitimate reason to limit the fundamental right to support candidates and parties of choice. Contributions to the parties were limited in order to prevent the parties from becoming vehicles for the quid pro quo exchange of government actions in return for donations from wealthy individuals and groups. But why was it then necessary to limit additionally the amount of money parties gave to their own candidates? If the amount of money a party received from any individual or group was limited, could a large or even unlimited party donation then corrupt the candidate?

This question was never seriously addressed by the court, let alone answered. The Court subsequently decided in *FEC v Colorado Republican Federal Campaign Committee* (2001) that political parties could spend unlimited amounts of money on behalf of their candidates as long as they did not coordinate with them. The implication was that a direct donation from the party to the candidate, not the amount per se, was the corrupting element. To put it another way, the Court believed that political parties were less potentially corrupting if they acted like independent outside interest groups, an odd legal fiction to be sure. Treating political parties as essentially large political action committees marginalized them and centered political campaigns even further on the candidates themselves. Candidates, especially incumbents, therefore became largely responsible for raising their own funds and for deciding how to spend that money for re-election purposes.

The *Buckley* system lasted until the mid-1990s, but was gradually eroded by the growing professionalization and resultant expenses of political campaigns. Campaign managers, pollsters, media buyers and the like were replacing volunteers and political operatives who used to provide the manpower for state and local political parties. As legislative districts got larger and community neighborhoods were transformed by new demographic trends and social mobility, American political candidates began to rely more on direct mail, TV and radio, and less on door-to-door campaigning and direct voter contact. The new forms of communication were expensive, which increased the fund-raising burden on candidates and their supporters, a burden that the party organizations alone could not shoulder.

The candidate-centered campaign finance system created by *Buckley* and the growing expense of campaigns significantly advantaged long-time incumbents in uncompetitive districts. These legislators began to raise significant sums of money that they then proceeded to stockpile. This was highly inefficient; in a party-centered system, that money would have been put to better use by helping to elect candidates in marginal seats. When Democratic Party domination ended in 1994 and the control of Congress became more uncertain, the inefficiencies of the *Buckley* system became more glaring. Controlling Congress in an era of relative competitive balance now hinged on redirecting donations and expenditures to the most vulnerable incumbents and promising challengers. As a result, party leaders in Congress began to create 'leadership PACs' (PAC standing for 'political action committee') which distributed excess campaign funds to vulnerable party candidates and encouraged intra-party transfers of campaign dollars from safe incumbents to more vulnerable legislators. This also provided opportunities for those aspiring to legislative leadership positions to demonstrate their worthiness and accumulate political debts that could be cashed in at leadership elections. Nevertheless, the effect of these quasi-party committees was limited: incumbents still banked most of their campaign dollars in order to scare away potential challengers.

In the mid-1990s, the official political party committees briefly appeared to be becoming more centrally involved in campaign fundraising, particularly at the presidential level. Taking advantage of favorable rulings from the regulatory agency that oversees federal campaign finance reform, the Federal Election Commission (FEC), political parties began collecting so-called unlimited soft money contributions for 'party building' activities. Although the intent of this was to allow parties to engage in registration and voter mobilization efforts, much of the money was diverted to pay for 'issue' advertisements that were actually thinly veiled candidate advertisements. As the 'soft money' loophole was more heavily utilized, many came to believe that this was undermining the purposes of the *Buckley* era limitations (money collected under these limits came to be called 'hard money'). Democrats, with the assistance of some Republicans like John McCain, passed legislation (the Bipartisan Campaign Reform Act of 2002 or BCRA), which closed the party-building soft money loophole and more closely regulated the issue advertisements. This short period, which lasted from the mid-1990s until the passage of the BCRA in 2002, marked a high point for the official political party apparatuses, placing them centrally in the increasingly important role of raising and distributing campaign funds.

The passage of the BCRA sidelined the political parties once again and, unintentionally, helped to elevate the role of outside groups. While the BCRA had plugged the party-building soft-money loophole, it did not address the more serious underlying problems: namely, elections were getting more expensive and campaign funds needed to be allocated more efficiently than by simply giving it to safe incumbents. Therefore with the political party path blocked, soft money flowed to independent groups that could help candidates fund their campaigns. The Supreme Court had exempted independent spending (i.e. expenditures that were not controlled by or spent in consultation with the candidates) from any regulation or limits other than the obligation to disclose the sources of their donations and the recipients of their expenditures. For thóse seeking paths around the new regulations, independent expenditures offered the best solution. Nonprofit organizations and independent spending PACs, with the help of favorable court decisions, filled the money void created by the BRCA limitations on the official political parties.

Three recent Federal Court decisions have been particularly important in increasing the role of outside groups in elections. First, *Wisconsin Right to Life v FEC* (2010) loosened the distinction between issue and candidate advertisements that had previously been tightened in the BCRA. This mattered because it allowed nonprofits that were restricted in their political activities by Internal Revenue Service (IRS) rules to make electioneering advertisements that indirectly favored or opposed candidates with fewer limitations than before. Secondly, the *Citizen United v FEC* (2010) decision permitted corporations and trade unions to tap into their treasury funds for independent election expenditures. Many believed that this would open the floodgates for corporate money in political campaigns. And then, in what actually may have been the most important decision, an appellate court cleared the way for unlimited contributions from individuals and interest groups to so-called 'Super PACs' that could advocate expressly for the election or defeat of candidates (*Speech-now.org v. FEC*, 2010).

The sum effect of these three legal decisions was to spur independent spending by individuals and interest groups and to spawn the creation of many new Super PACS. These organizations were often run by party insiders such as Karl Rove, but many were also more ideological or created solely to support particular candidates in party primaries. It also added yet another set of actors to the already very complex and fractured campaign finance environment, with Super PACs operating alongside state and national parties, Senate and House campaign committees, leadership PACS and various other partisan interest groups. Although broadly aligned with one party or the other, each operated with varying degrees of independence from one another and pursued often quite distinctive agendas.

The intersection of party primaries and the shadow party

The fracturing of funding intersected with another institutional trend, the proliferation of party primaries and the opening up of caucuses to broader participation. Political parties in all democracies experience tensions between the motives for winning elections and for satisfying the purer policy demands of their electoral bases. As attitudes in the party bases diverge more from one another and the median voter, these tensions increase. In the American system, this manifests itself in the difference between primary and general election incentives. The turnout in primary elections and caucuses is typically lower and skewed toward the more politically motivated voters. Primary electorates are thus usually more liberal or conservative than the November electorates, and candidates have to accommodate accordingly. This creates the odd strategic dance in which candidates move to the left or the right in order to win the nomination, and then try to move their positions back to the center to win over more centrist and independent voters in the final round.

No recent presidential candidate exemplified this tension more clearly than Mitt Romney. He first tacked to the right to gain the Republican nomination in 2011, for example raising his hand along with the other Republican candidates at a primary debate to signify that he would not accept a deal with the Democrats that raised taxes, even when such a deal included spending cuts ten times the size of the proposed tax increase. He then tried to move back to the middle in the general election by assuring voters that his positions on entitlements and fiscal austerity were not as draconian as they had seemed months earlier. The strategy allowed President Obama to remind voters of Romney's contradictory positions in the final months of the campaign.

Super PACs have added a new force to this tension. Long-serving conservative senators, such as Bob Bennett of Utah and Richard Lugar of Indiana, have failed to be renominated, losing to Tea Party aligned candidates that were heavily financed by outside groups. Many other 'establishment' candidates in 2012 – such as David Dewhurst in Texas and Sarah Steelman in Missouri – also failed to win their party's nomination, thanks in no small part to such Super PAC spending, which favored more conservative Tea Party opponents. These defeats have sent a strong signal to Republican candidates that any acts of policy heresy would be punished by a primary or caucus challenge. Money, which today moves flexibly and quickly across state lines, often allows Tea Party and other challengers to overcome the normal obstacles posed by incumbency. It can also exacerbate intra-party fighting and the length of presidential primary campaigns. For example, in the 2012 Republican presidential primary, Sheldon Adelson, the wealthy owner of a casinos and hotel resorts corporation, donated $20 million to keep former House Speaker Newt Gingrich in the campaign far longer than he would have otherwise been able to, prolonging the primary process.

The fear of Super PAC interventions in primaries contributes to polarization. After the 2012 election, negotiations between President Obama and House Leader John Boehner on a 'grand bargain' to cut spending and raise taxes failed because many Republican House members feared that voting to extend the Bush tax cuts to all but the wealthiest taxpayers would be construed as a tax hike, which in turn would lead outside groups to seek their defeat in a party primary. When groups or party factions with money and organization play the role of policy monitor, rewarding candidates that are loyal to their causes and working against those perceived to be disloyal, it can have the effect of fracturing the party along ideological lines. Within the type of centralized party system that exists in the United Kingdom and other European countries, leaders with an eye to the general election or the tradeoffs necessary for governance can deal with factionalism within the party structure, using rules and internal incentives to resolve matters. But in the United States system, with low membership barriers in party primaries and outside groups with large amounts of money, it is harder, if not impossible, for party leaders to control nomination races or to mediate disputes.

Parties in Congress: the rise of polarization

While the party organizations have remained relatively weak, scholars broadly agree that at the elite level (particularly amongst Members of Congress) the two parties have become significantly more polarized from one another since the 1970s. Analyses of voting patterns in Congress reveal that the median ideological distance between Democrats and Republicans has been steadily increasing since the early 1980s (Hetherington, 2009: 417). Figures 4.1 and 4.2, which measure the ideology of Members of Congress on a liberal to conservative scale (with −1 representing the most liberal Member and +1 representing the most conservative), clearly illustrate this trend. In both the House (Figure 4.1) and Senate (Figure 4.2), Democrats have become somewhat more liberal over time (though much of this is a result of the decline in the numbers of conservative Southern Democrats). Republicans, by contrast, today have voting records that are *significantly* more conservative than they were 30 or even 20 years ago, a fact that is particularly true in the House of Representatives. This raises the question: why has this dramatic ideological polarization between the two parties in Congress occurred?

Structural causes

To a large degree, contemporary polarization in Congress is a function of changes that occurred between the late 1940s and 1960s, when the two national parties were seen as being ideologically close to one another. The Democratic Party had to reconcile the policy demands of its conservative Southern members with those of more liberal members from other parts of the country. Southerners began to exit the Party, however, in the late 1940s, in part because of its embrace of civil rights for African Americans, a trend that accelerated after the passage of the Civil Rights Act of 1964 and the Voting Rights Act of 1965. Over time, as Democratic lawmakers retired, the increasingly Republican Southern electorate chose even more conservative Republicans to replace them, while the handful of newly redrawn majority African American districts in the South began to return more liberal representatives.

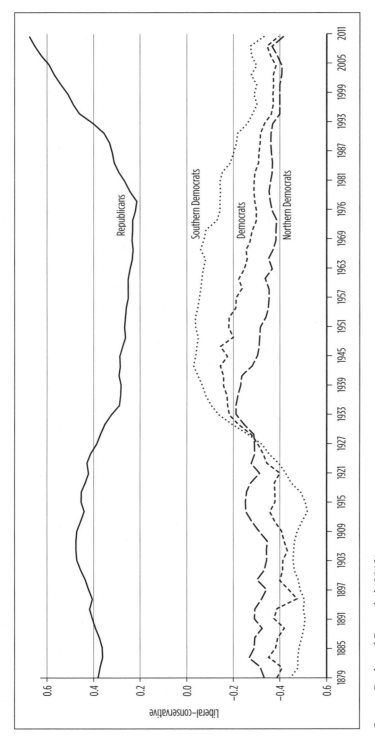

Figure 4.1 Mean ideological score of Members of the US House of Representatives based on roll call voting patterns, 1879–2011

Source: Poole and Rosenthal (2012).

Figure 4.2   Mean ideological score of Members of the US Senate based on roll call voting patterns, 1879–2011

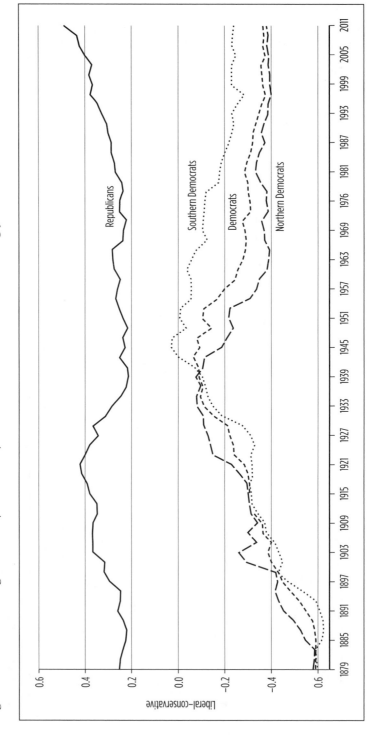

Source: Poole and Rosenthal (2012).

Over time this shift led the national Republicans to become more conservative on economic, racial and social issues, which produced a counter-reaction in other areas of the country. This was particularly true in the eastern part of the country, where more liberal Democrats have gradually replaced moderate Republican legislators. To illustrate: after the 1952 election, Republicans won just 6 percent of the Southern House seats but won 65 percent of the north-eastern and mid-Atlantic House seats; by 2012, the Republicans had won 70 percent of seats in Southern states, while winning just 28 percent of the seats in the north-east and mid-Atlantic. These regional shifts in voting patterns have produced two parties that are both ideologically more homogeneous and increasingly distant from one another.

However, this realignment process does not fully explain polarization, since the voting records of Republican Members have become increasingly conservative irrespective of the region they are from, while Democrats from all regions have also grown more liberal (Jacobson, 2003). This has led to a lively debate amongst American political scientists and commentators about the potential causes of polarization in Congress. Many (e.g. McDonald and Grofman, 1999; Carson and Crespin, 2004) argue that the decennial rearrangement of House districts – a process typically controlled by partisan state legislatures – has contributed to polarization by creating increasing numbers of 'safe' party districts. As these districts become more skewed toward one party or the other, candidates increasingly become concerned about winning their party's primary, an election in which more ideological and committed party identifiers vote, rather than the general election (McCann, 1995). The evidence for these claims is fairly weak, however. First, even if we hold boundary lines constant, House districts have become significantly more Democratic or more Republican in their voting habits over the past 20 years (Silver, 2012). Second, the fact that polarization in congressional voting has occurred in the Senate, albeit at a slower pace, suggests that partisan redrawing of district boundaries has had a limited effect.

Another cause of polarization may be the rise in ideologically motivated interest groups since the 1960s (McCarty et al., 2006, especially ch. 5). These groups tend to hold what are often extreme positions on the issue or set of issues they care about. As we have already discussed, these groups are able to mobilize committed supporters, particularly in primary elections, and are a critical source of campaign money, as demonstrated by the key role played by Super PACs in the 2012 presidential primary elections. Others argue that changes in the media environment have had an impact, both on elites and on the mass public. In particular, the rise of conservative talk radio, ideologically oriented cable news channels such as the conservative network Fox News and liberal-leaning MSNBC, as well as the proliferation of websites with overt political biases, may be playing a role in increasing polarization at all levels. Prior (2007) finds, for example, that partisan voters are increasingly self-selecting news sources that align with their preexisting ideological or partisan viewpoints.

Rising inequality in the United States could also be contributing to polarization in Congress. McCarty et al. (2006) argue that, as higher income voters have become significantly wealthier over the past 30 years, they have become less favorable to social welfare spending programs that they no longer benefit from and less willing to accept higher levels of taxation to pay for such programs. Since these voters tend to be an important source of votes and campaign money for Republican candidates, the Party's elected officials become increasingly opposed both to redistributive government programs and to tax increases. Conversely, those at lower income levels have become relatively poorer and therefore more favorable to government assistance programs. However these groups, which tend to favor the Democrats in elections, vote at relatively low levels, while many are non-citizen immigrants that cannot vote at all (Gerring, 1998). As a result, the incentives for the Democrats to move to the left on economic policy are not as strong as they are for the Republicans to move in a conservative direction, which may help to explain some of the asymmetry in elite polarization, as is evident in Figures 4.1 and 4.2.

Other structural changes in the population may be having an effect on polarization at both the elite level and amongst the voting public. There is a popular belief – expressed by academics such as Wuthow (1989) and Hunter (1991) – that the country is divided into distinctive 'red' and 'blue' Americas, each with vastly different values, religious orientations and lifestyles (see Frank, 2004; Fiorina et al., 2006). However, while scholars have found that cultural factors such as religion are important in structuring political behavior and party politics (Green et al., 1996; Kohut et al., 2000; Layman, 2001), there is little research to support the idea that society at large has polarized along religious, cultural or ideological lines (see Fiorina et al., 2006; Baker, 2005). Similarly, some have claimed (e.g. Bishop, 2004; Nunn and Evans, 2006) that the tendency of Americans to live in socially and economically homogeneous communities has contributed to greater homogeneity in the partisan or ideological views of the electorate as a whole, though Fiorina and Abrams (2008) note there is a lack of evidence for these claims.

Changes in the way Congress operates

Another contributing factor to increased polarization has been changes to the way Congress is run. Since the mid-1970s, party leaders have obtained significantly more institutional resources, while the once powerful chairs of congressional committees have seen their influence decline (Rohde, 2006; Zelizer, 2004;). The emergence of more powerful party leaders reflects the increasingly homogeneous ideological nature of the party caucuses that they lead (Hetherington, 2009: 425). However, it also has contributed to polarization by narrowing the legislative choices that Members can choose from and providing strong incentives for legislators to demonstrate party loyalty (Sinclair, 2002).

Although the party leadership in the Senate has become powerful in recent years, these institutional changes have mainly occurred in the House. In large part this is because the House, unlike the Senate, has a powerful Rules Committee that determines whether legislation will be considered on the floor of the House and whether amendments can be offered to legislation. Prior to the 1970s, the Rules Committee was largely comprised bipartisan coalitions of Southern conservative Democrats and Republicans, and functioned largely independently of the Speaker and the other majority party leaders (Sundquist, 1968). Reforms in the mid-1970s changed that, placing the power to appoint committee members in the hands of the party leadership.

This has led to changes in the way legislation is considered, with restrictions placed on the number and types of amendments that may be offered to a bill on the floor of the House, as well as strict time limits for consideration of measures. In many cases, House Members are prohibited from offering *any* amendments whatsoever to bills. Similarly, omnibus bills, single bills containing multiple provisions that often have little relationship to one another, have become increasingly common. Restrictions on amendments, time for consideration of bills and the proliferation of omnibus bills all have the effect of forcing Members to vote only for options that are approved by the party leadership, which in turn tends to reflect the median position of the members of their party caucus rather than the median position of the chamber as a whole. As a result, policy outcomes have moved further to the left (when Democrats are in the majority) and further to the right (when Republicans are in the majority) over time, leaving centrist legislators from both parties with little influence over the content of legislation (Krutz, 2001).

Polarization, particularly in the House, has also increased in part because of changes in the committee system, where most legislation is introduced and developed. Length of service or 'seniority' was traditionally the most important factor in who became chair of a congressional committee, a position that in turn could be held for as long as that Member remained in Congress. As a result, committee chairmen established bases of power independent of their party's leadership. However, the seniority system has progressively become weaker since the mid-1970s, particularly so after the 1995 Republican takeover of the House; party loyalty is now an important factor in the selection of committee chairs (Dodd and Oppenheimer, 2005), and, at least in the Republican Conference, such individuals may not hold their positions for more than six years. The increase in the number of subcommittees, as well as the willingness of party leaders to bypass committees on major pieces of legislation, have also weakened the power of committee chairmen while strengthening the party leadership (Oleszek, 2004; Rohde, 2006).

Finally, changes in interpersonal relationships and a growing 'team mentality' may be having an effect. Following the Republican takeover of both the House and Senate in 1994, the working week for Members of Congress was shortened to facilitate travel back and from districts/states. As Mann and Ornstein (2006) observe, this meant that Members had less time to develop relationships with their colleagues, particularly those from the opposing party. Relatedly, the families of Members of Congress tended to remain in their districts, also reducing the social interactions that once were commonplace in Washington (ibid.: ch. 2). Party unity may also be stronger simply because congressional elections are, at the aggregate national level, more competitive, which in turn may be producing a stronger 'team mentality' amongst caucus members (Hetherington, 2009). This could be one reason for the dramatic increase in incumbent contributions to fellow party candidates and party campaign committees (see e.g. Currinder, 2005; Heberlig and Larson, 2005; Heberlig et al., 2006).

Consequences of polarization

A 2004 *Washington Post* editorial, published shortly after that year's elections, argued that 'polarization is worrisome ... it can condemn Congress to gridlock ... [and] it can alienate citizens from their government' (*Washington Post*, 2004). On the first point, scholars have indeed shown that polarization has led to increasing levels of legislative inaction (e.g. Jones, 2001; Binder, 2003). Bond and Fleisher (2000) observe, for example, that opposition parties in Congress have become increasingly unified and reflexively hostile to initiatives emanating from a president of the other party. Unsurprisingly, therefore, the policy-making process has become particularly gridlocked during periods of divided government (ibid.; Sinclair, 2011b).

For example, since 1997 the parties have failed to agree on a formal budget to fund the government, forcing Congress to pass short-term stopgap funding measures known as 'continuing resolutions'. In the 112th Congress that lasted from 2011–12, previously routine matters, such as the raising of the United States' debt ceiling and the passage of a farm bill, became controversial amongst many Republican law-makers in the House, leading to protracted negotiations that prevented Congress from dealing with a variety of other policy issues. This pattern appeared to repeat itself in the negotiations surrounding the so-called 'fiscal cliff' at the end of 2012 and which continued into 2013.

Democrats and Republicans have also proved increasingly willing to use the Senate filibuster – a provision that allows for continuous debate – in order to block legislation and presidential nominations when in the minority, as well as employing other mechanisms to prevent consideration of measures, such as 'holds' (Sinclair, 2012). The number of filibusters is typically measured by the times a motion for 'cloture' is invoked, which is a formal procedure to end debate and move to a vote; to invoke cloture, a supermajority of 60 senators must consent. Such cloture votes were traditionally unusual as senators typically elected to proceed to votes by unanimous consent. However, the number of cloture votes began to increase between the 1970s and 1990s. By the mid-2000s, most legislation and important nominations were subject to cloture votes, meaning that they needed 60 votes to avoid a filibuster.

Polarization may have other negative impacts on public policy. Sinclair (2008) argues that the emphasis on party unity leads to suboptimal policy-making free from discussion, compromise and often the input of experts, all of which she believes produces better legislation (see also Mann and Ornstein, 2006: ch. 4). The emphasis on party unity may also hamper oversight during periods of unified government, e.g. the failure of Republican oversight before and after the Iraq War (Hetherington, 2009: 8). The increasing use of reconciliation measures – which can be passed by a simple majority in the Senate – may lead to budgetary outcomes that are more extreme, since they cannot be blocked by the minority party. As McCarty et al. (2006) contend, polarization has not only been caused by income inequality but has actually exacerbated it, in large part because increasing division leads to policy 'drift'. For example, laws dealing with the minimum wage or taxes are often not updated to take account of changing circumstances, such as increases in the cost of living (see also Hacker and Pierson, 2011).

On the other hand, many have argued that polarization has had some positive effects. The parties in Congress have greater ideological cohesion and discipline, which enables the winning party to act in a more coherent way and to try to enact the program that it presents to voters during campaigns, which in theory should increase accountability to voters (e.g. Crotty, 2001). This has led some, such as Pomper (2003), to claim that the United States is moving towards a UK-style parliamentary democracy in which parties contest elections based on a common policy platform that they then all commit to implement once in office. However, this ignores the fact that the party organizations themselves remain far weaker than those in parliamentary systems, while the divided structure of government means that some form of cooperation and compromise is necessary, blurring the lines of accountability that typically exist in the Westminster system.

Have voters polarized too?

Although it is clear that elected officials have become more ideologically polarized from members of the other party, there is some uncertainty about whether voters have similarly polarized. Although most scholars believe that the widespread cultural and social polarization implied by images of 'red' and 'blue' Americas is overstated (e.g. Fiorina et al., 2006), they do accept that, amongst the two-thirds of the electorate that identify with one of the two major parties, there has been a growing gap in terms of their attitudes on economic and social issues (e.g. Layman and Carsey, 2002; Jacobson, 2005). However, whether this constitutes 'polarization' (that is voters becoming more extreme in their views), the presence of more extreme options for voters to choose from, or some form of 'sorting' by voters into the 'correct' ideological party is a matter of considerable debate.

Fiorina et al. (2006), extending the work of DiMaggio et al. (1996), argue that the electorate has not polarized. They note, for example, that the US National Election Study consistently shows that a clear plurality of Americans characterize themselves as 'moderate'. Moreover, they suggest that there is little evidence that increased geographic homogeneity or social cleavages (such as age, race, gender and religious affiliation) have actually made Americans' views on public policy issues more extreme. Rather, elite polarization means that the *options* voters are able to select from have polarized (Jacobson, 2007; Rauch, 2007; Fiorina and Abrams, 2008), masking the relatively consistent ideological moderation of the electorate as a whole.

However, Fiorina et al. acknowledge that a growing gap has emerged between the ideological views of those who identify with either party on economic and social issues. This leads them to introduce the idea of 'sorting'. They claim that as the elites of the parties – their elected officials and visible activists – began to take clearer public stances on a wide range of economic, cultural and racial issues from the 1960s and 1970s onwards (Carmines and Stimson, 1989; Aldrich and Rhode, 2001), voters have responded by aligning themselves with the party that best fits their *existing* position on issues important to them.

For example, at the aggregate level, Fiorina notes that views on abortion have been relatively constant over time. However, those that felt strongly on the issue changed their party identification to reflect the elite cues sent by each party's leaders. Therefore Democrats have become more homogeneously pro-choice, and Republicans more unified in their pro-life stance, though very few voters have actually shifted their views (or the intensity of their views) on the abortion issue. This suggests that voters have not polarized per se, but rather that ideology and party identification are simply better aligned today than they were 30 or 40 years ago. This argument is consistent with scholars who argue that voters select their party affiliation based on their ideological viewpoints (Abramowitz and Saunders, 1998).

Others disagree. Bartels (2006), as well as Layman and Carsey (2002), have suggested that the increase in the correlation between party and ideology is too great to simply be explained by voters re-sorting themselves based on their existing ideological viewpoints. They also note that there is an increasing correlation between the economic preferences of voters, their social issue preferences and their party identification. Given that this correlation was not nearly as strong 30 or 40 years ago, it seems to suggest that voters are bringing their views in line with those of their party rather than simply sorting on the basis of pre-existing views. In short, that would seem to imply that, at least amongst partisan identifiers, some degree of polarization has occurred.

There is mixed evidence for this thesis. On the one hand, Green et al. (2002) demonstrate clearly that the realignment of the South was issue-based, which supports a sorting claim, while Abramowitz and Saunders (1998) demonstrate that ideology helped to shift patterns of partisan identification in the 1990s. Layman and Carsey (2002) show, however, that this type of sorting really only occurs when voters (a) perceive party differences on the issue (i.e. relatively high information voters) and (b) see the issue as salient to them. Thus for most voters on most issues, it is the shift in elite party attitudes that is causing identifiers in the electorate to change their preferences rather than the other way around (see also Goren, 2002). This is consistent with research that shows party identification is a deep-seated and stable identity (Campbell et al., 1960; Converse and Markus, 1979; Green et al., 2002), that partisanship is important in structuring attitudes toward policy issues (Campbell et al., 1960), and that individuals often change their issue positions in response to changes in the stands of elites who share their general political worldview (Zaller, 1992).

In summary, it appears that *both* partisan sorting and actual polarization amongst party identifiers has occurred, even though the idea of 'popular' polarization of the American public at large has been somewhat exaggerated.

Consequences of polarization and sorting

Studies have shown that these changes within the electorate are related to increasing levels of voting participation, activism, grassroots campaign donations, interest in elections and perceptions of government responsiveness amongst *all* groups of voters (Hetherington, 2009; though, as he points out, this is doubtless also a function of parties' increased efforts to mobilize voters). Indeed, these changes may have contributed to a resurgence in party identification in the electorate. The percentage of strong partisans has rebounded while the presence of so-called 'pure' independents has declined. The degree to which citizens express positive feelings toward one party and negative affect toward the other also has increased markedly (Hetherington, 2001). Most fundamentally, the relationship between party identification and vote choice in both presidential and congressional elections has grown significantly stronger (Bartels, 2000). In line with these findings, there has been a decline in voters 'splitting' their presidential and congressional tickets (Jacobson, 2005).

Although most scholars agree that polarization and/or sorting are primarily caused by elected politicians (Fleisher and Bond, 2001) or committed party activists (Layman et al., 2006), it is likely, as Jacobson (2007) argues, that polarization at the mass level also exacerbates elite polarization. As the bases of both parties become more ideologically homogeneous (and possibly more extreme), elites will feel less pressure to moderate their views than they would have when their constituencies were more heterogeneous.

Another important consequence of party sorting is that it has produced an environment in which the party acts as a far more important filter for information than it once did. As Jacobson (2007) notes, the partisan gap in approval ratings from President Eisenhower to President Clinton never exceeded 70 percentage points. However, under both the Bush and Obama presidencies, the gap has rarely been less than 70 percentage points. Much the same was true of opinions of the War in Iraq; for example, in 2004, Jacobson found that the gap between Democrats and Republican support for the war averaged 63 percent, which represented twice the maximum partisan difference during the first Gulf War. Similarly, Democrats and Republicans do not just hold different opinions, but appear to view facts differently, e.g. Republicans were 42 percentage points more likely than Democrats to think Saddam Hussein possessed weapons of mass destruction prior to the invasion.

The effects of polarization and its meaning for American politics

As recently as half a century ago, American political parties were completely unrecognizable from their European counterparts. Their party organizations were fragmented and decentralized; there was relatively little party unity or discipline amongst its elected officials; and the party leaders in Congress were weak. Moreover, both parties had ideologically heterogeneous coalitions amongst the electorate at large. In short, the US had a political system that was more candidate-driven than party-centered. Today, the major parties have evolved in some ways to become more like parties in parliamentary democracies: by many measures, party unity in Congress (and in state legislatures) is at its highest levels over the period of the past 100 years; party leaders in Congress exert far greater influence over legislative outcomes; while amongst voters that identify as party supporters, ideological unity has increased significantly. In some ways then, the US has moved toward a party system that more closely resembles the Westminster model of unified parties with clear national identities and distinct policy platforms.

However, there is an important difference: these shifts have occurred in the absence of the type of powerful, centralized, party organizations that are common in most European countries. In fact, the party organizations have played at best a marginal role in the revitalization of partisanship at the elite and mass levels. Instead, partisanship has become more important as the ideological polarization between the parties has increased. In turn, polarization has been shaped by a variety of forces: the rise of ideological, party affiliated groups that provide vital resources to candidates, an increasingly politicized media, growing economic inequality, the shift of the South away from the Democratic Party, and changes in congressional rules and culture.

After many years of increasing party unity in Congress, this marriage of increased polarization with weak party organizational structures has recently begun to contribute to party fragmentation and dysfunction in American government. Many elected officials, with an eye to primary challengers that could be financed by ideologically motivated outside groups, are increasingly wary of engaging in compromise with their counterparts in the other party. This phenomenon is particularly true for Republicans, whose base coalition has polarized significantly more to the right than the Democrats have toward the left.

As a consequence, the Republican Party in particular is finding it increasingly difficult to govern when it is compelled to share power with Democrats, as was the case after the 2010 mid-term elections. Whether on the issue of increasing the debt ceiling, cutting spending or raising taxes, the Party's leadership has been unable to strike significant agreements with their Democratic counterparts owing to rebellion from Members concerned about the threat of a conservative Tea Party challenge. Since the Party's leaders do not control the nomination process nor provide the bulk of financing to candidates, their ability to impose discipline on their Members is weak. In short, polarization, which up until this point has helped boost party unity, may now be leading to the fragmentation of the parties along ideological fault lines.

Although polarization may have arguably produced some benefits, such as boosting levels of voter participation in elections, the major consequence appears now to be fairly clear: policy gridlock. Recently, it has produced a seemingly never-ending round of fights over fiscal issues that pose a threat to the day-to-day ability of the US government to function and to the health of the American economy as a whole, as the 2011 fight over the debt ceiling and the debate over the so-called 'fiscal cliff' at the end of 2012 both highlight. These disputes over previously routine issues, which are typically resolved only by short-term fixes that ensure the battle will be reengaged in a matter of weeks or months, suggest that effective governance under conditions of divided government is currently nearly impossible.

These outcomes should not be surprising: the weak party organizational structure in the United States is a reflection of the fragmented structure of government itself, in which powers are separated and public officials are elected by highly divergent constituencies and at different times to one another. Such a system can ultimately only work when there are incentives to cooperate and compromise. However, polarization produces few incentives to engage in either, thereby making dysfunction and gridlock almost inevitable. Given that neither the current polarized party system nor the institutional structure of US government is likely to change significantly in the medium term, this type of governance style is likely to perpetuate over the next several years, particularly in the absence of unified party control of both Houses of Congress and the presidency.

Chapter 5

Interest Groups

Lee Drutman

On July 21, 2010, President Obama signed into law the Dodd-Frank Wall Street Reform and Consumer Protection Act, a sweeping piece of legislation that would substantially rewrite the rules of the American banking system and create an entirely new agency to regulate consumer financial products. The bill had been one of the most heavily lobbied pieces of legislation ever. According to one analysis, more than 850 businesses, trade groups and other corporate interests had paid more than 3,000 lobbyists to advocate on their behalf. The Chamber of Commerce alone had 85 lobbyists from 49 different firms working Congress, and the Securities Industry and Financial Markets Association had 54 lobbyists from 37 different firms making their case (Pell, 2010).

Yet, as the public attempted to make sense of what exactly had happened, the reviews differed. Did reform-minded lawmakers triumph over banking lobbyists to enact the toughest regulations on the financial sector in more than seven decades, putting an end to an era of financial deregulation that many believe caused the financial crisis of 2008–09? Or did the banks get away with half-measures that, while putting in place many new rules, still sidestepped the basic issues of 'too big to fail' by not breaking up the biggest banks? In many respects, it was a premature question: the bill mandated financial regulatory agencies to write more than 400 individual rules to implement the bill. Even two and a half years later, as this chapter is being written, barely a third of the rules has been completed.

It was also an impossible question because the bill was so large and sprawling that very few, if any, individuals were in a position to evaluate it in its totality. The legislation covered such topics as consumer credit, derivatives markets and products, investor protection, consumer protection, fair lending, bank capital, mortgage reform, insurance and resolution authority – 16 sections in all, each with their own argot-laden array of subtitles and sub-provisions, all written in dense legalese. Yet, even with all the sweep and heft of the bill, many reform provisions were defeated or set aside, often because some particular lobbying interest strongly opposed it. Other provisions were quietly inserted into the bill at the behest of a particular Senator, working closely with a particular lobbying interest.

Politicians spoke repeatedly of the bill in the simplistic terms of Wall Street versus Main Street, of ending bailouts versus preserving too big to fail. Journalists and pundits spoke of winners and losers, as the standard media narrative always directs them to do. But as is almost always the case, the complex reality lay somewhere in the middle, a series of compromises worked out in endless conversations, the vector of multiple competing interests and incentives. Tracing and measuring their exact influence is a difficult and quite likely an impossible task. But the claim that lobbyists played a large part in the outcome is beyond dispute. Without a doubt, the legislation was affected in some way by just about every major interest that participated in the process.

This legislation will illustrate many aspects of modern lobbying, serving as the backdrop for a basic overview of how interest groups work in American politics, and how and why these groups do (or do not) shape outcomes. (I should add that I worked as a US Senate staffer during the passage of the bill as part of an American Political Science Association Congressional Fellowship (December 2009 to July 2010). Some details of the bill's passage are provided, based on my first-hand experiences.) The basic argument in this chapter is actually quite straightforward: that interest groups succeed primarily by dogged involvement, particularly in highly technical details. Despite popular caricatures to the contrary, lobbying is not simply a bidding war where special interests purchase policy by agreeing to pay members more than their opponents. Rather, interest group politics more resembles a messy multi-dimensional, multi-stage tug-of-war of shifting alliances, unpredictable terrain and only occasionally participatory crowds, where most of the time nothing much at all happens, and where victory comes most easily when there is nobody pulling on the other side.

As the complexity of the issues with which Congress must deal continues to increase, and the fundraising demands of running for office continue to expand, lobbyists and the interests that they represent are put in increasingly powerful positions. Time and money continue to become dearer and dearer resources for the average member of Congress, increasing the importance of those who can help congressional offices to acquire both. At the same time, the competition to influence Congress has become ever fiercer as more and more interests have poured money into Washington. Such competition makes individual-level outcomes harder to accomplish for lobbyists and harder for social scientists to explain parsimoniously (Salisbury and King, 1990; Baumgartner et al., 2009). But the overall picture appears to be one of distortion, in which the aggregate priorities and positions of

Washington do tilt toward those who devote the most resources (Gilens, 2012; Kimball et al., 2012).

The distribution of political resources

In 2011, 14,483 unique organizations filed lobbying reports (or about 27 for each single member of Congress). The majority of these lobbyists represent businesses, either working directly for corporations or on behalf of trade or business associations. But Washington is also home to representatives of a diverse array of other interests: nonprofit advocacy groups organized for all manner of causes; local, state and foreign governments; colleges and universities; hospitals and nursing homes; identity groups; unions, professional associations, and so on.

What all these groups have in common is that they are in Washington because they care about some set of policy outcomes, and they are willing to spend resources to make their case. Some will win, and some will lose. And while there are many in Washington who claim to know (for a fee, of course) what it takes to win, the short answer is that there are no guarantees, and certainly no consistent pattern that spending more money leads to an increased likelihood of winning.

What we do know is that interest groups employ a wide range of tactics to get what they want. The following discussion considers the most common approaches and why and how they are likely to be effective. But first, let us pull back and gain a broader picture.

Who is represented and how has that changed?

More than 50 years ago E. E. Schattschneider (1960) quipped that 'the flaw in the pluralist heaven is that the heavenly chorus sings with a strong upper-class accent'. The 'pluralist heaven' referred to a claim, made by some at the time, that James Madison's ideal of competitive democratic pluralism, in which faction regularly counteracted faction, was alive and well, and that American democracy was accordingly thriving (or at least performing as well as could be expected). Schattschneider dissented, noticing that most of the participants in politics represented the very well-off.

Little has changed since. Indeed, one of the more persistent and consistent empirical findings in political science is that Washington influence (both lobbying and campaign contributions) is dominated by rich individuals and business interests (Schlozman and Tierney, 1986; Baumgartner and Leech, 1998). The most recent and most exhaustive tallies on the breakdown of Washington lobbying come from

Schlozman et al. (2012), whose book, *The Unheavenly Chorus*, is a 700-page testament to the wide-ranging nature of Schattschneider's seemingly timeless critique. By their count, business groups make up 53 percent of the organizations with lobbyists in Washington, hire 64 percent of the outside firms, and make 72 percent of the lobbying expenditures. They also provide half of the PAC donations. Moreover, Schlozman et al. estimate that, while 10 percent of adults in the United States could be classified as executives, about 74 percent of the organizations in Washington represent the interests of executives. Another 10 percent of adults they classify as professionals, and 17.3 percent of Washington organizations represent them. That means that less than 10 percent of organizations represent the other 80 percent of Americans (ibid.).

What has changed is the density of interests in Washington. Between 1981 and 2006, the number of organizations listed in the directory more than doubled, from 6,681 to 13,777. The fastest growing lobbies in Washington have been the education lobby, the health lobby, and the state and local government lobby, but the business lobby still remains the dominant group. Of the top-level categories listed, the only category that has not witnessed a growth in the absolute number of organizations represented is labor unions. The number of organizations representing unions has remained unchanged over 25 years.

Figure 5.1 shows an overview of the balance of Washington representation over a 25-year period, based on listings in the *Washington Representatives* directory (the most comprehensive source of lobbying organizations). The graph provides a visual representation of the fact that by far the most common type of interest in Washington is business – corporations and business associations consistently account for about half of all groups represented in Washington. State and local governments, followed by foreign groups (both foreign businesses and governments), followed by occupational associations, round out the five most well-represented interest types. Public interest groups of all types (the authors make no distinction between liberal and conservative groups that claim to speak for a broader public, and note that almost a quarter of these groups are organized on behalf of environmental and wildlife issues) only account for around 4 percent of all the groups with Washington lobbyists. Summarizing the distribution of organized interests, Schlozman et al. (2012) conclude that throughout the period considered 'pressure politics has been a domain hospitable to the representation of the interests of the advantaged, especially business. Any amelioration or exacerbation of its upper-class accent is secondary to the fact that the chorus has unambiguously become large'.

Washington influence is dominated by institutions, rather than citizen groups, for two main reasons. One is the simple fact that it is relatively easy for institutions to mobilize politically since they already

Figure 5.1 *Lobbying interests in Washington*

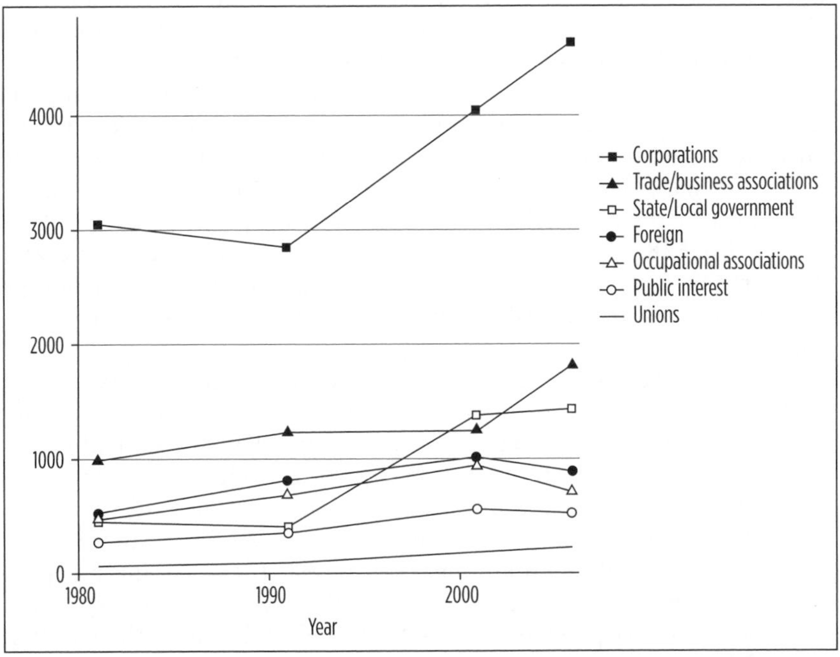

Source: Derived from Schlozman et al. (2012).

exist and can thus allocate some of their already existing budgets to political activity (Salisbury, 1984; Hart, 2004). Interested citizens, by contrast, must find a way to overcome the collective action problem, pulling together resources and commitments (Olson, 1965). Thus forming groups, especially when they rely on the contribution of many far-flung individuals, is notoriously difficult. Additionally, the nature of much political conflict, in which a particular policy affects a handful of companies greatly while it affects most citizens only marginally, also skews political activity toward companies who have the most incentive to remain vigilant and active (McConnell, 1966; Lowi, 1979; Wilson, 1980). All of this helps to explain the persistence of the participatory imbalance. With the basic contours of who is represented in place, let us now turn our attention to how lobbying works, looking more closely at the tactics that are used.

How much does money matter?

Perhaps the most common view of how interest groups work is that they buy policy through campaign contributions. The argument goes that since American elections are privately funded, lawmakers must solicit donations to get reelected. Because they need this money, they will trade their votes and other official actions in exchange for campaign support (Grossman and Helpman, 1994, 2001).

The traditional mechanism for organizational campaign giving has been the Political Action Committee (PAC). PACs allow like-minded individuals (often employees of the same company or members of the same association) to pool their contributions together and support candidates of their choosing. In 2008, there were 4,292 active PACs, including 1,578 corporations, 272 labor unions, and 928 trade and membership associations. Organizations also frequently encourage their employees to contribute independently and directly to campaigns.

Recent changes in US campaign finance law have expanded and diversified the sources of money, arguably making money even more important. While traditional PACs were limited in the contributions they could make to candidates ($10,000 per election cycle), new 'super PACs' now provide a vehicle for corporations and unions to make unlimited contributions. Unlike traditional PACs, these super PACs can spend unlimited amounts, as long as they operate 'independently' of campaigns. The 2012 election also witnessed the expansion of a new set of independent groups organized under the 501(c) section of the US tax code who were able to spend hundreds of millions of dollars on advertising and campaigning without having to disclose their donors.

There is wide consensus among both Washington insiders and political scientists that money at the very least buys access (Langbein, 1986; Hall and Wayman, 1990). But the connection between contributions and actual outcomes is much more tenuous. Scholars have conducted at least 40 studies trying to link PAC contributions to roll call votes. Some studies found relationships, while others did not. Ansolabehere et al. (2003), summing up the studies, conclude: 'overall, PAC contributions show relatively few effects on voting behavior. In three out of four instances, campaign contributions had no statistically significant effects on legislation or had the "wrong" sign – suggesting that more contributions lead to less support'.

When it comes to campaign contributions, the finance sector has consistently been the most generous source of campaign money. For the last seven cycles, roughly one in six itemized campaign contributions have come either from PACS or individuals affiliated with the FIRE sector (Finance, Insurance and Real Estate), the sector with most at stake in the Dodd-Frank bill, substantially more than any other sector (Drutman, 2012b). Goldman Sachs, for example, contributed $2.8 million to candidates in the 2010 election cycle between its PAC and its employees. JP Morgan Chase & Co contributed $2.0

million. Wells Fargo made $1.8 million in contributions. Would these supposedly savvy Wall Street banks be better off getting a subscription to the *American Political Science Review*? Were these contributions wasted, as the political science studies referenced above might indicate?

As with most issues, it is hard to say what exact influence the money had (and very difficult to test it quantitatively). All the money from the finance sector did not stop the Dodd-Frank bill from passing. But it may have prevented particular amendments from passing or particular provisions from being included in the various drafts that circulated throughout the House and Senate for months before the bill was passed. Clawson et al. (1992) make the case that money in politics does not buy votes, but it does build friendships. They also argue that money provides what they call 'effective hegemony' – that it helps to set the range of acceptable agenda topics: 'some alternatives are never seriously considered, and others seem natural and inevitable; some alternatives generate controversy and costs, and others are minor and involve noncontroversial favors' (Clawson et al., 1992). Lessig (2011) makes a similar argument: that measuring influence involves not just what is on the agenda, but what is off the agenda as well. Power is the ability to determine the scope of the debate. Since campaign contributions come disproportionately from businesses and wealthy individuals (Drutman, 2011; Schlozman et al., 2012), it's not surprising that members of Congress tend to be most responsive to their wealthiest constituencies (see e.g. Gilens, 2012).

The most useful way of understanding campaign contributions is that they are the price of admission. In a political world of limited time and limited attention, making campaign contributions can accomplish two major things. First, they often directly buy access to the politicians. Many large contributions are given as the price of admission to fundraising events, which provide rare opportunities to talk to an otherwise harried member of Congress, and an environment where that member is likely to provide a sympathetic ear. Second, they create the conditions for reciprocity, which is one of the most powerful universal norms (Whatley et al., 1999). Money may not be a guarantee of anything, but it helps lobbyists and the interests that they represent to build a positive relationship with a member, and often it buys a sympathetic hearing. And in an era in which the cost of running for Congress continues to increase with each passing cycle, reelection minded lawmakers have less and less leverage to upset potential donors. Though much attention is focused on campaign contributions, the majority of organizational money (about 90 percent) goes to actual lobbying activities (Milyo et al., 2000). Campaign contributions are but one tactic in a larger arsenal of influence.

Lobbying as information and argument

To understand truly legislative lobbying, one must first understand something very basic about congressional staff: turnover is high and most staff, particularly in the House, are quite young. According to a 2009 Congressional Management Foundation survey, 27 percent of House legislative directors are under 30 years old, and 87 percent are under 40 years old. More than half (55 percent) have only a bachelor's degree, and only one in six (16 percent) have a law degree. Typically, they have two to three legislative aides working under them, and 80 percent of those aides will have less than three years experience in Congress. Committee staffers tend to have more experience than personal office staff, and Senate staff likewise tend to be more experienced than their House counterparts. Still, turnover everywhere in the government is high because of relatively low pay, long hours and difficult working conditions, with only a handful of truly dedicated staffers making a career of it (Schuman, 2010; Jensen, 2011).

At the same time, legislation has grown ever more complex. The 111th Congress passed the two longest non-appropriations bills in Congressional history: the Dodd-Frank Wall Street Reform and Consumer Protection Act at 383,013 words, and the Patient Protection and Affordable Care Act at 327,911 words. (For the sake of comparison, the Oxford World's Classics edition of *War and Peace* is 561,093 words.) Congressional offices also have to deal with a remarkable range of issues. As one measure of the diversity, since 2009, the Library of Congress has used 1,023 unique codes to identify legislation.

The practical implication is that the average staffer cannot possibly know more than a fraction of what he or she needs to know, especially if he or she has only been in the job for a few years. As Esterling (2004) writes: 'it is difficult for Congress to know about the current research-based state of knowledge for the full array of policies before it'. High turnover also creates a problem of institutional knowledge (Whiteman, 1995). New staffers do not know what positions their boss has even taken in the past, and how he or she handled particular circumstances and constituencies.

This is where lobbyists frequently step in: 'in contrast, it is relatively easy for specialized interest groups to know about the state of knowledge for a policy' (Esterling, 2004). Esterling finds that demonstrated technical expertise improves access. In one recent survey, two-thirds of staffers described lobbyists as 'necessary to the process' as either 'collaborators' or 'educators'. Staffers also frequently referred to lobbyists as 'partners' (Policy Council, 2007). As Allard (2008) argues, lobbyists assist staffers 'by sifting information and noise, putting information into a coherent framework, and by challenging or checking facts on impossibly short time deadlines'.

In recent years, the outsourcing of expertise to interest group lobbyists has accelerated across all areas as a result of increasing turnover of staff and the increasing complexity of policy. It also does not help that members of Congress are also spending more and more time fundraising and less and less time in Washington or that Congress has increasingly limited funding for its own independent research capacity. Most notably, in 1995, Congress cut off funding for the Office of Technology Assessment, killing the 23-year-old agency that had become a trusted and valuable source for neutral policy expertise (Bimber, 1996).

The financial sector is arguably one of the most complicated parts of the economy. The sheer length of the Dodd-Frank bill alone is testament to that. One of the leading reasons for the financial crisis was that nobody understood the collective levels of risk because nobody could understand the entire financial system with its maddening array of interlinkages, from mortgage lending and consumer banking, to credit default swaps, to a complicated mix of financial derivative products. Congressional offices were forced quickly to become experts on a range of arcane technical workings of a remarkably diverse financial system as well as on a complicated regulatory system with many overlapping and unclear jurisdictions among 22 different government agencies that the bill delegated some authority to, each of which fought to maintain its own regulatory territory despite initial attempts in earlier drafts of the bill to streamline the regulatory process. All through the process, lobbyists tried to position themselves as helpful experts who could walk congressional offices through particular parts of the financial system. But of course, each lobbyist client had its own perspective, and its own particular story about the causes and effects of particular policies. For example, would breaking up the biggest banks end the 'too big to fail' problem by eliminating banks that were so systematically important that they would need to be bailed out? Or would it make the problem worse by creating more small banks without the capital reserves to weather the downs that are inevitable in market capitalism? It depended on who was making the case. But in the end, the so-called Brown-Kaufman amendment, which would have limited a bank's total deposits to 10 percent of all deposits, failed by a 61 to 33 vote, as almost the entire financial industry had advocated.

Providing a 'legislative subsidy'

Since members and their staff have limited time and resources, they frequently need the help of outside interest groups to enact their legislative priorities. Accomplishing anything in Congress is time-consuming and resource-intensive. It requires holding hearings, distributing briefing materials and most importantly getting other members to sign on. To accomplish this, members of Congress frequently enlist the help of like-minded lobbyists and interest groups. Hall and Deardorff (2006) have formalized this understanding into a theory they call 'lobbying as legislative subsidy'. In short, they view lobbying as 'a matching grant of costly policy information, political intelligence, and labor to the enterprises of strategically selected legislators' – not to change the mind, but to 'assist natural allies in achieving their own, coincident objectives' (ibid.).

While the popular press often depicts interest groups as twisting members' arms for votes (and this may occasionally happen), the modal relationship is far more cooperative. Most of the time, interest groups are working and strategizing with their allies, trying to figure out how they might accomplish their shared priorities. For example, most Republicans opposed Dodd-Frank and depicted it as a government overreach. Even after the bill had passed, Republicans in Congress continued to introduce legislation to try to repeal parts of it. Did they do so because they were rewarding financial sector donors? If so, why the Republicans but not the Democrats? After all, the financial sector has historically supported Republicans and Democrats in roughly equal proportions (Drutman, 2012b). A more convincing explanation is that many Republicans' anti-regulation, pro-free-market worldview just happened to coincide with financial groups' positions on a particular piece of legislation, creating a fortunate partnership. In the same way, many Democrats worked closely with members of a pro-reform coalition known as Americans for Financial Reform, utilizing the policy and politics expertise of a set of groups outside of Congress. Then again, one might ask where these preferences came from in the first place.

On a case-by-case basis, the lobbying-as-legislative-subsidy relationship can seem entirely benign. After all, if lobbyists are merely helping members of Congress to enact the policies that they already support, how is that a problem? But, as Hall and Deardorff (2006) ask: given that business has significantly greater resources to provide legislative subsidies, does this mean that members will defer to business priorities, since those are the ones with the backing to get accomplished? They wonder whether 'representation is compromised without individual representatives being compromised'. There is good reason to wonder.

Attention to the technical rule-making details

In 2011, the Federal Register, the daily digest of proposed and final rules, notices of hearings and meetings, and presidential orders and proclamations, ran to 82,419 pages. That is an average of 321 pages per working day. Between 2004 and 2010, the federal government issued 23,003 rules (more than 3,000 per year), 518 of which the Congressional Research Service deemed 'major', generally because they could have an impact of at least $100 million on the economy (Copeland and Carey, 2011).

While much public attention focuses on Congress and the Executive Office of the President, a significant amount of lobbying attends to the routine and detailed work of the massive federal rule-making bureaucracy. Here, technical expertise is at a premium. Administrative rule-making is about figuring out how actually to write and implement rules. And the bureaucrats writing the rule tend to be most interested in finding a workable one, especially one that will minimize headaches and complaints for the agency. This has two important consequences for interest groups. The first is that it puts technical expertise at a premium. The second is that it provides an advantage to those who pay the closest attention to implementation of the rules (i.e. those most likely to complain). Additionally, the bureaucrats making the decisions are not subject to the same constituency and fundraising pressures as individual Members of Congress.

On all counts, business interests are advantaged. They tend to have the know-how, resources and interest to provide the detailed analyses that the rule-writers want. They also pay the closest attention to federal rulemaking (Lowi, 1979; Furlong, 1997; Golden, 1998; Furlong and Kerwin, 2005; Yackee and Yackee, 2006; McKay and Yackee, 2007). McKay and Yackee (2007) report that agency rule-making is very often not competitive. This matters, because when lobbying is 'imbalanced' (as it often is), agency rule-making tends to be responsive to the side that participates most. As they note: 'lobbying requires considerable time and money to monitor agencies, research policies, and convince the bureaucrats that a group's position is the right one' (ibid.: 350).

The Dodd-Frank legislation passed in response to the financial crisis offers a good example. Despite being almost 400,000 words long, the legislation still delegated almost 400 rule-makings to the regulatory agencies. In October 2012, more than two years after the legislation passed, the law firm Davis Polk reported that only 127 of the 398 rule-makings had been finalized, while 237 had passed deadlines and 136 had yet to be proposed. In the two years following the bill's passage, the two most active banks (Goldman Sachs and JP Morgan Chase) met with the Treasury, the Federal Reserve and the Commodities Futures Trading Commission a combined 356 times, or 3.5 times per week. Those two banks by themselves also accumulated 114 more reporting meetings than all reform-oriented groups combined (Drutman, 2012a). Again, sheer numbers do not prove anything in any particular case. But more meetings mean more opportunities to press a case and to make arguments. Over time, this run of opportunities adds up.

Perhaps the most controversial Dodd-Frank rule was the 'Volcker Rule' – an attempt to prevent banks from engaging in what was known as 'proprietary trading' – basically taking gambles on clients' assets that would benefit the company. It began as a three-page proposal. It grew to ten pages in the Dodd-Frank bill. More than a year later, the proposed rule had grown to 298 pages, and regulators faced more than 1,300 question letters on 400 topics. As the *New York Times* reported at that time: 'even the helpful summary prepared by Sullivan & Cromwell, a law firm that represents big banks runs [to] a dense 41 pages' (Stewart, 2011).

Notably, the Volcker Rule was a rare case where citizens did engage in rule-making participation. An estimated 16,500 of the 17,000 comment letters came from individuals opposing what they believed to be banks' attempts to weaken the rule. However, since the letters were largely duplicated standard letters that lacked the sophisticated economic analysis that the bank letters included, it was unclear how much of an impact they would have (McGrane, 2012).

Of the 400 Dodd-Frank rules, only a handful saw any notable level of citizen or public interest group participation. Few public interest groups had the resources to participate at the level of detail that they knew would be meaningful to regulators. While the populist 'Main Street vs Wall Street' messaging can work well on the floor of Congress, coupled with media attention, the more specialized and less dramatic actual rule-drafting is a domain limited to technocratic experts.

More broadly, on issues where the public is not paying attention – which are actually most of the issues that the federal government deals with – those who are paying attention are much more likely to shape understandings and priorities, and thus outcomes (Lowi, 1964; Wilson, 1980; Smith, 1995; Smith, 2000). It is in the small details – the particular wordings of particular subsections of great interest to a particular company – where the access and friendship bought over time can have the greatest influence. Former Republican Eric Fingerhut once put it this way: 'the public will often look for the big example; they want to find the grand-slam example of influence in these interests. Rarely will you find it. But you can find a million singles' (quoted in Lessig, 2011).

Grassroots pressure

Visit almost any interest group's website and supporters of a cause will likely be urged to contact their Congressman on some issue of pressing concern. Kollman (1998) found that 56 percent of interest groups have their Members contact Congress on a regular basis, and an additional

38 percent of groups do so occasionally. Citizen groups (90 percent) and labor unions are especially reliant on grassroots efforts.

As technology has lowered the barriers to participation, email contacting has increased. In 2008, the CMF estimated that 44 percent of Americans had communicated with Congress at some point in the previous five years, and that Congress received almost 200 million communications in 2004 (90 percent through email), as compared with 50 million in 1995. In a 2010 CMF survey, the majority of staff (57 percent) said email and the internet made legislators more responsive to their constituents and 88 percent responded that email had the potential to influence their boss if he or she were undecided. At the very least, 90 percent of congressional staff do agree that responding to constituents is important.

But as Goldstein (1999) has shown, most constituent mobilization is not organic. It is stimulated by lobbying groups, who use constituents to target the few key swing votes that they think matter on a particular issue. As one trade association executive that Goldstein quotes coldly notes: 'grass roots mobilization is used for one purpose, period – to influence legislative policy. It's not about getting more Americans involved. It's not about educating people on the issues. It's not about making Americans feel good about their political system' (ibid.: 125).

Why is it likely to matter? Most political science assumes that lawmakers care about being reelected, and in practice this means keeping a majority of constituents happy enough. Arnold notes that among a lawmaker's constituents are numerous 'attentive publics' – that is, groups of citizens who care very much about particular issues and pay close attention to them (Arnold, 1990). There are also many 'inattentive publics' – other groups of citizens who could be made to care if an issue achieved public salience, but otherwise would be likely to ignore it.

Arnold argues simply: 'legislators' decisions are dependent on how they believe constituents will react'. Some of it is a guessing game, but grassroots mobilization can take the guessing away. For the 'attentive publics' – the groups that tend to have the Washington lobbyists because they care very much about particular issues – a grassroots campaign is a way of sending a message to Congress that that particular constituency is paying attention. Many groups also set up scorecards of 'key votes' that they broadcast to their members. Gun owners are a good example of an attentive public. Through the National Rifle Association (NRA), millions of gun enthusiasts are made aware of particular legislation that would affect their gun ownership and are encouraged to call Congress (Patterson and Singer, 2006). This gives the NRA enormous influence in Congress. The NRA succeeded in defeating key amendments that would have banned assault weapons and required more extensive background checks for gun purchases.

A telling example from the Dodd-Frank bill involves the case of automobile dealers. One of the many questions surrounding the legislation was whether or not automobile dealers should be exempted from regulation by the new Consumer Financial Protection Bureau created under the law. The original legislation included car dealers, since the vast majority not only sell cars, but also originate auto loans. But as then Senator Sam Brownback (R: Kansas) argued on the dealers' behalf, auto-dealers 'are the quintessential Main Street business throughout the country. There's not a single auto dealer on Wall Street. None of them. Not a one. You can go up there today and try to buy a car and you can't get one. These are Main Street businesses' (Senate Floor speech, May 24, 2010). Behind Brownback's rhetoric was a massive grassroots organization of auto dealers, the National Automobile Dealers Association. There are auto dealers in every community, and they organized a coordinated effort to tell Representatives and Senators how onerous the new regulation would be for them, and how it would cut their already razor-thin profit margins, possibly putting them out of business. It was an exemption that meant a great deal to the auto dealers, but did not attract a lot of public attention otherwise. The one-sided grassroots pressure worked, and the auto dealers got their exemption in the final bill.

While it has certainly become easier to contact Congress, each individual communication has come to seem less meaningful. If it used to be the case that the time it took to write a heartfelt letter or the courage it took to make a phone call were a signal that a citizen actually cared (Ainsworth, 1993; Kollman, 1998) then sending an email may not have the same impact. Still, one study (Bergan, 2009) found that an email lobbying campaign did influence roll call votes in New Hampshire on tobacco legislation. But it is unclear how generalizable those results are.

As new platforms and new technologies make it easier than ever for citizens to share their opinions with Congress, the role of grassroots is inevitably changing. Like so much in Washington, there is much noise, and it increasingly seems like the answer to cutting through the noise is even more noise.

People who know people (the revolving door)

As we have noted, turnover among legislative and executive branch staff is relatively high. Many who leave both the legislative and executive branches become professional lobbyists upon leaving, lured by the better pay, the more flexible hours and the chance to take credit for one's work (Drutman and Cain, 2013). Typically, the lobbyists are rewarded financially for their connections. One study (Blanes i Vidal et al., 2010) estimates that lobbyists earning potential drops when the lawmakers they are associated with leave Congress (when they were senior legislators on key committees). It also estimates that a sub-group of former top Congressmen who became firm lobbyists earn on average $319,000. The rewards are similarly high for top Congressional staff. Another study (Bertrand et al., 2011) finds that 'well connected' lobbyists earn a premium over their less well-connected peers. There is no doubt that lobbying is a lucrative career.

The reasons for such salary premiums are no secret. Those who have spent substantial time in government tend to have personal relationships with their colleagues who remain. They have built up networks of friendship and trust, and they are able to reach their former colleagues in ways that strangers are not able to. Former staffers also have insider knowledge of the quirks and idiosyncracies of the processes and personalities of decision-making within their former institutions. They know what makes different key people tick – what they are likely to do in response to what, and how best to approach them. Arguments and approaches that may work well with one key decision-maker could play out horribly with another. Additionally, having these relationships also makes these former staffers privy to intelligence that others may lack. In a town where things can happen very quickly and there are many first mover advantages, having networks of former colleagues who are in the know can make a difference. Finally, having worked in government on a variety of issues, former staffers cannot help but pick up some knowledge of particular policies. If they have been specialists on particular issues in Congress, there is a good chance they will bring that expertise to their lobbying clients (LaPira and Thomas, 2012). In short, as Drutman and Cain (2013) write: 'the value of a Congressional staffer to a lobbying firm is likely to be a function of their Knowledge of Congressional Procedure (KCP), their Personal Contacts (PC) and Policy Expertise (PE) related to bills that come before Congress'.

Thus, one way for a lobbying organization to boost its chances of success would be to purchase the services of a particularly well-connected lobbyist (or, as is more often the case, the services of multiple well-connected lobbyists). As with any of the factors discussed in this chapter, there are no guarantees of success in lobbying. There are plenty of tales of so-called Washington 'fixers' who do not always get what they ask (Heinz, 1993). And there are plenty of organizations that succeed despite the lack of insider connections and knowledge. But all things being equal, the more connected one is, generally the better.

On Dodd-Frank, one report (Frates, 2010) found 243 former government employees registered to lobby on behalf of financial sector interests. Citigroup had hired the most: 55. Additionally, there were 33 former chiefs of staff, 54 former staffers to the House Financial Services or Senate Banking Committees, and 28 former legislative directors who were lobbying for financial sector interests. It is almost certain that these lobbyists helped their clients to gain access to key offices and used their valuable understanding of the personalities and procedures involved to help to plot strategy.

But the same analytical problem we have faced arises again with hiring revolving door lobbyists: it's hard to prove that, on any given issue, hiring a particular lobbyist made a difference, especially when both sides have major players representing them. As with any service provider, not all lobbyists are the same. Choosing which lobbyists to hire will continue to be a strategic choice for interest groups, and hiring those with the most direct access to and experience of Congress will continue to give those who can afford it an edge. Whether this edge is determinative depends on many other conditions.

The power of persistence

Finally, there is the value of sheer persistence, an often under-appreciated aspect of lobbying. In American politics, few issues are ever resolved, a point made perhaps most trenchantly in an exchange in the film *Thank You for Not Smoking*, in which the tobacco lobbyist Nick Naylor responds to a question from his son for a school assignment about American government:

> *Joey Naylor*:   Dad, why is the American government the best gov-
> ernment?
> *Nick Naylor*:   Because of our endless appeals system.

'Our endless appeals system' captures the ways in which no political loss (or victory) is ever permanent. There are always new venues in which to continue the fight, always the hope (or fear) that a new Congress or a new administration will change course or pick up an issue that had been previously ignored. As Patashnik (2008) notes: 'the losers cannot be counted on to vanish without another fight'. He finds evidence that many reforms wind up being undone simply because the losers patiently stick around, waiting for the moment when reformers have moved on and most attention is elsewhere. It is then that they can win back what they lost.

As we have discussed, Dodd-Frank created almost 400 rule-makings and, as of two years later, less than one-third had been completed. While representatives from the financial sector continued to participate actively in the rule-making procedure, the coalition of reform groups that had come together to advocate for reform had become a shell of its already stretched-too-thin self during the passage of legislation (Stanley, 2013). Meanwhile, the potentially equalizing force of public attention had moved on, and few journalists outside of the financial sector trade presses continued to cover the rule-making.

The US tax code also provides an excellent example. In 1986, Congress passed a major tax reform, eliminating many loopholes and deductions and simplifying the code. Yet, 20 years later, most of the losers won their exemptions and subsidies back, as well as much more. As a 2005 report noted, 'since the 1986 tax reform bill passed, there have been nearly 15,000 changes to the tax code – equal to more than two changes a day. Each one of these changes had a sponsor, and each had a rationale to defend it. Each one was passed by Congress and signed into law' (President's Advisory Panel on Federal Tax Reform, 2005).

The future of Washington lobbying

The Dodd-Frank Wall Street Reform and Consumer Protection Act of 2010 was one of the most heavily lobbied and complicated bills that Congress ever passed. Hundreds of millions of dollars were poured in to influence the legislation and thousands of lobbyists were hired. Thousands continue to work on the slow-moving rule-making processes set in motion by the legislation, though increasingly out of sight of the limited attention of the mainstream media and, thus, the public. That, overall, the lobbyists involved helped to shape the legislation in some way is beyond doubt. But whether they did so in any systematic or consistent way is impossible to prove. The trail of evidence covers the millions spent on campaign contributions and lobbying, including the wide array of ex-Congressional staff hired and the many comments provided along the way. On issues where the interests on both sides were active and the issue was relatively salient, the outcomes are generally more likely to be public-opinion-satisfying compromises. On issues where Congress only hears from one side of the argument, and where there is little press coverage or public knowledge, the active parties are more likely to get what they want. From the wide-angle view, Dodd-Frank was a very public fight, with interests on all sides, and the result was a compromise that reflected that. But zoom in, and pockets of one-sidedness come into focus. Keep the camera rolling as time passes, and while the public moves on, the lobbyists for the financial sector continue to stick around, diligently working to shape the intellectual framework as the agencies begin to write the rules, dealing with the complex technical details.

Certainly, few bills approach Dodd-Frank in terms of sheer size. But the major problems that Congress faces become more and more complicated and interlinked as the complexity of the modern global economy inevitably expands and the US Code continues to grow. In an era of specialization, a short-staffed generalist institution like the US Congress has a harder time making good decisions without out-sourcing expertise. And in an era of increasingly costly campaigns, members of Congress have less and less freedom to upset existing or even potential donor bases.

The challenge in studying lobbying and campaign finance is that influence is often contingent on a range of other factors, and each issue brings with it its own unique characteristics: the balance of geographic and partisan interest, the level of public saliency, the balance of inter-ests on both sides, the particular legislative history. Yet, the stakes are so large that ever-increasing dollars continue to flow into politics and lobbyists continue to expand their range of tactics and strategies. None of this is likely to change in the foreseeable future.

But while resources do not reliably correlate with outcomes on any particular case, they do matter in the aggregate. Resources do not only determine outcomes. They tug on agendas and attention, and they alter priorities. They make certain outcomes easier and certain outcomes more difficult. The imbalanced nature of the lobbying system has been a persistent feature of Washington. It is unlikely to change without active intervention.

Chapter 6

Media and Politics

Philip J. Davies

'From the Mall to the Ball: CNN Won Big on Inauguration Day' said the eye-catching display advertisement placed by CNN in the *Wall Street Journal*. 'CNN Beats MSNBC & Fox News Combined', it went on, adding in smaller type, 'Among Adults 25–54 & Adults 18–34', who are key groups as far as advertisers are concerned. '#1 Cable News Network In Total Viewers for the Day – This is CNN', completed the text of the advertisement, which was illustrated with images of half a dozen key CNN journalists and presenters who had followed up their very well-received coverage of the election, and particularly of election night, with another success covering President Barack Obama's second inauguration (Weprin, 2013). At a time when American newspaper sales have declined sharply and it has become increasingly difficult to find a newspaper stand on that nation's streets, it may seem odd that a cable television news service felt moved to validate its success with an announcement in a respected and high profile hardcopy press outlet.

There may be a number of things at work here. The ability to segment and target an audience is important to anyone wishing to get their message out. Traditional newspaper audiences in the United States are not generally considered to be routes to audiences targeted by demographic group, except by geography. Other media outlets, from television to internet based sources, have a stronger ability to narrowcast to specific audiences. Clients with commercial and political messages to deliver have taken advantage of this ability to find specific audiences. Simultaneously, audiences have turned away from sole reliance on broadcast and traditional newspaper media and have embraced a plurality of news and information sources.

Media outlets have undergone dramatic changes in the 21st century, but in the midst of general sales decline some traditional media have managed to retain their significance as sources of record and as conduits to key audiences. Newspapers have been identified as America's 'fastest-shrinking industry' between 2007 and 2011, with overall decline calculated at 28.4 percent (Nicholson, 2012). A growth in online publishing (24.3 percent) and the internet industry (24.6 percent), although these categories clearly cover very much more than new ways of replacing daily newspapers, might give some indication of the shifts that have been taking place. But the traditional news industry has not been inflexible, with some rising to the challenge to incorporate new platforms into their structure, some strengthening their positions as key channels to important national audiences, and others retaining a role as carriers of in-depth journalism with a role in the local or national daily political news cycle.

Communication is a key element of political life in any nation. Political actors at every level, elected and appointed office holders, opinion leaders, campaigners, whether recently engaged in the debates of the day or long established contributors, rely on the various available media to take their points to larger audiences and to contribute to their influence on political outcomes. When he opined that 'the medium is the message', Marshall McLuhan was warning his readers that any medium extends the reach of thoughts, but can also have an independent effect on the delivery and interpretation of the message (McLuhan, 1964; Federman, 2004).

Media significant to politics in the USA have evolved considerably in recent years. Diversity in local newspaper outlets has declined as readership has gone down and advertising revenue with it. The power of major television broadcasters has been challenged with the greater cost effectiveness of cable and satellite channels to more narrowly defined audiences. The internet has democratized journalism as well, and entirely new contributors have explored the tools made available. Fresh voices, often more opinionated and jarring, have been liberated by these changes. In this chapter I explore these changes in major media formats in the USA before moving on to an examination of the 2012 election for examples of the interaction between politics and the media.

Newspapers

As of September 2012 the *Wall Street Journal* had become the largest circulation newspaper in the USA, with an average daily circulation of 2,293,798 of which 794,594 were accounted for by the newspaper's digital edition. The biggest print edition newspaper was *USA Today*, with 1,627,526 print copies supplemented by 86,307 digital copies. There were another five newspapers with an average daily circulation over half a million: the *New York Times* (1,613,865, 55 percent digital); the *Los Angeles Times* (641,369, 27 percent digital); the *New York Daily News* (535,875, 27 percent digital); the *San José Mercury News* (529,999, 8 percent digital); and the *New York Post* (522,868,

34 percent digital) (Alliance for Audited Media, 2012). Sunday newspapers have a different sales pattern, and the 2012 figures showed a dozen with sales averaging half a million or more.

In 2005, when digital editions were less common, there were nine newspapers with average daily sales over half a million and 14 Sunday papers exceeding half a million sales each (Burrelles Luce, 2005). This finding fits with the general evidence of steady newspaper decline, but examined in detail it presents a slightly more complex picture. The figures for America's top 25 newspapers in 2012 show 16 of them gaining circulation against nine losing audience, compared to the previous year. Given the continuing impact of a poor economic climate on all sales activity, and accepting that there will be other impacts potentially caused by regional differences, population shifts and direct competition in those few cities that still have more than a single newspaper, it might be plausible to perceive a potential bottoming out of the decline of the late 20th and early 21st centuries.

Some newspapers have maintained, and even increased, their circulation by successful promotion of their online editions. The *New York Times* daily edition, with the digital edition accounting for more than half of its daily circulation and 40 percent of its 2.1 million Sunday circulation, is a prime example of this shift. Between 2006 and 2010 the Pew Research Center measured a fall from 38 to 26 percent of the population reading a print newspaper, and an increase from 9 to 17 percent in online readership of news (Pew Research Center for the People and the Press, 2010b). This same report points out that the newspaper reading population is older than the general public, and that the problem of declining readership may accelerate if this readership dies and is not replaced with a younger cohort.

Some outlets appear to be facing this threat more successfully than others. Two-thirds of *New York Times* readers are under 50, compared with 55 percent of the national adult population. *USA Today* and the *Wall Street Journal* have readerships that come close to matching the national profile. For the *New York Times* and the *Washington Post* their strong shift to digital provision may help account for their younger than average reader profile. *USA Today* has been slower in building its digital presence, but is a print news product that has always been designed to attract a broad audience. The total time that people reported spending 'with the news yesterday' in 2010 was 70 minutes, slightly less than reported in the earliest data from 1994, but higher than in most of the intervening years. 'Got news online' does not register until after 1996, but by 2010 accounted for 13 minutes of the total, and appeared steadily to be rising.

If newspaper audiences are showing signs of holding up in spite of the decline in newspaper print circulation, newspaper income is not. Advertising revenue for digital platforms is much lower than for the print versions of the newspapers. Research recently published has reported that while the US newspaper industry's online advertising revenue grew by $207 million in 2011 compared with the previous year, print advertising fell by $2.1 billion in the same period, a loss of about $10 for every $1 gained online. This followed a similar 7:1 loss in 2010, and losses both in print and online in the previous two years. Aggregate advertising revenue fell from its 2000 peak of $48.7 billion to $23.9 billion in 2011. Circulation revenue was relatively stable around $10 billion (Edmond et al., 2012).

The shift towards a business model leaning more on digital provision is well under way, and appears inevitable for most newspapers. An increasing proportion of this digital content will be enclosed by paywalls, with local and community newspapers joining the specialist vehicles that have already shifted in this direction. An article on the *Financial Times* website predicted that one in five American newspapers would be charging for access before the start of 2013, and reported the weighty support for this opinion of Berkshire Hathaway chairman and newspaper investor Warren Buffet (Edgecliffe-Johnson, 2012).

In getting this far the US newspaper industry has compensated for its loss of revenue not only by adjusting its delivery system, but also by drawing on the assets built up over years of pre-internet profitable existence and by making substantial cuts in expenditure, including staffing. A few newspapers have closed. Future stability or growth in this news sector depends on developing a new business model that provides a firm financial base in the long run.

The newspaper industry has faced challenges before. Radio, then television, had already taken their places as transmitters of those stories most important to the nation. Television grew to be the medium through which most Americans get the bulk of their information about politics. Nevertheless the newspaper, particularly the major newspapers of record, retained a serious and in-depth role in the news cycle. As Robert Spero points out: 'the word-count of a half-hour news programme would not fill up much more than one column of one page of the *New York Times*' (Spero, 1980: 177).

Television

While the post-inaugural advertisements by CNN celebrated a genuine ratings victory on January 21, 2013, it is understandable that they did not mention the fall in audience compared to the same event four years earlier. CNN's 2013 audience average for the oath and speech was 3.136 million, MSNBC was viewed by 2.273 million and the Fox News Channel (FNC) by 1.316 million. For the evening coverage, which included the inaugural balls, CNN again led their competitors, a victory no doubt especially relished given the usual dominance of FOX among these three providers in evening television provision. Nevertheless the CNN audience was 61 percent lower than four years earlier. The MSNBC audience was 25 percent lower than in 2009 and the FNC audience collapsed by 82 percent (Carter, 2013; de Moraes, 2013).

There are plausible explanations for these audience declines. President Obama's inauguration was a cause for massive national celebration and self-congratulation. Public approval of Obama's predecessor had fallen by the beginning of 2009 to historic lows, and there was a widespread sense of relief that a new administration, with a new political agenda, was being installed. There was also a perhaps exaggerated sense that at a time of considerable political, international and financial stress, a new president would bring a new dawn. And of course a historic inauguration for an African American to the office of president was a very important event. Even many of the Republicans who had campaigned for their party's candidates in the 2008 elections were proud that their nation had matured to the point that an African American could be elected to occupy the White House.

The same general sense of celebration did not apply in 2013. The Obama campaign had won a famous reelection victory after a bitter interparty campaign, the temper of which was prefaced by a line in a 2010 interview given by Republican Senate Minority Leader Mitch McConnell stating that the 'single most important thing we want to achieve is for President Obama to be a one-term president' (Garrett, 2010). While said in the context of a broader ranging interview, McConnell's comment captured the spirit of the period. Party political positions in Washington over the next two years appeared entrenched and uncompromising, setting battle lines for the election campaign. For some the reelection of the USA's first African American president may have been a cause for particular celebration – after all, the reasoning would go, what would be the effect on unorthodox candidate choices in the foreseeable future if the first president who was not a white male fell after one term? But the more general sharing of a feeling of national pride in having a black president had been replaced by stronger, traditional, partisan opposition to the incumbent. This entrenched partisan opposition was accompanied by disappointment among some of his 2008 supporters with the Administration's lack of progress in tackling the nation's economic problems. These factors undoubtedly acted to deflate the potential television audience for the second inaugural.

The partisan nature of the audience might also go some way to explaining the variation in audience decline between 2009 and 2013. While US newspapers attract some criticism for political bias, it is rare to find a major newspaper that identifies itself very closely with any particular political ideology; and in general American newspapers refrain from acting as the partisan voice of a particular political persuasion. Partisanship has been more identified with some participants in the electronic media – including radio channels carrying a large proportion of 'shock jock' opinion based programming, and television outlets cleaving to a well-defined part of the political spectrum. As the spectrum of television delivery services has expanded, space has been created for a greater diversity of ideological approach.

Research on the 2008 presidential campaign found that MSNBC, a satellite and cable station, broadcast a significantly higher proportion of negative news items on Republican John McCain, and a higher proportion favorable to Obama, than the average for all channels. FNC was more critical of Obama than the average. The nightly newscasts of the three major networks, NBC, ABC, CBS, were more neutral and less negative than other news outlets. To a considerable extent these channels are reflecting the ideological convictions of their audiences. At the time of the 2008 elections three times more Fox News viewers identified themselves as Republican than Democrat, with the MSNBC audience being a near mirror of this. The traditional major news programs drew audiences more typical of the broad political divisions in American society (Pew Research Center's Project for Excellence in Journalism, 2008; Pew Research Center for People and the Press, 2008). This pattern was confirmed in 2012 when the difference between MSNBC's positive coverage of Obama and FNC's favorable coverage of Romney became even more pronounced and marked these two as sharply different in their coverage to CNN and to the major networks (Pew Research Center's Project for Excellence in Journalism, 2012). The very much larger decline in viewers of FNC between the inaugurations of 2009 and 2013, compared to the relatively modest decline in the audience for MSNBC, will at least in part be a reflection of the relative pleasure and disappointment felt by those channels' very differently politically inclined audiences.

Another thing not covered in the CNN newspaper announcement was the performance of the major broadcasting networks – NBC, CBS and ABC all outperformed their cable based competitors, with NBC averaging over 5 million viewers through the daytime period. In every case the viewing figures were down more than half from four years earlier, although they were higher than the 2005 audience for George W. Bush's second inaugural, perhaps a more comparable occasion.

The segmentation of the 2013 television audience for this major political event demonstrates effectively a media landscape that has emerged during the past generation. In 1984–85 primetime viewing for 57.1 percent of American households was conducted through network, independent or public television channels, with just 7.6 percent tuning to the relatively new cable services. By 2008–09 almost all the independent channels had consolidated into networks, though network, independent and public television viewing was down to 27.7 percent of households, while all forms of cable, and an emerging category of 'other tuning', stood at 46 percent (Gorman, 2010).

While overall viewing figures appear to have risen, the delivery systems have diversified and the available content has changed. Much of the programing used and developed over the past 30 years by cable-delivered channels contains no element of current affairs or news. While specialist news channels have been created, and the traditional broad based programing channels with news shows, are now delivered in multiple ways, including cable and satellite, a very substantial proportion of the newly available channels specialize in sport, music, comedy, drama, shopping, movies and other entertainments. All of these may be interpreted to transmit some kind of cultural or ideological politics to their audiences, but they are not at all engaged in the distribution and interpretation of hard news and political information and debate. As audiences have shifted away from broad content channels to more specialized outlets, the opportunity has increased to live in a news- and politics-free zone.

New and social media

The internet has become a delivery mechanism for traditional media in adapted formats and has been the context within which entrepreneurs both commercial and amateur have created entirely new media and communications systems for recent elections. The Facebook social networking site started in 2004 was valued at $104 billion when it was launched on the stock market and was reported as having a billion users by September 2012. It was nevertheless losing stock market value as investors expressed concerns about its profit making potential (Fowler, 2012). This new giant was feeling the stress of competition from even newer communications platforms, such as Twitter, as well as competing with other burgeoning new companies in the development of products that might prove profitable and that might maintain customer loyalty to the brand.

The print news probably felt the impact of the internet first, and has continued to feel it as new media platforms have been established in that new environment. 'Perhaps the most profound change in journalism', according to Stephen B. Shepard, former senior editor at *Newsweek* and editor-in-chief of *Business Week*, 'has been the extraordinary transformation wrought by social media' (Shepard, 2013: 293). This is an impact beyond that of the internet alone. The internet is a tool that can provide platforms for the distribution of traditional newspapers, radio and television, and those industries are changing in form to incorporate the new delivery opportunities. Not all who try to adapt will necessarily be successful, but the major organs of traditional print and electronic media have the resources, expertise and branding that gives them some room to experiment and come up with corporate and business forms that will project them into the future. The news and social media that have evolved in the environment afforded by the internet, however, provide direct and novel competition with existing news sources.

The internet and its social media forms have provided an environment in which news sources are increasingly democratized. This pluralized world of sources also comes with the caveat that readers are left personally responsible for judging the quality and reliability of every individual item. The blogosphere is an anarchy which may host conspiracy theorists, whistleblowers and skilled investigative journalists. Facebook, Twitter and other social media act as locations where news can be shared, and where things can gather such momentum that they are described as viral. It encourages a perspective among users encapsulated in a *New York Times* interview with a college student: 'if the news is that important, it will find me' (ibid.: 295).

In 2001 the internet was nominated as one of their main sources of 'news about national and international issues' by 13 percent of respondents, behind radio with 18 percent, newspapers with 45 percent and television with 74 percent. Mention of television rose to 82 percent of respondents in 2002, but after that steadily declined to 66 percent in 2010. The figures for newspapers reached 50 percent in 2003, before sliding steadily to 31 percent in 2010. Radio remained relatively steady throughout: 18 percent in 2001, 16 percent in 2010. Respondents naming the internet as a main news sources rose over the same period from 13 to 41 percent. Among 18–29 year olds the figures were: internet, 65 percent; television, 52 percent; newspapers, 21 percent; radio, 15 percent. The loyal audience for television, as for newspapers, is an aging one, and the new forms of delivery are likely to get more important if these age cohorts continue their current media behavior, or if the trends intensify as new young cohorts come of age (Pew Research Center for People and the Press, 2011).

For anyone with a political message to get across, these changes are critical for media strategy and expenditure. Television remains the most efficient broadcast media and gives some opportunity for targeting through the use of particular timeslots, channels with highly defined audiences and with regional footprints. Some newspapers have a national profile and a potential for in-depth reporting that retains for them a place in the news agenda-setting process, while others have to rely on their local appeal to stem the newsprint decline. The internet can deliver newspaper branded products, and both real time and recorded television and radio, and may prove a valuable partner to these traditional media; but it is also the breeding ground for a still rapidly changing range of social media whose impact has already been large and is not yet complete. The interaction between ongoing politics and the available media is nowhere more evident than in the course of an election campaign, and the 2012 elections have provided a fine laboratory for this.

Media spending 2012

The cost of election campaigns in the USA has attracted attention for decades. Some observers have consistently criticized the escalating role of money in the American electoral process, with others defending it on the grounds that democratic practice should not necessarily be expected to come cheap, and that America's constitutional guarantee of free speech covers campaign expenditure. On occasion the debate has swung to favor greater regulation. The Federal Election Campaign Act of 1972, amended in 1974, 1976 and 1979, and the Bipartisan Campaign Reform Act of 2002 form the most recent corpus of legislation forming the backdrop to current elections. They in their turn have been interpreted and somewhat remodeled in impact in major Supreme Court cases such as *Buckley v Valeo*, *Citizens United v Federal Election Commission* and *speechnow.org v Federal Election Commission*.

Campaigners, being engaged in an entrepreneurial and competitive business, have to take the best advantage they can of the regulatory environment in which they work. New ways are developed of channeling money into campaigning and to expand the resource available. In 2008, candidate Obama refused federal campaign funding, freeing the campaign to raise and spend money without a formal cap, signaling the end of the aggregate limits set in the 1970s. Alongside the liberalizing decisions taken recently by the Supreme Court, this created the opportunity for massive spending by and on behalf of federal candidates.

Most campaign spending is reported through the Federal Elections Commission, but it can still be difficult to collect wholly accurate aggregate figures and reliably to break those aggregates into categories of expenditure. The respected Center for Responsive Politics reports a total expenditure on the Obama/Romney race of $2,335,803,281 – including spending by candidate campaigns, the national party and independent spending intended to influence the election (Center for Responsive Politics, 2013). The Center's coverage of presidential campaign expenditures only covers about $1.05 billion of these funds, but the largest spending category, as always in recent elections, is the

$583.8 million (55.5 percent) on media. The amount of $349.7 million reported as spent on media consultants and miscellaneous media resists further breakdown, but the Center also traces $157.3 million spent on broadcast media and $74.8 million on internet media. The *Huffington Post* in its own more detailed analysis reported the Republican campaign as spending $270 million and the Democrats spending $420 million on 'television/radio ads, including "media production" and "placement" services', with the Republicans' $100.6 million spend on online advertisements almost matching the Democrats' $118.1 million. Telemarketing took a further $74.5 million of the Republican budget and $35.2 million of the Democrats' costs. The Republicans spent more on fundraising consultants, $31 million to $6.5 million, while the Democrats outspent the Republicans $32.1 million to $19.3 million on polling (Stein and Blumenthal, 2012).

New and social media 2012

The figures indicate strongly, and reasonably enough, that the business of the campaign is communication – to get out the message, consolidate support, raise funds and get out the vote – and that this is pursued vigorously through all available media by the campaign organization. It is also clear that while television advertising still dominates media expenditure, spending on internet advertising, virtually non-existent two elections previously, has become very significant. Furthermore the pattern of expenditure on internet media is likely to be different. The internet gives targeted reach that may be inexpensive in terms of media buying, but can be enhanced by personal intervention. Purchasing advertising time on sites visited by target voter groups is a campaign activity that might be compared to targeted advertising buys in other media. The use of the internet to establish followership groups, to communicate through email, to respond, organize and reassure, is perhaps more comparable to traditional door-to-door activities, but is given huge reach and efficiency by the new media and the addition of peer-group reinforcement through social media sites. These activities are probably more intensive in their use of personnel and are more likely to turn up in campaign staff budgets or volunteer numbers than in the core advertising expenditure.

There was a general response after the 2008 election that the Obama campaign had grasped the nettle of new social media more successfully than any opponents, and, even with four years to catch up, the Romney campaign found that Obama's team had taken further strides in its understanding of the effectiveness of these formats. In 2008 the Pew Center found that, while Republicans formed a larger proportion of all internet users, Obama voters took the lead in online activism as measured by the proportion who were sharing files related to the election, signing up online for campaign information, contributing money to the campaign, signing up for campaign news alerts, and volunteering through the internet (Smith, 2009).

Congressional Quarterly's Tom Price summed up the response to the Obama 2008 campaign: 'Obama's command of the Internet proved a key to his victory over Arizona Sen. John McCain in 2008 ... all candidates are striving to emulate Obama's 2008 online success' (Price, 2012: 867). But, as Price points out, the Obama campaign was doing more in 2012 than before. Facebook, Twitter, YouTube and other social media platforms were being used extensively to rally the faithful, and these outlets had grown massively in the intervening years. Average daily Twitter use in 2012 was 340 million tweets daily, compared to a mere 1.8 million tweets on election day 2008. Use of the internet had grown to encompass nearly two-thirds of US adults. President Obama and his team demonstrated their comfort with the new media and their old-fashioned strategic skills when the president logged into the social media site reddit with the message 'I am Barack Obama, President of the United States – AMA [ask me anything]'. Obama spent half an hour responding to questions. Within two days the conversation had been viewed 5.3 million times. This was all timed to coincide with the Republican National Convention. Throughout, the Obama campaign retained the edge in social media. The President's victory tweet, 'four more years' with a photograph of himself and Michelle Obama hugging, became the most re-tweeted message to date.

Media strategy 2012

Post-election discussions within a Republican party that had been convinced of its prospects of victory focused on a number of factors. Perhaps the most significant of these topics concerned the demographic shifts in the USA that meant while Ronald Reagan in 1984 could build a landslide victory on 69 percent of white voters Romney in 2012 could achieve the same popularity with whites, but lose the election. Skill and proficiency in the delivery of new and established political media was also a big topic. Research from the 2010 election indicated that relevant social networking could influence voter turnout, but while all campaigns were aware of this, the Obama campaign was better able to take advantage of this development (Markoff, 2012).

Sasha Issenberg (2012) puts the case that new expertise has joined the new media in the campaign process, adding the latest research result in persuasion, mobilization and statistics to a well-established armory of campaign pollsters and consultants. The Washington voter research group Analyst Institute, founded in 2007 to help Democratic candidates, is given much credit, but there is also mention of the 'consortium of behavioural scientists' who used their research knowledge to help create tools that would work in various media formats, from advertisement design to interpersonal reinforcement of voting intentions (Carey, 2012). The Obama campaign also had the support of a team of engineers from Facebook, Twitter and Google building their election software (Madrigal, 2012). Other candidates will plan similar campaign organizations in the future, but in 2012 the President's reelection organization maintained an edge.

The sources used by the American electorate for 2012 campaign news reflected the general shifts in media preference, but with an even stronger showing for the internet. Television was identified as a main election news source by 67 percent, newspapers and magazines by 30 percent, and radio by 20 percent, all close to their general performance as news sources, but public use of the internet as a main election news source rose to 47 percent.

Television and traditional media 2012

The campaigns' continuing expenditure on non-internet media is primarily on paid advertising, and this punctuates airtime in the American household throughout the primary and general election campaigns. There was a general impression that 2012 was a more negative campaign than that leading to Obama's first election, although the saturation advertising that accompanied the NBC Olympics coverage presented an opportunity for statesmanlike, and often fairly content-free, television advertisements.

Free media continues to be sought, and invitations to appear on television continue to be accepted, though even free media opportunities have shifted from the declining number of hard news slots towards the expanded 'infotainment' program sector. Late-night US television has become a familiar location for leading candidates who want to reach out to an audience that takes less of its news from traditional hard news outlets. Barack Obama appeared on Jon Stewart's *Daily Show*, Jay Leno's *Tonight Show*, *The David Letterman Show*, and took part in a sketch with Jimmy Fallon of NBC. Michele Obama appeared with Jimmy Kimmel on ABC. The Obama appearances gained high viewer ratings and contrasted sharply with Mitt Romney's apparent unwillingness to appear in this format (Carter, 2012).

The long Republican pre-primary and primary season featured many televised candidate debates – totalling almost 30, even before the party nominees began to face up to each other. The impact of these less structured forms of political media cannot always be controlled. Texas

Governor and leading Republican hopeful Rick Perry could not remember one of the federal departments (Energy) that it was his policy to close down during a televised debate on November 10, 2012, providing one minute of television that fatally holed his campaign. President Obama put on a weak performance in his first debate against Mitt Romney that immediately had an impact on his standing in the polls. Mitt Romney's claim that as Governor of Massachusetts he had collected 'binders full of women' as potential appointees undermined his standing with the very group he was trying to reach.

Even in these cases, the impact of the television appearances was filtered and magnified by the internet and social media. Perry's brief television failure could be replayed endlessly on the computer, and was not confined to a limited region or timespan. MoveOn.org posted 35 Facebook messages during the Romney/Obama debate, viewed by 3 million people, but Romney's slip provided an excellent opportunity for his opponents to show their mastery of the new media. BinderFullofWomen.com was established within minutes by an Obama supporting PAC to spread the word and to raise funds. Other Obama supporting groups used Facebook and Twitter to spread the news of Romney's gaffe, and the news spread as recipients 'shared' the item with their own friends and followers (Lorber, 2012).

It may be that the internet will give a longer shelf life as well as a larger footprint to political stories, news and opinion. Motifs based on relative trivia such as the Romneys' dog being strapped to the top of the car for hundreds of miles, or Mrs Romney's horse performing in the Olympics, the organization of which Mitt Romney had expressed doubts about, can be kept alive. Much more important gaffes, such as Republican Todd Akin's mention of 'legitimate rape' during his campaign to be Senator for Missouri, and Republican Richard Mourdock's comment that pregnancy due to rape still constitutes a conception that is a 'gift from God' during his Senate campaign in Indiana, are also less containable in the age of the internet than in previous media eras.

Post-Inauguration

The 2012 campaign confirmed recent trends in that part of the US media world that concerns itself with politics. Hard copy media readership has continued to decline. Newspapers have begun to embrace media beyond their traditional hard copy, though this has yet to prove itself viable. Media only a generation old – cable and satellite television – is also finding itself challenged for market share. Internet-carried media continue to develop, extending existing outlets and providing a fertile space for new developments. Even here there is a hint of danger. The share value of Facebook has declined since its launch, and its search for new and viable media products within its business model has not been without difficulty.

One of the most commented on elements of the Obama campaign success was its 'ground game'. In essence this boils down to traditional campaigning using the best contemporary methods, a symbiosis of social media, traditional media, social intelligence and the latest analytical tools to get the message most efficiently to people on the ground. A similar evolution is likely to take place in media provision and its political use. Certainly there does not seem to be evidence of a decline in overall exposure to political information through the US media – the proportion of people acquiring political news has increased slightly, although the more common use of narrowcasting to targeted audiences may mean that a larger proportion of this information is ideologically charged.

After the exhilaration of Inauguration Day, Washington returned quickly to its usual business of politics. The news media spent a few days discussing President Obama's second inaugural address, agreeing that it was as forthright a statement of a political agenda as this president had ever made. As after election day, when many Republicans were shell-shocked at the degree of the Obama victory, there was some indication of potential cooperation across party political lines, though this was counterbalanced by other voices who wanted no capitulation but instead a regrouping to take advantage of Republican election potential in the 2014 and 2016 elections. That potential, it was agreed, could only be achieved if lessons were learned from the Obama campaign operation – especially its use of communications media of all kinds.

The temporary ascendancy of CNN – a channel of choice for the 'big occasion' – was replaced by its normal ratings, near the bottom of the pile, below Fox News and MSNBC. CNN's new head, Jeff Zucker, indicated that he felt charged with finding a new format for the channel to stop and reverse the ratings failure – its greater reliance on hard news presented in a relatively balanced fashion seems less attractive to audiences than the approaches taken by its nearest competitors (Harris, 2013). And within a few days the event seemed remembered most for the question of whether Beyoncé Knowles lip-synched or sang live the national anthem.

Chapter 7

The Presidency

Jon Herbert

The euphoria of election night 2008 was extraordinary. Confronting economic crisis and engagement in two foreign wars, the American electorate had chosen a new political direction, electing the first black president along the way. An intelligent, relatively young president-elect, blessed with a phenomenal gift for rhetoric, offered the people 'hope' and 'change' for the future. Particularly, he emphasized his willingness to stand above the petty squabbles of party politics, offering instead a commitment to a post-partisan presidency.

As the celebrations rolled on, two groups did not join the party. First, many Republicans bemoaned their defeat and began to plan strategies to resist the new president's initiatives. Only 53 percent of American voters had chosen the Senator from Illinois, offering good reason to believe that resistance to his leadership could be both effective and, thinking forward to elections in 2010 and 2012, productive. Second, many political scientists of a certain age sighed deeply, muttered 'No, you can't' and turned back to their datasets. Calling on extensive scholarship, these scholars believed that the new hopeful's aspiration to lead dramatic change from the Oval Office would prove unattainable.

Political scientists have long emphasized the contrast between expectations of the presidency and the office's capacity for leadership. Presidential campaigns often build images of super-human candidates possessed of magnificent skills and vision, allowing the candidate to promise transformative change for the United States. The reality, meanwhile, is one of a Constitution designed to issue the presidency with limited power and imposing structural constraints that render leadership near impossible. Presidents confront a system of multiple power centers in Washington, including the legislative and fiscal powers of Congress, the federal bureaucracy's control of policy implementation and the Supreme Court's power of judicial review. A presidency cannot control public sentiment or, under most conditions, shape the key intellectual currents prevalent in the political culture (Skowronek, 1993; Edwards, 2009). The presidency confronts a system of myriad players, each with their own incentives which drive their behavior. These incentives rarely encourage these officials to throw their lot in with the presidency. The idea that this system should then generate radical reforms to presidential order could be considered eccentric or far-fetched.

Some political scientists regard the constraints upon the president's leadership to be so great that the abilities and behaviors of the individual president should not even be the primary focus of study (Moe, 1993). Instead, the presidency could be understood best as an institution driven by its context. In any decision-making situation, a presidential choice may be most easily explained by identifying the incentives attached to each policy option available, rather than by studying the president's psychology or leadership style. While a president may appear to lead, he is simply following paths made available to him by his context. Incapable of influencing opinion, either in Congress or among the public, this 'responsive presidency' can only facilitate change using the limited opportunities presented (Edwards, 2009).

Yet Obama suggested that one individual's leadership could overcome the resistant structures and cultures of the US political system. Those supporting him pointed to an impressive set of individual skills that could aid him. As considered in the previous volume of this series, Obama seemed well-equipped to be president (Roper, 2010). Fred Greenstein, who has articulated a framework for understanding the skills necessary to conduct the office effectively, offered an extremely positive assessment of Obama's capacities. He likened Obama's talents in public communication to the most lauded of presidential speakers, including Franklin Roosevelt, Kennedy and Reagan (Greenstein, 2009). Obama's organizational capacity seemed good, given the steady and focused approach of his 2008 campaign and his willingness to recognize the importance of designing thorough and well-informed decision-making processes (Greenstein, 2011: 10). Events during Obama's pre-presidential career suggested a degree of tactical judgment and hard-headedness that belied the high idealism of his 2008 rhetoric: his political skills seemed strong. Equally, his cognitive style was exceptional, 'marked by analytic detachment and a capacity for complex thinking' (ibid.: 11). While Greenstein hesitated to assert that Obama had a very clear policy vision, instead considering him a pragmatic problem solver, his assessment was, nevertheless, distinctly positive. No president is likely to score highly in each of Greenstein's categories, but Obama was closer to this status than most of his predecessors.

This chapter describes three forms of presidential leadership, examining this apparently talented leader's attempts, as an individual president, to overcome the structural challenges confronting him. First, Obama's relations with Congress are examined. Obama promised a new spirit of bipartisanship with which to reshape Washington politics, replacing the more usual partisan conflict. Second, Obama's capacity to inspire through rhetoric suggested that the new president might achieve change through leadership of the public, despite presidents' limited success on this front over the preceding 30 years. Third, he promised to rein in the growth of executive power, reversing the trend of increasing presidential influence.

Obama, Congress and the rise of the partisan presidency

One particular institutional barrier to presidential leadership warrants special attention. The presidency now operates amid levels of partisanship not seen in a century. American politics was once marked out from similar Western democracies by the openness and ideological indiscipline of its party system. The limited power of party ties allowed presidents trying to steer legislation through Congress to choose their strategies. On the one hand, the president could employ a partisan strategy, working with his own party to support his legislative proposals, designing the program to correlate with party concerns and inspiring the party base to deliver the congressional votes needed to pass the legislation. On the other hand, the president also enjoyed the opportunity to build cross-party coalitions in support of his preferred policies. The option of pursuing bipartisan strategies compensated, to some degree, for a president's inability to depend upon his own party's support. However, as detailed in Chapters 4 and 8, the US political system has undergone a significant transformation, which has generated more rigid party structures. A more partisan and more ideologically polarized Congress has narrowed the strategic options available to the presidency. Bipartisan strategies are less likely to be successful, as the changes of the last two decades have reduced the opportunities for the presidency to attract votes both from the opposition party and from ideological moderates. Meanwhile, the potential of partisan strategies has increased. Media partisanship encourages presidents to trigger favorable coverage from editorial teams predisposed to supporting presidential positions. In approaching the public, presidents see the potential to mobilize their own party's base by taking policy positions they will favor and reaping easy dividends by criticizing the opposition party. If they align themselves ideologically with their own party, presidents can have reasonable hopes of both high partisan support from a relatively stable own-party coalition and assistance from their party's congressional leadership. Presidents have more reason, compared to 30 years ago, to believe that a governing strategy designed around partisanship will succeed. The George W. Bush presidency presented an object lesson in the possibilities of partisan strategies; many of Bush's significant legislative victories were based on partisan votes, from tax cuts to prescription drug benefits, while his bipartisan strategies often failed, perhaps most spectacularly in the case of immigration reform. Forces shaping presidential conduct now channel presidents into more partisan behavior.

The rise of this partisan presidency does, though, generate a fundamental problem for presidential leadership. Partisan strategies have significant weaknesses, including their limitations in Congress and their potential electoral costs. Presidents are rarely blessed with the substantial own-party majorities in Congress needed to ignore the other party entirely. In the Senate, the increased use of the filibuster, often as a weapon in partisan conflict, means that presidents need 60 of the 100 senatorial votes to pass their preferred legislation. It is rare that either party holds 60 Senate seats, meaning that presidents are normally obliged to work with the opposition party to get anything done. Equally, while the House of Representatives continues to take floor decisions by simple majorities, the narrow majorities there in recent Congresses have demanded that presidents win support from among the few remaining ideological moderates within their party to pass legislation, or find opposition votes if members of their own party defect. Hence, a partisan strategy designed around simply mobilizing the party's ideologically coherent base is not always enough to get the law changed. Presidents must design congressional strategies to appeal to moderates as well. Mobilizing the base and winning moderates are not goals that sit comfortably alongside one another: to succeed, the presidency must develop the compromises to win moderate support, while persuading an ideologically committed base to rally behind the very compromises which leave that base disappointed.

Partisan strategies also hold the potential to damage the presidency's image and future electoral prospects. Hinckley (1990) details presidential attempts to don the 'head of state' role by rising above terms that will associate the president with a party. A 'partisan' leader directs a particular clan, not the whole people, therefore a president so labeled is demonstrating a failure of character that compromises his ability to perform as president of all the people. The 'adult in the room' should rise above such partisan bickering. Hinckley's evidence suggests a clear connection between the ideological center and projecting the image of being presidential. Furthermore, presidents may need votes from moderates and independents. To these centrists, who may make the difference between winning and losing the presidency, partisanship is often alienating. Each presidential campaign pitches its own candidate as a sober moderate, while employing negative campaigning to push perceptions of their opponent away from the ideological center ground:

firmly attaching the 'partisan' label to an opponent is a key weapon in establishing that opponent as a dangerous radical. This phenomenon has only been exaggerated by the American public's alienation from the extended partisan wrangling in Washington.

Thus, presidents have the incentives to sell themselves as bipartisan. George W. Bush, campaigning during the 2000 election cycle, highlighted his experiences of working with Texan Democrats and labeled himself 'a uniter, not a divider'. Obama's 2008 condemnations of party warfare and promises of post-partisanship were cut from the same cloth. However, bipartisan strategies are rarely adopted by presidents and often fail. Obama's promises of policy change allied to a post-partisan presidency defied recent scholarship and experience. He would either need to find a capacity for bipartisan leadership without recent precedent, or sacrifice his pledge of post-partisanship and govern as a partisan, or reveal a new, third approach to governing.

The Obama Presidency and the 111th Congress: unified government

Obama had promised to show more respect for the constitutional prerogatives of other institutions in the political system. He certainly demonstrated some deference to Congress. Obama often encouraged Congress to take the initiative in drafting legislation, limiting his administration's direct input to statements of broad principles. George W. Bush had employed the same approach to great effect over education policy and Obama encouraged Congress to design major initiatives including his healthcare reform and proposals for changes in energy and environmental policy. He often seemed to be on the sidelines for substantial periods while Congress hammered out legislative detail, only bringing the power of his office to bear when the process became particularly contentious.

His approach to delivering his broader pledge, to rise above partisan battles, was more complex. Obama came to office with his party holding a 257 to 178 majority in the House and a 58 to 40 majority in the Senate. The latter brought the new administration tantalizingly close to the point where party-line votes in Congress would allow his legislation to pass. For a few months during 2009, the Democrats, working with independent Joe Lieberman, held the 60 votes in the Senate required to curtail filibusters. Yet, Obama did much to sustain the impression that he was governing in a bipartisan manner. He employed much bipartisan rhetoric in office. Substantial energy was committed to communication with congressional Republicans. High profile events were organized to demonstrate

Obama's openness to Republican ideas on economics and healthcare policies, such as bipartisan policy summits and presidential visits to Capitol Hill. The symbolism was unambiguous. More substantively, the administration encouraged bipartisan cooperation to develop legislation on pressing policy problems. A potential opportunity for Democrat Senator John Kerry and Republican Senator Lindsey Graham to cooperate in planning energy and environment reform was praised. When a cross-party 'Gang of Six' from the Senate Finance Committee met to discuss healthcare reform, the administration allowed the group time to discuss potential compromises. When these efforts did not bear fruit and the administration pursued reforms more closely aligned with Democratic party priorities, the administration still tried to court Republican support for its proposals. Indeed, some accused the administration of desperation in its attempts to win even a single Republican vote for its healthcare legislation. This approach would extend to Obama's attempts to negotiate a 'grand bargain' over the federal budget in 2011. To some observers, Obama was 'wedded to a naïve and platonic ideal of bipartisanship' (Remnick, 2010).

Judging by the legislative results, Obama's bipartisanship was a failed initiative that hindered his presidency, rather than assisted it. There were a few successes. Most notably, the 'Dodd-Frank' re-regulation of the financial markets became law with support from both parties, despite controversy over its consumer protection measures. The 'lame duck' session after the 2010 midterm elections generated abolition of the 'Don't ask, don't tell' measure that had constrained gay service in the military and agreement to extend tax cuts initiated in the Bush era. However, the bipartisan approach did not directly deliver healthcare reform or major economic measures. The failed negotiations between Kerry and Graham over energy and environmental reform sounded the death knell for any legislative action on climate change.

Different interpretations of these events offered different explanations of the failures of bipartisanship. Republicans emphasized the administration's underlying partisanship and argued that Obama had never approached negotiations with their congressional caucus in good faith. The impression of a willingness to negotiate was generated by cleverly choreographed symbolism, while the administration and congressional Democrats quietly wrote the legislation in private. Republicans noted the limited presence of their ideas in Obama bills. To them, the bipartisan strategy was a cover for the application of a traditional big-government, budget-busting liberal ideology. Democrats made similar accusations of bad faith in the negotiations, unsurprisingly against the Republicans. They recorded the ferocity of Republican opposition to Obama proposals. For instance, only six months into Obama's first term, the Republican National Committee had organized a national advertising campaign labeling Obama's healthcare proposals a 'dangerous experiment' (Sinclair, 2011). Republicans were accused of adopting uncompromising resistance to Obama's proposals as a strategy to make the Democrats look ineffective and responsible for lingering economic problems. They were seen to be pursuing 'strategic disagreement' by which circumstances were engineered to make the other party fail (Gilmour, 1995).

Some felt Obama himself had blundered. Liberal observers argued that Obama was strategically inept: 'Obama erred by offering self-defeating concessions to Republicans who had no good-faith intention of seeking compromise ... It took the administration far too long to realize that the overall Republican strategy was not to negotiate but simply to say no – even to the point of rejecting ideas the party had supported in the past' (Robinson, 2010). Others read his attempts to bargain as a lack of commitment to particular policy goals. While the phrase 'leading from behind' was derived from the administration's decision to allow the Europeans to lead military action in Libya, it might also have been used to describe the administration's restraint in dealing with Congress. To some, this restraint increased the opportunity for a bipartisan consensus to emerge, while to others it was a lack of leadership. Obama's personal style in dealing with Congress also drew criticism. Television commentator Tom Brokaw (2012) noted a widespread perception that 'the president doesn't work hard enough at bringing everybody into the White House and rolling up his sleeves, having them in the living quarters, getting them around the table and saying how do we get this deal done'. His high-handed and didactic manner in dealing with legislators was not greatly appreciated either. Journalist David Brooks suggested that Obama 'governs like a visitor from a morally superior civilization' (Brooks, 2012a). These shortcomings hindered Obama's ability to build working relationships with a range of Republicans.

These partisan and personal criticisms neglect the more fundamental structural problems associated with greater partisanship and polarization. Particularly, the increased ideological distance between the two parties renders bipartisanship harder, because the parties disagree more sharply over policy. The challenges Obama and the Republicans faced in pursuing compromise were simply greater than those confronted by previous generations.

While bipartisanship had not lived up to Obama's promises, there was substance to Republican accusations that Obama had behaved as a partisan. For all the apparent efforts to encourage bipartisanship, Obama used his party's majorities in Congress to follow a partisan strategy when required. Despite the public consultations with Republicans over an economic stimulus package, drawing the package together was largely a partisan operation. Chief of Staff Rahm Emanuel, whose service in the House had won him a reputation for uncompromising partisanship, ran the White House campaign to plan and pass the stimulus. Initially, Obama's team proposed few specifics, asking congressional Democrats to provide the spending plans for the package. As Obama's transition teams prepared the legislation, his staff met the Democratic congressional leadership almost daily. Equally, when the bipartisan 'Gang of Six' failed to offer a healthcare proposal, the administration pivoted swiftly to a more partisan approach: in describing the genesis of Obama's healthcare plan, Hacker (2010) argues that it resulted from concessions made among Democrats to one another, not to Republicans. Once interparty cooperation broke down, it left congressional Democrats to design much of the policy detail. The administration's planning of policy was, therefore, often partisan. Furthermore, Obama worked closely with, and depended upon, the Democratic leaders in Congress. Senate Majority Leader Harry Reid and House Speaker Nancy Pelosi were integral to Obama's success in Congress and, unsurprisingly, policy proposals bore their party's ideological stamp. The administration may have preached bipartisanship, but partisanship was an undercurrent in dealings with Congress from the first day, as relationships and policy proposals were developed to allow a switch to partisanship when working with Republicans failed.

This approach allowed Obama to achieve his two most significant legislative successes through partisan votes. His party passed a massive $787 billion stimulus package, the American Recovery and Reinvestment Act (ARRA). The bill passed the House without a Republican vote and only three Senate Republicans voted for it. His extraordinary healthcare reform did not win a floor vote from a Republican in the Senate and only a single House Republican vote. These were momentous policy achievements, based on partisan votes. Such partisan votes were anything but exceptional in the 111th Congress. Overall party unity scores ran at around or over 90 percent for each party in both House and Senate, meaning that, when the parties opposed one another on a vote, there were very high levels of party loyalty (Poole and Rosenthal, 2013).

While Obama had promised bipartisanship, the Congress he confronted delivered partisanship. Despite the accusations of strategic naivety leveled against him, Obama seemed to deliver contingent bipartisanship. He would search for consensus across the parties, but resort to exploiting the opportunities presented by his party's congressional majorities if those were the only means to achieve legislation. He could not generate a post-partisan presidency, but the legislative victories of 2009 and 2010 represented substantial rewards for falling back upon a partisan approach.

The Obama Presidency and the 112th Congress: divided government

Despite legislative successes, the administration suffered what Obama termed a 'shellacking' in the 2010 midterm elections. The public reduced the Democrats' representation in Congress substantially. In the Senate, a Democrat majority of 51 (plus two independents) facing 47 Republicans had no chance of overcoming filibusters without winning some Republican support. The Democrats had lost control of the House altogether, Republicans holding a 242 to 193 majority. The Obama Administration now faced divided government. Republicans could block the passage of Democrat legislation and use their control of the House agenda to highlight the issues they chose for media and public attention.

At one level, the new congressional context appeared to provide the perfect opportunity for Obama to pursue bipartisan leadership. Incapable of passing legislation with his party alone, Obama now had additional incentives to reach for the center ground, both to steer preferred legislation through Congress and to project an image of moderation in anticipation of the 2012 election.

Bipartisanship, though, relies on cooperation from both parties. Obama did not need the support of all Republicans, but at least some would be required to join with Democrats if majorities were to pass legislation. Republican incentives, however, had not changed greatly after the 2010 midterms. Those elections appeared to have rewarded Republican intransigence. Resisting Obama appeared an effective electoral strategy. Given the strong tendency for legislators of a party to vote together, each individual Republican could position him or herself with the rank-and-file and expect that the party line would hold. The purpose of the Republicans' resolute opposition was captured by Senate Minority leader Mitch McConnell (R: Kentucky): 'the single most important thing we want to achieve is for President Obama to be a one-term president' (Kessler, 2012). Increased partisanship endowed Obama with legislative victories under unified government, but under divided government it disadvantaged him as he confronted an opposition party less prone to fragmentation.

Scholars expect a presidency confronting such obstacles to resort to other forms of leadership, perhaps using executive power or employing public opinion to bully poll-sensitive legislators into changing their policy positions. Furthermore, Obama was expected to exploit opposition obstructionism to position himself favorably for reelection. He too could use strategic disagreement to his electoral advantage by presenting himself as attempting to address public concerns despite an uncooperative and unreasonable Republican party. Once again, the structures and incentives within the political system directed Obama away from his promise of a post-partisan presidency.

Each side recognized that the public's primary concern was the slow economic recovery, particularly high unemployment. To win in 2012, each party had to demonstrate engagement with the issue. The parties articulated very different stories about the crisis. Democrats argued that government spending was vital, both to the well-being of those suffering the recession's effects and in boosting the economy. Republicans argued that the burden of government on the economy had to be cut to allow the private sector to grow and provide new jobs. The ideological disagreement was intense and the electoral stakes, given the issue's prominence, were high.

Even though cooperation seemed unlikely, the parties could not simply posture, as hard decisions would be required during the 112th Congress. The normal business of government continued, presenting a genuine problem in that it had to be funded, demanding congressional agreement on spending, taxing and borrowing. Republicans, particularly new Tea Party representatives, saw opportunities to highlight what they believed to be popular priorities of cutting the spending and size of government. During 2011, they exploited budget procedures to highlight these concerns; a series of partisan conflicts over fiscal policy resulted. In the spring, Republicans took advantage of the budget process. The federal government was so short of money that it was very close to a shutdown and Republicans refused to approve more spending without budget cuts. A shutdown was averted very late on. In the summer, Republicans refused to accept an increase in the federal government debt ceiling, suggesting that it might not continue to borrow money to fund its programs. In December 2011, hostilities broke out over a cut in the 'payroll tax' used to fund social programs.

The most telling of these clashes was the summer's debt ceiling fight. Raising the limit of how much the federal government could borrow was normally uncontroversial, but Republicans saw a chance to highlight growing federal debt and to emphasize their belief that it should be controlled through spending cuts, particularly in entitlement programs of Medicare and Social Security. If the debt ceiling was not raised, the federal government would not be able to pay its bills. This default could have jeopardized its capacity to borrow, throwing the American economy into chaos.

As both parties postured publicly over the debt limit, Obama opened up secret negotiations with Republican House Speaker John Boehner. They both hoped to achieve a budgetary 'grand bargain' to address the federal government's fiscal problems in the long term. Each felt they could reach a historic agreement which would serve the US economy and people well. They embarked upon complex and secret talks on future levels of federal spending and taxation. The secrecy was required because, to design any such grand bargain, each participant had to take a risk. Amid the intricacies of the budget numbers, each demonstrated a willingness to contradict their own party's economic orthodoxies. To generate a position between those contrasting orthodoxies, Obama came to the table willing to achieve spending cuts by reducing entitlement benefits. Many Democrats would have loathed the cuts in social spending and the implied acceptance of a core Republican argument that the federal government was spending too freely, was generating an unsustainable debt and should cut spending rather than do more. Meanwhile, Boehner agreed to consider increased federal tax revenues of $800 billion. Republicans would have been horrified by such a concession, even if it might have been presented as a process of closing tax loopholes and eliminating subsidies. Furthermore, Boehner would have appeared to be conceding that the federal government needed to raise more money to deal with the debt, despite Republicans' public conviction that lower taxes and smaller government would resolve the country's economic problems. Each party's sacred ideological cows and electoral narratives were under threat from the 'grand bargain'.

Despite Obama and Boehner's willingness to make policy concessions, the 'grand bargain' proved impossible. This failure is best explained by imagining the two party leaders meeting close to a common center ground, while their parties looked on warily from the ideological periphery. Each leader worried whether he could bring his own party round to accepting the centrist settlement. Indeed, so great were the partisan tensions that neither believed he could be seen to be giving much ground. The negotiations were characterized by each participant explaining that their party would not accept excessive concessions. Each side believed that they had to demonstrate to their own party's mainstream that they had achieved a good deal. Indeed, at one point Republican negotiators even admitted that they needed an 'Obama scalp' to win their rank-and-file's support (Wallsten et al., 2012). Obama feared the impact within his own party of achieving only a small increase in federal revenues (Bai, 2012). Neither leader's credibility within his party could sustain the suggestion that he had been taken advantage of, such is the fervent hostility underpinning Washington's partisan conflict. Ultimately, from the core of each party, whatever centrist agreement could be reached looked like a bad deal engineered by bad leadership. That assumption triggered the second set of concerns: each leader feared that the other would not be able to deliver his legislators' votes when the deal was agreed. Even if Obama and Boehner developed some degree of personal trust, they did not trust each other's parties to honor an agreement, making for complicated discussions over mechanisms to force each party not to renege. Poisonous partisanship added layers of complexity to the deal, making it harder to negotiate. As journalist Matt Bai (ibid.) wrote, 'the only thing holding Washington back from a meaningful step toward reducing debt and modernizing government isn't any single policy dilemma, but rather the political dynamic that makes compromise such a mortal risk'.

Rather than take that risk, Obama and Boehner fell back on strategic disagreement, recognizing the benefits in opposing one another. Each could be seen as defenders of his party's own orthodoxy and protectors of the party mantras intended to lead to victory in the 2012 elections. Rather than a grand bargain, the two sides could only agree to 'kick the can down the road' by establishing temporary measures to delay a proper settlement until the end of 2012. Unimpressed, the credit rating agency Standard and Poor's downgraded its rating of the US debt, condemning the American political system: 'the downgrade reflects our view that the effectiveness, stability, and predictability of American policymaking and political institutions have weakened at a time of ongoing fiscal and economic challenges' (Standard and Poor's, 2011).

Obama moved his focus onto his American Jobs Act, a $447 billion proposal to boost employment in the US economy, which drew on ideas from both parties. The Republicans refused to consider it seriously. Obama's experiments in bipartisanship had failed when confronted by structures of presidential–congressional relations that one man's talents and will could not overcome. As the 112th Congress approached its conclusion, it seemed that it would set a record for low levels of legislative achievement. Obama had, though, pursued other forms of presidential leadership in parallel with his efforts to win congressional support.

Obama goes public

The rhetorical capability demonstrated during Obama's rise to the presidency had won extraordinary praise. Therefore, many believed that he could employ the presidency's 'bully pulpit' to win support for his chosen policies. Some even wondered if Obama was a new 'great communicator' of the Reagan ilk, by implication ascribing transformative capacities to his rhetoric. Others noted his campaign's successful exploitation of social media, suggesting a new means of persuasion for the presidency's use. Obama seemed likely to 'go public', pursuing enhanced public approval ratings through public events in order to convince legislators to support the president's preferred policies, as legislators would find it hard to cross a popular presidency (Kernell, 2006).

Despite the expectations, Obama's public opinion ratings, and those for his preferred policies, did not suggest an effective communications strategy. In line with recent presidencies, his job approval ratings dropped perilously during his first year in office, falling to under 50 percent in November 2009. A majority of Americans continued to believe that the country was on the 'wrong track' throughout his first term and, by late 2011, over 70 percent of Americans believed this to be the case. Nor was he able to win the American public's support for his specific policies. Neither the stimulus bill nor healthcare legislation inspired widespread public support. Worse, Obama seemed to lose control of his own image, Republicans defining him in the public mind as a high-spending, big-government liberal who could not resolve economic problems.

Observers offered a range of narratives to explain this failure. Some blamed the White House communications operation, headed by Obama's Senior Advisor, David Axelrod (Leibovich, 2010). Obama aides acknowledged, if not in conciliatory style, that the administration might have been distracted from public presentation issues: 'sue us. We were trying to save the country' (Thrush, 2012). A more damaging accusation suggested that the problem was an absence of message. Obama recognized that 'the nature of this office is ... to tell a story to the American people that gives them a sense of unity and purpose and optimism, especially during tough times' and that he had sometimes failed to fulfill this role (Boerma, 2012). Even as the president ran for reelection, *Politico* complained that the president lacked a 'cohesive political identity' (Thrush, 2012). Others criticized Obama's personal style. Greenstein (2011: 10) argued that 'his presidential communications have been too pedagogical and insufficiently persuasive. His ubiquity is also a problem'. Obama's tendency to discuss policy in too much detail, rather than keeping the message simple and clear, was a weakness. In contrast, others suggested that the administration was liberal and argued that Obama's message did not resonate with the public because they were ideologically ill-disposed to accept it. According to this argument, only 22 percent of the 2008 electorate had declared themselves liberals, so it is unsurprising that public appetite for Obama's programs was limited (*New York Times*, 2008).

Scholars of the presidency offer a different explanation. While the public and journalists might entertain fantasies of presidential leadership, these scholars argue that 'going public' is ineffective. George Edwards, particularly, has shown how rarely public addresses impact on public opinion significantly. Presidents may have some ability to draw attention to particular issues, but they rarely influence what the public think about those issues (Edwards, 2003). Kernell's (2006) core observation was to record the increasing tendency for presidents to speak publicly, particularly in the form of minor addresses. At the same time, he also identified a 'strategy' of leadership. Presidents, he argued, would 'go public' to make themselves personally popular. This popularity could be used to lever a recalcitrant Congress to support presidential policies because legislators would fear the electoral repercussions of crossing a popular president. However, Kernell's 'strategy' label has often been over-interpreted, as though it offered a form of presidential leadership independent of Congress. 'Going public', in its crudest form, implies that presidents attempt to win public support and presidential leadership thrives or founders according to the ability to make an appeal. Edwards undermined the latter concept, dismissing the naïve conception of a direct connection between presidency and public.

Edwards's conclusions pose an awkward question. If 'going public' is ineffective, why do presidencies continue to expend such extensive effort on public communication? Some have suggested that the Obama administration has not done so. Hacker (2010) noted the absence of an intense public campaign for healthcare reform. No obvious 'Facebook model' of governing emerged, by which a social media campaign marshaled support for Obama reforms. However, the growing understanding of the presidency's public communication offers more subtle explanations of Obama's behavior than can be accommodated by the most basic 'going public' model of 'President speaks to public, public responds, Congress quakes'.

First, considering public communication by the president as nested within congressional strategy draws attention to narrower targets than Congress as a whole. To win a specific congressional vote, an administration identifies particular legislators they need to persuade; going public is one weapon in the presidency's armory to address those selected legislators. Persuasion could take numerous forms, given the sophistication of legislators' electoral calculations (Herbert, 2013). The institutional complexity of Congress also suggests that presidencies may need to influence different parts of the legislative process. The target might be a particular committee or agenda, rather than the legislator (Eshbaugh-Soha and Miles, 2011).

Second, there are limitations to approaches based on treating the public as a monolithic recipient of presidential communication. As Jacobs and Shapiro (2000) argue, there are a myriad of publics. New media technologies, media fragmentation and marketing databases offer presidencies the means to target their communication to selected audiences. Rather than being limited to national appeals through three major television networks, presidents can target an audience of constituents in the district of a particular legislator. Particular groups likely to have strong views on a policy area or specific proposal may be targeted. Communication could be designed to mobilize the party faithful, demotivate opposition activity or appeal to non-partisan independents.

Third, the message delivered by presidential communication, rather than being an attempt to enhance presidential approval ratings, could take many forms, depending on administration aspirations. Various dimensions of presidential image could be addressed, such as perceptions of the president's ideology, priorities or personal characteristics. Presidential performances could also be designed to shape perceptions of other players in the political system, such as Congress or either political party. Communication might be designed to raise an issue's profile. Equally, rhetoric could identify special features of a policy alternative for attention. Presidents may try to manipulate the dimensions of an issue that the public notice, selecting dimensions to cut across unfavorable circumstances and advantage a presidential proposal. The public communication of presidents constructs the choices available to the public by defining the available alternatives and how they should be understood. The presidency's proposal will act as a foil for all other arguments in the policy area, so that foil must be chosen strategically.

The last of these ideas raises a further key issue in understanding presidential communication. Most ideas in the field revolve around the assumption that presidential efforts are designed to change the opinions of members of the public. Brandice Canes-Wrone's work (2001, 2006) identifies other possibilities. She suggests that presidents will 'go public' not to change minds, but to exploit preexisting public sentiment. She notes that, if a president's position is already popular with the public, televised appeals are likely to increase congressional funding in that policy area. That is, presidents choose to bring the public into a Washington debate when it suits their needs. Presidential communication serves an 'activating' role by highlighting, for legislators, the stakes of crossing public sentiment. Hence, presidential appeals can move policy in the direction of majority opinion.

Canes-Wrone's work recognizes another level to the presidential 'game', of whether to engage public attention with Washington debates or not and what surrounding contexts may encourage them to do so. Another level of the game would be the consideration of how to use this public sentiment in Washington. Administrations usually attempt to influence perceptions of public sentiment among elected officials, for example, by prioritizing publicity for the opinions of some groups among the public over others and choosing where in Washington to bring those opinions to bear. The presidency attempts to intercede in the process of translating public sentiment into a political force.

The simple notion that presidents try to generate an unambiguous public super-majority in support of a policy option, or expect that support to generate a mirroring super-majority in Congress, is misplaced. Those circumstances will virtually never occur, because public support is rarely so clear cut or consistently engaged with Washington politics. Rather, the imperative for presidents is to maneuver around the indifference, confusion, ignorance or outright skepticism of a fragmented public. In most circumstances, a presidential proposal is intended to replace a status quo likely produced by similarly unrepresentative maneuverings; the president's aim is simply to generate a new, but from his perspective preferred, unrepresentative status quo.

The Obama Administration's use of public communication reflected a number of these considerations. The situation Obama confronted in the 111th Congress, and the strategy chosen to address it, was particularly orientated against a classic 'going public' approach. The administration's partisan strategy in Congress depended upon winning Democratic party majorities, including a small group of pivotal legislators: a handful of Senators and the conservative 'Blue Dog' Democrats in the House. Winning their support demanded an intricate, insider, bargaining approach by which Obama relinquished control of drawing up legislation to allow his congressional allies to develop a consensus bill. This strategy, designed around the needs of wooing Capitol Hill, imposed a series of costs on any administration attempts to influence the public. Most standard presidential 'going public' involves an initial coherence. The presidency reveals a reform in messages carefully tailored for public consumption. It holds the natural advantage of striking first in the battle over public sentiment on the plan, as objectors may take time to develop effective criticisms of a new proposal. The Administration's insider strategy precluded this approach. Instead, the presidency was cast as responsive, rather than leading the process. In the healthcare debate during the summer of 2009, particularly, Obama appeared uncommitted, and supporters struggled to defend a set of amorphous promises, rather than a concrete plan. The congressional squabbles over the legislation were often conducted in public, as were the processes of bargaining, which did little to encourage public support. Intense media scrutiny focused on the processes, including sordid deals done to win key legislators' votes, rather than the policies or their purposes. Obama seemed to preside over some particularly egregious examples of 'politics as usual', such as the notorious 'Cornhusker Kickback' by which Nebraska Senator Ben Nelson nearly managed to negotiate an extra $100 million in Medicare funds for his state, in exchange for his support. Sending coherent messages about the policies to the public was impossible in this fluid and unfavorable environment. Also, the bargaining process meant that the opposition had plenty of time to organize attacks on the president's proposal. Even the timing weighed against coherent communication strategy; given the eccentric rate of congressional progress in developing legislation, the administration could not tell when best to schedule public events to coincide with legislative processes. Unsurprisingly, Republicans used the opportunities presented by Obama's partisan strategy to shape perceptions of his reforms and presidency.

Nevertheless, Obama did achieve some notable successes. Particularly, he managed to win public attention for the issue of healthcare despite the economic troubles of the period. When asked to name the most important problem facing the United States, unusually high percentages named healthcare as the legislative trials and tribulations played out in Washington. Including presidential appearances on an unprecedented five different Sunday news shows on September 20, 2009, the Administration continued to tout the need for reform, even when the prospects of success looked bleak. Arguably, keeping public attention on healthcare was crucial to the passage of reform, as it presented wavering Democratic legislators with an unpleasant decision: to vote for healthcare reform and risk looking liberal, or to vote against healthcare reform and destroy Obama's presidency. Obama's personal image was also unusually strong in the face of economic difficulties, as he maintained levels of personal favorability significantly out of line with his job approval and other ratings. Americans might have thought he was struggling with the economy, but they liked him. His communication was not irredeemably flawed.

During the 112th Congress, the Administration had even less reason to use a classic 'going public' approach to leadership. Under antagonistic partisan conditions, Obama could not expect to win majority support in Congress for much legislation, so his communication strategy was not so much rooted in aspirations to persuade and bargain as in the public pursuit of partisan conflict. Public communication was integral to the pursuit of strategic disagreement, as the presidency attempted to shape perceptions of the conflict and all participants within it. Obama attempted to portray himself as the 'adult in the room', developing his image as a reasonable moderate open to negotiation amid partisan hostilities. Offering the right image on economic issues was crucial. Obama presented himself as a competent manager of the economy operating against difficult headwinds, but with the right priority (jobs) and with the interests of the American people at heart. Meanwhile, Republicans were cast as the demons of the piece, as incapable of thinking beyond the failed policies of the Bush era and dangerously out-of-touch with the concerns of ordinary Americans. In the election year of 2012, this criticism was neatly attached to Republican candidate Mitt Romney even before he had had the opportunity to define himself clearly to the public.

Obama's experience showed the presidency to be constrained by its context. Whatever his rhetorical talents, Obama could not transform the United States from his 'bully pulpit'. The classic 'going public' approach, however, is only one strategy available to the presidency and possibly one of the least effective. Obama demonstrated the diverse range of communication opportunities available to presidencies, using the office to shape the Washington agenda, to develop his personal image, to mobilize select publics and to shape perceptions of many Washington officials and organizations.

Executive power

Greater recognition of the presidency's executive power has been a major development in presidential scholarship. Substantial work emerged as George W. Bush took office, offering new emphasis on the presidency's capacity to exert power without persuading other participants in the political system. Scholars noted that presidencies could exercise substantial sway over the activities of the federal executive through a series of unilateral instruments, such as executive orders and presidential memoranda (Cooper, 2002; Mayer, 2002; Howell, 2003). The actions of the Bush presidency only concentrated attention further. The Bush team's claim to have unilateral power to prosecute military conflicts was extraordinary and was accompanied by a swathe of 'War on Terror' measures such as the use of torture as a means of interrogation, illicit domestic surveillance, military tribunals and extraordinary rendition. The Administration used signing statements to justify decisions to avoid implementing laws properly, cited executive privilege to resist legislative and judicial oversight and worked to politicize the executive branch. These and other exertions encouraged Andrew Rudalevige to catalog the rise of a 'new imperial presidency', suggesting that the constitutional system of checks, balances and separated powers was under assault from the power of the executive (Schlesinger, 2004; Rudalevige, 2005). These observers noted a gradual, if uneven, rise in executive power over time.

Obama's 2008 campaign promised to rein in the excesses of previous presidencies. Liberals had been outraged by Bush, and Obama promised to restore the constitutional balance by respecting the authority of other political institutions. However, there were substantial reasons to distrust such promises to restrain the presidency. Obama would face the same institutional imperatives to gather power in the White House as did his predecessors. The temptation to take action using power that did not rely on congressional consent would surely prove difficult to resist.

Initially, Obama appeared to pursue his pledge to restrain his new office. During the 2008 campaign, the closure of the Guantanamo Bay prison camp, established to receive suspected terrorists, became a symbol of Obama's desire to overturn Bush's excesses. He issued executive orders to close the camp shortly after taking office. The administration expended substantial energy to try to provide normal legal trials for a number of the alleged terrorists, most notably arguing that Khalid Sheikh Mohammed, a planner of the 9/11 attacks, should stand trial in New York. Although these efforts failed, Obama clearly attempted to reverse Bush's concentration of power in the Oval Office. Obama's use of signing statements, to explain presidential interpretations of congressional legislation, was much narrower than Bush's. Executive privilege, withholding information from Congress and the courts to prevent oversight, was rarely used. One notable exception was the administration's refusal to provide evidence on the Justice Department's failed 'Fast and Furious' operation, by which the department appeared to facilitate the transport of illegal guns into the hands of drug traffickers in Mexico. Making a familiar executive privilege claim, that policy discussions on sensitive issues could not become public, Attorney General Eric Holder became the first sitting member of the US Cabinet to be held in contempt of Congress.

The Obama Administration exerted executive power more consistently in foreign policy, most notably asserting the right to mount military operations against terrorism wherever in the world it chose. The administration claimed to have its own internal review process, but that was hardly an equivalent constraint on presidential power to that embodied in the Constitution's statement that Congress holds the power to declare war. Administration beliefs in this area were reflected in a series of actions. Obama asserted the prerogative to assassinate suspected terrorists anywhere in the world, even if they were US citizens. The Administration pursued its 'kill list' through unmanned drone strikes in at least five countries. Covert cyberwar operations against Iran were employed without substantial congressional involvement. These presidential actions raised complex constitutional questions about the power of the presidency to conduct war without committing troops to direct military action. The operation to assist anti-Qaddafi rebels in Libya, using US air power and special forces on the ground, was never brought to Congress for approval. It would have been extraordinarily unusual for the Administration to have asked for a congressional declaration of war, a process only observed in five previous conflicts. The more normal path is to request a congressional resolution of support for action. Bush, often regarded as extreme in his assertions, had gone to Congress for authorizations to use military force both against terrorists and Iraq. However, even this option was not pursued by Obama. Instead, the administration labeled their commitment to Libya as not a 'war', but a 'kinetic military action'. The failure to achieve normal criminal trials for alleged terrorists led to the administration adopting a revived military tribunals system, with limits upon defendants' rights, such as the use of secret evidence and administration refusal to accept judicial review of the prisoners' status. Despite improvements, the echoes of the Bush abuses were unmistakeable and much lamented by liberals.

The most significant shift in the administration's use of executive power came in late 2011. Frustrated by the failed budget negotiations of that year, Obama despaired of working with Congress. Divided government offered him only frustration and an appearance of inaction as he faced a truculent economy and a reelection campaign. The structures of government made a less constrained form of power, executive action, seem very appealing. His Deputy Chief of Staff, Nancy-Ann DeParle, was nominated to head a team to identify changes the president could make through executive action (Savage, 2012). The bypassing of Congress to achieve action was treated as a virtue in Obama's public discourse. In a Las Vegas speech he argued that 'we can't wait for an increasingly dysfunctional Congress to do its job. Where they won't act, I will' (Obama, 2011). The 'We Can't Wait' initiative even had its own White House webpages.

DeParle identified a series of major initiatives which were rolled out during 2012. For example, the administration exploited an opportunity presented by Bush's No Child Left Behind Act to further its chosen education policy. The original act had set proficiency standards for pupils' educational achievements, which each state was required to reach. The proficiency standards were unrealistically high, but failing to achieve them would have generated punishments for the states. The act also allowed the federal government to issue waivers, releasing states from having to achieve these impossible standards. Recognizing that states would want to avoid the sanctions imposed by the existing legislation, the Administration allowed state waivers, but only with substantial strings attached. The waiver would be issued if states adopted new systems for evaluating teachers and school proficiency. Without needing new legislation from Congress, the Administration fashioned state-level education policies.

Obama's administration also used executive power to shape immigration policy. Thousands of children brought to the United States illegally are raised as Americans, receiving American public schooling and having little direct experience of their country of birth. Despite this upbringing, these children remain illegal immigrants and so face deportation and find it difficult to find employment. The DREAM Act, designed to address their situation by providing a route to permanent residency status, had been considered by Congress for over a decade, but failed to become law. In June 2012, the Obama Administration took executive action to address this situation, announcing that federal prosecutors would defer deportation proceedings against certain types of immigrant brought to the US illegally as children. Those enrolled in university, or having graduated, or serving or having served honorably in the military were all eligible for a deferral of deportation and work authorization if they had paid taxes and had not committed any felonies or serious misdemeanors. This action was particularly contentious as the administration had adjusted the policy in a manner that Congress had repeatedly and explicitly rejected. Administration claims that this was simply an enforcement issue, and so well within presidential authority, seemed disingenuous, especially as the Administration touted the new policy loudly to Hispanic-Americans during election season.

Education and immigration policies were only two elements of the 'We Can't Wait' initiative. Obama used executive power to change policies on, among others, welfare, federal support for mortgages, student loans, fuel economy standards, veterans' jobs, pharmaceutical shortages and domestic violence.

Republican responses to Obama's actions were surprisingly muted, but in a manner that reflects the developing literature on the presidency's executive power. The *New York Times* reported that Republicans judged opposition to Obama's executive actions as politically risky, as it would reinforce Obama's narrative on the dysfunction of Congress (Savage, 2012). While some literature on executive action details the growth of executive action as a power grab and an exceeding of authority, a more nuanced interpretation has emerged. This approach considers the presidency's action as less unilateral and more conditional, as the rest of the American political system retains the capacity to respond by constraining presidential assertion. Howell argues that many executive actions reflect the views and interests of other politicians in Washington and therefore presidential actions are tolerated (Howell, 2003). Sometimes it may even be in the legislators' interest to allow the presidency to take responsibility for a policy through executive action, allowing legislators to duck the potential political costs of action. On other occasions, courts, Congress or the public may choose to resist. Hence, executive action is a question of calculation for the presidency: will an assertion be challenged successfully or not (Howell, 2003; Howell and Pevehouse, 2007)? Hence, on education policy Obama knew that many, including vociferous Republican governors and legislators, were frustrated by Congress's inability to revise the No Child Left Behind legislation. He acted knowing that waivers of unrealistic proficiency standards would be welcomed.

Obama employed executive action to demonstrate his leadership, often to particular electoral constituencies within the Democratic Party, because the congressional route did not offer opportunities to do so. Despite his 2008 campaign pledges, Obama made an unambiguous and conscious turn to executive power. Responding to pressing policy problems, or being seen to do so, was more important to the president than maintaining his initial deference to others' constitutional prerogatives. However, the 'We Can't Wait' initiative revealed the subtleties of executive action that had been disguised by some of Bush's more blunt claims of authority. Obama's actions were not ill-considered, but rooted in strategic calculations on whether he could bypass Congress without incurring damaging levels of political criticism.

The second term: a new approach?

Candidate Obama made many pledges and raised many expectations in 2008. Above all, he promised the leadership to achieve change after the Bush years. Part of that change was expected to be in the conduct of the presidency. Obama seemed to offer a new post-partisan presidency, perhaps led by a president capable of inspiring the people through rhetoric, but willing to restore the institutional balance outlined in the Constitution.

At the end of his first term, Obama could claim substantial changes had been achieved. He had overseen an arresting of the American economy's perilous descent and a sluggish recovery, an unprecedented reform of healthcare policy and re-regulation of the financial markets. He had achieved reelection, with his party retaining a majority in the Senate. However, these achievements were often testament to Obama's recognition of the structures within which the presidency operates and his willingness to shape his leadership strategies accordingly. Dreams of a post-partisan presidency had been vanquished by the resolute partisan forces shaping the political system. Leadership through public communication was often a marginal element within Obama's strategy and little suggests that he could have used his rhetorical abilities to generate overwhelming public support for his policies. His restraint in exercising executive power, although notable compared to his predecessor's, was hardly complete.

Furthermore, these constraints prevented Obama from addressing many pressing problems facing the United States as he began his second term. Whether, and how, the economy could recover fully was unclear. The federal government's long-term budgetary problems, compounded by slow economic growth, had to be addressed. The United States had already teetered close to a borrowing crisis during 2011, and the continuing pressure exerted by spending on social entitlement programs suggested that this problem would not subside without painful sacrifices. Having spent 60 years allocating resources among conditions of abundance, the American government was only slowly engaging with the rather greater challenge of allocating resources under conditions of relative scarcity. The United States also faced substantial foreign policy challenges, most obviously managing the decline of American power relative to other nations, especially China. Other domestic policy issues also required attention, as the challenge of implementing Obama's new healthcare reform would pose numerous problems, as would climate change and immigration policy.

Obama would have to address these problems while working within many of the constraints suffered in his first term. Although he won reelection by a 3 percent margin, on the surface the 2012 results appeared to maintain the conditions of 2011–12. Obama faced divided government, with a Democrat-led Senate and a House Republican majority. The ideological center in Congress still appeared denuded, particularly in the House. The partisan presidency, which shaped much of his first term, still suggested that he would face resolute opposition. The nature of Obama's 2012 victory, though, did seem enabling, as it changed the governing environment in subtle ways. While proving that a president received a direct policy mandate from an election is impossible, an intense bout of public argument defines how returns should be interpreted, potentially helping or hindering a presidency (Dahl, 1990; Jones, 1998). Obama won by a clear margin, but commentators also highlighted the importance of high turnout among the young, Obama's success in blaming Republicans for continuing economic problems, and the Democrats' impressive results among the Hispanic-American community. Furthermore, his victory confronted Republicans in Congress with revised calculations. Their strategic obstruction in the 112th Congress had not rendered Obama a one-term president. Republicans had to ask whether four more years of persistent resistance would damage perceptions of the Democrats' ability to lead or merely reinforce the Republicans' image as 'the party of no'.

There were reasons for Obama to worry. Second-term presidents should expect to face distracting scandals as first-term actions are investigated during the second, particularly if the opposition party has a platform for their investigations through control of a chamber of Congress. Obama would also find himself a 'lame duck', as second terms often generate low public approval ratings, the media and public are distracted by the processes of choosing the next president, and the incumbent has a reduced capacity to bargain through pledges of future favors. Second terms rarely generate extensive legislative achievements. Previous experience suggests that the main hope for substantial, presidentially led reform lies in crises. A foreign or economic policy disaster, perhaps derived from the US finally exhausting the international markets' tolerance for its debt levels, might create an environment in which the country would turn to the presidency to lead change. Nevertheless, changes in Obama's strategy also suggested potential for significant achievements.

Facing a House Republican majority during the 112th Congress left a lasting impression upon Obama and his staff. Before the 2012 elections, the experience triggered reevaluations of both the president's loudly professed bipartisanship and his use of executive power. Starting his second term, Obama seemed to have adjusted his approach to governing further. He outlined a very clear and full policy agenda and offered more legislative specifics. He declared a plan to go public far more directly than in his first term. He appeared to downplay bipartisanship and promised to extend his use of executive power.

After two years of budgetary quarrels with the Republicans, the same concerns threatened to engulf the agenda throughout Obama's second term. Before this second term had even started, Obama had to negotiate the so-called 'fiscal cliff', and he delivered his inaugural facing looming battles over the federal government's debt limit, a planned 'sequester' of spending cuts and the need for a continuing budget resolution to keep the federal government functioning. The Administration feared being, as it were, nickeled and dimed to death by budgetary battles dominating the agenda. Instead, Obama articulated other issues on which he would act. The heart-rending massacre at Sandy Hook Elementary School in Newtown, Connecticut, in December 2012, prompted Obama to promise greater regulation of gun ownership. The presidential election result opened the way to new discussions of immigration reform, as Republicans confronted a future in the minority if they could not attract non-white votes. Obama's inaugural address highlighted the threat of climate change and the controversial nomination of Senator Chuck Hagel to be Secretary of Defense suggested a new direction for the military. Obama also seemed willing to offer more legislative specifics, rather than leading from behind on policy detail. Appointing Vice President Joe Biden as head of a task force to develop policy recommendations on gun control marked a change from allowing Congress to develop legislation. Such direction was not used in every policy area, though, as reflected in the administration's initial deference to Congress over immigration policy.

Obama also pledged to 'go public' in support of his agenda. The attention to climate change in his inaugural address reflected this commitment and he was explicit about the public's role in achieving reform of gun laws: 'I tell you, the only way we can change is if the American people demand it ... if Americans of every background stand up and say: "Enough. We've suffered too much pain and care too much about our children to allow this to continue." Then change will come. That's what it's going to take' (Obama, 2013). He demonstrated uncharacteristic determination to change the issue's politics, trying to act as a director, not a facilitator of change.

Furthermore, Obama showed signs of abandoning his post-partisanship. Attempting to negotiate the 'grand bargain' over the budget deficit during 2011 had, according to White House Counselor Pete Rouse, made Obama 'more realistic ... about who he's negotiating with' (Baker, 2013). His 2013 inaugural address was notably short on the 'good government' rhetoric of repairing Washington politics that had featured heavily in 2009. The implication was unambiguous: Obama had decided that opposition from congressional Republicans was absolute, so bipartisan reforms would be exceptional. Obama was no longer 'inhibited' by a desire to be post-partisan and 'by the need to not offend the Republicans with whom he was negotiating' (Brooks,

2013). He would attempt to act, casting his reforms in his own terms with Democrat support, and so presenting Republicans with the awkward strategic choice of either negotiating to temper the reforms or standing in resolute opposition at the risk of being labeled obstructionist.

Having resorted to executive action to further his policy priorities in 2012, Obama openly acknowledged that administrative action would serve the same purpose in 2013. For example, his promise to take meaningful action on gun regulation was backed by presidential memoranda to revive federal government research into gun violence, to improve the background check system used to scrutinize gun purchasers and to reduce illicit trade in firearms. The Administration recognized that legislative action on climate change was unlikely, instead arguing that executive action would have a significant impact. Action was promised to regulate power plant emissions more strictly, to raise standards for energy efficiency in building regulations and to reduce pollution emanating from federal government activities.

Early in his second term, Obama promised more decisive leadership through far more assertive use of the presidency's tools. Once again, he seemed ready to defy the structures of American politics and their orientation against action, attempting to conquer expectations of second-term presidencies and the partisan presidency.

Chapter 8

Congress: The Causes and Consequences of Partisanship Deadlock

Aaron Ray and James A. Thurber

In this chapter we examine the institutional and policy consequences on Congress that flow from increased partisanship, the absence of winning majorities, and the relative unpopularity of the institution. Addressed in detail are public and scholarly views of Congress, the impediments to institutional effectiveness and productivity, and opportunities for reform. The 111th and 112th Congresses illustrated both the capacity for legislative productivity when faced with crisis and under unified party control and the tendency toward gridlock when Congress is divided. In the fall of 2012, President Obama won a second term in office, the Democrats expanded their majority in the Senate and Republicans maintained their hold on the House. These results raised significant questions about the ability of a divided Congress to go beyond deadlock and address major issues facing the nation in the 113th Congress and beyond.

The 111th and 112th Congresses

The 111th Congress, which spanned the first two years of the Obama presidency with a Democratic majority in both chambers, was exceedingly productive. Unified party government and strong party unity on the Hill allowed the Democrats to pass significant legislation to address instability in the financial sector, to supply stimulus to an economy in recession, and to reform the nation's health insurance system. Between July 7, 2009 and February 4, 2010, the Democrats held a filibuster-proof super-majority of 60 votes in the Senate. (On July 7, 2009, Al Franken (D) won the contested Minnesota seat giving the Democrats 60 votes. On February 4, 2010, Scott Brown (R) replaced Paul Kirk (D) in the Massachusetts delegation. However, Ted Kennedy's (D) illness kept him away from the Senate from March to

August 2009. Until Kirk replaced Kennedy on September 24, 2009, the Democrats lacked the necessary 60 votes.) The Democrats used this advantage to enact major legislation including the American Recovery and Reinvestment Act (economic stimulus), the Patient Protection and Affordable Care Act (health insurance reform) and the Dodd-Frank Wall Street Reform and Consumer Protection Act (financial reform). This period of legislative productivity in part inspired a conservative backlash in the 2010 midterm elections.

The 2010 midterm elections changed the dynamic in Congress as Republicans gained a majority in the House and narrowed the Democrats' advantage in the Senate. The 112th Congress saw historically limited legislative productivity in the run up to the 2012 elections. The success of Republican candidates in 2010, many associated with the Tea Party movement, came to dominate coverage of the midterm elections and had a significant effect on the workings of the 112th Congress. A response to what was seen as an unwarranted expansion of the power of the federal government, the Tea Party movement involved a loosely organized collection of conservative groups focused on influencing policy and electing conservative candidates. Tea Party groups effectively exercised this power in, and after, the 2010 elections (Bailey et al., 2012). During the 112th Congress, divided government led to gridlock. Tensions came to a head in May 2011 when Republicans objected to raising the debt ceiling without instituting a plan to reduce the deficit. This impasse resulted in a downgrade of the nation's credit rating and the creation of a bipartisan Congressional committee (the 'Supercommittee') to recommend a deficit reduction plan. The Supercommittee failed to reach an agreement, triggering significant cuts to military, education, transportation and healthcare spending (referred to as sequestration), set to take effect in January 2013. (Sequestration is a budget procedure created in the Gramm-Rudman-Hollings Deficit Reduction Act of 1985 in which appropriations in excess of the spending caps adopted in the annual Budget Resolution are 'sequestered' by the Treasury Department and not allocated to agencies.)

The combination of a large deficit and debt, automatic sequestration of defense and domestic discretionary spending, and the expiration of previously instituted Bush tax cuts, also in 2013, came to be known as the 'fiscal cliff'. How to address these looming deadlines became a primary theme of the 2012 campaign. In November of 2012, Republicans retained control of the House, Democrats retained control of the Senate, and President Obama was reelected to a second term. These 2012 election results set the stage for continued divided government as Congress was faced with how to address the fiscal cliff and other pressing policy issues in the 2012 lame duck session and in the 113th Congress.

134

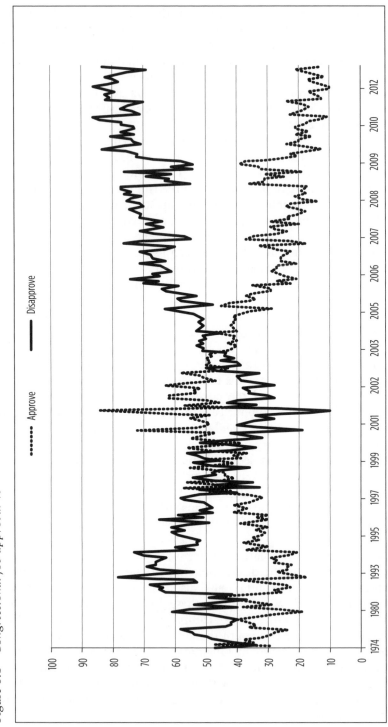

Figure 8.1 *Congressional job approval %*

Source: Adapted from Gallup (2012b).

Assessing Congress

Both the public and scholars have developed a poor opinion of congressional performance. For the public, dissatisfaction with Congress reached a historic low in February and August of 2012 with only 10 percent of the public expressing approval of the way it was doing its job.

Nevertheless, as important as the overall job performance rating is, how the American public evaluates the various functions of Congress more precisely illuminates the areas of prime dissatisfaction. Indiana University's Center for Congressional Studies 2010 survey of public attitudes about Congress found profound negative evaluations concerning the performance of the institution (Center on Congress, 2012). The major result of the survey was that, on all questions where the public graded Congress, it was rated as an underperforming institution: 'Dealing with key issues facing the country' – D; 'Keeping excessive partisanship in check' – D-minus; 'Conducting its business in a careful, deliberate way' – D; 'Holding its members to high standards of ethical conduct' – D; 'Controlling the influence of special interest groups' – D-minus. In response to the question, 'Do members of Congress listen and care about what people like you think?', 33 percent said no, not most of the time. On the question, 'What do you think is the main thing that influences what members of Congress do in office?', 43 percent said it is special interests, and another 41 percent say it is personal self-interest. On the broadest-gauge question, 'Overall, do you approve or disapprove of the way Congress is handling its job?', 84 percent disapproved.

Ironically, despite the low grades, personal feelings about the institution's characteristics and general negative attitudes about Congress, Americans still see it as an important institution in the system of government. The survey found that when asked 'How much of an impact does the work of Congress have on your life?' a majority, 52 percent, said 'a great deal' and another 36 percent said 'some'. There is also a strong belief that Congress has a legitimate claim to share power with the president. In response to a question about which institution should take the lead, Congress or the president, in setting the national agenda, determining the federal budget and deciding to go to war, very solid majorities said both the president and Congress should play a role. The conclusion is that Congress is important in the system of government, but it is failing to do its job.

A 2011 survey of political scientists that asked the same questions as the public survey found that the experts gave the institution similarly negative reviews. The experts gave Congress a grade of C on 'exercising its proper role in setting the legislative agenda' and Ds for 'focusing on the key issues facing the country' and 'generally fulfilling its national policymaking responsibilities'. The survey found that political scientists thought accessibility and openness were areas of strength with Congress. The institution earned Bs on being 'accessible to constituents' and 'open to the public', and a C for 'broadly reflecting constituents' interests'.

Scholars gave Congress weak grades for 'keeping excessive partisanship in check' – the House received an F and grades for the Senate split between D and F in that area. In response to whether the legislative process in each chamber 'involved a proper level of compromise and consensus', the Senate got a C and the House an F. The political scientists also gave Congress D grades on the questions 'Does Congress keep the role of special interests within proper bounds?' and 'Does Congress consider the long-term implications of policy issues, not just short-term?'. When scholars turned their attention to the voters, they gave them D grades for 'following what is going on in Congress on a regular basis' and for 'understanding the main features of Congress and how it works'.

The public has clearly given Congress failing grades while political scientists are only somewhat more satisfied with the institution. Procedural wrangling and partisan gridlock have created the perception that Congress is tied in knots at a time when the nation needs a functioning government more than ever. Congressional polarization along both ideological and party lines is a reflection of the American body politic itself with both the House and Senate dominated by fierce, uncompromising partisanship. Leaders demand ideological purity and lockstep voting and routinely make use of strong-arm procedures to enforce partisan views and subsequent behavior.

Functions of Congress

Congress serves multiple functions, including lawmaking, representation, deliberation and oversight. Scholars often use how well the institution performs these functions as a set of criteria for assessing the effectiveness of Congress as a branch of government. The effectiveness of Congress to fulfill each of these functions has been compromised in recent years by structural and political impediments. The current deadlocked and politicized environment in Congress arguably limits its ability to serve these functions and therefore undermines the effectiveness of the institution.

Lawmaking and legislative procedural maneuvers

Congressional procedural changes have undermined the normal legislative process over the past four decades. For the most part, these changes have not been structural, but have merely involved the use of long standing legislative tools. However, they have helped to undermine trust in the institution. Current concerns focus on today's majority congressional leadership, but the same tactics were practiced in the past by the minority party leadership. Thus, this process cannot be blamed solely on one political party. Both parties use House and Senate rules to deny the opposition a full debate or effective votes and to make significant alterations to legislation passed by the committees of jurisdiction.

An additional problem is the increasing use of filibusters, amendments and holds to clog the legislative work in the Senate. Figure 8.2 shows the rise of cloture motions to stop filibusters in the Senate since 1967. The term 'filibuster' is applied to many different actions in the Senate including objections to unanimous consent requests, efforts to delay proceedings and the anonymous 'hold' that originally was meant as an informational tool for majority leaders trying to arrange floor schedules. 'Holds' are an informal senatorial custom unrecognized in Senate rules and precedents. They allow Senators to give notice to their respective party leader that certain measures or matters should not be brought up on the floor. The party leaders will usually honor holds placed by a member. Holds provide significant leverage to members who wish to delay action on nominations or legislation. The mere threat of a filibuster prompts the majority leader to halt action on a bill or to move quickly to cut off debate, meaning that the minority can block legislation without actually holding the floor and talking for hours on end. Filibusters are currently rarely invoked but often threatened to gain political bargaining power and negotiating leverage. After the Democrats retained control of the Senate in the 2012 elections, Majority Leader Harry Reid indicated a desire, with the support of President Obama and some other Senate Democrats, to reform the cloture process in order to reduce the amount of obstruction in the Senate. In December 2012, Reid announced, 'We're going to change the rules. We cannot continue in this way'. In response, Minority Leader Mitch McConnell expressed opposition to the proposed reform. A bipartisan group of Senators lead by Republican John McCain of Arizona and Democrat Carl Levin of Michigan put forward a proposal to provide the Senate Majority Leader the ability to limit debate on some motions and to speed consideration of lower-level nominees to the executive and judicial branches. A separate proposal by Democratic Senators Jeff Merkley of Oregon and Tom Udall of New Mexico garnered the support of almost 50 Democratic senators. The Merkley–Udall proposal would ban filibusters on motions to proceed and would require Senators to speak continuously on the floor to keep a filibuster going. Without action in the 2012 lame duck session, filibuster reform was left to the 113th Congress.

Figure 8.2   Cloture motions filed in US Senate, 1967–2010

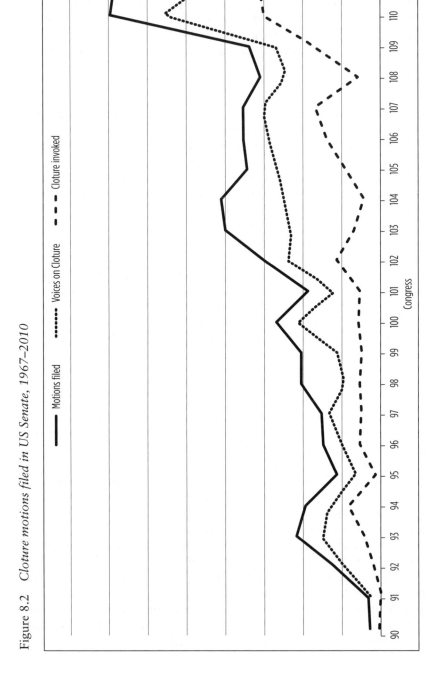

Source: Adapted from Wolfensberger (2012).

The 113th Congress did enact modest procedure reforms to limit the filibuster. Two measures, agreed to by Senators Reid and McConnell, passed with bipartisan support. One measure reduced the amount of debate time following a cloture vote from 30 hours to 4. The second measure prevents a filibuster if eight members of the minority party, including the minority leader, agree to sign a cloture motion. These reforms, while less ambitious than those proposed by Senators Merkley and Udall, represent a small step in the direction of filibuster reform.

Lawmaking and the power of the purse

The Constitution gives the Congress the power of the purse by providing that 'No money shall be drawn from the Treasury, but in Consequence of Appropriations made by Law' (Article I, Section 9). The entire government will shut down if appropriations are not enacted annually. In recent years, there has been heavy reliance on omnibus appropriations bills, 'minibus' appropriations, and additional riders and earmarks added to must-pass appropriation bills. There is also a growing tendency toward government by continuing resolution.

Continuing resolutions are a temporary stopgap funding measure whenever Congress cannot complete action on one or more of the 12 regular appropriations bills by the beginning of the fiscal year (October 1). In the past, continuing resolutions were only used for short periods (one or two months). However, the concurrent budget resolutions have been passed on time only twice since 1976. The federal government has been forced to run on continuing resolutions and supplemental appropriations. Partisan deadlock over a continuing resolution in the spring of 2012 came within a few hours of shutting down the federal government as happened in late 1995 to early 1996. The 2011 experience with multiple continuing resolutions and the debt limit negotiations revealed a deadlocked Congress.

Lawmaking and committees

Committees are necessary for Congress to have a rational division of labor and to work both effectively and efficiently. However, the proliferation of committees and other bodies has contributed to policy fragmentation and jurisdictional overlap. This was evident in the battles over healthcare reform and climate change legislation. Examples of policy fragmentation are extensive: the number of committees and subcommittees with jurisdiction over homeland security is 108; for energy/environment 56; and for jobs/economic security, potentially all 218 committees and subcommittees. There is also a problem of policy balance with committees being captured by specific interests that represent only one view of the issues, such as the agriculture and armed services committees, whose members typically reside in farm states or close to military bases or defense companies. When there is little policy equilibrium within committees in the deliberation of various competing policy positions, there is a perception of unfairness and unequal access for policy preferences.

Although there have been periodic attempts to reduce the number of committees, rationalize jurisdictions and decrease the number of committee assignments, potential reforms of the committee system in the House and Senate have all failed since the overhaul of the Senate committee system in 1976. There have been 13 committee reform efforts since the Joint Committee on the Organization of Congress in 1946, which established the present system of committees. The consequences of an antiquated congressional committee system are unequal workloads of committees and members, and unnecessary duplication, delay and gridlock.

Representation and the role of money

The drive for reelection is a logical part of a representative democracy, though it continues to get more expensive. The growth of the 'permanent campaign', with its negative campaign tactics, threatened to weaken the institution of Congress. Deregulation of campaign finance has reduced transparency about who is giving and for what. In the wake of *Citizens United v Federal Election Commission* (2010) an avalanche of non-transparent campaign money from corporations and unions raised questions about the fairness of the campaign process and its implications for governing.

Campaign spending has grown rapidly from $3.08 billion in 2000 to $5.29 billion in 2008 for presidential election years and from $1.62 billion in 1998 to $3.65 billion in 2010 in non-presidential election years. According to the Center for Responsive Politics, an estimated $6 billion was spent in 2012. Campaign costs have become so monumental that Members must spend most of their time raising money, leaving less time for legislating and working with their fellow legislators. There is intense pressure constantly to raise money and campaign. Moreover, Members often win by criticizing Congress, which undermines trust in the institution. Many members stay with their families in the home district and commute to 'work'. With fewer Members in Washington, the infamous 'Tuesday-through-Thursday Club' is all too real. The House in 2011 spent fewer than 100 days in session, the smallest number in 60 years, and even fewer than the 108 days clocked by the 1948 'Do-Nothing Congress'.

Representation and lobbying

Lobbyists and money from special interests in campaigns are certainly part of the dynamic Congress; however, even after President Obama's lobbying and ethics reforms in 2009, deadlock, extreme partisanship and the hostility the public sees in Congress continued. Nevertheless lobbying can be an essential part of congressional policy-making, as when lobbyists provide expertise that would not be available to the members. But the influence of lobbyists in Congress gives rise to concerns about conflicts of interest and whether the advent of massive lobbying campaigns wrinkles rather than levels the playing field. The number of registered lobbyists increased – from 16,342 in 2000 to 34,785 in 2005, but dropped to around 13,000 in 2010 and 8,500 in 2011 after the 2007 lobbying reforms. The drop in the number of lobbyists does not mean there is less lobbying in Washington. The decline in registered lobbyists is due at least in part to failure to register by sliding in under the requirements, in the letter but not the spirit of the reforms. In 1998, registered lobbyists reported spending $1.427 billion; in 2004, lobbyists spent at least $2.128 billion on reported activities; and in 2010 and 2011 that grew to $3.5 billion, but there is likely much more spent in 'grassroots lobbying' and other unregulated efforts. Spending by registered lobbyists has grown 62 percent in the last five years. This averages out to over $9.7 million in lobbying expenditures each day Congress was in session in 2008 or over $6.5 million per year for every Member of Congress. This does not include money spent for strategy, public relations, grassroots, coalition building, issue advertising on television advertisements and in the print media, and advocacy on the internet. The 1995 Legislative Disclosure Act (LDA) and the 2007 Honest Leadership and Open Government Act (HLOGA) do not cover most advocacy in Washington. The definition of a lobbyist fails to capture most of the advocacy activity in Washington.

Deliberation

There is a difference between deliberation and dysfunction. The right to talk a bill to death, the filibuster, has been allowed by the Senate's rules since 1806, but at first it was used sparingly. Its use is on the rise, as shown in Figure 8.2. Senators often feel very little compunction about stopping the work of the Senate. The collapse of comity is also a serious problem undermining deliberation. The influx of more partisan former House members into the Senate has undermined its capacity for bipartisan deliberation. There appears to be a lack of true deliberation and comity and civility in both the House and Senate. There are fewer committee meetings and hearings, conference committees meet less often, laws are frequently written or substantially revised behind closed doors by the party leadership, and there has been a shortcircuiting of the traditional legislative process. Figure 8.3 illustrates an increase in the use of closed and structured rules and a concomitant decline in the use of open rules for initial consideration for the amendment of legislation.

Figure 8.3   *A decline in open rules*

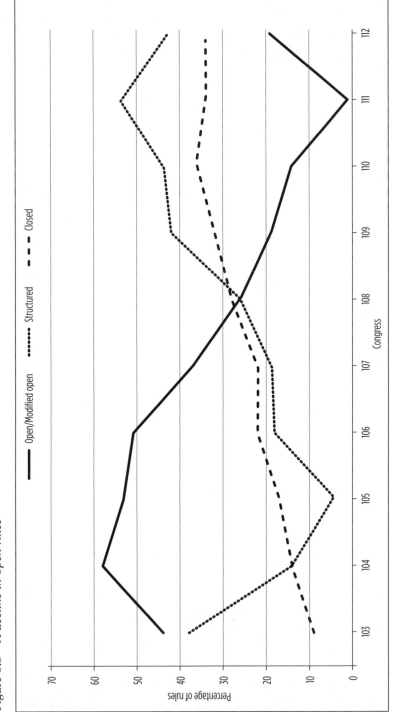

Source: Adapted from Wolfensberger (2012).

Oversight

Rigorous oversight of federal agency actions is essential to ensure Congress is aware of the president's policy initiatives and that the laws Congress has passed are properly implemented. Congress is often too timid when there is unified party government and too aggressive with divided party government. Congress practices 'fire alarm' oversight, waiting until the alarms go off before it begins to review in detail agency activities, rather than 'police patrolling' with regular, planned and active oversight. There has been a long-term decline in the ability or even willingness of Congress to make thorough use of its oversight powers to keep the executive branch in check. Robust oversight could have potentially prevented or lessened the banking and housing crises and the Gulf oil spill and could have improved agency response. Members of Congress are typically not involved in laws after they are passed. In some cases, there are too many friendly alliances between committees that authorize programs, the interest groups that benefit from the programs, and the agencies that administer them. In other instances, the committee chooses to distance itself from the implementation, knowing the results will not please every constituent. All laws have intended and unintended consequences and they need to be monitored carefully by Congress. Former Democratic Representative Lee Hamilton of Indiana argues that 'if we want to make sure that federal agencies are doing their jobs appropriately, with the best interests of the American people constantly in mind, then Congress must do a better job of oversight, looking into every nook and cranny of their activities' (Hamilton, 2010).

Impediments to legislative productivity

The missing middle

A fundamental reason for gridlock and dysfunctionality is the disappearance of the moderates or what some call the vital center in Congress. There has been a steady decline in the number of moderates in Congress since 1960. Figure 8.4 illustrates this decline as measured by DW-NOMINATE scores. (These scores are a commonly used measure of the ideology of legislators and are produced by applying a spatial model to roll-call voting in Congress. They allow for the comparison of members of different Congresses across time. Poole and Rosenthal (2012) argue that the first ideological dimension, capturing differing views on economic policy, explains most roll-call-voting decisions. A second dimension, capturing views on race, has diminished in importance since the 1960s. See also McCarty et al., 1997.)

Figure 8.4   *Decline of Congressional moderates*

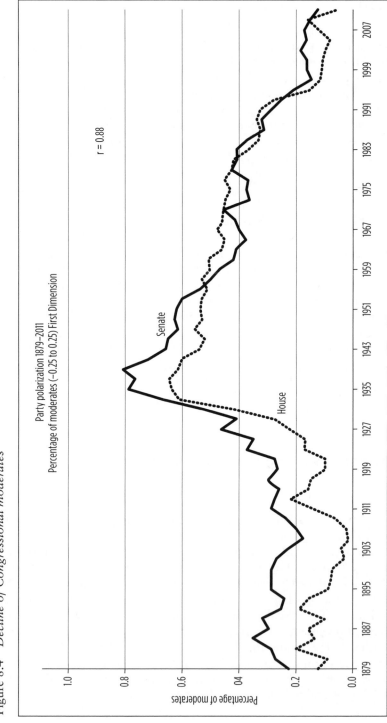

Party polarization 1879–2011
Percentage of moderates (–0.25 to 0.25) First Dimension

r = 0.88

Source: Poole and Rosenthal (2012).

Four decades ago, there was a vigorous middle in Congress. Both parties spanned the ideological divide that exists today. Figure 8.5 illustrates the decline in members in each party who overlapped ideologically with the opposition. For much of the 20th century, each party had a large liberal and conservative wing. On divisive issues such as civil rights, liberal Democrats and Northern moderate Republicans would join forces against the conservatives of the Confederate South. Getting the votes needed to stop a filibuster required a coalition of Senators from both parties. Paul G. Kirk, Jr, a former aide to Senator Ted Kennedy who was appointed to fill his seat temporarily in 2009, explains: 'more commonly than not, the conservatives in the two parties would be together, the progressives in the two parties would be together, and then you'd kind of have a moderate center and find the 60. The breath of political thought overlapped' (Schatz, 2010). Polarization has reduced these forces of moderation in both chambers.

Related to the lack of a middle in each party, it is the movement of both parties to more extreme partisanship which has also helped to create congressional dysfunction. Over 80 percent of the roll call votes have pitted a majority of Democrats against a majority of Republicans, a measure of partisanship. This is the highest percentage of party unity votes since Congressional Quarterly began measuring voting patterns of Members of Congress in 1953. In the 1960s, the yearly average was less than 50 percent. Polarization has reduced the frequency of consensus in the House, reduced legislative productivity in the Senate, and increased legislative productivity in the House (Sinclair, 2009). In addition, movement of former House members into the Senate has contributed to increased partisan polarization in the upper chamber (Theriault and Rohde, 2011).

In addition to the challenges of legislating under divided party government in an area of intense polarization, ideological divisions within the Republican Party complicated the efforts of House Speaker John Boehner and Senate Minority Leader Mitch McConnell to organize their members. In the 2011 negotiations between Speaker Boehner and President Obama to reduce the deficit and raise the debt ceiling, initial reports suggested that conservative members of the House Republican Caucus rejected a tentative deal. A similar split in the Republican caucus occurred in the 2012 lame duck session when the Speaker proposed a measure (referred to as Plan B) to avert the fiscal cliff. Although the influence of the Tea Party seemed to be on the wane after the 2012 election, ideological conservatives, particularly in the House, continued to exert significant influence (Williamson et al., 2011).

Not only does the decline in centrist members increase polarization, but also high levels of polarization may in turn drive centrists out of Congress. The decision to forgo reelection by two moderate Senators, Democrat Kent Conrad and Republican Olympia Snowe, was attrib-

Figure 8.5 *Polarization in the Senate*

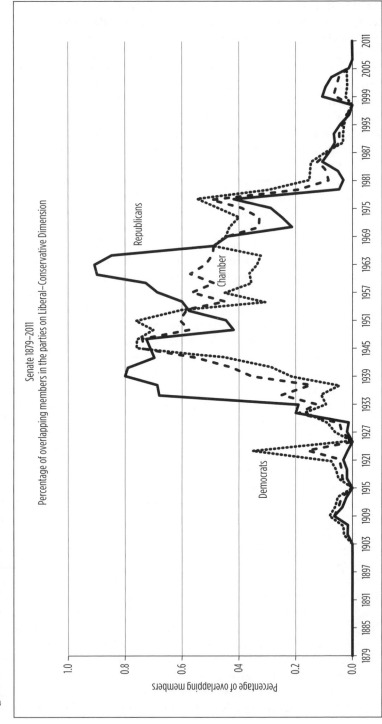

Senate 1879–2011

Percentage of overlapping members in the parties on Liberal–Conservative Dimension

Source: Poole and Rosenthal (2012).

uted in part to the polarized atmosphere in the Senate. In a speech to her Senate colleagues in December 2012, Snowe decried 'excessive political polarization' and argued that 'it hasn't always been this way. And it absolutely does not have to be this way' (Sharp, 2012).

Redistricting

Among the potential causes of polarization is the redistricting of House districts. Partisan gerrymandering occurs in most states. Scholars disagree about the role that redistricting has played in the increase in polarization. Some argue that it is one driver of polarization in the House (Carson et al., 2007; Grainger, 2010); others dispute the link between gerrymandering and polarization (McCarty et al., 2009). Despite this disagreement, practitioners perceive that redistricting has negatively impacted on Congress and its members. Republican John Tanner describes the negative consequences of partisan gerrymandering: 'when Members come here from these partisan districts that have been gerrymandered ... they have little incentive to really work across party line in order to reach solutions. If one comes here wanting to work across the aisle, one has to watch one's back, because the highly charged partisans don't like it' (Tanner, 2008).

The House has been redistricted to safe seats; only 85 seats were competitive in 2010, and 85 in 2012. The creation of these safe House districts has led to the election of increasingly 'ideologically pure' representatives with a relatively harmonized constituency, little institutional loyalty and an unprecedented degree of partisan homogeneity within the two parties. This has increased the importance of the party primary, with an 18.8 percent turnout on average since 1986 and activist organizers focused on the ideological party vote. Moderate voters are easily shut out of the process; appeals to the 'base' drown out serious debate on broad issues of national concern. This has increased the importance of ideology in legislating and lobbying activities – creating deadlock, a divided, partisan House, and a subsequent lack of comity and civility in the way decisions are made, or not, in Congress. In effect, the Representatives choose their voters – hardly a democratic ideal.

A case in point: the Supercommittee

The Joint Select Committee on Deficit Reduction (the 'Supercommittee') was established on August 2, 2011, after months of conflict and abortive negotiations between President Obama and congressional leaders over how to slow the growth of the government's deficit and debt. The Budget Control Act (PL 112-25) raised the federal debt ceiling (thus preventing the debt default of the federal government), cut spending and created the Supercommittee, granting it extraordinary scope and power. These powers included the charge of crafting a recommendation by November 23, 2011, encompassing at least $1.5 trillion in additional deficit reduction over a ten-year period, beyond the $917 billion cuts made as a first installment in the Budget Act. Everything was supposed to be 'on the table' for negotiation: revenue tax increases; tax reforms, such as simplifying the tax code and eliminating some tax breaks and loopholes; and reforms to slow down the growth of entitlement programs, such as Social Security, Medicaid and Medicare. Should the Supercommittee not agree on a recommendation or the full Congress fail to pass the Supercommittee's recommendation, a 'trigger mechanism' requiring enactment of $1.2 trillion in automatic spending cuts was included.

The $1.2 trillion across-the-board spending cuts had to be split between the national security and domestic programs, with the some of the biggest entitlement spending, Medicaid, food stamps, jobless benefits and veterans' pensions excluded, thus setting up for the Supercommittee a full table of choices, but removing the largest targets from the automatic cuts. The threat of the automatic across-the-board spending cuts was intended to be sufficiently 'distasteful to lawmakers' to provide a strong incentive for them to adopt a bipartisan agreement.

The compromise did not occur. On November 21, 2011, the Supercommittee informed Congress, the President and the public that they had been unable to reach agreement on a deficit reduction plan by the statutory deadline. After this failure of the Supercommittee, there were partisan statements condemning the outcome. Senate Majority Leader Harry Reid, D-Nevada, said Democrats 'were prepared to strike a grand bargain that would make painful cuts while asking millionaires to pay their fair share, and we put our willingness on paper', but that Republicans 'never came close to meeting us halfway' (Barrett et al., 2011). Senate Republican Minority Leader Mitch McConnell of Kentucky argued that an agreement 'proved impossible not because Republicans were unwilling to compromise, but because Democrats would not accept any proposal that did not expand the size and scope of government or punish job creators' (ibid.). The primary reasons for the failure of the Supercommittee were both internal and external to Congress: polarization of the members, weak presidential and party leadership, and unfavorable public opinion.

The structure and membership of the Supercommittee

House and Senate Democrat and Republican leaders selected Supercommittee members with an equal number from each party in the House and the Senate with the goal of building a bipartisan agreement to reduce the deficit (Table 8.1). The twelve Supercommittee members

Table 8.1 *Senate and House Supercommittee members*

Senate Republicans	Senate Democrats	House Republicans	House Democrats
Jon Kyl, Arizona	Patty Murray, Washington, Co-Chair	Jeb Hensarling, Texas, Co-Chair	Xavier Becerra, California
Rob Portman, Ohio	Max Baucus, Montana	Fred Upton, Michigan	Jim Clyburn, South Carolina
Pat Toomey, Pennsylvania	John Kerry, Massachusetts	David Camp, Michigan	Chris Van Hollen, Maryland

were generally part of and reflected the views of the leadership; they were experienced and individually and collectively had extensive knowledge about issues surrounding attempts to reduce the deficit. The Republicans and Democrats selected for the Supercommittee also represented key powerful committees and constituencies in the House and Senate.

The stature of the Supercommittee members, the seriousness of their charge and the importance of deficit reduction guaranteed substantial publicity that raised expectations for success. However, the proposals from Democrat and Republican members failed to bridge the partisan divide between the two parties on deficit reduction through tax increases and spending cuts. Democrat panel members proposed a combination of spending cuts and revenue increases of between $2 and $3 trillion over ten years. The Republican proposal plans focused on saving over $2 trillion primarily through cuts in spending. Both sides attempted to compromise, with Republicans offering $300 billion in new tax revenue, a proposal that was untenable to their own members who had taken a 'no new tax' pledge. Democrat members proposed to cut hundreds of billions of dollars from federal healthcare programs, a proposal that angered the base of the congressional Democrats. Ultimately, the Republicans who made a no new tax pledge did not make tax reform offers that were large enough to satisfy Democrats. Democratic committee members did not make proposals to cut entitlement programs (Medicare and Medicaid) sufficiently to please the Republicans. Ideological polarization fundamentally undermined the capacity of the Supercommittee to find common ground (see Figure 8.6). The ideological divide was most evident in the Republicans' refusal to shift or fudge their no-tax pledge and Democrats insistence on tying spending cuts to tax hikes. In the end, this was almost certainly the biggest single factor influencing the committee's failure.

Figure 8.6 *112th House and Senate common ideological space scores highlighting Supercommittee members*

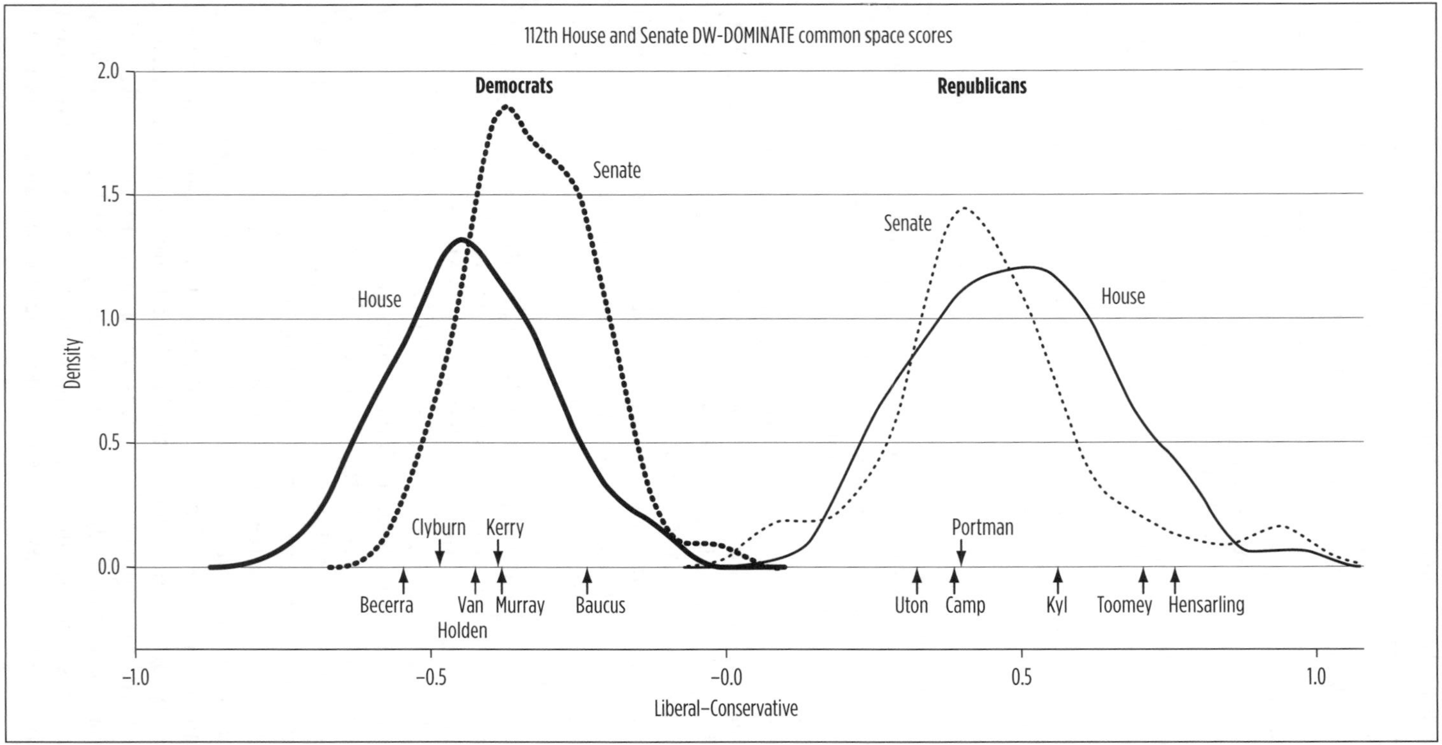

112th House and Senate DW-DOMINATE common space scores

Source: Poole and Rosenthal (2012).

Weak presidential and party leadership

President Obama and Republican and Democrat congressional leaders never pushed very hard publically for a bipartisan agreement (even later during the 'fiscal cliff' negotiations in December 2012). The President offered his own package of tax hikes and spending reductions, but he seemed not to put the personal weight of his office behind it. In fact, he left the country as the Supercommittee talks came down to the wire. House Speaker John Boehner and Senate Minority Leader Mitch McConnell were neither vocal nor visible during the final negotiations. Senate Majority Leader Harry Reid and House Democratic Leader Nancy Pelosi were also unwilling to work for a deal. The leaders did not push in public for a deal, and if they exerted private pressure, it was not effective. This seeming inaction can be interpreted in several ways: the leadership believed the Supercommittee would function best if left alone; the leaders exerted their influence through private meetings and phone calls, but to no avail; the leaders either did not care or did not want a deal; or the President and congressional leaders felt their party would have an advantage in the upcoming 2012 election by blaming the other party for the failure. After the 2012 election, President Obama definitely felt he had a mandate to take a tougher stand with the Republican congressional leaders on large tax hikes on the wealthy and to limit spending cuts. The deal to avert the fiscal cliff reached in the waning hours of the 2012 lame duck session did result in higher income taxes for the wealthy and a temporary delay of automatic spending cuts.

Public opinion and interest groups did not back a specific plan

A *National Journal* survey (Cooper, 2011) found that only slightly more Americans favored a Democratic proposal to reduce the deficit with cuts and revenue increases on the wealthy rather than the Republican cuts-only approach. By a margin of 49 to 44 percent, the public favored the Democratic plan suggested in October 2011 that would include '$4 trillion in deficit reduction through a combination of federal spending cuts and tax increases on wealthier Americans' over 'a Republican plan that calls for $3 trillion in deficit reduction through spending cuts alone, with no tax increases'. The survey of voters showed that the American people seemed no more unified than the Members of Congress and the Supercommittee members who represent them on deficit reduction solutions. The poll and many other surveys showed a decided lack of confidence in Congress to get anything done with historic low evaluations of Congress shortly after the Supercommittee failure. Without strong public support for a balanced deficit reduction plan of cuts and tax increases, and with the public blaming Congress for the Supercommittee's failure, there was fresh political fodder for the 2012 campaign.

The 2012 election

Much of 2012 was spent campaigning, with Republican nominee Mitt Romney challenging President Obama and both parties trying to protect and pick up seats in the House and Senate. After vigorous campaigning, the outcome of the election did little to change the numerical balance of power in Washington. President Obama won reelection with 332 electoral votes and received 51 percent of the votes cast to 48 percent for Mitt Romney. In the Senate, the Democrats held 53 seats after the election compared to 45 held by the Republicans. Two independent Senators also caucused with the Democrats. These results constituted a swing of four seats to the Democrats. In the House, the Republicans held 234 seats after the election compared to 201 held by the Democrats. This constituted a swing of 15 seats to the Democrats.

In the aftermath of the election, a still divided Congress was left to resolve the impending fiscal cliff as well as address other pressing issues such as tax reform, immigration, gun control, the debt ceiling, climate change and a multitude of other problems. Despite holding the majority in Congress, Democratic gains and President Obama's strong performance left the Republicans examining the strength of their coalition. Early signs from the Republican leadership indicated a willingness to accept increased tax revenues (although not necessarily higher tax rates) as part of a deal to address the fiscal cliff. There were also proposals to take up immigration reform, widely seen as an attempt to restore the Republican brand in the minds of Hispanic voters, who represented a growing portion of the national electorate. However, the lame duck session illustrated the continued challenges of legislating under divided party government. President Obama and Speaker Boehner failed to craft a grand bargain to address the deficit with a comprehensive package of revenue increases and spending cuts. Conservative members of his own caucus also rebuffed the Speaker when he tried to introduce an alternative measure (referred to as Plan B) to avert the fiscal cliff.

Ultimately, Vice President Joe Biden and Senate leaders crafted a deal to avoid the most dramatic elements of the fiscal cliff. The deal passed the Senate by 89 to 8 votes. In the House, the vote was 257 to 167, with 151 Republicans opposed. The opposition of conservative Republicans to the bill highlighted the divisions within the Republican caucus.

The American Tax Payer Relief Act of 2012 included a number of reforms. The most notable portions of the deal included raising income and capital gains tax rates for individuals making more than $400,000 per year while the Bush era tax rates were made permanent for individuals below that threshold. The automatic spending cuts were delayed for two months and unemployment insurance was extended for one year. However, the deal did not address another looming deadline to raise the Federal debt ceiling, did not extend the payroll tax cut, and did not address the long-term deficit problem. In the immediate aftermath of the deal, pundits warned of continued partisan conflict over these issues.

Possibilities for reform

Most of the problems in the way Congress works are linked to increasing polarization and a lack of true bipartisanship. The chambers are more partisan and deadlocked than at any time since the 1860s (just prior to the Civil War). There is little consensus about major policy problems and solutions. It is harder than ever for a majority to get its way. However, important reforms could improve lawmaking and lead to more consistent and careful oversight, encourage deliberation and fulfill Congress's Constitutional mandate to represent the people. Here are some suggestions:

- Reforms should be made to the congressional budget process by enforcing the calendar and stopping the growth of continuing resolutions and omnibus spending bills and by establishing a biennial appropriations process with one year for appropriations and the next year for oversight of government programs. A two-year process is reasonable, as now the budget is often passed right on the heels of the next year's budget talks. Other reforms include: establishing a true Pay-As-You-Go (PAYGO) rule covering expenditures, taxes and authorizations; abolishing earmarks in both the House and Senate by requiring open access to and discussion of all narrowly cast appropriations; stopping all new 'backdoor spending' by authorization committees and requiring all permanently authorized legislation to be reviewed on a regular basis. Wolfensberger (2012) suggests restoring the use of conference committees to resolve differences between House and Senate versions of legislation.
- Improve lawmaking through legislative procedural reforms by returning to the regular order, limiting restrictive rules and improving protection of the minority in the House. The Senate needs immediate filibuster reform by making it easier to invoke cloture so as to stop the filibuster, say with a vote of 60 on a first vote to 51 on the fourth vote. Moreover, Senate filibuster rules must be changed to force the members actually to perform, rather than simply threaten,

a filibuster. A face-saving route to reduce frivolous filibusters and the resulting deadlock in the Senate must be found. Secretive and lengthy holds on bills and nominations must also be limited.

- Of particularly critical importance is requiring members of both chambers to spend more time on their jobs in Washington. The 'Tuesday-to-Thursday' Club needs to be stopped with an enforceable required schedule of work in Washington. Members should be in Washington doing the work of committees, oversight, lawmaking and educating themselves. It is time for the party leadership in both chambers to set rules of attendance that have consequences. There needs to be a new schedule for Congress in session, which includes not only the show time on the floor, but the work time in committees and their offices. Congress also needs to return to real post-enactment conference committees that are transparent to the public and fair to both parties.
- A key part of representation in America is pluralism, the expression of interests and lobbying through organized groups. The 2007 lobbying and ethics reforms were a weak down payment on improving the regulation of lobbying. There needs to be better definition of lobbying and better enforcement of the Congressional rules and laws. Codes of ethics in both House and Senate are rarely enforced, but, coupled with greater enforcement, the Senate should create an office of public integrity and the House should step up its investigations and public reporting of ethical violations. There should be an absolute ban on lobbyists raising money for those they lobby. Leadership political action committees have no role in good government and should be abolished. Fund raising quotas set for committee chairs and ranking members are an invitation to practice undue influence; the quotas benefit no one.

The inability of Congress – in the absence of a vigorous, bipartisan center – to address effectively such known and crucial issues as job creation programs, tax reform, the rising accumulation of public debt, a looming Medicare and Medicaid shortfall, immigration reform, gun control, a failing education system and serious energy and environmental problems is a legitimate cause of public dissatisfaction. A Congress that cannot confront these critical public policy challenges will surely lack the reserves of comity and trust to face any unknown and sudden – and perhaps even more dangerous – crisis.

Chapter 9

The Supreme Court

Cornell W. Clayton and Lucas K. McMillan

Writing for a bitterly divided Court in *National Federation of Independent Business v Sebelius* (2012), Chief Justice John Roberts gave President Barack Obama a major constitutional victory only a few months before the 2012 presidential election by upholding Obama's signature legislative achievement, the Affordable Care Act. Although Roberts agreed that the act's mandate provision, requiring individuals to purchase healthcare insurance, had exceeded Congress's Commerce Clause powers, he concluded that the mandate *could* be upheld under Congress's taxing power instead. Roberts, it was later learned, had initially voted with the four other conservative justices on the Court to invalidate the law, but later switched sides and joined the four more liberal justices to uphold it (Crawford, 2012). Furious with this betrayal, the remaining conservatives – Antonin Scalia, Anthony Kennedy, Clarence Thomas and Samuel Alito – wrote an unusual, scathing, joint dissent, accusing Roberts of 'rewriting' the Affordable Care Act in order to save it.

John Roberts's role in upholding the Obama administration's healthcare law surprised most Court observers. Roberts is usually considered a reliable conservative, if not the leader of the conservative bloc on the Court. His switch, however, took place in the context of a unique, highly public feud between the Court and the executive branch. During his 2010 State of the Union address to Congress, President Obama took the unusual step of publically castigating the Court for its recent decision in *Citizen's United v FEC* (2010), which overturned restrictions on corporate campaign expenditures (Silverleib, 2010). Then, while the Court was still considering arguments in the *Sebelius* case, Obama returned to the bully pulpit, warning the Court's conservatives that striking down the healthcare law would be a betrayal of their putative commitments to 'judicial restraint' (Marcus, 2012). Against this backdrop, Roberts's switch in *Sebelius* was viewed by some as an effort to protect the Court from further politicization and attacks on its institutional legitimacy (Tribe, 2012). For conservatives, however, Roberts's move was a severe disappointment. At a crucial moment, he had failed to embrace core constitutional principles that the Republican Party had sought to advance and that a 'Roberts Court' was supposed to embody.

The *Sebelius* case illustrates both the enormous political power of the United States Supreme Court as well as the delicate balancing act that the justices must engage in during an era of polarized politics. The fact that the Court is routinely characterized as sharply divided between conservative and liberal justices underscores its dual role as both a legal and a political institution. As a court of law, it is the highest appellate court in the country; thus the frequent description 'the Court of last resort'. Nearly all of the cases heard by the Court come as appeals from lower courts, and nearly half of these are routinely decided unanimously and without dissent. Many of these cases raise technical legal issues or they are the result of simple disagreements between lower courts over how to interpret a particular statute or legal provision. In these cases the Supreme Court's primary function is to enforce legal norms and bring uniformity to judicial enforcement of federal law.

The Supreme Court, however, also plays an important policy-making role in American politics through its exercise of judicial review, the power to declare that an act of Congress or the president violates the Constitution. Unlike many European nations that vest judicial review power in a single constitutional court, in the United States lower courts also can exercise this power. However, lower court decisions invalidating acts of Congress or the president usually wind up on appeal and are ultimately resolved by the Supreme Court. The Court's exercise of this authority in cases such as *Sebelius*, *Citizens United* or *Bush v Gore* (where the Court actually decided the outcome of the 2000 presidential election) usually occurs during the times that ideological divisions manifest themselves on the Court, whence its role in the political system becomes controversial.

The Court's exercise of judicial review powers, however, does not take place in a vacuum. The Roberts Court, like those before it, is deeply influenced by the broader electoral forces that also structure the political system of which it is part. For most of the past 40 years, American politics, especially at the presidential level, has been shaped by an electoral regime that is at once more conservative, but also more divided and polarized, than the earlier 'New Deal electoral regime' that it replaced. The Court reflects these developments in electoral politics. It has at once become increasingly conservative, advancing a constitutional jurisprudence promoted by the post-1968 Republican Party, while at the same time its decision-making has become more polarized and fragmented. With five conservative-leaning justices appointed by Republican presidents, and four liberal-leaning justices appointed by Democratic presidents, the Roberts Court is today more closely divided along partisan and ideological lines than any in recent history.

While it is too early to tell what Obama's reelection to a second term portends for the future of electoral politics in the United States, it is certain that it will continue to complicate the role of John Roberts. As Chief Justice, Roberts must try to lead a conservative, but sharply divided, Court whose constitutional decisions will likely continue to be in conflict with the policies of the President. Before examining the Court's role in advancing conservative constitutional objectives, we turn first to examine more precisely how the Roberts Court has been structured by post-1968 electoral politics.

The Roberts Court: conservative, divided and polarized

Contrary to the popular image of the Supreme Court as a heroic, counter-majoritarian institution protecting the rights of vulnerable minorities against the majorities or powerful elites, the Court's relationship to democratic power is often more complex and even counter-intuitive. More than 50 years ago the prominent political scientist Robert Dahl (1957) demonstrated that the Court usually acts in concert with, rather than counter to, the policy values and constitutional views of elected elites. Dahl's explanation was simple: since justices are appointed by party leaders, and party leaders appoint individuals who share their attitudes and values, except for short transitional periods, the Court was 'inevitably a part of the dominant national governing alliance'. This is not to say that the Court never behaves contrary to the will of elected majorities. However, overtime, the Court's policy-making role tends to harmonize with the views and values that also dominate the elected branches (Whittington, 2007; Gillman, 2008).

The behavior of the Roberts Court must also be understood within the broader context of electoral politics over the past several decades, and especially with reference to the Republican Party (GOP) which has most often controlled the White House and appointed the majority of justices since 1968. Chapter 4 in this volume explains how the Republican and Democratic Parties were transformed in the mid-20th century. Starting in the 1960s, for example, the New Deal Democratic Party's electoral coalition that dominated national elections since the 1930s began fragmenting over a series of issues, particularly civil rights, and was gradually replaced by an electoral regime marked by a more conservative and more competitive, if not dominant, Republican Party. Indeed, between 1968 and the election of Barack Obama in 2008, the GOP won seven out of ten presidential elections (compared to having won only two of the nine presidential elections in the previous 36-year period). Moreover, the GOP controlled one or both chambers of Congress during 33 of the last 44 years between 1968 and

2012 (compared to doing so in only 10 of the 36 years before 1968) (Rosenburg, 2009).

The GOP's electoral success since 1968 accounts for the rightward drift in American public policy over the past 40 years, as documented by many scholars (Hacker and Pierson, 2005; Bartels, 2008). However, it also had a dramatic impact on the federal judiciary and constitutional law. Indeed, the role of the Court was a key cleavage issue that helped to break apart the New Deal electoral coalition and led to the creation of a more conservative Republican coalition. During his 1968 presidential campaign, for example, Richard Nixon emphasized 'law and order' issues, linking rising crime rates and the decline in public morality to the 'liberal' decisions of the Warren Court. His promise to appoint 'strict constructionists' to the Court played a major role that appealed to southern white voters who were angered by the Court's role in racial desegregation and the liberalization of many areas of social policy, moving them into the Republican electoral coalition. Republican presidents since that time have viewed appointments to the Court both as an electoral strategy in campaigns and as the primary tool in a 'judicial counterrevolution' against the New Deal and the effort to advance a conservative constitutional agenda (Tushnet, 2003). During the 1980s the Reagan Administration in particular set out to entrench in the federal courts a more conservative vision of the Constitution based around a jurisprudence of 'original intent' and a commitment to rein in federal regulatory power, expand the protection of businesses and corporate rights, and to reverse earlier Supreme Court decisions that liberalized policies in areas such as criminal justice, abortion, affirmative action and the role of religion in public life (Balkin and Levinson, 2001; Johnson, 2003).

There have been 16 justices appointed to the Supreme Court since 1968; 12 of these appointed by Republican presidents and only four by Democratic presidents. In previous periods, partisan affiliation was not always a reliable predictor of a justice's ideological behavior once they were on the bench. President Eisenhower for instance famously complained that his appointment of Earl Warren, a former Republican Governor of California, was 'the biggest damn fool mistake I ever made' (Sitkoff and Foner, 1992). Since the 1960s, however, the two major parties have become more ideologically unified or 'sorted' (with Democrats becoming more consistently liberal and Republicans more consistently conservative) and polarized (with Democrats becoming more liberal and Republicans more conservative than in the past) (see Chapter 4). When combined with the Court's elevation as a cleavage issue in electoral campaigns, the ideological polarization of the parties has led to a judicial appointment process where partisanship has become an increasingly more reliable predictor of ideological behavior on the Court (McMahon, 2007).

159

Figure 9.1 *Ideological voting on the Supreme Court*

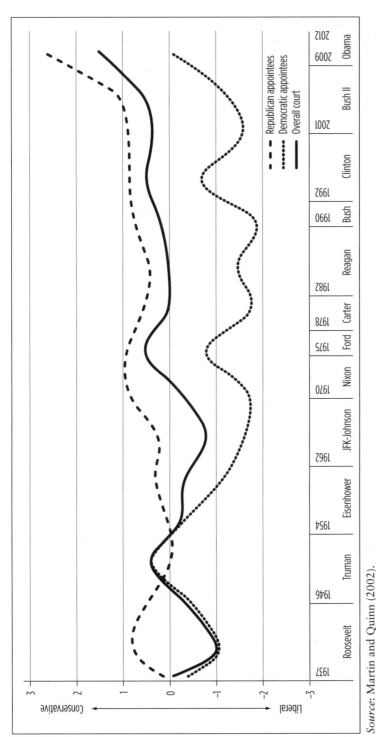

Source: Martin and Quinn (2002).

Notes: Martin and Quinn (2002) scores are dynamic measures that place a justice's ideal preference point on a common ideological continuum. They do so for each justice in each term since 1937 and are estimated using longitudinal data in the form of per-term merit votes derived from the Supreme Court Judicial Database (http://mqscores.wustl.edu).

The impact of GOP appointments to the Court since 1968 in shifting its ideological behavior is clearly depicted in Figure 9.1. Using data gathered by Andrew Martin and Kevin Quinn (2002), which estimate the ideal ideological position of each justice based on their voting records in each term, we calculated the Court's mean ideological position over time, as well as the position of its mean Republican and Democratic appointees between 1937 and 2011 (negative scores reflecting more liberal voting behavior and positive scores more conservative voting behavior).

The solid black line represents the ideological position of the mean justice during this period. During the New Deal regime period between 1937 and 1968 the Court's mean justice voted in a liberal direction (averaging −0.382 across the period). Beginning with the election of Richard Nixon in 1968, the Court's behavior shifted. Nixon appointed four justices between 1968 and 1972, and since that time the mean justice on the Court has voted in a conservative direction (averaging 0.333 for the period between 1969 and 2011). Today the voting behavior of the mean justice is more than twice as conservative as it was in 1968.

The Court's voting data in Figure 9.1 also demonstrate that the shift in the ideological direction of the Court should be understood as a consequence of partisan appointments and the growing divisions between the parties. The broken line on top reflects the mean Republican appointee on the Court, while the dotted line on the bottom reflects the position of the mean Democratic appointee. Despite year-to-year variations, the mean Republican score was consistently more conservative than Democratic appointees (except for 1948–52, when no Republican appointees served on the Court). Moreover, the gap between the mean Republican and mean Democratic justice has widened since 1968, although it has done so in an asymmetrical way as the appointees from both parties have become more conservative in recent years. This asymmetrical polarization reflects the fact that GOP appointees have become substantially more conservative while Democratic appointees have remained more liberal, even while moving in a conservative direction since 1968.

If it is clear that the Court has become more conservative, it is also true that electoral politics during this period has been more closely divided and polarized than in the past. Indeed, divided government – where one party controls the presidency and the other controls one or both chambers of Congress – has been a distinctive feature of post-1968 electoral politics, and although the GOP has controlled the White House during most of this period, three Democratic presidents were elected – Carter, Clinton and Obama. The divided, polarized nature of post-1968 electoral politics has also left its mark on the Supreme Court. As already noted, the Court's voting behavior became both more conservative and more polarized since 1968 (similar to members of Congress, Republican appointed justices became much more conservative and Democratic appointed justices remained liberal). In addition, although there were no vacancies on the Court during President Carter's term, the other two Democratic presidents each appointed two members of the Court. President Clinton appointed Justice Ginsburg and Justice Breyer, while President Obama appointed Justice Sotomayor and Justice Kagan. Thus the Roberts Court is currently composed of five Republican appointees and four Democratic appointees, and it is as evenly divided along partisan and ideological lines as ever.

The closely divided, ideologically polarized nature of the Court is most evident in its fragmented decision-making and opinion-writing practices. Typical of the more fragmented style of decision-making that has come to characterize the Court's opinions is the headnote explaining the Court's decision in the *Sibelius* case:

> ROBERTS, C. J., announced the judgment of the Court and delivered the opinion of the Court with respect to Parts I, II, and III–C, in which GINSBURG, BREYER, SOTOMAYOR, and KAGAN, JJ., joined; an opinion with respect to Part IV, in which BREYER and KAGAN, JJ., joined; and an opinion with respect to Parts III–A, III–B, and III–D. GINSBURG, J., filed an opinion concurring in part, concurring in the judgment in part, and dissenting in part, in which SOTOMAYOR, J., joined, and in which BREYER and KAGAN, JJ., joined as to Parts I, II, III, and IV. SCALIA, KENNEDY, THOMAS, and ALITO, JJ., filed a dissenting opinion. THOMAS, J., filed a dissenting opinion.

One way to measure the fragmentation of the Court's decision-making practices is to examine the frequency with which it reaches unanimous decisions in comparison to bare-majority or closely divided decisions. Figure 9.2 shows the percentage of cases decided unanimously (9–0, 8–0), as well as those by closely divided votes (with 3 or more justices in dissent) for each of the four Court periods between the chief justiceships of Earl Warren and John Roberts (1953–2012).

Although the Rehnquist and Roberts Courts decided a slightly higher percentage of their cases with unanimous decisions than their predecessors, the percentage of severely divided decisions has grown steadily. Indeed, the Roberts Court is the first to experience a higher percentage of its cases decided by sharply divided votes than unanimously, with 43 percent decided with at least three dissents while 42 percent were decided unanimously.

Although it is sharply divided and polarized, the Roberts Court nevertheless tends to be controlled by the bloc of five Republican-

Figure 9.2   *Unanimous and divided decisions on the Supreme Court*

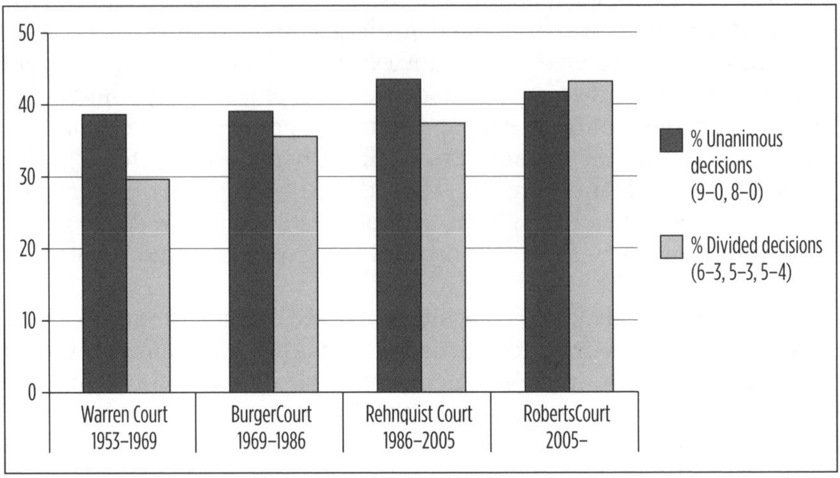

Source: Supreme Court database 2012.

appointed, conservative justices (consisting of Chief Justice Roberts, and Justices Scalia, Kennedy, Thomas and Alito). In fact, when the Court decided cases by sharply divided 5–4 votes, the bloc of five Republican-appointed justices constituted the majority 69 percent of the time during the 2008 term, 72 percent of the time in 2009, 73 percent of the time in the 2010 term, and 50 percent of the cases during the 2011 term (Clayton and McMillan, 2012).

Originalism: back to the future in constitutional interpretation

The conservative but polarized nature of the Roberts Court is clearly reflected in many of its major constitutional decisions in recent years. Although a thorough review of the Court's development of constitutional law is beyond the scope of this chapter, examining a few areas of its recent decision-making illustrates the extent to which the Court continues to be shaped by the values and ideas of the post-1968 Republican Party, even during the era of Obama.

The impact of Republican electoral politics on constitutional jurisprudence is most evident in the way the Court now approaches constitutional interpretation. Chief Justice Roberts's opinion in the *Sebelius* case, for example, began by discussing Alexander Hamilton's views in the *Federalist Papers* to explain what the Framers might have thought about Congress's healthcare mandate passed some 220 years later. The dissent likewise appealed to 18th-century dictionaries in order to argue the opposite about the Framer's views. Although constitutional debates have paid some attention to the founding period, turning the 'Framers' intent' into the primary mode of constitutional interpretation is a recent development. Indeed, prior to the 1980s, few federal judges or justices thought the Framers' specific attitudes about a policy question emerging two centuries later were even relevant, much less dispositive to a case. This change in the mode of constitutional debate is the direct result of the modern Republican Party's embrace of originalist jurisprudence and its efforts to implant this view on the courts.

Throughout much of the latter half of the 20th century a debate has raged between so-called 'interpretivist' and 'non-interpretivist' approaches to constitutional analysis (Ely, 1980). Non-interpretivism emerged out of the legal realist thought in the early part of the century and tends to view the Constitution as a 'living document' that should be interpreted to reflect the nation's 'evolving senses of justice' or changing views of 'human dignity'. This approach to constitutional interpretation has been generally embraced by political leaders and judges associated with the Democratic Party, especially during the 'Great Society' period of the 1960s and 1970s. As a jurisprudential approach it reached its peak on the Warren Court and early Burger Courts when the justices decided cases establishing expansive new individual rights in cases like *Brown v Board* (1954) (prohibiting racial segregation), *Engel v Vitale* (1962) (ending school prayer), and *Roe v Wade* (1973) (establishing abortion rights).

Interpretivists on the other hand argued that the Constitution should not be viewed as evolving, but as a static document, and interpreted according to the values it embodied at the time of its enactment. 'Original intent' jurisprudence in particular suggests that judges should rely on the explicit text of the Constitution or the intention of the framers when adopting those words to decide cases. Since 1980 the GOP has explicitly embraced originalism as the preferred mode of judicial interpretation of the Constitution and advanced it in its presidential platforms, government litigation strategies and judicial selection process (Clayton, 1992; Johnson, 2003).

Most commentators agree that some variant of originalism now dominates constitutional decision-making on the Roberts Court. Even justices and legal scholars who are identified with the concept of a living Constitution today often feel compelled to 'dress up their theories in the garb of originalism' (Fleming, 2007). Given that only a few decades ago there were few originalists of any stripe on the federal bench, it is all the more remarkable that originalism is today reflected in nearly all the major constitutional decisions of the Roberts Court (Toobin, 2012).

Gun rights and the Second Amendment

The Court's use of original intent jurisprudence to advance a conservative vision of the Constitution can be seen in recent decisions interpreting the Second Amendment. In 2008 the Roberts Court gave the National Rifle Association (NRA) and the Bush administration a long sought after policy victory, declaring for the first time that the Constitution protects a personal right to possess firearms. The case, *District of Columbia v Heller* (2008), grew out of a challenge to a federal law banning the possession of private handguns in the District of Columbia. Enacted in 1976, the law had gone without serious challenge for nearly 30 years before Dick Heller, a police officer denied a permit to keep a private handgun at his home, brought a suit arguing that it violated his rights under the Second Amendment. The Bush Administration filed a brief supporting Heller, leaving the District of Columbia government to hire its own counsel to defend the law in court.

Neither the language of the Second Amendment nor the Court's decisions interpreting it over the years recognized a personal right to possess firearms. Indeed, the Court had always permitted reasonable regulation of personal firearms by both national and state governments. Although the NRA and other groups had been waging a well-financed campaign to alter this understanding of the Second Amendment, overcoming an established line of legal precedent stretching back more than a century would not be easy.

From the outset the arguments in *Heller* turned on the Framers' intent. During oral arguments there was practically no reference to the nature of modern guns or the dangers that such weapons might pose to urban societies. The debate focused on whether the Framers of the Second Amendment merely sought to protect state militia from being disbanded by the national government or whether they sought to protect a more expansive individual right to personal protection. The Court's 5–4 decision split along familiar conservative–liberal lines. Justice Scalia's 64-page opinion for the conservative majority was a magnum opus of originalist analysis, deconstructing in exhaustive detail each word of the Amendment and declaring that the Framers intended to protect a personal right to firearms (in the process reflecting on the Glorious Revolution in England, King George's efforts to disarm the colonists, and repeatedly discussing the views of Sir William Blackstone). In response, Justice Breyer and Justice Stevens wrote separate dissents (combining to more than another 100 pages) that also excavated 17th- and 18th-century documents to discern the intentions of the Framers, but they of course came to a different conclusion about the Framers' views.

While the Court's ruling in *Heller* established a personal right against *federal* gun regulation, it did not address whether the right also barred state and local gun control laws. Under the Court's modern rights jurisprudence, the Second Amendment would offer protection against state and local regulation of firearms only if the right was deemed 'fundamental' enough to be part of the Due Process protections of the Fourteenth Amendment. That question – whether the personal right to possess firearms also applied against state and local governments – came to the Court two years later in *McDonald v City of Chicago* (2010).

Otis McDonald, a retired maintenance engineer, lived in a Chicago neighborhood that had been over-run by gang violence and wanted a handgun for protection. A 1982 city ordinance banning handguns prevented him from purchasing one. The vast majority of gun control laws in the United States come from state and local governments. Thus, the *McDonald* case was more important than *Heller*, both for conservative gun activists and for gun control and law enforcement groups that opposed them. Not surprisingly, the *McDonald* case attracted substantial attention. More than 33 groups filed amici curiae ('friends of the Court') briefs, including one signed by 58 Senators and 251 Members of the House of Representatives, mostly Republican, asking the Court to apply the Second Amendment to the states.

The Court's decision in *McDonald* reflected the same 5–4 split as in *Heller* (with Justice Sotomayor replacing Justice Souter in the dissent). Writing for the majority, Justice Alito held that ownership of guns for personal protection was a fundamental right protected by the Fourteenth Amendment. The Court's earlier decisions upholding state gun regulations, Alito argued, were irrelevant. Justices Stevens and Breyer once again wrote separate dissents challenging the majority's history. In summary, Breyer wrote that 'the Framers did not write the Second Amendment in order to protect a private right of armed self-defense' and that there 'has been, and is, no consensus that the right is, or was, "fundamental"'.

The Court's decisions interpreting the Second Amendment are striking not only because they took place in the political context of heightened concern about gun violence in the wake of shootings in Columbine, Aurora, and more recently Newtown, but because a sharply divided Court overturned more than a century of case law to advance the policy objective of conservative politicians and the interest groups supporting them. It did so using a debate that took place entirely within the GOP's jurisprudential framework of constitutional originalism. Indeed, in much the same way that evolving conceptions of justice and human dignity had been the constitutional methodology for advancing liberal policy goals during the Warren Court, originalism and the framers' intent has become the constitutional framework for advancing a conservative agenda on the Roberts Court.

The First Amendment and campaign financing

The Roberts Court's decisions involving campaign finance and the First Amendment also reflect the constitutional priorities of the post-1968 Republican Party. The Court's first major venture into campaign finance law was *Buckley v Valeo* (1976), where it struck down a federal law limiting how much money candidates could *spend* in campaigns but upheld restrictions on how much money groups and individuals could *contribute* to campaigns. As extensively discussed in Chapter 4, the Court's distinction between campaign spending and campaign contributions created several practical problems for campaign finance reform efforts in the United States. Without the ability to limit expenditures; Congress could do little to stem the skyrocketing cost of campaigning in the era of television. Moreover, the Court's distinction eventually created a two-tiered system of campaign finance where so-called 'hard money' (funds given directly to a candidate's campaign) was subject to contribution limits and public disclosure, but 'soft money' (funds given to political parties or political action committees or PACs for 'party-building activities' or 'issue advocacy') was not subject to such limitations.

By the 1990s soft-money contributions and expenditures by corporations, labor unions and wealthy donors was eclipsing the regulated hard-money contributions and expenditures made by the candidates themselves, thus raising new concerns about the corruption of money in elections. Congress responded by passing the Bipartisan Campaign Reform Act of 2002 (BCRA) prohibiting PACs from funding advertisements that mentioned a candidate within 60 days of a general election or 30 days of a primary election. Although John McCain was a co-sponsor of BCRA, the law passed Congress largely on party lines; with 49 Senate Democrats and 198 House Democrats voting in favor, and 37 Senate Republicans and 176 House Republicans voting against. Republicans may have believed that the law infringed on free-speech rights but they also clearly understood that conservative candidates benefited from less regulation of corporate spending during campaigns.

In 2003, the Court upheld BCRA in *McConnell v Federal Election Commission*. Writing for a 5–4 Court, Justice Stevens said that the restrictions it imposed on speech were minimal and closely related to the government's interest in preventing corruption in elections. But three years later Justice Sandra Day O'Connor, a key member of the *McConnell* majority, retired from the Court and was replaced by President Bush's appointment of the more conservative Samuel Alito.

In *Citizens United v FEC* (2010) a small conservative advocacy group challenged the FEC's classification of a documentary film, *Hillary: The Movie*, as prohibited 'electioneering communication' under the BCRA. The film, deeply critical of Hillary Clinton, ran just prior to Democratic primaries in which she was a 2008 presidential candidate. The Court could have decided the case on narrow grounds limited to whether the film was 'electioneering', but it instead reached out to revisit its decision in *McConnell*. Writing for a divided 5–4 Court, Justice Kennedy (joined by Roberts, Scalia, Thomas and Alito) reversed *McConnell* and struck down the BCRA law, concluding that corporations have the same free-speech rights as individuals: 'political speech is indispensable to a democracy, which is no less true because that speech is coming from a corporation'. Justice Stevens took the rare step of reading his dissent from the bench. Scolding the conservative majority he asked where their commitment to judicial restraint was if they were willing not only to overturn a recent congressional statute but reverse the Court's own precedent of just a few years earlier. The Court's decision, he went on, invited corporations to spend unlimited amounts of money with little or no accountability, and effectively put American democracy 'up for sale'.

Within days of the decision, President Obama attacked the Court in his State of the Union address (with three of the five justices from the *Citizens United* majority sitting only a few feet away). Accusing the Court of 'overturning a century of law', Obama said they had opened the 'floodgates for special interests'. Justice Alito, who joined the majority opinion, was captured on television shaking his head and mouthing 'not true'. Chief Justice Roberts sat stoically, but later complained publicly about the presidential scolding (Reeves, 2010).

Obama's rebuke seemed to have little effect, however, because the following year, in *Arizona Free Enterprise Club v Bennett (2011)*, the Court struck down another campaign finance law. The Arizona statute did not restrict campaign spending but merely provided extra money to candidates who opted for public funding if independently financed opponents exceeded certain spending limits. The same 5–4 majority of *Citizens United*, however, held that Arizona's law burdened the free-speech rights of privately financed candidates by 'level[ing] the playing field' with public funds. The Court followed that decision with *American Tradition Partnership v Bullock* in 2012. There the Montana Supreme Court had upheld a state law restricting corporate campaign expenditures by distinguishing *Citizens United* on the ground that Montana's law was justified by the state's unique interest in addressing a long, documented history of corporate corruption in its elections. The Court, however, disagreed. In an unusual, one-page, per curiam opinion (an opinion issued 'by the Court' without indicating specific authorship) from which the four liberal-leaning justices dissented, the Court simply said that its holding in *Citizen United* also applied to state restrictions on campaign spending.

Other areas of the Court's First Amendment jurisprudence also reflect the influence of the post-1968 Republican Party's constitutional vision. For instance, the Court significantly lowered the wall that separates church and state in cases such as *Zelman v Simmons-Harris* (2002), where a 5–4 majority upheld a Cleveland school voucher program allowing parents to use taxpayer funds to send their children to private, religious schools. That decision, a major victory for religious right groups that had chafed under Warren Court decisions restricting public funding of religious education, was recently expanded by the Roberts Court in *Arizona Christian School Tuition Organization v Winn* (2011). Writing for a 5–4 Court, Justice Kennedy held that Arizona taxpayers lacked standing to challenge a private school tax credit that funneled state funds even more directly into religious schools. Similarly, in *Hosanna-Tabor Evangelical Lutheran Church and School v EEOC* (2012), the Court for the first time recognized a 'ministerial exception' to federal employment discrimination laws covering religious schools, another area that the religious right has bristled over. Writing for the Court, Chief Justice Roberts said that churches and religious groups must be free from government interference in how they hire and dismiss certain employees even when, as in this case, the jobs they perform are primarily non-religious.

Federalism and federal preemption

If gun rights, campaign finance and the separation of church and state demonstrate the increasingly conservative but polarized nature of the Court's constitutional decision-making, federalism is an area where cross-cutting cleavages within the Republican electoral coalition are manifesting themselves on the Court. 'New federalism', or the idea that certain powers should be transferred back to the states from the federal government in order to restore some of the autonomy states lost after the New Deal, has been a major policy priority of the post-1968 Republican Party. While both Democrats and Republicans have supported some forms of devolution of political power, the GOP also embraced a new 'judicial federalism' that rejects the view that the balance of power between states and the national government should be determined primarily by the political process. The GOP has instead insisted that courts should enforce federalism's boundaries under the Tenth and Eleventh Amendments and strictly interpret the enumerated powers of Congress. Indeed, every GOP platform since 1980 has explicitly mandated the Party to appoint judges committed to the 'constitutional sovereignty of states' and to 'decentralizing federal power' under the Constitution (Clayton and Pickerill, 2004).

The commitment to judicial federalism began to bear fruit in the mid-1990s when a bloc of five Republican appointed justices began holding for the first time since the 1930s that Congress had exceeded its authority under the Interstate Commerce Clause. In cases such as *United States v Lopez* (1995) (striking down a federal law that banned the carrying of firearms close to schools) and *United States v Morrison* (2000) (striking down the federal Violence Against Women Act) the Court began placing new limits on congressional regulatory power. The same bloc also began reasserting a more expansive notion of state sovereignty under the Tenth and Eleventh Amendments in cases such as *New York v United States* (1992) (invalidating a federal statute requiring states to pass legislation regarding the disposal of toxic waste) and *Printz v United States* (1997) (striking down part of a federal law requiring local law enforcement officials to conduct background checks on individuals purchasing handguns).

The Court's new commitment to policing the boundaries of federalism, however, at times appeared more political than principled. The Court invalidated federal statutes that conservatives disapproved (i.e. laws involving gun control, domestic violence and environmental protection), but upheld ones conservatives favored, such as in *Gonzales v Raich* (2005), where it held that Congress's interstate commerce clause powers were sufficient to outlaw the use of medical marijuana, even if the marijuana was never bought or sold or crossed state lines.

Against this backdrop came the *Sebelius* case. Prior to the Court's recent federalism decisions, a challenge to Congress's authority to regulate the interstate healthcare market, which makes up nearly one-sixth of the US economy, would have seemed frivolous. Indeed, despite the bitter partisan fights surrounding the passage of the Affordable Care Act (ACA), most legal scholars thought that court challenges stood little chance of success and were intended more as political theatre. So it surprised many, including the Obama administration, when the Court took the *Sebelius* case and scheduled it to be decided just months prior to the 2012 presidential election (Toobin, 2012).

Not since *Bush v Gore* (2000) had the Court willingly inserted itself in a high-stakes, high-risk, political case in the midst a presidential election. The last time the Supreme Court had struck down a president's key legislative achievement was during the conflict between Franklin Roosevelt and the Court over the New Deal in the 1930s. That period ended with Roosevelt launching a frontal challenge to the Court's institutional authority in the form of the now infamous Court-packing plan (Carson and Kleinerman, 2002). Moreover, the Roberts Court was still reeling from public fall-out over its decision in *Citizen's United* as well as from *Bush v Gore*, the decision that essentially put in office the president who had appointed Roberts as Chief Justice.

It is perhaps not surprising then that Roberts was conflicted in *Sebelius* and wished to avoid another decision that would be perceived in highly partisan terms (Tribe, 2012). Yet, even as Roberts upheld the act as an exercise of Congress's taxing and spending powers, his opinion deftly finessed the conservative constitutional issues in the case. Not only did Roberts's opinion agree that Congress lacked interstate commerce clause powers to impose an individual mandate, his opinion also struck down as a violation of state sovereignty provisions of the law that sought to coerce states into expanding their Medicaid programs to cover the poor (Toobin, 2012). Thus, while the decision was an important short-term victory for the Obama administration, it was not a defeat for GOP constitutional principles.

Similar cross-pressures are also evident in the Court's cases involving federal preemption. In contrast to the Rehnquist Court's preoccupation with constitutional federalism, when it comes to preemption (or the question of when congressional policy trumps conflicting state policies) the Roberts Court often has appeared more concerned with expanding federal power in order to protect businesses and corporations from over-zealous state regulators (Pickerill, 2009). For example, in *National Meat Association v Harris* (2012) the Court held that that the Federal Meat Inspection Act preempted a California law that sought to prohibit the sale of non-ambulatory animals. Similarly, in *Kurns v Railroad Friction Products Corp.* (2012), the Court held that a state law allowing a tort claim by an employee exposed to asbestos was preempted by federal employment safety laws.

However, preemption can run both ways. In *Arizona v United States* (2012), the Court struck down most of a controversial Arizona immigration law that was opposed by the Obama administration. In the 5–3 opinion authored by Justice Kennedy, the Court held that three of the four main provisions of the law, which aimed at making it easier for Arizona to apprehend and deport illegal immigrants, were preempted by federal immigration statutes. However, in another case involving illegal immigrants, *Chamber of Commerce v Whiting* (2011), the Court maintained its larger devotion to protecting state sovereignty. In that case, the five conservative justices on the Court held that a state law requiring employers to use the federal E-Verify computer database to check the immigration status of job applicants was not preempted by federal immigration statutes.

The Roberts Court in the Obama era

Despite President Obama's reelection in 2012, the Roberts Court's constitutional decisions demonstrate that the Court is still dominated by the appointments and ideas of the post-1968 Republican Party. This is likely to continue at least in the near future as none of the five Republican-appointed justices on the Court are expected to retire or give President Obama the opportunity to fill their seat. Indeed, one consequence of the more polarized nature of judicial politics in recent decades is the tendency of justices to coordinate more rigorously their retirements with presidential elections in order to assure they are replaced by an ideologically like-minded justice (Ward, 2003).

Nevertheless, the closely divided nature of the Court means that in some areas of law liberal inroads will be made. Here Anthony Kennedy, the most moderate of the five Republican appointed justices, will continue to play a key role. Appointed by Ronald Reagan in 1987, Kennedy is usually a reliable conservative vote in cases involving federalism, protection of business interests or limiting federal regulatory power. Indeed, Kennedy was reportedly the most upset of his fellow conservatives when Chief Justice Roberts switched sides in *Sebelius* and prevented the Court from striking a major blow to federal regulatory power (Toobin, 2012). He also recently sided with his fellow conservatives in the most important voting rights case to come to the Court in many years, *Shelby County v Holder* (2013), in which a 5–4 majority struck down the congressional formula used to select state and local governments into the preclearance requirements of the 1965 Voting Rights Act.

However, in cases pitting the government against individual liberty interests, Kennedy is less predictable. He tends to support individual liberties against state power whether the case involves politically conservative rights (i.e. gun control or corporate speech) or liberal ones (i.e. abortion or gay rights). In *Boumediene v Bush* (2008), for example, Kennedy wrote the opinion for a 5–4 Court, holding that detainees at Guantanamo Bay had a right to the habeas corpus review and that the Military Commissions Act of 2006 was an unconstitutional suspension of that right. Kennedy also sided with liberals in a string of cases curbing states' use of the death penalty, writing the majority opinions for a 5–4 Court in *Roper v Simmons* (2005) (prohibiting minors from being executed) as well as a 5–4 decision in *Kennedy v Louisiana* (2008) (prohibiting capital punishment for non-capital crimes). In both cases, Kennedy abandoned his four conservative colleagues who dissented. Finally, Kennedy was also the author of the Court's landmark decision involving the rights of gays and lesbians. In *Lawrence v Texas* (2003), he wrote for a sharply divided Court, striking down state anti-sodomy laws and recognizing a constitutional right to private sexual conduct; and in *United States v Windsor* (2013) he wrote the opinion for another 5–4 Court, striking down the federal Defense of Marriage Act as a violation of constitutional equal-protection rights.

Beyond the isolated liberal victories that Kennedy's swing role might produce, and despite Roberts's effort to sooth tensions between the

Court and the executive in the *Sebelius* case, it is likely that the Court will continue to find itself in conflict with the Obama administration during its second term. President Obama will no doubt continue to use the bully pulpit to criticize the Court, and on occasion may even seek legislative responses to decisions that he opposes (such as *Citizens United*). In addition, Obama can also expect to fill at least one vacant seat on the high bench in his second term. Justice Ruth Bader Ginsburg has signaled that she may be ready to retire before 2016, when she will be 83. However, even if this was to occur, replacing Ginsburg will not allow Obama to shift significantly the ideological direction of the Court, since he would be replacing one of the most liberal justices.

Similar to his first two appointments of Justice Sonia Sotomayor and Elena Kagan, any second-term appointment by Obama is likely to be moderately liberal but also to reflect a concern about bringing greater diversity to the bench by nominating another woman or member of an ethnic minority (Goldstein, 2012). Although it is unlikely any of the five conservatives will leave the bench while Obama is in office, should that happen, any nominee would have to survive intense scrutiny by Senate Republicans (including the possibility of a Senate filibuster) as a replacement would create the first Democratic-appointed majority on the Court since 1972. Thus, in the short term Obama's reelection will likely preserve the sharp ideological divide on the Court.

Obama is also unlikely to undertake any broader strategy aimed at restructuring the judiciary or advancing an overarching constitutional philosophy in his second term (say similar to that undertaken by Ronald Reagan). Despite his public rebuke of the Court, Obama's approach to judicial appointments and other court initiatives during the first term evidenced apathy about the judiciary more than anything else. This probably reflects Obama's long-standing belief in grassroots democratic action and the limited role judicial power should play in policy-making. Indeed, Obama's view about courts may be summarized as: the best thing judges can do is 'stay out of the way of progressive policymakers' (Driver, 2011). Thus, Obama's second term will probably continue to see opportunistic uses of executive litigation and judicial selection as a way of limiting and preempting the conservative drift of constitutional law, but not a broader effort aimed at advancing a competing constitutional agenda (Goldstein, 2012; Toobin, 2012).

In the long term Obama's reelection may portend something more. We have argued that the Supreme Court can be understood as an institution that is structured over time by broad developments in the elected branches. Obama is the first Democratic president since Franklin Roosevelt to win two presidential elections with more than 50 percent of the popular vote. Although divided government continues, his reelection also brought Democratic gains in both the House and the Senate. Moreover, the younger, more ethnically diverse, demographic shape of Obama's electoral coalition augers well for future Democratic electoral prospects. While it is too early to tell whether Obama will be viewed by future historians as a transformational president leading to a new period of electoral politics, if he is they are also likely to view the Roberts Court as a holdover institution reflecting constitutional values of a declining electoral regime.

Chapter 10

American Federalism at a Crossroads

Paul L. Posner

Woodrow Wilson told us that the federal–state relationship is the cardinal question for the American system, destined to be reformulated for each generation. As the United States faces a daunting range of policy challenges in the second decade of the 21st century, these words remain timely. The federal system continues to be a central vehicle used by national officials to satisfy an ever expanding range of policy goals, from health reform and climate change to fiscal consolidation and tax reform. While state and local governments are central actors in these emergent policy initiatives, the outcome for the federal system is troubling. In short, the flexibility of state and local governments to satisfy their own unique and diverse interests and needs has become encumbered by the growing reach of these increasingly prodigious and ambitious national policy goals. Ironically, many of these national policy issues originated with the state and local sector, but they often get transformed when making the intergovernmental roundtrip. The Obama administration's health reform provides a powerful illustration of these trends, with the reforms borrowed from Massachusetts and setting the agenda for an ambitious policy regime relying on states as the critical workhorses to expand coverage through Medicaid and new health insurance exchanges.

Yet, as the federal role has expanded, state and local governments have retained vital roles in implementing these far flung national initiatives. Simply put, the policy ambition of the federal government far exceeds its administrative, legal, fiscal and political capacity to implement federal programs, mandates and preemptions. Accordingly, states and local governments, as well as a wide range of nonprofit and private corporations, are bought in as third parties to carry out federal initiatives through a host of governmental tools, including grants and loans in addition to regulatory tools. States have strengths in implementation, stemming from their bargaining position as experts who can exit national programs, leaving federal officials with little or no recourse.

174

Recently more polarized parties have served to weaken the ability of national officials to undertake concerted policy action while strengthening the resolve of state officials to resist new and existing federal policy mandates. The conservative governors' resistance to health reform through Medicaid expansion, as well as broader state restiveness over No Child Left Behind, illustrate the continuing leverage states can deploy in a federal system that remains decidedly interdependent in all major policy initiatives. In such a system, political dissensus can destabilize national programs, empowering state and local officials with new leverage in policy formation and implementation. The 2012 election campaign has revealed major disagreements between the two parties over the federal role in healthcare, with Democrats promoting strong national policy and Republicans advocating new block grants to decentralize policy to the states. Notwithstanding the nationalization of policy over the past 50 years, these recent trends suggest that the federal relationship will remain the cardinal question in a nation with continuing ambivalence about the reach of national government.

Federalism and the history of the republic

Until the 1860s, American federalism in practice resembled what has come to be known as 'dual federalism'. In dual federalism, there is little overlap in the functions and responsibilities of the federal government and the states. Each level has its own, largely separate, sphere of responsibilities. In this system, the national government concentrated on defense, foreign affairs, developing the western territories and the promotion of American industry and commerce through the use of tariffs and 'internal improvements'. The states were almost wholly responsible for the administration of justice, public education, welfare and most public infrastructure. While national officials in practice did engage states in partnerships for infrastructure improvement and other national programs, dual federalism kept national activism in check through presidential actions and Supreme Court decisions (Nathan, 2008).

However, even during the early years of the republic, the roles of the federal government and the states proved to be critical lines of cleavage dividing political parties and factions. Underlying economic and social factors fed political conflict over the nature of American federalism and led eventually to southern secession and civil war.

Following the civil war, a long period of gradual government expansion ensued, along with the first tentative ventures into so-called 'cooperative' federalism. As the nation's economy expanded, the limits of state economic regulation were exposed. States attempted but ultimately proved unable to regulate effectively the developing national systems of rail transportation, food processing, mining and heavy industries (Beer, 1973). Their jurisdictional reach was inadequate to the geographic scope of the economic externalities created by national markets and industries. Consequently, the later 19th and early 20th centuries saw the gradual growth of federal railroad regulation, anti-trust legislation, food and drug safety legislation, and the creation of the Federal Reserve Bank system (Walker, 1998).

While incremental growth of grants continued for many years, cooperative fiscal federalism came of age during and after the 1930s. The New Deal readjusted the balance of power and the operational practices of the federal system as profoundly as the civil war had done. State and local finances collapsed under the pressure of the Great Depression, as tax revenues contracted sharply and demands for services increased. Consequently, states and localities turned increasingly to the federal government for assistance, as the federal share of public expenditures equaled combined state and local spending for the first time during peacetime (Leuchtenburg, 1963; Patterson, 1981).

This system of cooperative federalism, marked by shared involvement by all types of general purpose governments across most domestic functions, became the norm in American governance in the 1950s. It was greatly expanded during the 1960s with the so-called 'Great Society' program of President Lyndon B. Johnson. Hundreds of new federal grant programs were adopted: the total number of federal grants tripled from 132 in 1960 to 397 in 1969 (Walker, 1998). Some of the largest and most important federal aid programs in existence today, such as education grants for disadvantaged children and Medicaid, were established during this period.

This explosion of new federal spending programs, and the conflicts caused by the federal government's new focus on civil rights, poverty and governmental reform, created a political backlash and intergovernmental policy changes in the Nixon and Reagan administrations. President Richard M. Nixon launched a so-called 'new federalism' initiative that sought to reduce the strings on federal grant programs and decentralize decision-making. Although he failed to enact all of his proposed reforms, President Nixon succeeded in winning congressional approval of General Revenue Sharing – a multi-billion dollar program of largely no-strings aid to state and local governments – as well as broad flexible block grants for community development and employment and training programs. President Ronald Reagan, too, sought to reduce federal power and influence by cutting federal spending (and taxes) and by consolidating smaller, more tightly controlled, federal grant programs into more flexible block grants.

Notwithstanding these episodic federalism reform initiatives, the federal grant system remains highly categorical and restrictive. There are more than 950 federal grant programs according to the

Congressional Research Service (Dilger, 2009). Only 25 of these programs are block grants, reflecting the continuing propensity of Congress to claim credit for highly specific programs.

Nationalization of the policy agenda

The congressional aversion to block grants and revenue sharing reflected a deeply rooted nationalization of politics and policy-making in the system. Federal policies were extended to an ever broader range of issues traditionally in the purview of state and local governments. Whether it be health care, homeland security or education, national policy-makers of both parties advocated more far reaching national policy reforms premised on the emergence of a broad consensus supporting the nationalization of both problems and solutions.

Systemic political factors previously serving to institutionalize restraint on the exercise of federal power had become eclipsed by secular shifts in political incentives and national policy-making processes. As late as 1960, the federal system was undergirded by political, social and economic forces that placed limits on the role of the federal government, reflected in a general forbearance and restraint that federal officials demonstrated in policy formulation. The position of state and local governments in the federal system was protected by the party system itself. As late as 1960, Morton Grodzins noted that the party system was decentralized, with its power base concentrated at the state and local level (Grodzins, 1969). National office holders, whether they be presidents or congressmen, owed their nominations and political allegiances to state and local party leaders, embedding a sensitivity to the prerogatives of state and local officials in fundamental political incentives. Federalism was an important line of cleavage between the parties, with the Republican Party dedicated to preserving states' authority and constraining the growth of federal power. The interest group system served as a bulwark of federalism as well – business was the preeminent interest in the American system and their interests were viewed as being better protected by the states than by the federal government.

In fact, national policy-makers did observe forbearance and restraint on federalism issues prior to the 1960s. Daniel Elazar (1962) wrote that, before the 1960s, Congress generally protected states in federal legislation. Even as the federal role expanded over the economy in such landmark statutes as the Fair Labor Standards Act, the Social Security Act and Title VII of the Civil Rights Act of 1964, state and local governments were exempted. Indeed, federalism was accepted as one of the primary 'rules of the game'.

By the mid-1990s, many of these factors had shifted dramatically, leading to the unraveling of the constraints that bolstered the position of states in the system. Since Grodzins's time, the party system has fundamentally changed as candidates for national office have been forced to assemble their own coalitions to compete for nominations and elections. Interest groups and the media have eclipsed state and local parties as gatekeepers of candidate recruitment and legitimation. National elected officials have converted from being ambassadors of state and local party leaders to independent political entrepreneurs anxious to establish their own visible policy profiles to appeal to a diverse coalition of interest groups, media and an increasingly independent base of voters. Far from allies, the relationship between congressional officials and state and local elected colleagues from their districts resembles more of a competition among independent political entrepreneurs for money, visibility and votes.

These trends toward congressional and presidential policy activism span partisan boundaries, obscuring differences on federal role questions that used to define the party system. The Congressional Quarterly discontinued its Federal Role Index as one of its measures of congressional voting behavior in 1969 as the gap between the parties withered on this dimension. Reinforcing these structural changes in the political system have been changes in conservative ideology. Liberals in the United States have been broadly supportive of an active and largely centralizing federal role in the federal system since the New Deal of the 1930s. Traditional conservatives have become national policy activists as well, welcoming federal power to implement social values of religious conservatives and economic policies advanced by libertarians. Hence, on issues ranging from federal preemption of state economic regulation, school choice, gay marriage or medical marijuana they are prone to support novel and even aggressive expansions of federal authority vis-à-vis the states to advance their political, economic or social policy goals.

These nationalizing trends were echoed and bolstered by other trends in the political system and the broader economy. The growth of national media institutions focused on Washington created a powerful resource for those groups wishing to nationalize problems and issues, and reporting increasingly sought to find national dimensions or applications for state and local problems or solutions. The advent of lobbies representing broad and diffuse interests, the so-called public interest groups, has fueled national policy advocacy as many of these groups have settled in Washington rather than in the states. Another important development in the interest group sector was the pronounced, but little noticed, shift of business groups from allies of the states to advocates of national regulation by federal agencies, underscoring the impact of the nationalization and globalization of the economy on the federal system.

Faced with newly empowered and mobilized interest groups pressing for national policy expansion, states and localities were left in a weaker political position. No longer able to rely on organic political alliances with national party officials in the White House or the Congress, these governments had to form their own interest groups in Washington. While these groups could count such victories as the enactment of general revenue sharing and unfunded mandates reform, more intensely organized and funded advocates of program and regulatory expansions often outflanked them. Most critically, state and local governments were unable to marshal sufficient internal consensus across the wide range of governors, mayors and state legislative leaders sufficient to mount effective interest group campaigns in Washington or among grassroots constituencies beyond the beltway (Posner, 1998).

These trends have only worsened in recent years as greater polarization among parties has further undermined the cohesion necessary for any interest group to gain attention. Thus, for instance, the National Governors Association was unable to take positions on two of the defining domestic policy reforms in recent decades – welfare reform in 1996 and health reform in 2010 – due to deep disagreements between Democratic and Republican governors. On health care, Republican govenors felt obliged to renounce changes to the bill advancing state financial interests to join their Republican Congressional leaders to oppose the reform in its entirety. This development reflected a stunning reversal from the days when party positions in Washington reflected state and local party interests. Such positions are now articulated by national party leaders.

Coercive federalism

The nationalization of politics had consequences for the federal system. With a stronger impetus to nationalize problems, federal officials increasingly found that cooperative federalism tools were insufficient to pursue more insistent and compelling national goals brought to the federal doorstep. The cooperative model expanded the federal role while at the same time strengthening the state and local foundations for that role. State and local governments retained vital bargaining power with national leaders since they could at least threaten to withhold their cooperation that was so vital for national programs to succeed. From the federal perspective, gaining participation was more critical politically to program survival than promoting compliance with goals (Ingram, 1977).

Most studies of the etiology of federal policy initiatives during this period show that grants were usually the initial tool used to stimulate interest and adoption throughout the intergovernmental system, only to be followed by more coercive mandates as the federal role became more legitimate and gaps in implementation became less acceptable (Kincaid, 1990). Intergovernmental regulations can range from direct orders imposed on state and local governments by federal statute to more indirect actions that force state and local policy change as a consequence of other independent federal policies, such as the implications of federal immigration policies for local health clinics. Such policy actions could consist of either affirmative obligations for state and local governments to take action on a policy issue – what might be generically termed a 'mandate' – or a constraint preventing or pre-empting certain actions.

Thus, the instruments of coercive federalism go well beyond the popular concept of 'unfunded mandates'. This conceptualization was formalized when Congress passed the Unfunded Mandates Reform Act (UMRA) in 1995. While the passage of this Act did indeed mark an attempt to reverse, or at the very least arrest, the growth of intergovernmental regulation or coercive federalism, in fact UMRA primarily addressed only one of these instruments – statutory direct orders – leaving federal grant conditions and rules and preemptions of state authority outside of its purview. The relatively narrow definition embraced in UMRA has served to limit the potential effectiveness of this reform in influencing these policy decisions (Fantone, 2011).

The secular trends toward a more coercive and centralized federalism have survived the passage of both Republican and Democratic administrations, as well as Democratic and Republican Congresses. Recent centralizing actions succeeded in overturning cooperative federalism frameworks that had evolved over many years. The Bush administration accelerated centralization of the federal system, working with a Republican controlled Congress. Whether it was No Child Left Behind, the Real ID Act or elections administration, President Bush and the Congress followed a muscular domestic policy agenda relying on federal mandates and preemptions on states and localities to carry out national policy priorities (Conlan and Dinan, 2007). The Obama administration has added health reform to the list – states have become the primary instrument used to extend health insurance to the uninsured through both expansive new Medicaid coverage mandates and the new health exchanges which states will administer under close federal supervision and standards.

The vital role of states in national policy expansion

As the earlier discussion suggests, the federal role in the federal system has become far more prominent and centralized than it has at any time in American history. The explosion of issues demanding federal responses has continued unabated in both Republican and Democratic regimes. With stronger incentives for national political officials to respond with national programs and policies, federalism no longer serves its former role as a primary basis defining political choice. Federalism is now more important in shaping how national leaders respond to the growing agenda of national problems than in determining whether those officials will respond.

As the agenda of national policy issues has become more complex, the national government has extended its reach into areas where it had little historic role or legitimacy. The federal system nonetheless continued to play a vital role as enabler and legitimizer of the expansion of federal programs. Given the continuing aversion to expansion of direct federal bureaucracies, national policy-makers improvised by designing policy initiatives which appeared to minimize direct federal roles by attempting to leverage, cajole, entice, mandate and otherwise engage the resources of independent actors such as states and localities in a highly pluralistic society. Robert Stoker has suggested that the tools of third-party government are both centralizing – by permitting the federal government to gain access to authorities, resources and political consent that it would never have been able to do on its own – and decentralizing – by inviting in third parties as federal implementers (Stoker, 1991).

The states as policy laboratories and administrative partners

Historically, many national programs in fact often have their origins at the state and local level carrying out their long-standing roles as policy laboratories of innovation in the system (Nathan, 2008). In issues ranging from global warming to healthcare coverage for the uninsured, states have often piloted new approaches to public issues. Their policy innovations have provided them with a stronger voice in shaping the agenda and in formulating policy responses at the national level as well. There are reasons to believe that the reliance on states to generate national policy ideas has accelerated in recent years. Frustrated by political and policy gridlock at the national level, many groups championing policy reforms find states to be more hospitable and eager champions of new policy ideas and reforms than the federal government. This has been facilitated by the significant political and administrative transformation in state governance and administrative capacity that has occurred over the past 50 years, going from what some called the sleepy fallen arches of our system to the active champions of new policy innovations.

Responding to many of the nation's critical challenges has increasingly become the joint responsibility of all levels of government. The effectiveness of federal programs is, therefore, dependent on state and local management and resources, as well as constructive interactions between federal, state and local actors. As a result, third-party actors are increasingly joining with government officials to develop, fund and carry out national policies and programs. Thus the fiscal and policy fortunes of each level of government in the system are increasingly intertwined.

While state and local governments have traditionally assumed central roles in grants, even under more coercive instruments such as preemptions, federal officials often have been forced to rely on state and local regulatory regimes to supplement paltry staff levels and to promote greater political support. Partial preemption strategies, for instance, provide states with vital opportunities to exceed federal regulatory standards when participating in federal regulatory enforcement regimes. While perhaps falling short of the cooperative partnerships observed for federal grants, nonetheless the substantial state roles promote a degree of decentralization, thanks to the critical role played by states in implementing federal standards, and in some cases in promulgating the standards themselves (Zimmerman, 2005).

State resistance to national mandates

Even under direct order mandates, states have collectively shown a resilience that has prompted greater resistance to centralized programs hatched in Washington. Mandates have a political life cycle that is centralizing in passage and decentralizing in implementation. During the initial passage, state and local government officials are prone to being divided, ambivalent and actually supportive of the purposes. However, these political dynamics are reversed during the implementation cycle. State and local cohesion grows as the costs and program design challenges become more salient to officials throughout the country; conflict between the goals and priorities of state and local and federal officials heightens at this stage as well, not surprisingly (Posner, 1998). Thus, for instance, while state and local officials offered little opposition to initial passage of No Child Left Behind, many have joined forces with teachers' unions to mount vigorous protests of the program's standards and constraints, including attempting to gain court injunctions against the program's most onerous mandates. Ultimately, states' opposition forced federal education officials to offer significant new flexibility to states and, therefore, has contributed to the gridlock preventing the Act's reauthorization in Congress. Most states refused to pass broad sweeping changes to their driver's license procedures to comply with the federal Real ID Act of 2005, forcing the federal government to back off and search for a compromise with state leaders (Government Technology News, 2009).

Looking ahead, states are likely to become even more resistant and assertive in responding to new federal policies. The 2012 elections brought even greater polarization to state governments. The proportion of states with unified government has grown, continuing a trend away from divided government that started ten years earlier. After the 2012 elections, only 12 states have divided government, the lowest number since 1952. Fully half of the states now have a single party that controls a super-majority in the legislature, up from only 14 states ten years ago (Kurz, 2012). Importantly, 23 states now have unified Republican Party control of both the governor's office and the legislature. This gives Republican conservative governors greater support to challenge federal mandates and policy prescriptions authored by a Democratically controlled administration in Washington.

Indeed, the resistance that states showed in defying federal mandates ushered in during the Bush era was redoubled with the advent of the Obama administration. Ideologically conservative Republican governors, such as Governor Kasich of Ohio and Governor Scott of Florida, stepped up to refuse new federal funds for high speed rail, expanded unemployment insurance and Race to the Top education provided under the 2009 Recovery Act, the stimulus program enacted by Congress at the behest of the Obama Administration. From a strict political economy standpoint, states have much to gain from accepting federal grants, particularly those with little encumbrance of state resources. After all, federal grants could be viewed as obtaining a return on federal tax revenue provided by the state's citizens, and governors face some political risk in subsequent elections from refusing large pots of federal money. Nonetheless, one study noted that high profile state refusals of federal grants are not new; in fact, state leaders have found it politically advantageous to draw attention periodically to their opposition to federal policies when the national administration was controlled by the opposite political party. However, this study also noted that state refusals of federal funds have been far higher than previous periods, reflecting higher levels of polarization between a Democratic administration in Washington and ideologically conservative Republicans controlling the states. Over 40 percent of Republican governors refused federal money from the Obama Administration (Nicolson-Crotty, 2012).

State push back on health reform

The signature moment for conservative state resistance was President Obama's healthcare reform program. Expanded state Medicaid and state-based health exchanges are the foundation for the major increase in health coverage provided under the Patient Protection and Affordable Care Act of 2010. Of the 34 million additional people expected to receive health insurance, 18 million would be through the expanded mandates and financing under Medicaid. State Medicaid programs would face significant new mandates to expand coverage to adults with incomes up to 133 percent of the federal poverty level. The federal government will fully pay for this coverage for the first several years, declining to 90 percent by 2020. An exchange must be established for each state to provide individuals with incomes higher than the Medicaid threshold a broader range of health insurance choices, both for individual and small business employees. Within basic standards set by the federal government for benefit coverage, choices and rates, states can choose to operate the exchanges, ensuring compliance with federal standards as well as gaining the opportunity to add more stringent state standards. If states do not choose to participate, the federal government will step in to establish exchanges in that state, possibly by contracting with a nonprofit entity.

The state push back came in two phases. First, a majority of state attorneys general brought a suit in the federal courts to have the entire Act declared unconstitutional, partly due to the impact that the Act's mandates would have on the states' sovereignty protected under the 10th Amendment to the Constitution. Second, even after the Court affirmed the constitutionality of the law, states retain enhanced ability to opt out of both Medicaid and health exchange roles. While the federal government can step in to ensure that health exchanges operate in states that refuse to participate, they have no such recourse for states like Texas that have pledged to renounce the expansion in Medicaid eligibility. About half of the states have announced they would not run exchanges in their states. While many governors refuse to participate in federally mandated health insurance schemes, ironically those states who choose to operate exchanges will have a greater influence in putting the imprint of state interests on these health insurance offerings (Vestal, 2013).

State officials are actively deliberating on Medicaid expansion, with 14 Republican governors having announced that they will oppose the expanded coverage. However, states will have longer to consider and reconsider their Medicaid decisions; already several conservative governors have announced that their states will apply for Medicaid expansions. It is expected that other states will ultimately make the same decision because the stakes are so high – billions of federal dollars will be left behind in Washington for states renouncing participation, leaving potential beneficiaries without coverage and reducing incomes for influential doctors and hospitals who agreed to lower payments under the health reform with the anticipation of gaining additional patients from the ranks of the uninsured. The stakes are high with significant benefits and costs from any decision that states make. If Texas opted for expansion of Medicaid, its rolls would grow from 3.7 million to 6.1 million – a boon to lower income residents and medical doctors alike. However, even with the federal government footing most of the bill, the state would still pay an additional \$5.7 billion over the next ten years (Holohan et al., 2012).

The role of the Supreme Court

The Supreme Court has buttressed states in their battles with the federal government over authority and influence. The Rehnquist Court reversed years of federal expansionary rulings by establishing boundaries limiting federal policy expansions. Congress's ability to use the interstate commerce clause as the basis for federal expansion was limited by the 1995 *United States v Lopez* decision overturning federal mandates restricting guns on school property. The ability of Congress to engage state and local resources and authorities in the service of national goals was crimped by the 'commandeering' cases; the 1997 *Printz v United States* decision, for instance, ruled that the federal government may not directly order local sheriffs to help screen the criminal records of prospective gun purchasers.

While the Court has been increasingly assertive in establishing limits for federal direct orders on states, it had been reluctant to limit grant conditions and spending power in general. The argument is that grants are voluntary agreements freely entered into by the state government, which vitiates their coercive nature (see *Oklahoma v United States Civil Service Commission*, 1947). Thus, it is not surprising that most federal mandates are carried out not by direct order but by conditions of aid. With federal assistance approaching nearly \$700 billion, the federal government uses the Trojan Horse of grants to project a wide range of requirements on the states and localities. When one looks at recent controversies between federal and state governments, it is the grant conditions that states protest about most vehemently – No Child Left Behind, Medicaid mandates predating health reform, and emergency management requirements are examples.

In its seminal 2012 ruling, affirming the Obama Administration's healthcare reform (*National Federation of Independent Businesses et al. v Sebelius*), the Court broke new ground in constraining grant conditions as well. The Court's majority asserted that the grant condition in the health reform act for state Medicaid expansion had become equivalent to direct commandeering of states by federal officials in the service of national goals. Both the sheer extent of funds at risk and the potential loss of not only the new Medicaid matching funds but also of existing Medicaid funding for recalcitrant states was the equivalent of aiming a 'loaded gun' at the heads of state officials.

This path-breaking court decision left many gasping for bright lines defining when the Court would consider grant conditions too onerous and coercive to be acceptable under the Constitution. In a decision nearly 20 years ago, the court ruled that withholding 5 percent of highway grant funds was not sufficiently powerful to constitute coercion. But since Medicaid accounts for a far higher percentage of state revenues, federal penalties threatening the entire grant appear to have crossed that undefined coercion line. Would special education or Title I education mandates be considered equally as coercive? The Court's health decision avoided providing clear criteria to answer this question.

Clearly, these new judicial constraints have further boxed in federal officials in responding to new national needs appearing on the federal doorstep. What options do federal officials have in working through states in the future? Given limits on federal coercion through either direct orders or grants, one scenario favored by conservatives might be for the federal government simply to foreswear national policy, leaving it in the states' hands. Another option would be for the federal government to carry out new federal programs itself – an outcome replete with irony for the federal system and conservatives alike.

More immediately, the Court's decision fortified the bargaining position of conservative states in dealing with a Democratic administration seeking to implement the new health reform law. States reluctant to expand Medicaid no longer had to foreswear their existing Medicaid program. The decision made it more realistic for states to threaten to exit the process so as to enhance and supplement their rather weak and diluted representational voice in the federal system (Hirschman, 1971). Given the limits on representational federalism already demonstrated, states needed some additional leverage to enhance their bargaining position. Owing to their critical position as implementers of major national policy initiatives, states and localities have always enjoyed a monopoly on the means of delivering promised federal benefits across most domestic programs. After all, the federal government often has little or no recourse for implementing national domestic policy beyond state and local governments. However, this asset was often under-utilized due to the superior enticement that federal financial assistance offered to states and localities. Should ideology trump financial incentives, states may collectively gain new leverage in dealing with both Congress and the administration by resisting the blandishments of new federal assistance programs and regulations.

The federal system and fiscal challenges

A system with greater political tensions and ideological disagreements must now cope with a new challenge that will undermine cooperation from all sides – the short and longer-term expenditure and revenue pressures occurring at all levels of government. In the short term, the recent economic downturn and stock market declines have caused revenues to slide, while other developments, such as healthcare cost increases, have greatly increased spending demands at all levels of government. Longer-term trends, such as the aging of the population, will continue to put spending demands on all governments, while other trends, such as globalization and advancing technology, will affect traditional sources of government revenues by eroding tax bases.

The federal budget is on an unsustainable course. With deficits already exceeding 7 percent of GDP in 2012, long term projections by the US Government Accountability Office (2012a) show deficits exploding to unsustainable levels exceeding 20 percent of the economy over the next several decades, thanks to population aging, higher healthcare costs and slower revenue growth. For the state and local sector, the Accountability Office's projections show continuing fiscal stress thanks to these very same forces. These sectors will have to struggle perennially to meet balanced budget requirements in the face of underlying fiscal deficits of 2 percent of the economy. Rising employee pensions, growing healthcare costs stemming from the financing role of states in Medicaid, and slower-growing revenues arising from slower workforce growth and the limited reach of sales taxes all contribute.

The financial challenges facing all governments threaten to erode the fiscal foundations that have underwritten cooperative federalism in the past and enabled partners to join together in expanding public services to meet rising public expectations. In its place, the fiscal future of the federal system could feature heightened intergovernmental conflict where all levels of government vie to preempt revenues and shift costs and blame for the difficult choices that will be necessary to resolve fiscal deficits. A prolonged period of austerity will challenge state and local governments like never before to find fiscal space to address their own unique needs while at the same time assuming stewardship for the growing agenda of national priorities placed in their hands. Under this scenario, it is unlikely that the federal government could afford to play the role of the fiscal white knight in bailing out fiscally stressed states and localities like it did in the depths of the Great Recession with the $800 billion stimulus ushered in by the Obama Administration. Indeed, it is more likely that federal fiscal officials will serve to exacerbate state and local fiscal stress as they compete for tax bases and scarce resources.

National policy leadership and intergovernmental conflict

The trends covered in this chapter present a quandary to national officials. On the one hand, there are greater pressures than ever before to nationalize problems and present them on the federal doorstep for immediate resolution. Increasingly anxious national officials, courting a shifting alliance of interests, active publics and media, campaign as problem solvers, ready to fix old problems festering on the agenda, even as they target new ones to solve.

Yet, in doing so, they will have to find ways to work within the federal system, for states and localities will invariably be involved in nearly every major national domestic issue. With all of their conflicts and tensions, intergovernmental systems remain well suited for many of the 'wicked' problems faced today – problems with contestable definitions, a wide distribution of the resources and capacities necessary to solve them, and uncertainties about how best to implement these solutions. Complex public policy problems like climate change, healthcare costs and coverage, and educating the future workforce will call on the compound republic to find ways to work in effective partnerships across boundaries.

The political difficulties involved with rising to these intergovernmental policy challenges should not be underestimated. This system was once viewed as a win–win, as the federal government gained state participation while states gained significant new federal dollars to help expand programs. Increasingly riven with conflicting ideological agendas and fiscal constraints, the federal system now radiates increasing conflicts and tensions between activist policy-makers in Washington and wary officials in states and communities.

The Obama Administration illustrates the balancing act that national leaders must play in this more delicate and tension filled environment. The initial promises and actions of the Administration created widespread concerns and occasionally loud complaints about policy centralization and standardization resulting from presidential policies to establish national programs to reform healthcare, climate change, financial markets regulation and infrastructure. However, the Administration actually followed a path that was far more nuanced and cooperative than that suggested by early expectations or contemporary rhetoric. While coercive federalism strategies were deployed in healthcare and sought in climate change, the Administration relied on older regimes of cooperative grants and regulatory flexibility to engage the states in collective initiatives to achieve economic recovery and regulate the financial sector. A large infusion of new federal funds and nearly unprecedented intergovernmental consultation between the White

House and governors over the Recovery Act were intended to promote state support for expedited and error-free spending of stimulus funds. Thus it was hoped to jump start an early economic recovery from the worst downturn since the Great Depression. Even in the case of healthcare, the strategy adopted by Congress and the Administration enabled conservative states to opt out of administering new national programs, thereby accommodating the heightened ideological polarization among the states (Conlan and Posner, 2011).

The reliance on the states by an Administration devoted to a more active federal role may come as a surprise to some, as would the use of more cooperative and decentralizing policy tools to carry out the new initiatives. At the same time, the Administration faced the challenges of dealing with states that had become politically more polarized and conflictual than at any time in recent memory. These state differences came to constitute a source of policy drag that would slow the pace of policy change, frustrating the policy ambitions of new federal officials. It also called on national officials to design policy tools in ways that accommodated the wider variance of policy interests and priorities among the states and localities – a familiar challenge that has become more central and vexing for national policy centrists.

Going forward, the Obama Administration's domestic policy initiatives carry lessons for the future of the federal system. Unlike Ronald Reagan or Richard Nixon, this President had no deep-seated commitment to restoring states to their 'rightful place' in the federal system. Indeed, the Obama Administration, like others including the Bush Administration, came to the federal system not through principle but through an opportunistic strategy to gain adoption and implementation of national policy goals. From this vantage point, national officials nonetheless had compelling incentives to engage with a federal system that was absolutely vital to whatever success and policy legacy they would ultimately enjoy. Federalism may not have informed the decisions about *whether* to undertake the growing agenda of national policies, but it most certainly was instrumental in shaping *how* those initiatives would be designed and implemented.

The foregoing discussion suggests that the fealty of national officials to federalism rests not on philosophical or ideological anchors but on the sheer self-interest of anxious national officials who have strong and continuing incentives to accommodate state and local governments in nearly all domestic policy initiatives. In the American system, engaging states and localities is the essential enabler that legitimizes the creation of many new federal programs in the first place, given the nation's long-standing resistance to national bureaucracies and direct federal policy interventions. Ultimately, federal systems can advance federal policy interests perhaps more effectively than more uniform or nationalized systems of policy governance. Federal systems have the potential

to promote political legitimacy and support both by delegating decisions and political hard choices and by engaging and delegating part of
the job to those with highly divergent interests and views. They also
promote another vital function for public leaders – policy learning.
Given the wide range of unknowns that often accompany ambitious
new national policy ventures, engaging state and local officials provides national leaders with the benefits of learning from the experiences of numerous decentralized actors. Engaging a diverse federal
system in managing and adjusting national goals to unique local conditions may, thus, help national political actors to gain both greater
political support and better public policy.

Chapter 11

The Troubled Economy

Christopher J. Bailey

The economic problems confronting President Obama in his second term are enormous. First, the fall-out from the financial crisis of 2007–08 and the Great Recession that followed continues to cast a deep shadow over the economy. Economic growth remains fragile, unemployment is high, the standard of living for many Americans is lower than a decade ago, and high levels of government debt threaten the delivery of services. Second, the economic preeminence of the United States that has underpinned its hard and soft power for 50 years or so is increasingly threatened by emerging economies such as China, India and Brazil (Fouskas and Gokay, 2012; Moran and Roubini, 2012). A study published in December 2012 by the National Intelligence Council forecast that China would overtake the United States as the world's leading economic power before 2030 (Shanker, 2012). The growth of these economies not only poses a threat to American competitiveness but also raises the specter of intense struggles over resources and raw materials. However, not all is gloomy and predictions of the country's demise should be treated cautiously. Boosters can point to the fact that the United States has considerable energy resources and a deep-rooted entrepreneurial culture that show signs of powering an economic recovery. The country has a comparative advantage over many of its competitors in sectors such as services and commodities that may help to revive the economy (Brooks, 2012b; *The Economist*, 2012c).

In this chapter I examine the economic challenges confronting the United States, the debates over policy, and the intense ideological and political divisions that structure policy-making. I show that the policy debates about how to respond to these challenges have ranged from discussions about the role of government in managing the economy that have challenged some of the precepts of the New Deal to technocratic wrangling over the efficacy of various policy tools. Revealed in these debates are deep ideological and political divisions that not only point to fundamental tensions in the American polity, but also structure policy-making as political rivals strive to advance their own ideo-

191

logical vision and compete for partisan advantage. An institutional landscape that divides power, and profound ideological rifts between the major political actors, have combined to create a dysfunctional policy process dominated by short-term or stop-gap measures.

The troubled economy

In September 2008 the collapse of the investment bank Lehman Brothers brought to a head a long fermenting financial crisis that pushed an already fragile American economy deep into recession. Excessive bank lending over the previous decade had fueled a housing bubble that had eventually burst leading to the collapse of major financial institutions, loss of homes and savings, a credit crunch, business failure, and rising levels of unemployment. The collapse of the housing market was dramatic. US Census data shows that between 2007 and 2009 the mortgage delinquency rate rose from 5.4 to 9.4 percent, the foreclosure rate increased from 2.0 to 4.3 percent, mortgage lending fell from $1.14 trillion to $664 billion, while the number of houses sold fell from 891,000 in January 2007 to 396,000 in October 2009. Median house prices fell by nearly 20 percent between the first quarter of 2008 and the third quarter of 2009. Bank lending dried up as financial institutions lost confidence in balance sheets contaminated by 'toxic assets', pushing large numbers of businesses into bankruptcy and the country into recession. Bureau of Economic Analysis data shows that GDP declined by 3.7 percent in the third quarter of 2008 and continued to decline for another three consecutive quarters (see Figure 11.1). Between August 2008 and October 2009 the official seasonally adjusted unemployment rate produced by the Bureau of Labor Statistics (BLS) rose from 6.1 to 10.0 percent (see Figure 11.2). Broader measures of unemployment, or under-employment, that include 'involuntary' part-time working and those who stop looking for employment suggest the 'real' rate of unemployment was even higher: rising from 10.8 percent in August 2008 to 17.5 percent in October 2009, a level that analysts believe had not been seen since the Great Depression of the 1930s (Leonhardt, 2009). The proportion of the working age population in employment in October 2009 was 58.5 percent, the lowest figure since 1947. Towards the end of 2008 the term 'The Great Recession' began to gain currency as a description of the economic crisis confronting the country (Rampell, 2009).

The economic collapse of 2008 not only revealed individual and institutional shortcomings in the financial sector but also laid bare deep structural problems in the American economy that had been obscured beneath mountains of debt. Over the previous decade the manufacturing preeminence of the United States had been challenged by emerging

Figure 11.1 *Percentage change in GDP 2005–12, quarters (2005 US dollar)*

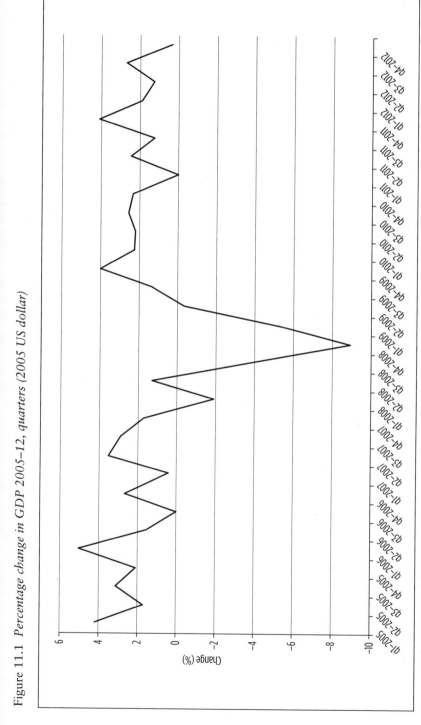

Source: Compiled by author from Bureau of Economic Analysis data.

Figure 11.2 *Seasonally adjusted unemployment rate, 2009–13 (%)*

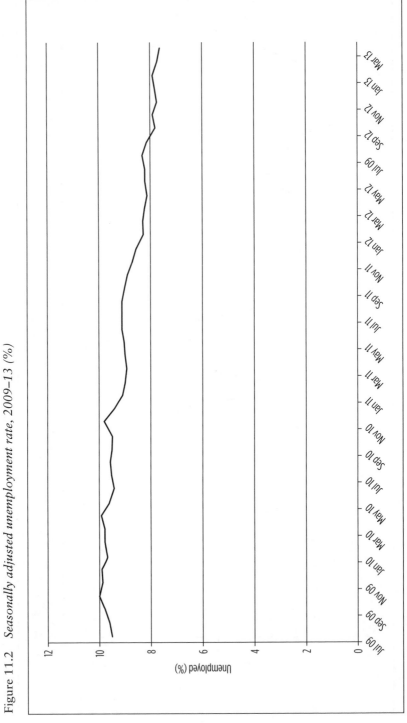

Source: Compilede by author from Bureau of Labor Statistics data.

countries like China, India and Brazil leading to a loss of jobs, downward pressure on wages and a balance of payment problem. A report published by the Economic Policy Institute (EPI) in 2012 calculated that China's entry into the World Trade Organization in 2001 cost the United States 2.7 million jobs between 2001 and 2011, including 2.1 million in manufacturing, and drove down wages as manufacturers sought to reduce their labor costs. The downward pressure on wages caused by efforts to compete with manufacturers in emerging economies contributed to a lack of growth in median household incomes in the United States for much of the first decade of the new century and led to increased borrowing as Americans tried to maintain or improve their standard of living. Federal Reserve data show that consumer debt doubled between 2000 and 2009 and amounted to 97 percent of GDP by the end of the decade (Federal Reserve, 2012; Krugman, 2010). This surge in credit fueled both the housing bubble and a worsening balance of payments as Americans bought computers, electronic goods and other items produced overseas. US Census data reveal that the value of imported goods rose from $1.4 trillion in 2000 to $2.5 trillion in 2009 while exports rose at a much smaller rate (US Census, 2012). Structural problems caused by long-term economic trends such as de-industrialization and globalization meant that Americans were living beyond their means for most of the early 21st century.

The financial crisis and deep-rooted economic problems facing the United States posed two challenges for policy-makers. First, ways had to be found to stabilize the financial system and get Americans back to work. Action needed to be taken to stop banks collapsing, restore confidence in financial instruments and encourage economic growth. Second, the challenges posed by de-industrialization and globalization needed to be addressed. Ways had to be found to reorder the American economy, to revitalize manufacturing and to meet the competitive challenge from the emerging economies. The difficulties in meeting these challenges have been immense and in some cases intractable. Finding solutions to problems requires knowledge of their causes, and this has proved problematic. As Nobel Laureate Joseph Stiglitz has noted, 'finding root causes is like peeling back an onion' with each explanation generating further questions (Stiglitz, 2010: xvii). Even when the causes of a problem have been successfully identified, the question of what to do is often a matter of considerable debate dictated by partisan and ideological viewpoints. Policy choices are often taken with thoughts of political or some other advantage in mind. Finally, some problems may be beyond the capability of policy-makers to solve. They may know the answers but lack the power to do anything meaningful. The reality of the globalized economy means that the solutions to America's economic problems may lie in Beijing, Delhi and Berlin as much as in Washington, DC.

Responding to the financial and economic crisis

The scale of the financial crisis of 2008 and subsequent recession challenged policy-makers in ways that had not been seen since the 1930s and raised questions about the adequacy of the tools available to the government to restore the economy to health. A form of neo-liberalism which stressed the efficiency of the free market had dominated American political and economic thinking since the early 1980s. A number of important sectors of the economy (including banking) had been deregulated, tax breaks given to the wealthy to encourage enterprise, and interest rates used to encourage or discourage borrowing. Government was seen as the problem not the solution. The events of 2008 swept away many of these certainties. Markets did not seem to be either effective or self-correcting, deregulation (or lax regulation) was identified as a factor behind the housing bubble, tax cuts for the wealthy did not appear to have produced a vibrant economy that could respond to the challenge posed by emerging economies, and the manipulation of interest rates failed to kick start borrowing and investment. Government began to be seen as having a role in solving problems rather than being the cause of the problems.

Early efforts to deal with the crisis resembled the struggles of fire fighters attempting to put out blazes before they led to a general conflagration. The Federal Reserve and US Treasury used their regulatory and financial powers to force the sale of the failing investment bank Bear Sterns to JP Morgan Chase in March 2008, and placed the troubled mortgage companies Fannie Mae and Freddie Mac under 'conservatorship' (or federal control) in September 2008. As the scale of the financial crisis and the recession became apparent the Federal Reserve began to employ conventional and unconventional methods to stabilize the financial system as a whole and stimulate the economy. When a reduction in interest rates to levels close to zero failed to produce an increase in bank lending the Federal Reserve announced that it would begin buying corporate bonds and mortgage-backed equities in a massive program of what became known as 'quantitative easing'. Between September and December 2008 the Federal Reserve pumped over $1 trillion into the economy in this way, leading to some objections that it was usurping the constitutional spending powers of Congress, by engaging in quasi-fiscal operations, and had effectively become an unaccountable fourth branch of government (Wessel, 2010). Further episodes of quantitative easing in 2010 and 2012 confirmed that the Federal Reserve had moved beyond its traditional central bank role of curbing inflation and acting as 'lender of last resort' to playing an active role in stimulating the economy (Goldfarb, 2012a). In December 2012 Ben Bernanke, Chair, announced that the Federal Reserve would continue to boost the economy in this way until unemployment fell to 6.5 percent or inflation exceeded 2.5 percent. This was the first time that the Federal Reserve's goals for the economy had been made public (Goldfarb, 2012b).

The Bush Administration responded to the worsening economic climate of late 2008 with further action designed to prevent more large financial institutions collapsing. On October 3, 2008 President Bush signed into law the Emergency Economic Stabilization Act of 2008 which created a Troubled Assets Relief Program (TARP). TARP sought to prop up large financial institutions by providing $700 billion to remove 'troubled' (or 'toxic') assets from their balance sheets. Critics denounced the program as a bloated example of 'corporate welfarism' that gave succor to banks deemed 'too large to fail' while ignoring the fate of small banks and businesses (Stiglitz, 2010). Citibank, Bank of America, JP Morgan Chase, Wells Fargo and the insurance company AIG received billions of dollars of support from the federal government under TARP but nothing was given to medium and small banks, which led to the collapse of nearly 100 banks in the first nine months of 2009 (Kiel, 2009; Dash, 2009). Although nowhere near the scale of bank failures during the savings and loan crisis of the late 1980s, and probably not important to the wider economic picture, these bank failures reinforced a popular impression that the federal government was providing life support to Wall Street at the expense of Main Street. TARP gave no assistance to families struggling to pay their mortgages, small businesses finding it difficult to raise capital, and the growing ranks of the unemployed. Critics argued that the Federal Government was effectively sustaining a failed financial system without addressing either the need to stimulate economic growth or the deep-rooted structural problems that plagued the American economy (Stiglitz, 2010).

Efforts to stabilize large financial institutions continued under President Obama. In February 2009 the administration ordered 19 of the country's largest banks to undergo 'stress' tests to determine whether they had sufficient capital to survive if the economy deteriorated further. The results of these tests led to the Federal Government forcing ten of the banks to raise $75 billion in extra assets (Andrews, 2009). In March 2009 the administration announced a new plan to buy 'toxic' assets, called the Public Private Investment Program (PPIP), which used remaining TARP funds to support private sector purchases of distressed assets. The Administration argued that PPIP allowed toxic assets to be priced correctly, would restore liquidity to the banks, and would boost confidence in the financial sector. Although banks initially proved unwilling to sell toxic assets at prices that private investors wished to pay, PPIP eventually helped to revive the market for mortgage based bonds and even provided a return for taxpayers (Dash, 2010). This meant that the Federal Government effectively became the country's largest 'vulture' investor (an investor who buys distressed assets in the hope of later selling them at a profit). In June 2009 President Obama proposed a major overhaul of the financial regulatory system designed to ensure that the conditions that had led to the financial crisis would not recur. These proposals formed the basis of the Dodd-Frank Wall Street and Consumer Protection Act of 2010. The Act tightened regulation of the financial sector and restricted the ability of commercial banks to invest in high risk equity and hedge funds.

Wall Street banks were not the only companies regarded as 'too large to fail' as the Great Recession took hold in the last quarter of 2008. Plummeting car sales during the year pushed General Motors and Chrysler to the brink of collapse and threatened the loss of over a million jobs in the auto industry as a whole. In September 2008 the 'Big Three' car manufacturers (General Motors, Ford and Chrysler) asked the Federal Government for a $50 billion bailout. President Bush agreed to an emergency bailout of $17.4 billion from TARP funds to ensure the short-term survival of the companies but left the decision about whether to approve a larger bailout to his successor. Propping up companies like General Motors and Chrysler raised questions about the appropriate role of government in supporting private industry that had not resonated as loudly in discussions about the future of large financial institutions. President Obama decided that the consequences of allowing General Motors and Chrysler to collapse, particularly the effect on unemployment, outweighed concerns about the end of capitalism, and agreed a comprehensive rescue plan for the industry. The two companies agreed to enter into a managed bankruptcy process that restructured their operations, streamlined their products, required the production of more energy-efficient cars, and reduced worker benefits in return for financial help that left the Federal Government as a major shareholder in both companies. Questions about the wisdom of the auto bailout would resurface in the 2012 presidential election.

President Obama realized that combating the recession required more than bailing out the banks and auto industry and moved quickly to stimulate the economy when he took office in January 2009. In February 2009 he signed into law the American Recovery and Reinvestment Act (ARRA) which provided approximately $800 billion in federal spending over two years to reduce unemployment. Funding for a variety of 'green' projects, particularly efforts to develop and promote renewable energy and energy conservation technology, constituted a significant part of the stimulus package. Obama had outlined a vision of a clean energy economy which would create millions of green jobs and provide the country with an improved infrastructure to meet the economic challenge posed by China in numerous speeches during his election campaign. ARRA provided a vehicle to advance this agenda and can be construed as articulating an industrial policy as well as an effort to stimulate the economy. Critics have cast considerable doubt on the success of this policy with accusations that large sums of money have been wasted on unneeded projects, but it may be too early to assess its ultimate impact.

The effectiveness of ARRA in stimulating the economy was undermined by reductions in state and local government spending. With revenues from property and other taxes falling rapidly, state governments had to reduce spending and raise taxes to meet balanced-budget requirements. A report by the National Conference of State Legislatures in February 2009 concluded that state governments faced a budgetary shortfall of $135 billion in Fiscal 2010, while a Pew Center on the States report published in June 2012 revealed a $1.35 trillion gap between state assets and their obligations for public sector retirement benefits in Fiscal 2010 (PEW, 2012a). Public sector job losses and battles over pensions and other benefits resulted. BLS data show that state governments shed 43,000 jobs in the 12 months from September 2008 to September 2009, and local governments lost 88,000 jobs. Many state and local governments controlled by Republicans also took action to weaken job security for public sector workers, to attack collective bargaining rights and to reduce pensions and health benefits of public employees under the banner of 'right to work' measures (Sonmez and Fahrenthold, 2012). In Wisconsin these actions eventually led to an unsuccessful effort in June 2012 to recall (i.e. remove from office) the Republican Governor Scott Walker.

Signs that the economy was beginning to recover began to appear in the first half of 2009 with data showing a slowdown in the decline of GDP in the first two quarters (see Figure 11.1). Growth in the third quarter of 2009 signaled the technical end of the recession but few Americans noticed the difference. A backdrop of continued high rates of unemployment meant that public perceptions of employment prospects remained low (see Figure 11. 2). In December 2009 a Gallup Poll tracking American perceptions of the job market revealed that 89 percent of respondents believed it was a 'bad' time to find a quality job; a figure that had changed little over the year (Morales, 2012). Fragile growth and unchanging unemployment rates in the first half of 2010 did little to improve the public mood. A PEW report published in April 2010 revealed that 88 percent of Americans rated national economic conditions as only fair or poor (PEW, 2010a). The same report showed increasing public skepticism about the effectiveness of government action on the economy. Just 33 percent of respondents believed that the stimulus package of 2009 had helped the situation while only 31 percent said that the government had made progress in fixing the problems that had caused the financial crisis. Just 31 percent approved of President Obama's handling of the economy.

Concern about the public finances added to the growing discontent about the Administration's handling of the economy. The annual budget deficit had jumped from $151 billion in 2007 (1.2 percent of GDP) to $415 billion in 2008 (3.2 percent of GDP) as the Bush Administration began to bail out the floundering financial sector and tax revenues fell as the recession took hold, but this increase almost paled into insignificance compared to the dramatic rise in the deficit that occurred in 2009 when the difference between the federal government's spending and revenue reached $1.27 trillion (10.1 percent of GDP) as a consequence of further bailouts and stimulus spending (see Figure 11.3). The deficit fell slightly in 2010 but still remained well above $1 trillion (9 percent of GDP). A deficit of this size had not been seen since 1945 when, in the last year of World War Two, it accounted for 21.5 percent of GDP. The large budget deficits incurred during the Great Recession had a predictable effect on the national debt (see Figure 11.4), which grew from $8.9 trillion in 2007 (64.6 percent of GDP) to $13.5 trillion in 2010 (94.2 percent of GDP). The last time the national debt had approached this level was in 1946 after five years of war when it reached 121 percent of GDP.

Public skepticism about claims of economic recovery and the Administration's handling of the economy, and rising concern about public finances, had important electoral and political consequences in 2010. First, Republicans and Tea Party activists took advantage of rising discontent about the economy to attack the Democrats in the midterm congressional elections. A warning sign that the Democrats could expect electoral problems had occurred as early as January 2010 when the Republican Scott Brown won a special election in Massachusetts caused by Senator Edward Kennedy's death. Brown's victory in a normally safe Democratic state provided evidence of the Party's electoral vulnerability on economic issues that Republicans exploited in the midterm elections held in November 2010. In these elections the Republicans regained control of the House of Representatives and increased their numbers in the Senate. Second, increased concern about the deficit changed the focus of economic policy. Support for further stimulus measures faded as Republicans took advantage of their new political strength to challenge President Obama on a range of issues related to the deficit. Battles over the level of federal spending, rates of taxation and the debt ceiling came to dominate the politics surrounding economic policy in the period leading up to the elections of 2012.

Deficit politics

President Obama had recognized the political problems presented by the burgeoning deficit and had tried to depoliticize the issue early in

Figure 11.3 · *Federal budget surplus/deficit 1990–2012*

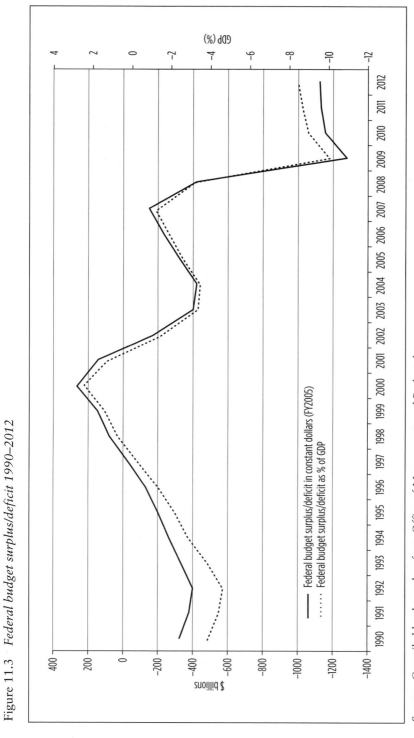

Source: Compiled by the author from Office of Management and Budget data.

Figure 11.4 *Gross federal debt at end of year, 1990–2012*

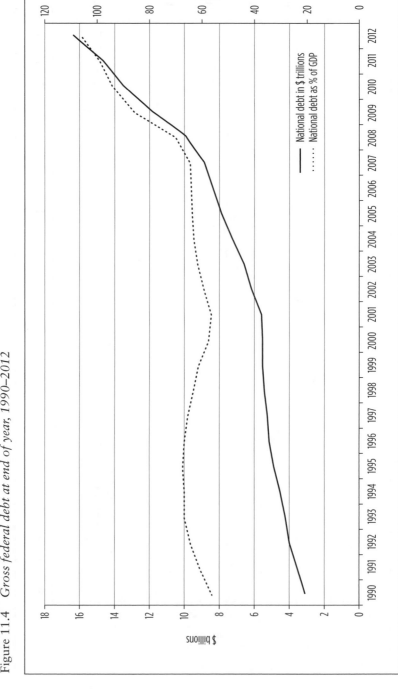

Source: Compiled by the author from Office of Management and Budget data.

2010 by creating a bipartisan National Commission on Fiscal Responsibility and Reform (popularly known as the Simpson-Bowles Deficit Commission after its co-chairs former Republican Senator Alan Simpson and President Clinton's former Chief of Staff Erskine Bowles) to suggest solutions. The Commission produced a report in December 2010 that proposed cuts in discretionary spending and entitlement programs, such as Social Security, Medicare and Medicaid, and increases in revenue largely achieved through tax reforms that would reduce the deficit by $4 trillion by 2014 and eliminate it by 2035. Although supported by 11 of the 18 members of the Commission, the report failed to achieve the 14 votes needed to send it to Congress for a vote. Three Republicans (including House Budget Committee Chair Representative Paul Ryan (R: Wisconsin)) and four Democrats voted against the proposal. Republican opponents of the plan produced by the Simpson-Bowles Deficit Commission claimed that the proposed spending cuts in domestic programs were not large enough, while Democratic critics opposed proposals to means-test entitlement programs.

Partisan battles over the deficit escalated in 2011 when the need to raise the federal government's debt ceiling provided a focus for this struggle. The debt ceiling sets a legal limit on the amount of money that the federal government can borrow to meet its obligations (paying interest on the national debt, federal salaries and other payments). Most other countries do not set legal limits on their borrowing of this sort. Congress has usually raised the debt ceiling level automatically when borrowing has threatened to exceed legal limits, but in 2011 the Republicans decided to use the issue to try to force President Obama to agree to large spending cuts in domestic programs. The opportunity to do this arose in April 2011 when federal government borrowing reached its legal limit. With congressional Republicans rejecting calls to raise the debt ceiling, Treasury Secretary Timothy Geithner declared a 'debt issuance suspension period' which enabled him to take 'extraordinary measures' (including the sale of assets) to meet borrowing requirements. These extraordinary measures provided the means for the federal government to meet its legal obligations until early August 2011. Geithner warned that if the debt ceiling had not been increased by that date the consequences would be catastrophic as the United States would be unable to pay its creditors and a sovereign default was a real possibility. The specter of another financial crisis loomed.

The debt ceiling crisis provoked an intense period of conflict and bargaining between President Obama and Congress. Republicans offered to consider tax reform (though not increases in marginal tax rates) if the Democrats would agree to large spending cuts. President Obama and congressional Democrats agreed to consider a combination of spending cuts and tax rises but only after the debt ceiling had been raised. A compromise was agreed days before the August deadline that

Treasury Secretary Geithner had stated threatened a sovereign default. The Budget Control Act of 2011, signed into law on August 2, 2011, raised the debt ceiling level with immediate effect, specified $917 billion of spending cuts over ten years, and created a Joint Select Committee on Deficit Reduction (known as the 'Supercommittee') to produce a plan for a further $1.5 trillion reduction in the federal deficit by the end of November 2011. Failure to produce a plan would lead to $1.2 trillion in automatic spending cuts in January 2013 in a process known as sequestration. Wall Street delivered its verdict on the agreement when three days after enactment of the Budget Control Act of 2011 the credit rating agency Standard & Poor's downgraded the federal government's credit rating from AAA to AA+.

Standard & Poor's concern that the Budget Control Act of 2011 failed to resolve the problem of the deficit proved prescient. In late November 2011 the Supercommittee announced that it had been unable to reach agreement on a deficit reduction plan acceptable to both sides of the partisan divide. Failure to reach agreement raised the prospect of what Federal Reserve Chair Ben Bernanke labeled a 'fiscal cliff' in testimony to a congressional committee in February 2012 posing a threat to the economic recovery in early 2013 (Geoghegan, 2012). Sequestration and the expiry of Bush-era tax cuts promised a fall in government and individual spending that might push the economy back into recession. One report claimed that falling over the 'cliff' would lead to the loss of two million jobs and raise the unemployment rate by 1.5 percent in 2013 (Fletcher and Goldfarb, 2012). To compound matters the debt ceiling also looked likely to be reached around the same time. In short, the Budget Control Act of 2011 alleviated an immediate crisis but did little to solve the problem of the budget deficit.

The economy, the 2012 election and the 'fiscal cliff'

The conflict over the debt ceiling took place against a backdrop of an economy that stubbornly refused to grow at a pace that restored employment and living standards to levels seen before the Great Recession. Economic growth since the second half of 2009 had been hesitant and had almost stalled on a couple of occasions (see Figure 11. 1). This hesitant recovery produced only limited improvement in the unemployment rate (see Figure 11.2), which appeared stuck at the 9–10 percent mark with the ratio of employment to population remaining historically high (Whoriskey, 2012). Unemployment and under-employment combined with downward pressure on wages to reduce median family income levels, while the housing crash contributed to a fall in the median net worth of families to levels last seen in the early 1990s (Appelbaum, 2012; Mui, 2012). Middle-class families were hardest hit by the collapse in house prices as property constituted a large proportion of their wealth. An economic recovery seemed a long way from the experience of many Americans and led some conservative commentators to talk about 'the worst economic recovery in history' (Lazear, 2012) and the 'weakest non-recession economy in US history' (Pethokoukis, 2012c).

The hesitant nature of the recovery prompted a debate about President Obama's handling of the economy that became increasingly heated as the presidential election of 2012 approached. On one hand, liberal economists such as Joseph Stiglitz (2010) and Paul Krugman (2012) argued that Obama underestimated the depth of the recession and that the stimulus package of 2009 was far too small. Research by Carmen Reinhart and Kenneth Rogoff (2009) suggested that recessions caused by financial crises tend to be deeper, and subsequent recoveries less robust, than economic downturns caused by other factors. Some accounts of the Obama Administration claim that arguments were made for a larger stimulus package in 2009 but that these were scaled back to secure congressional approval (Scheiber, 2012). On the other hand, conservative economists such as John Taylor (2009), and right-wing think tanks such as the Cato Institute and the American Enterprise Institute, argued that President Obama's actions prolonged the recession and slowed the recovery. They claimed that the stimulus package was ineffective and uncertainty about tax and regulatory policies deterred enterprise and the creation of new jobs. Anti-tax groups such as Americans for Tax Reform, led by Grover Norquist, also argued that high taxes damaged the economy. Although the niceties of these disputes between economists may have passed over the heads of most Americans, the public concurred in viewing the government's efforts to resuscitate the economy as inadequate. Opinion polls revealed that the public continued to have major doubts about Obama's management of the economy. A Pew poll conducted in August 2011 showed that only 34 percent approved of the way that he had handled the economy (PEW, 2011).

President Obama offered a major new initiative to boost employment levels on September 8, 2011. Addressing a Joint Session of Congress Obama detailed plans for an American Jobs Act that contained $447 billion of spending on infrastructure projects and tax cuts for small businesses and individuals to stimulate the economy. He claimed that this stimulus would not add to the budget deficit as the cost would be off-set by savings elsewhere. He also announced that the Federal Housing Authority (FHA) would offer loans to struggling homeowners to refinance their mortgages at a lower rate. Although he described the American Jobs Act as non-controversial, as many of its elements had previously enjoyed bipartisan support, his speech reiterated a vision of a networked economy, with an improved infrastructure that could compete with China, and contained an explicit statement of the appropriate role of government that distanced him from both his Republican opponents in Congress and in the forthcoming presidential election. Taking aim at those who believed that government interference in the economy hindered enterprise, he argued that 'this larger notion that the only thing we can do to restore prosperity is just dismantle government, refund everyone's money, and let everyone write their own rules, and tell everyone they're on their own, that's not who we are'. He continued to note that President Abraham Lincoln, a Republican, had provided support for the intercontinental railway, the National Academy of Sciences and land-grant colleges during the Civil War, and that presidents of both parties had supported basic research that had led to the development of the internet, among other things.

The American Jobs Act received a frosty reception from Congress. Republicans derided the plan as 'son of stimulus' that simply revisited failed economic policies, while many Democrats expressed concerns about granting additional tax breaks and increasing spending at a time when the public were concerned about the public finances (Steinbauer, 2011). Action on the legislation stalled in October 2011 when Senate Majority Leader Harry Reid (D: Nevada) failed to secure enough votes to invoke cloture on the measure and subsequent efforts to split the American Jobs Act into separate bills suffered the same fate. Electoral calculations, as much as economic or ideological considerations, lay behind Congress's rejection of the American Jobs Act. Republicans believed that Obama's management of the economy would prove an electoral liability and had no wish to offer him any help in improving his approval ratings on the issue, while Democrats were fearful of damaging their own election prospects by voting for a measure that contained additional government spending. Obama's Address to Congress on September 8, 2011 may have presented a forceful defense of a particular role for government in economic management but it failed to persuade Congress to act.

President Obama offered another stimulus package in the 2013 budget request sent to Congress on February 13, 2012. Obama called for $350 billion in new spending on infrastructure projects, worker retraining programs and hiring more teachers. He proposed to meet deficit reduction targets through modest cuts to Medicare and raising taxes on corporations and individuals earning over $250,000 a year. The highly partisan budget message that accompanied the request contained many of the themes that Obama had developed in his speeches urging action on the American Jobs Act. He repeated his attack on Republican calls for limited government. '[This budget] rejects the "you're on your own" economics that have led to a widening gap between the richest and poorest Americans that undermines our belief in equal opportunity and the engine of our economic growth', he told Congress before offering a vision of the way forward: 'to succeed and thrive in the global, high-tech economy, we need America to be a place with the highest-skilled, highest-educated workers; the most advanced transportation and communication networks; and the strongest commitment to research and technology in the world'. Republicans dismissed Obama's budget as a blatant piece of electioneering. Senate Minority Leader Mitch McConnell (R: Kentucky) described the budget as 'a campaign document' while GOP presidential candidate Governor Mitt Romney called it 'an insult to the American taxpayer' (Montgomery, 2012).

The gap between President Obama and Mitt Romney on economic policy grew wider as the campaign progressed as poor growth and unemployment figures in the summer of 2012 made the economy the primary issue in the election. Economic growth slowed in the second quarter of 2012 and unemployment remained stubbornly high at just over 8 percent in July 2012 (see Figures 11. 1 and 11.2). Campaign speeches highlighted not just differences of opinion between the two candidates on the performance of the economy but also important ideological differences about the role and size of government. Obama claimed that his policies had helped the American economy slowly to recover from the deepest recession since the 1930s and offered a vision of a modernized economy in which government played a major role in educating workers and promoting investment in infrastructure. Romney argued that Obama's policies had slowed the recovery by creating conditions inimical to enterprise, and offered a vision of a competitive economy fueled by low taxes and reduced government regulation. He called for a 'fairer, flatter, simpler' tax system that would lower all marginal rates by 20 percent, reduce taxation of investment and abolish inheritance tax, and proposed capping federal spending at 20 percent of GDP (Noah, 2012). The prominence and vehemence of these exchanges constituted more than the simple campaign rhetoric of two candidates who understood the importance of perceptions of economic well-being to electoral success; they also reflected deep-rooted ideological differences about the role of government in American life. Both candidates made explicit reference to these different visions of the role of government in their campaigns. In a speech to the Business Roundtable in Washington, DC, on June 13, 2012 Romney observed that 'I think this election is a watershed election, which will determine the relationship between citizen and enterprise and government'. The following day Obama agreed that Americans were being offered an important choice. In a major speech on economic policy at Cuyahoga Community College in Cleveland he claimed that 'at stake is not simply a choice between two candidates or two political parties, but between two paths for our country'.

The result of the presidential election surprised many political scientists and commentators who believed that President Obama would not win reelection against a backdrop of a poorly performing economy. A number of factors account for Obama's victory but two stand out when considering the impact of the economy on the result. First, *national* economic indicators were less important to the electoral outcome than the performance of *local* economies in key, swing states. Unemployment rates in states like Ohio, for example, were lower than the national average allowing Obama to tell a story of economic improvement in those states. Second, voters realized that the economic problems facing the country were deep-rooted and would need more than four years to turn round. Obama was reelected because he was able to offer the voters a more convincing explanation of the causes of America's problems and the best way to make the country more competitive. This was not an unconditional endorsement, however, of 'Obamanomics'. Exit and opinion polls taken at the time of the election, or just after, showed that the voters supported higher taxes for the wealthy and reduced government spending (Cassidy, 2012). They supported government intervention to help the economy but believed that high budget deficits should be reduced. Republican success in maintaining control of the House of Representatives also confused the message that the voters were sending on economic policy. Americans may have preferred Obama's economic vision, but they also returned many proponents of 'you're on your own' economics to office. The difficulties this would cause became apparent when President Obama returned to Washington to seek a solution to the 'fiscal cliff' facing the country in January 2013.

Negotiations to avoid the fiscal cliff of tax rises and cuts in government spending scheduled for January 1, 2013 dominated economic policy-making in the weeks following Obama's reelection in November 2012. Obama sought to take advantage of his electoral victory and opinion polls showing widespread public support for raising taxes on the wealthy to force Republicans to agree to a plan that would avert the threat of the cliff. He proposed that Bush-era tax cuts due to expire at the end of December 2012 should be extended indefinitely except for those earning over $250,000 per year, that $400 billion should be cut from Medicare and that targeted reductions in government spending should be identified to replace the across the board cuts mandated under the Budget Control Act of 2011. Republican leaders countered with proposals to extend the Bush-era tax cuts in their entirety, overhaul the tax code to remove a number of deductions and dramatically cut government spending. Resolving the differences between the two sides, particularly over the question of taxes on the wealthy, proved difficult as both sides claimed an electoral mandate for their position. Disagreements between Republican leaders and a very conservative Republican caucus in the House of Representatives further complicated negotiations with Speaker Boehner unable to command unconditional support from Majority Leader Eric Cantor or a majority of Republicans on the issue. Eventually a last minute deal brokered by Vice President Joe Biden that raised taxes for those individuals earning more than $400,000 per year (and families earning more than $450,000), left the taxes of other Americans unchanged and postponed a decision about spending cuts until March 2013 proved acceptable to both sides and was finally agreed by Congress on January 1, 2013. President Obama signed the American Taxpayer Relief Act of 2012 into law on January 2, 2013.

The American Taxpayer Relief Act prevented the United States from tumbling over the fiscal cliff by postponing hard decisions for a few months but did little to tackle the underlying issues that had caused the problem in the first place. President Obama spent the next two months trying to persuade congressional Republicans to accept further tax rises and targeted cuts in government spending rather than the across-the-board spending cuts due to come into effect in March 2013, but he was unable to reach a compromise. Two months after passage of the American Taxpayer Relief Act the country finally stumbled over the fiscal cliff when Obama was forced to sign a sequestration measure that required more than $25 billion of cuts in government spending over the next six months and $1.2 trillion in cuts over the next decade. Sequestration not only undermined the economic vision that Obama had articulated during his reelection campaign, and which he reaffirmed in his Inaugural Address on January 21, 2013 and his State of the Union Address on February 12, 2013, but also threatened to stall the country's economic recovery (Goldfarb, 2013). Cuts in spending, rather than increased investment, started to take place just four months after Obama's reelection leading a number of economists to predict the loss of around 750,000 jobs and a 0.6 percent fall in economic growth.

Conclusion

Partisan and ideological differences in Washington, DC, have produced a short-term or stop-gap approach to economic policy-making in which medium-term planning and budgeting have all but disappeared. Fundamental disagreements about the role of government in American life, and associated arguments about levels of taxation and spending, form the basis of these differences. Data produced by the Office of Management and Budget reveal that federal spending in recent years has been significantly higher than average over the last 50 years while average rates of taxation in the same period have been lower than at any time since 1960 (Cook, 2013). Reactions to these findings is shaped by partisan and ideological factors. Democrats focus on the evidence of low rates of taxation and argue that more revenue has to be raised, while Republicans concentrate on the data about levels of spending and insist that this needs to be cut. In the battle to avoid the fiscal cliff President Obama initially managed to focus attention on taxation and forced the Republicans to face difficult choices, but the subsequent effort to avoid sequestration revealed the limits of Republican willingness to give further ground. Future battles over the budget will likely focus on spending and will undoubtedly force Democrats to face difficult decisions about which programs to cut. The result will almost certainly be further stop-gap measures which postpone hard decisions on the budget deficit and leave economic policy-making in a muddled state.

Chapter 12

American Social Policy

Richard C. Fording

It has long been conventional wisdom that public spending on social welfare is relatively small in the United States compared to the rest of the industrialized world. Yet, over the last century the share of American government spending (combined federal, state and local) on social welfare programs has increased from a mere 0.5 percent of gross domestic product in 1914 to nearly one fifth (18.5 percent) in 2011. (Federal government spending data reported in this chapter were obtained from the Executive Office of the President, Office of Management and Budget, 2010; state and local spending data were obtained from United States Census Bureau.) On a per capita basis, this amounted to $7,786 per person in 2011. Although the United States still spends less than most other affluent industrialized nations, social welfare programs clearly represent a significant source of government spending. In 2012, spending on social programs (excluding education) comprised nearly half (45 percent) of all government spending, and a majority (56 percent) of all federal government spending. Consequently, it is not surprising that social programs have been at the center of recent political debates over alternative strategies to reduce the federal debt.

In this chapter I summarize recent trends and controversies surrounding American social programs. The chapter begins with a brief history and descriptive overview of the broad array of social programs that comprise the American welfare state. I then turn to a more focused discussion of the current challenges facing some of the most important social programs, beginning with a discussion of the looming revenue shortfalls projected to occur within the Social Security and Medicare programs, as well as the range of solutions proposed to fix them. I then move to a discussion of recent trends and policy changes in the major public assistance programs that make up the 'safety net' for the poor. The remainder of the chapter addresses debates over the effectiveness of the social welfare programs, particularly in the light of recent expansions of public spending during the economic downturn. This question has been the subject of much debate, especially considering the fact that American poverty rates have consistently increased over the last several years.

Social welfare programs in the United States: an overview

The growth of the American welfare state during the last century has largely been the product of two bursts of policy-making activity. Prior to the 1930s, social welfare provision in the United States was generally left to private charities. Although the federal government funded a few small programs, the vast majority of the disadvantaged were left to rely on private sources or a patchwork of programs that were designed and funded by state and local governments. This changed dramatically during the Great Depression, when the foundation for the modern welfare state was first laid with the passage of the Social Security Act of 1935 (SSA). Some of the most important social welfare programs operating today can be traced in one form or another back to this original legislation, including Social Security, Unemployment Insurance (UI), Supplemental Security Income (SSI) and Temporary Assistance for Needy Families (TANF).

The second important period of policy innovation occurred during the 1960s, amidst a wave of protest movements and Lyndon Johnson's War on Poverty. This era saw the passage of legislation that created two of the largest public assistance programs in the country today. The Food Stamp program was passed in 1964 to provide food vouchers to poor people across the country. Today, this program is known as the Supplemental Nutritional Assistance Program (SNAP). The Medicaid program was created in 1965 to provide access to healthcare for a large segment of the nation's poor. Its passage was coupled with that of the Medicare program, which provides healthcare for the population covered by Social Security. This era also witnessed a significant expansion of many existing public assistance programs. One of the most controversial expansions was the increase in benefit generosity and the broadening of eligibility rules within the Aid to Families with Dependent Children (AFDC) program, which eventually evolved into the TANF program in 1996.

The significance of these two historical periods, as well as their impact on the trajectory of social insurance and public assistance spending, can be seen in Figure 12.1. The figure plots the total amount of government spending (combined federal, state and local) on social welfare programs as a percentage of gross domestic product for three different categories of social welfare spending. Spending on 'pension' programs largely consists of spending on Social Security, but it also

Figure 12.1 *US Social welfare spending by expenditure category, 1913–2010 (GDP %)*

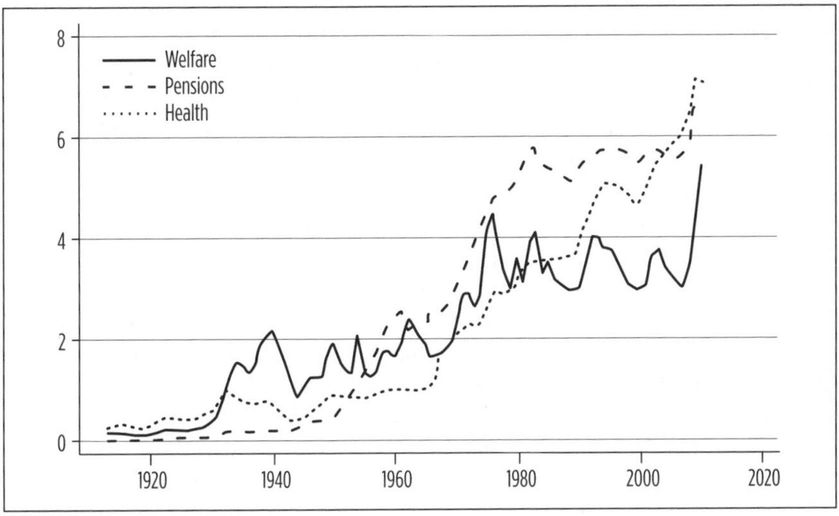

Source: data from www.usgovernmentspending.com (2003).

includes other government pension programs for retired government workers and veterans. 'Health' spending is dominated by spending on Medicaid and Medicare but also includes smaller government-funded healthcare programs. Spending on 'welfare' programs reflects government spending on programs targeted on the poor and the unemployed (including UI). Collectively, these programs comprised only 0.8 percent of GDP at the onset of the Great Depression in 1929. Spending within each category has significantly increased over time, and total social welfare spending now comprises nearly 20 percent of GDP.

The structure of the American welfare state

The American welfare state stands out from those of other Western nations in two important ways. First and perhaps most importantly, social policy experts have frequently described the American system as 'two-tiered'. The 'upper tier' consists of 'social insurance' programs, which are funded by contributions from program beneficiaries and generally cover broad segments of the population, regardless of income. The three most important social insurance programs that are still in existence today include Social Security, Medicare and UI. The 'lower tier' consists of what are termed 'public assistance' programs.

These are purely redistributive in the sense that they are funded mostly by nonparticipants through taxes; participants pay a relatively small share, if any, of the program costs. These are also the programs that most Americans have in mind when they use the term 'welfare'. The largest such programs today are Medicaid, SNAP, SSI and TANF. This lower tier also consists of state and local General Assistance (GA) programs, which provide cash assistance to a wide range of poor persons who are ineligible for federally funded (or subsidized) public assistance programs.

In contrast to social insurance, public assistance programs tend to be highly targeted and limited to the poor. As a consequence, they also tend to be far less popular than social insurance programs, which are universal in coverage. Indeed, public opinion data over the last four decades has consistently shown that a majority of Americans have favored increasing the generosity of the Social Security program. In contrast, approximately half of Americans polled since the early 1970s consistently support reducing the generosity of 'welfare' programs (Gilens, 1999). This remains true today, despite historic increases in poverty and inequality in recent years. Indeed, as of 2012, according to the General Social Survey only 19 percent of Americans supported increasing 'welfare' spending, while 48 percent believed it should be reduced. In the same survey, 56 percent of respondents supported increased spending on Social Security, while only 8 percent supported spending reductions. This contrast in support continues to be reflected in the political debates surrounding these programs and it is undoubtedly an important reason why social insurance programs tend to be better-funded than public assistance programs.

A second distinctive feature of the US welfare state is that much of its financing and administration is decentralized. State and local governments have traditionally been responsible for a sizable share of social welfare spending and have enjoyed a good deal of discretion in setting benefit levels and eligibility requirements for many programs. This is especially true for public assistance programs targeted on the poor. This fact has had important consequences for the generosity of many social programs. Decentralized programs tend to reflect a significant amount of variation across states in benefit levels and eligibility rules due to differences in state political environment and culture. In addition, many scholars believe that allowing states to choose benefit levels leads to a 'race to the bottom' in which states keep benefit levels relatively low to reduce the possibility that poor people might migrate to their state to enroll in their welfare programs (Peterson and Rom, 1990).

Although spending has dramatically increased over the last 80 years, the two-tiered structure of the social welfare system, as well as its relatively decentralized design, remain largely intact. Table 12.1 helps to illustrate this fact by providing a descriptive summary of some of the most important social insurance and public assistance programs in the United States today. The table reveals several key differences between the two sets of programs that are important in understanding the politics that surrounds them. First, eligibility for the three social insurance programs – Social Security, Medicare and UI – is much broader. Anyone can participate in Social Security and Medicare as long as they have contributed to the programs through payroll taxes for at least ten years. UI is financed by a tax on employers, but in effect the design is very similar since it is generally agreed that the tax is partly passed down to employees through lower wages. Each of these programs now covers over 90 percent of the labor force. In contrast, eligibility for public assistance is much more restrictive as all applicants must pass an income test. The test varies from program to program, and some are more restrictive than others. Public assistance programs are also much more likely to be targeted to specific demographic groups than social insurance programs. In particular, families with children (including non-disabled adults), the elderly and disabled are most likely to be eligible for assistance.

It is also clear from the table that public assistance programs are likely to be decentralized. That is, state and local governments tend to have significantly more policy-making discretion and financial responsibility for public assistance than they do for social insurance programs. The federal government is entirely responsible for financing the Social Security and Medicare programs, and as a result benefit levels are determined in an identical fashion in every state. UI is an important exception, but even though there is significant variation in UI benefits, they are considerably higher than those offered by public assistance programs.

Most public assistance programs, on the other hand, reflect at least some degree of state government discretion when it comes to setting benefit levels or establishing conditions for receiving aid, or both. The two most significant examples of decentralization can be seen within the Medicaid and TANF programs, and this has resulted in a great deal of variation in eligibility and benefit levels across the states. For example, as can be seen in Table 12.1, there is significant variation in Medicaid payments, which can be explained by the discretion that states have in deciding which types of medical services to cover. The federal government reimburses states for about two-thirds of program costs as long as the states cover certain basic services, such as physicians' services, inpatient and outpatient hospital services, and laboratory and x-ray fees. However, state governments have many options to cover additional services with the same level of federal reimbursement, or with state funds. Some of the more common optional services include diagnostic services, intermediate care facility services, prescribed drugs and prosthetic devices, optometrist services and specta-

Table 12.1 Characteristics of major US social welfare programs, 2010

	Social insurance programs			Public assistance programs			
	Social Security	Medicare	UI	SNAP	SSI	Medicaid	TANF
Historical origin	1935	1965	1935	1964	1935	1965	1935
Eligibility	Retired workers, their survivors, and disabled	Retired workers, their survivors, and disabled	Unemployed workers	Individuals and families living below the poverty threshold	Elderly and disabled people living below the poverty threshold	Limited-income families with children, SSI recipients	Low-income families with children
Recipient rate (% of US population)	17.5	15.0	4.6	13.0	2.6	20.2	1.4
Average monthly benefit	$1,074 per person (cash)	$410 per person (medical services)	$1,268 per person (cash)	$133 per person (food voucher)	$570 per person (cash)	$461 per person (medical services)	$232 per person (cash + services)
Funding source	Payroll tax	Payroll tax	Employer tax	General revenue (federal)	General revenue (federal and optional state)	General revenue (federal and state)	General revenue (federal and state)

Total cost ($ billion)	713	248	79.5	68.3	43.3	389	35.8
Total cost (% GDP)	4.9	1.8	0.6	0.5	0.3	2.7	0.3
Administration	Federal	Federal	Federal and state	Federal and state and local	Federal	Federal and state	Federal and state or local
State variation in monthly benefit level (minimum and maximum)	Uniform benefits across states	Uniform benefits across states	MS: $784 HI: $1,692	Uniform benefits across states	ND: $423 HI: $989	CA: $294 CT: $798	Cash benefit for three-person family: MS: $170 AK: $923
State variation in eligibility rules	Uniform eligibility across states	Uniform eligibility across states	Significant variation in eligibility	Uniform eligibility across states	Uniform eligibility across states	Significant variation in eligibility	Significant variation in eligibility

Sources: data from Social Security Administration (2012); US Dept Agriculture, Food and Nutrition Service (2013); US Dept of Labor, Employment and Training Administration (2013); US Dept Health and Human Services, Administration for Children and Families (2010); Kaiser Foundation (2009).

cles, rehabilitation and physical therapy services, hospice care, and family planning services.

The states also have a significant amount of discretion in deciding who is eligible for Medicaid. The federal government has long required that states cover most poor or near-poor families with children, as well as those who are eligible for SSI. However, beyond the federal requirements, states have significant flexibility to extend coverage. The clearest example of this flexibility is the option to cover a state-defined population that is deemed 'medically needy'. As a result, we see a significant amount of variation in Medicaid coverage across the states that cannot be explained by variation in poverty rates. For example, in the state of Maine approximately 21 percent of the population participated in Medicaid in 2010, despite the fact that the poverty rate in the state was only 11 percent. In contrast, the poverty rate in New Hampshire (13 percent) significantly exceeded the Medicaid participation rate of 8 percent because Maine has used its discretion to extend Medicaid to a significantly wider pool of families and children.

There is even greater variation in the benefits and eligibility requirements within the TANF program. As Table 12.1 indicates, Mississippi, the state with the lowest monthly benefit level in 2010 (for a family of three with no other income), provided a mere $170 a month. Alaska had the highest benefit level for an equivalent family at $923 a month. The average benefit level across all the states was $436. The states also vary a great deal in their TANF eligibility policies. The federal government requires that all states enforce a number of different rules, yet they are free to set their own standards for these rules as long as they are stricter than the federal government's. For example, although the federal government requires that TANF recipients be engaged in at least 30 hours of work activities a week within 24 months of receiving TANF benefits, about a dozen states require TANF recipients (single parents) to work more than 30 hours (up to 40 hours). And although the federal government requires states to enforce a maximum 60-month time limit on the lifetime receipt of aid, 11 states have adopted stricter times limits. Finally, 14 states have taken advantage of state options to implement a 'family cap' on additional benefits when children are born to families on welfare.

A third difference between social insurance programs and public assistance programs is that the former tend to be more generous than the latter. The one exception to this in Table 12.1 concerns healthcare, where Medicaid and Medicare benefits appear to be relatively similar when spending is calculated on a per recipient basis. However, for cash (or in the case of SNAP, near-cash) programs, the benefits paid by public assistance programs are much smaller than the cash payments provided by social insurance programs.

The financial solvency of Social Security and Medicare

The last two decades have witnessed both stability and change in American social policy. There has been relatively little change in policies governing the two most important social insurance programs – Social Security and Medicare. Although the challenges facing both programs have been the subject of much debate, competing interests have caused a political stalemate that threatens the financial future of both programs. In contrast, there has been significant change in public assistance programs over the last two decades. In response to rising welfare caseloads, public assistance programs were transformed through national legislation in 1996 (The Personal Responsibility and Work Opportunity Reconciliation Act) that has had profound consequences on program rules, participation rates and ultimately the lives of the poor. Although the federal government has recently increased the investment in public assistance programs to respond to rising need during the economic downturn, important gaps remain in the safety net, and poverty and income inequality continue to rise.

The funding structure of Social Security and Medicare is relatively simple. Future beneficiaries (workers) contribute a portion of their earnings through a payroll tax. The revenue collected from this tax goes into a trust fund that is used to pay for the benefits received by current program beneficiaries. Throughout most of the program's history, Social Security has regularly generated a surplus because the number of workers has been large relative to the number of beneficiaries. Over the years, however, increases in life expectancy and the resultant increase in the percentage of retired workers have caused this surplus to shrink. As of 2000, there were approximately 3.4 workers paying payroll taxes for every Social Security recipient. Since 2000, that ratio has been declining and is expected to level out at approximately 2.0 workers per beneficiary by 2020. Expansions of Social Security to survivors of beneficiaries and disabled workers, in addition to increases in the real value of benefits, have also contributed to the shrinking revenue surplus. As a result, Social Security expenditures began to exceed payroll tax revenues in 2010. Although the trust fund is large enough to keep the program afloat for several more years, according to the most recent report of the Social Security Board of Trustees, under the current program rules the fund would be completely exhausted by 2034.

Although the funding problem within Social Security is relatively straightforward, the politics of Social Security has ensured that correcting the problem is extremely difficult. There would seem to be four possible strategies that have been offered in recent years. The first and perhaps most unpopular proposal today is partially to privatize Social Security by diverting a portion of workers' contributions into private saving accounts based on the stock market. This strategy was more popular when it was proposed by President George W. Bush during the early 2000s, but the volatility of the stock market in recent years has effectively ended the viability of privatization as a serious alternative, at least for the time being.

Although the remaining solutions to the problems with Social Security have been used in the past to keep the program solvent, they also face significant opposition from voters. One of the most commonly debated strategies would slow the growth in the beneficiary population by gradually increasing the minimum retirement age to receive full benefits. A change of this kind would be most preferred by current retirees since this change would not affect their benefits. Throughout the entire history of Social Security, this has only been successfully accomplished once, when Congress increased the retirement age from 65 to 67 in 1983. However, to avoid political fallout from non-retired workers at the time, the increase was not scheduled to be fully implemented until 2017. A proposal to increase the retirement age to 70 was the centerpiece of Mitt Romney's strategy to fix Social Security, but it is unclear whether there is bipartisan support for such a proposal.

A third strategy for dealing with the revenue imbalance would be to reduce the benefit levels received. Although the history of Social Security has been largely one of benefit increases, legislation passed in 1983, and later expanded in 1993, allowed benefits to be subject to federal income taxes. These taxes are used to help fund Social Security itself. This policy has effectively reduced Social Security benefits for higher-earning retirees. During the 2012 presidential election campaign, Mitt Romney proposed adjusting the benefit formula in a way that would further reduce the benefits of higher-earning retirees. President Obama, on the other hand, has recently proposed applying a new cost of living index to Social Security that would effectively slow the growth in benefits by reducing the magnitude of the cost of living adjustments through the use of something called the 'chained' consumer price index. As of mid-2013, this proposal had yet to be passed by Congress.

A fourth strategy for solving the financial problems within Social Security is to increase the amount of revenue generated by increasing the payroll tax. This strategy has been used fairly often throughout the history of the Social Security program. Indeed, between 1970 and 1990, the employee share of the total payroll tax for Social Security and Medicare steadily increased from 4.8 percent to its current rate of 7.65 percent. Yet, there have been no increases since 1990. One proposal that has been supported by President Obama and other Democrats has been to increase the tax rate among higher-income workers by raising the maximum taxable earnings level, which currently stands at $113,700 for 2013. According to current program rules, if a worker earns more than $113,700 in 2013, those earnings are not subject to the Social Security payroll tax. For example, this means that workers who earn twice this amount – $227,400 – are subject to a payroll tax on their total 2013 earnings that is only half the rate of workers earning less than $113,700. And of course, the payroll tax does not even apply to non-wage income, which is more likely to be received by higher-income workers. The regressive nature of the payroll tax is partly offset by the fact that the Social Security benefit formula ensures that high-income retirees receive a lower percentage of their average pre-retirement income than lower-income retirees, but most Americans still seem to believe that the financing system is unfair. Indeed, public opinion research finds broad support for either raising the 'tax cap' or eliminating it entirely and ensuring that all workers are subject to the same tax rate on their total annual earnings (Page and Jacobs, 2010).

The Medicare program shares the same funding formula as Social Security, and therefore it suffers from very similar problems. Yet, there are a few important differences. First, the problems with Medicare are much more urgent. The program already operates at a deficit (since 2008) and according to the most recent projections, published by the Medicare Board of Trustees, the trust fund will be entirely exhausted ten years sooner than Social Security in 2024. But even this projection may be too optimistic. This forecast assumes that the projected future costs of Medicare reflect significant savings due to the implementation of the Affordable Care Act (ACA), the national healthcare reform bill passed in 2010, which is often referred to as 'Obamacare' (see Chapter 13). Most importantly, the ACA requires a large reduction in payment rates for physician services that was scheduled to take effect in 2013. However, there is some concern that lawmakers may prevent these payment decreases from being implemented, largely due to opposition by the providers. If the full savings of the ACA are not realized, the state of Medicare may be even more urgent.

Even if the savings from ACA do in fact materialize, the Medicare program faces significant financial challenges. Unfortunately, solving the financial imbalance would appear to be even more challenging than fixing Social Security. Like Social Security, there is widespread support for preserving Medicare. Yet, the costs of the program are far less predictable because they depend on the rate at which program beneficiaries utilize healthcare services, as well as the costs of those services. Neither of these factors is within the strict control of policy-makers. Like Social Security, one possible strategy is to raise the payroll tax. This approach is being implemented with the ACA and will result in a tax rate increase of 0.9 percent for workers earning more than $200,000 a year (or married couples earning more than $250,000 a year). It is hard to imagine that the public will support similar increases in tax rates for middle-class and working-class Americans earning less than this amount.

There seems to be more support for increasing the minimum retirement age for Medicare. Unlike Social Security, the retirement age for Medicare has remained at 65 and there appears to be some support for aligning the retirement age across the two programs (the Social Security retirement age will reach 67 in 2017). The idea has received strongest support from congressional Republicans, but President Obama has indicated that he might be open to it as well. Yet, critics of raising the Medicare retirement age claim that it might have several undesirable consequences. Most importantly, adding 66 and 67 year olds to the private insurance rolls may result in increased private health insurance premiums due to the fact that health care costs for the 66–67-year-old population are greater than those for younger workers (Neuman et al., 2011). The Congressional Budget Office has also projected that increasing the Medicare eligibility age to 67 may cause an increase in the number of uninsured. Finally, many have criticized this option because the burden will be disproportionately felt by low-income workers, who are more likely than high-income workers to suffer from significant health problems prior to age 67. Unsurprisingly, this proposal has been strongly opposed by the American Association of Retired Persons (AARP), one of the most powerful interest groups in Washington.

One reform proposal that aims to deal with the long-term challenges of Medicare and which has generated a great deal of discussion is Representative Paul Ryan's (R: Wisconsin) proposal to turn Medicare into a 'premium support' system, or as critics charge, a voucher system. Under Ryan's plan, new Medicare beneficiaries would receive their health coverage through competing private insurance plans rather than traditional Medicare. The federal government would contribute a fixed amount to pay the premiums for the private insurance plan. Supporters of the plan argue that the costs of providing health care coverage would ultimately grow at a slower rate due to the introduction of competing plans. Critics of a premium support system argue that it is not clear that any savings would materialize. They claim that the Medicare Advantage program, which offers supplemental health coverage to Medicare beneficiaries, already operates in such a fashion and there has been little evidence of cost savings. Rather, opponents claim that moving to a premium support system may result in a higher cost for beneficiaries. This is due to the fact that if the private insurance premiums prove to be higher than the federal contribution, seniors would be required to pay the difference. There is also concern that under the current proposal in Congress, government contributions would not increase as fast as the cost of the premiums. With the reelection of President Obama, it is doubtful that a premium support program will materialize, at least in the near future. Rather, if Obama has his way, the financial challenges of the Medicare program will be fought through a variety of strategies that include reforms to the payment structure, a reduction in fraud and an emphasis on preventative care.

Public assistance programs and the erosion of the safety net

In contrast to social insurance programs, which have generally withstood the efforts of politicians to trim program costs, public assistance programs have not fared nearly as well over the last two decades. There are several reasons for these divergent trends. One important explanation is the resurgence of neo-liberalism and its influence within the Republican Party since the election of Ronald Reagan. Welfare programs have also become increasingly associated with racial minorities, thus leading to further stigmatization of public assistance recipients within the (majority) white electorate. As a result, public opinion data consistently find that relatively few Americans support increases in public assistance programs, and that opposition to public assistance is strongest among conservatives. According to the General Social Survey, by 2012 nearly half of all Americans, and approximately 70 percent of Republicans, responded that the national government was spending 'too much' on welfare programs. In contrast, only 19 percent of Americans (and a mere 10 percent of Republicans) throught that the government was spending 'too little'.

Finally, unlike the target populations for social insurance programs (e.g. the elderly and the average citizen), public assistance recipients are among the most politically weak constituencies. Thus, given the increased fiscal stress experienced by state governments in recent decades, it is no surpise that welfare generosity has decreased in every state since the early 1970s, while the sharpest declines have been seen in states with conservative political leadership and in those where racial and ethnic minorities comprise a significant share of the poverty population (Soss et al., 2011).

This decline in public assistance generosity is partly evident in Figure 12.1, where we see that in contrast to government investment in health and pension programs, public spending on 'income maintenance' peaked in the 1970s and declined slightly with each economic recovery through the mid-2000s. Yet, the trend in aggregate spending does not tell the full story, as some programs have suffered more than others. And despite recent increases in public assistance spending in response to the Great Recession, significant holes remain in the safety net.

One of the most dramatic decreases in public assistance program generosity has occurred within the TANF program, which has historically been the largest cash assistance program for poor families with children. According to a recent study, TANF benefits have fallen by 20 percent or more in 34 states since 1996, leaving benefit levels below 50 percent of the poverty line in every state (Finche and Schott, 2011). The decline in TANF benefits has coincided with a long-term reduction in the generosity of state General Assistance (GA) programs. As late as the mid-1970s, every state had some type of GA program in place to provide state-funded assistance for poor individuals and families who were ineligible for other federally-funded programs. As of today, many states have abolished GA entirely, and GA benefits in many other states have been severely restricted (Gallagher, 1999). As a result, the safety net has been left with significant gaps in coverage, and those who are not eligible to receive benefits from federally-funded programs – most non-disabled, working-aged men – have nowhere to turn if they fall beneath the poverty line.

Recent research has shown that one of the most significant consequences of the decline in TANF benefit levels has been a decline in its participation. Prior to 1996 when it was terminated, AFDC was the largest cash public assistance program in the country and the participation rate among eligible families was over 80 percent. Since the introduction of TANF, the national caseload has declined by over 60 percent. Today, less than 40 percent of eligible families participate in TANF. In addition to the erosion of benefit levels, research has also found that the decline in TANF caseloads is linked to a tightening of eligibility requirements adopted in 1996, including such reforms as strict work requirements, time limits for the receipt of aid, various behavioral requirements, and strict financial penalties for noncompliance with program rules. Although many poor families have lost benefits due to lifetime limits on the receipt of benefits, it appears that the majority of the decline in TANF participation is due to the fact that many poor families are discouraged from applying for it in the first place due to strict work requirements (30–40 hours per week) and benefit levels that fall well below the poverty line in every state.

Concerns over the adequacy of TANF in meeting the needs of poor families have heightened during the Great Recession. Under AFDC, caseloads usually increased during a recession in response to the increase in program eligibility. Over the last several years, however, TANF caseloads have continued to decrease and remained virtually flat during the most recent recession. This can be seen in Figure 12.2, which displays recent trends in the national caseloads for AFDC/TANF, SNAP, SSI and UI. As can be seen, state TANF caseloads barely grew during one of the most severe economic crises in American history. The same cannot be said, however, for the other programs. Indeed, SNAP caseloads reached their highest level in program history during the recession and have doubled since 2000. There are likely several reasons for these

Figure 12.2   *Trends in UI and major cash assistance programs, 1970–2011*

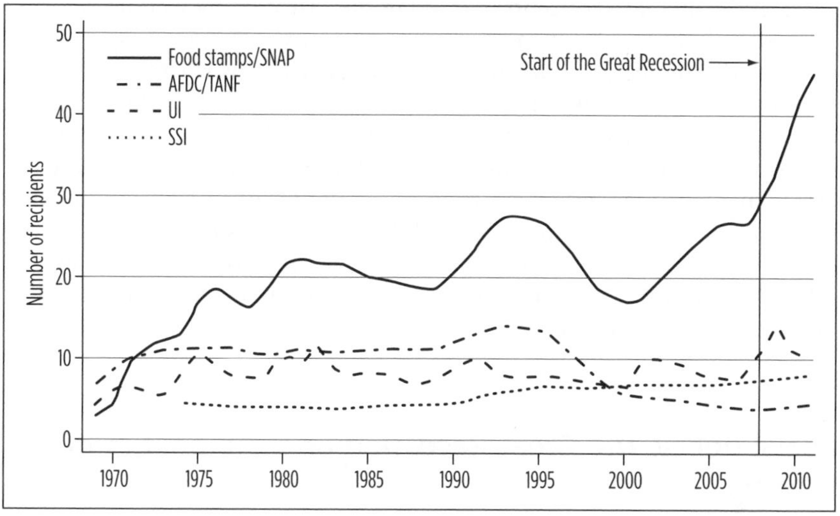

Sources: data from Social Security Administration (2012); US Dept Agriculture, Food and Nutrition Service (2013); US Dept of Labor, Employment and Training Administration (2013); US Dept Health and Human Services, Administration for Children and Families (2010).

divergent trends in TANF and the other programs. Most importantly, the other programs are not subject to the same strict eligibility requirements as TANF. It is generally easier to qualify for all of the other programs and it is easier to maintain eligibility once enrolled. In addition, benefit levels for all of these programs have increased steadily over time, in contrast to TANF. Finally, SNAP and SSI benefits are entirely funded by the federal government, while a significant portion of the costs of the TANF program are shared by the states. As a result, states have a greater financial incentive to enroll their poor families in SNAP and SSI compared to TANF. Many experts believe this is an important cause of the historic increases in the SNAP caseload.

Although it appears that TANF has been successful in reducing the welfare rolls, its lack of responsiveness during the Great Recession raises serious doubts about whether the program has been successful in achieving the goal of promoting economic self-sufficiency among the poor. The most recent studies which examine the long-term effects of TANF, as well as its impact across individuals at different income levels, are not optimistic and suggest that the most disadvantaged poor women are actually worse off (Ziliak, 2009). Concerns over the possible negative effects of TANF on the well-being of the poor are also heightened by several alarming trends. The number of families living in extreme poverty (earning less than $2 per person a day in a given month) increased sharply from 1.46 million in 1996 to 2.4 million in 2011, with most of the increase concentrated in families affected by welfare reform.

Finally, there has been increasing concern over the growing population of 'disconnected women', a term used by poverty researchers to describe low-income women who report themselves as neither working nor on welfare. According to some estimates, the size of this population doubled between the mid-1990s and mid-2000s and now stands at 20–25 percent (depending on the precise definition) of all low-income women (Blank and Kovak, 2008). Relatively little is known about how these women are surviving, but even if they are working in the informal labor market, research has shown that such jobs are less likely to lead to advancement.

Social policy, the Great Recession and the politics of poverty

Despite spending nearly 20 percent of GDP on social welfare programs in recent years, the poverty rate in the United States remains relatively high compared to other rich, industrialized nations. Even more distressing is the fact that poverty in the United States has been increasing for the last several years. This is evident in Figure 12.3, which displays the historical trend in US poverty rates – the percentage of the population that lives beneath the poverty line ($22,811 for a family of four in 2011). At the same time that poverty has been increasing, so too has the level of income inequality. Evidence of this fact is also displayed in Figure 12.3, which presents the ratio of annual income at the 90th percentile of the income distribution to that of the 10th percentile. According to the most recent Census Bureau data, the national poverty rate stood at 15.0 percent in 2011, relatively unchanged from 15.1 percent in 2010. Since 1965, the poverty rate has exceeded the 2010 value only once, and that was in 1983 during the presidency of Ronald Reagan.

Similarly, by 2011 the income level of Americans at the 90th percentile was 12 times that of the income level at the 10th percentile. This trend has been fueled in part by the erosion of the safety net and the growing poor population, but it has also been fed by reductions in the marginal tax rates for the richest Americans. These tax cuts, which have since become known as the Bush tax cuts, originated from legislation passed in 2001 and 2003 and remain largely intact. This has contributed to a level of income inequality that is unprecedented in recent American history and which has not been seen since prior to the Great Depression.

Over the last decade, the increase in poverty has been concentrated among working-age adults and children, reflecting the erosion of the safety net for poor families. Indeed, between 2001 and 2011 the

Figure 12.3   *US poverty rates and income inequality, 1967–2011*

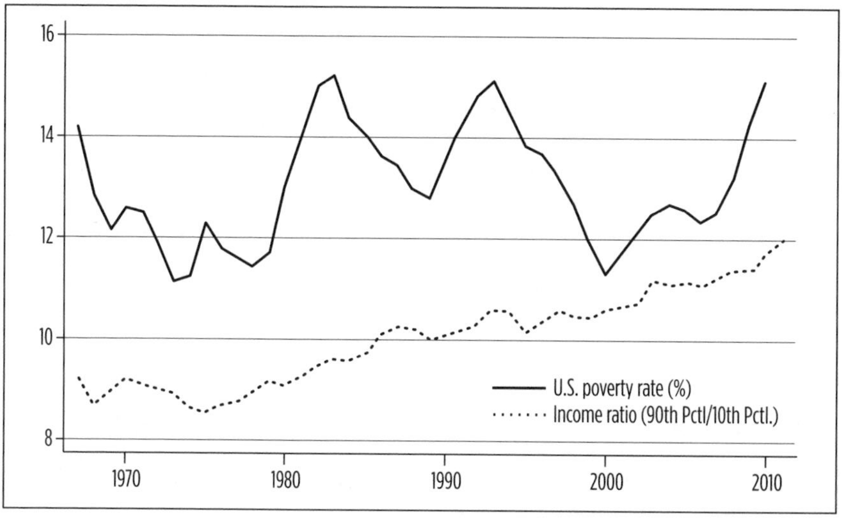

Source: DeNavas-Walt et al. (2012).

poverty rate for children increased from 15.8 to 21.4 percent – an increase of 27 percent in the number of children in poverty. In contrast, poverty rates among the elderly actually decreased during the same ten-year period, from 10.1 to 8.7 percent. This is reflective of a long-term reduction in the poverty rates of the elderly that is due in large part to the relative generosity of the Social Security program. Further evidence of the effectiveness of Social Security as a poverty-reducing force is provided in Table 12.2, which displays two sets of estimates of the number of poor Americans – one set of estimates that counts Social Security benefits in the calculation of income and an alternative set of estimates that does not. As can be seen, Social Security lifted over 21 million people out of poverty in 2011, approximately two-thirds of whom were elderly. Without Social Security, the poverty rate among the elderly would be nearly 44 percent, but after counting Social Security income that rate is reduced to a mere 8.7 percent.

As one might expect, President Obama has increasingly come to be blamed, at least in part, for the historic increases in poverty. Some of this criticism has come from the right, which has used the poverty statistics to attack the President's 'failed' economic policies. What is less expected, and perhaps even more problematic for Obama, is the fact that the harshest and most vocal criticism has come from his progressive base. Members of the Occupy movement have openly criticized him for not doing enough to halt rising levels of income inequality that began during the George W. Bush years. Black leaders, including members of the black congressional caucus, have also criticized him for

Table 12.2   *Effect of social security on poverty, 2011*

Age group	Percent in Poverty		Number lifted out of poverty by Social Security
	Excluding Social Security	Including Social Security	
Children under 18	23.4	21.9	1,107,000
Adults 18–64	16.7	13.7	5,829,000
Elderly aged 65 and over	43.6	8.7	14,480,000
Total, all ages	21.9	15.0	21,415,000

Source: Center on Budget and Policy Priorities based on data from the US Census Bureau, *Current Population Survey*, March 2012.

abandoning the black community and people of color. Indeed, by 2011 black and Hispanic child poverty rates had risen to alarming rates – to 38.8 percent and 34.1 percent, respectively.

Despite the criticism of Obama's record on poverty, a closer look at policy-making during the first term of his presidency suggests that there is good reason to suggest that the policies implemented during the first two years may have had a significant antipoverty effect. The most important source of this effect has likely been the package of program expansions bundled within the American Recovery and Reinvestment Act of 2009 (ARRA), known more generally as the 'stimulus'. ARRA was signed into law by President Obama less than one month after he had officially assumed the presidency; however, he began working on the legislation almost immediately after being elected. The primary goals of ARRA were to reduce unemployment; invest in infrastructure, education, health and 'green' energy; and to provide relief to those most impacted upon by the recession through an expansion of several social welfare programs. The Congressional Budget Office estimated that the total cost of ARRA would be nearly $800 billion by 2019, but the majority of the spending was front-loaded and approximately $500 billion had been spent by the end of fiscal year 2011 (US Congress, Congressional Budget Office, 2012). The key poverty-reducing provisions of ARRA included measures to expand federal spending for several important public assistance pro-grams, in addition to changes to the tax code that would benefit the working poor. Some of the most important specific provisions are (Sherman, 2011):

- an expanded Child Tax Credit for lower-income working families with children;
- an expanded Earned Income Tax Credit (EITC);
- additional weeks of emergency unemployment compensation benefits;
- an additional $25 per week for unemployed workers to supplement their unemployment benefits;
- a $250 one-time payment to elderly people and people with disabilities who receive Social Security, SSI or veterans' benefits;
- an increase in food stamp benefit levels;
- supplemental 'emergency' funding for states to use for the TANF program.

Evidence of the effectiveness of ARRA in reducing poverty can be gauged by examining the poverty-reducing effect of the major programs targeted by ARRA, both before and after its implementation in 2009. Compared to 2008, recent research has shown that this collection of ARRA-targeted programs and policies lifted an additional five million people from poverty in 2009, of which nearly two million were children (Fording and Smith, 2012). The poverty-reducing effect fell slightly in 2010, but the percentages are still significantly higher than what was seen during the pre-ARRA period. In other words, despite the fact that poverty rates have increased to historic levels, it would appear that conditions for the poor would be even worse if it were not for the stimulus.

Conclusion

Given the pressure to reduce the federal budget deficit, there is likely to be significant reductions in social spending in the coming years. For social insurance programs, reform will likely proceed despite political opposition from a broad spectrum of interest groups. Due to the popularity of Social Security and Medicare and the political power of the interests involved, reform is most likely to be modest in scope and take the form of a combination of strategies that spread the costs of reform across all major interests involved in the debate.

Public assistance programs are likely to suffer a similar fate, despite the fact that poverty rates and income inequality remain at record levels. However, an important difference is that the politics surrounding the debate over public assistance spending is likely to play out much differently. Because public assistance programs are relatively unpopular and the groups they serve are politically weak, elected officials can rarely afford to oppose spending cuts in these programs as this may provide ammunition for their opponents. The most recent examples of this fact were witnessed during the 2012 presidential election, when Republicans tried to portray President Obama as overly supportive of TANF and SNAP. In response to rising SNAP caseloads, Newt Gingrich even began to refer to President Obama as the 'Food Stamp President'.

Unless tax rates for the richest Americans are restored to the levels seen prior to the implementation of the Bush tax cuts, further reductions in social welfare spending are likely to fuel continued growth in poverty and income inequality in the United States. In addition to creating greater hardship, the continuation of this trend is likely to slow the economic recovery from the Great Recession. As economist Joseph Stiglitz has argued, rising income inequality in America has contributed to a sluggish recovery due to the fact that the average American is too weak to sustain the level of consumer spending necessary to produce a robust recovery. And as a result, 'the American dream – a good life in exchange for hard work – is slowly dying' (Stiglitz, 2013).

Chapter 13

Health Policy in the United States: 'Obamacare' and After

B. Guy Peters

Attempts to reform the healthcare system have been a part of American politics for decades. Unlike other industrialized democracies the United States does not have health insurance, public or private, for all citizens; and well over 50 million citizens lacked coverage in 2012. Some of these uninsured citizens had made a conscious gamble not to purchase insurance, but most were people who could not afford the rapidly increasing premiums. And over one-third of these uninsured were working full-time, and another third part-time, but their employers did not provide them with health coverage. These citizens had to rely on various stopgap measures such as emergency rooms or simply receive no care at all. And if they use the emergency room this tends to be the most expensive locus for receiving care.

In addition to the citizens who have no insurance, a significant proportion of those who are insured are covered for only catastrophic accidents or diseases or are in some other way significantly under-insured (Meltzer, 2011). The under-insured spend more than 10 percent of their total income on out-of-pocket medical expenses (5 percent, if low-income earners). The number of under-insured has been increasingly significantly as employers provide insurance with higher deductibles and co-payments as they confront rising medical costs (Schoen et al., 2008). There are no standards on the quality of insurance that is offered by employers, and many are now providing only minimal coverage.

Even for those who have health insurance the premiums are extremely expensive unless paid by their employers. In 2011 the average health insurance premium for a family was $13,375 (Agency for Healthcare Research and Quality, 2013). And for those who do have insurance through their employers the proportion of the total cost has been shifting toward the employee rather than the employer in a period of rapid price inflation in medicine. For example, from 1999 to 2009 health insurance premiums increased by 131 percent and workers' contributions increased by 128 percent (Kaiser Family Foundation, 2010). Further, most policies have annual and lifetime limits on payments so that medical bankruptcies occur frequently for people who thought they were adequately covered. A lifetime limit of $3 million in coverage may appear ample, but is often exhausted by cancer or other major diseases. Although determining the exact impact of medical debts is difficult, some studies have found that up to half of all bankruptcies are caused by debts related to healthcare issues.

President Obama campaigned on the healthcare issue in 2008 and during his first term was able to get the Patient Protection and Affordable Care Act (PPACA), or 'Obamacare' as his critics dubbed it, passed in 2010 (see Jacobs and Skocpol, 2010). Although this Act has a number of severe problems and remains unpopular with a majority of Americans, it represented a first step toward a comprehensive health insurance system. The PPACA also survived a challenge to its constitutionality (Cohn, 2012). Some aspects of the Act have already been implemented, and the remaining components are on track to be implemented, especially after President Obama won reelection. Even with that legislation in place, however, addressing the healthcare needs of the American public remains a significant policy challenge, not least because any attempts to provide health insurance for all citizens remain embedded in an extremely high cost and inefficient medical care system.

The American healthcare system

When running for office, and especially when opposing public intervention in the health system, American politicians like to boast that the United States has the best medical system in the world. Unfortunately, the facts do not substantiate those claims. The World Health Organization ranks the US system as 37th in the world, behind (among numerous others) Morocco, Dominica and Costa Rica. The National Research Council (2013) has documented that the health status of Americans under 50 is significantly worse than that of other affluent countries, although the health of those 65 and older is as good or better. Infant mortality rates (deaths in the first year of life per 1,000 live births – a standard measure of healthcare quality) in the United States are also higher than other industrial democracies, and the infant mortality rates for African Americans resemble those in some developing countries. The same poor performance can be found for other standardized health indicators such as life expectancy and morbidity for some major diseases.

The absence of health insurance for millions of people is an obvious cause of much of the poor outcomes in the healthcare system, but it is not the only one. Physicians and medical care facilities are also not distributed equally across the country. There are 817 doctors per 100,000 population in the District of Columbia, but only 171 in Idaho; and some counties in western states do not have a single physician, much less a hospital. And the high-tech character of American medicine tends to devalue the importance of basic care and prevention that can save substantial amounts of money in the long run through investment in early detection. Thus, less than 9 percent of physicians in the United States are in general practice – the type of medicine that would be most likely to emphasize prevention. Despite efforts from government and from the medical profession itself the proportion of general practitioners continues to decline.

What the United States does have is the world's most expensive healthcare system. Roughly 16 percent of the gross domestic product of the United States is spent on healthcare. The closest rival in the health spending race is France (13.8 percent of GDP), though it is ranked by the WHO as the best healthcare system in the world. Several aspects of the healthcare system, to some degree addressed by the Affordable Care Act (ACA), tend to drive up the costs. Perhaps the most important of these factors is that the payment system remains a fee-for-service one. This fact means that medical care providers are paid only when they provide services and they therefore have little incentive *not* to provide those services. Insurers attempt to control this compensation system through co-payments and deductibles paid by the patients, but the underlying incentive system makes cost-containment difficult. In this medical care system not only are the total costs high but there is a danger of over-treatment, with unnecessary surgeries and diagnostic procedures driving up the total healthcare bill.

The complex and competitive nature of healthcare also contributes to the excessive costs within the system. Although most Americans believe that their healthcare system is private, the finance is in fact roughly half public and half private. And within each of those sectors there are multiple providers and multiple insurers, all of which attempt to shift costs onto other insurers or onto patients themselves. As a consequence of these multiple actors involved in health financing, the administrative costs for private health insurance tend to be substantially higher than in other systems, or in public insurance programs such as Medicare. The only exception to this generalization is Medicare Advantage, technically Part C of Medicare, that operates more like a private health insurer and has many of the same administrative difficulties of the private insurance market. For example, administrative costs in American medicine are approximately 39 percent higher than the single-payer plan in Canada. That is, the multiple insurers spend a great deal of time and money trying to shift costs onto other insurers, especially Medicare. Further, the different rules and practices used by the various insurers impose costs on the providers when they file for reimbursement.

The lack of coverage for so many people within the population also contributes to the high costs of medical care. Many, and probably most, people who are not covered by health insurance do not seek medical care until there is a crisis and then they go to hospital emergency rooms. The emergency rooms are mandated to treat genuine emergencies, but this is the most expensive locus in which to receive care. As the uninsured generally have no means of paying for the care, the costs they incur in the emergency room are amortized over all the other patients in the hospital that do have coverage. This cost-shifting from the uninsured to the insured contributes to the high and increasing health insurance premiums paid by the insured and their employers. And that in turn contributes to the declining proportion of employers who have offered adequate health insurance coverage to their employees.

Finally, American healthcare does not promote preventative care as much as most other medical care systems and a great deal of care is supplied in hospitals and other 'high tech' facilities. Only 9 percent of doctors in the United States are in primary care and that proportion is declining. In addition, the emphasis on advanced diagnostic procedures such as CAT and MRI scans tends to drive up the costs of care significantly. That utilization of technology is in part a function of defensive practice by physicians who fear malpractice suits if they were to miss some potentially dangerous conditions in a patient.

Public sector health programs

As noted, despite the perception that the healthcare system is dominated by the private sector, there is a large and growing public sector component. Even before the passage of PPACA over 90 million people had health insurance from the government. Approximately half of those are people over 65, insured through Medicare; and most of the others are insured through Medicaid, the program for the medically indigent. A smaller number of children are insured through the State Children's Health Insurance Program (SCHIP). In addition to the public insurance programs several million veterans receive some or all of their medical care from the Department of Veterans Affairs and some Native Americans receive theirs through the Department of the Interior.

Medicare is the product of President Lyndon Johnson's Great Society, which represented the first major intervention of the federal government into the healthcare system. Medicare is an insurance program for the elderly, with Part A covering hospitalization and some nursing home care, and which is financed primarily through payroll taxation.

Part B of Medicare covers doctors' visits financed by premiums paid by the participants. Medicare also has a Part D that provides limited coverage for prescription drugs was added during the administration of George W. Bush.

For both major components of the program there are deductibles and co-payments for participants, designed to deter consumption and also to defray some of the costs of the program. Although the program is designed for the elderly who may often have significant vision and hearing problems, Medicare does not provide coverage for things such as spectacles and hearing aids. Nor does the program have significant coverage for long-term care, and many participants who require those services must spend down their assets so that they can be eligible for Medicaid. Given these deficiencies the majority of participants in Medicare purchase 'Medigap' insurance to cover some or all of the gaps in the coverage provided through the public program.

Medicaid is a federally subsidized program that is administered not through the federal government but through the states. Although there are some minimum standards in the program, there are also marked differences in coverage and benefits across the states. Medicaid is designed for people who are receiving other means-tested benefits such as TANF and SNAP, but many states extend the eligibility to people who are 'medically indigent' although they may have incomes a good deal above poverty levels. Indeed, a significant number of the recipients of Medicaid are employed but not in jobs that provide healthcare benefits.

Although the federal government pays roughly 60 percent of the total costs, Medicaid is a significant, and growing, expenditure item for state governments. In 2011 the states spent 17.4 percent of their general revenue on Medicaid, and that figure was projected to continue to increase by approximately 11 percent per year. The federal government provides approximately 60 percent of the funds expended through Medicaid and, while the Stimulus Act was in effect, the federal government was paying up to 70 percent. When the Stimulus Act expired the effects of growing medical costs became very apparent to state governments and is part of the reason why some states reject the expansion of Medicaid, which was called for in the ACA. This Act is projected to reduce Medicaid expenditures to some extent, although the states will also be required to participate in the state exchanges that are a central component of the program. Thus, the federal government will continue to impose substantial costs on the states.

SCHIP was passed in 1997 to provide health insurance for children in families whose income is higher than the limits set by Medicaid. In 2010 over eight million children were covered under this program. Like the elderly covered by Medicare, children are considered a group with special claims for public sector protection. SCHIP is technically a component of Medicaid, and like that larger program is funded jointly by the states and the federal government. The states also have some latitude in setting eligibility requirements. Also like Medicaid, SCHIP will to some extent be integrated into the ACA as that legislation is implemented.

The state governments also have been significant actors involved in reforming healthcare. For example, the health program implemented in Massachusetts was in many ways the model for Obamacare. Prior to that Minnesota, Tennessee and Hawaii had all adopted various programs that came close to providing universal coverage for the residents of the state (Gruber, 2008). These programs were to some extent successful but also were extremely expensive for the states and most have been eliminated or downsized significantly. Although the states, and at least one Republican state (Tennessee), had initiated their own versions of healthcare reform, many now are resisting involvement with the federal program.

The federal and state governments also have a variety of smaller and politically less visible health programs. For example, the Department of Defense provides medical care for millions of servicemen and their dependents. The Indian Health Service provides healthcare to federally recognized tribes. Governments are also major regulators of healthcare, including the regulation of pharmaceuticals and medical devices (such as through the US Food and Drug Administration). State and local governments also are heavily involved in public health and in providing mental health services.

Again, it is difficult to argue that healthcare in the United States is really a private sector activity; all levels of government are to some extent involved with healthcare policy. The majority of the funding for public sector healthcare programs comes from the federal government, although much of the implementation is done through state governments. In the emerging politics of healthcare the states that have been innovators are becoming impediments in many instances, given the opposition of many state governments to the ACA.

The Affordable Care Act

In the 2008 campaign for the presidency Barack Obama stressed the need for significant reform in the healthcare system. The majority of Americans agreed with this, although not on exactly what the reform should be. Citizens have been unhappy about costs, the large numbers of uninsured and restrictions on coverage, even for those who have insurance; but that discontent had never produced a workable political majority to generate change. President Clinton, along with Hillary Clinton, had proposed major change in his first term as president, but the complexity of the program, combined with strong opposition from small business and the insurance industry, led to its defeat. The opposition was so clear that Congress never took the issue to a vote.

The ACA had a long and tortuous passage through the legislative process, and the outcome was equally elongated and complex. Perhaps unfortunately, President Obama did not craft his own legislative proposals, but instead left that task to Congress. That delegation to Congress meant that a number of disparate pieces of legislation emerged from committees in the House of Representatives and the Senate. In addition, initiating the legislation in Congress left the process more open to lobbying, and the healthcare and insurance industries weighed in effectively. As a result, the legislation became something of a Christmas tree on which a number of benefits for various parts of the healthcare industry were hung.

The eventual passage of the legislation was aided by the bipartisan group of six Senators from the Finance Committee who beginning in June 2009 worked to draft the legislation. These Senators, along with health policy experts such as Jonathan Gruber, produced a bill that attempted to overcome standard problems in insurance programs, especially health insurance, such as adverse selection (Cohn, 2010).

The above having been said, the bill that emerged from the House – the Affordable Health Care for America Act – did contain numerous benefits for low income Americans and also imposed numerous regulations on the healthcare and insurance industries. It did not, however, contain as strong provisions for mandates as did the final legislation adopted and may not have been able to produce the type of changes required in healthcare.

The Senate, however, did not consider the House bill but drafted its own, with the title that became the name of the final legislation. The Senate bill was drafted under the guise of amendments to another House bill, so that the constitutional provision of taxation bills being initiated in the House could be fulfilled. After Senate passage, this bill had to return to the House for its consideration. At this point, however, the President intervened with a proposal that reconciled differences among the possible pieces of legislation, a proposal that in essence became the bill finally passed in both chambers of Congress and which was then signed by the President on March 23, 2010.

What is perhaps most remarkable politically about this legislation is that it was passed in the context of very strong divisions between the parties in Congress. A filibuster in the Senate, requiring 60 votes to break, was the major barrier to passage. Having a veto-proof majority in the Senate revolved around Ted Kennedy's seat from Massachusetts. After Senator Kennedy – a leading advocate of healthcare reform – died, a Democrat was appointed as his successor. However, the legislation got through the Senate before the special election to fill this seat was won by a Republican. Republicans in Congress have tried repeatedly to repeal the legislation, but have never been able to get a majority to do so in the Senate.

Although the principal provisions of the legislation would not become effective for several years, some important provisions became effective almost immediately. The most important of these initial federal interventions into the health system was the regulation of several aspects of health insurance policies. Perhaps most importantly, health insurers could no longer exclude pre-existing conditions from coverage, a practice that had long prevented people from getting adequate coverage when they changed insurance and also kept people immobile economically. Further, the Act permitted young people up to the age of 26 to remain covered by their parents' insurance, even if they were no longer dependents in tax terms. These provisions are regulatory means for addressing the need for extending coverage to a range of citizens who were being excluded by the regulations in private health insurance.

There are three primary operative elements in the ACA. The first is the individual mandate. If an individual does not have health insurance through his or her employer, from government programs such as Medicare or Medicaid, or through purchasing it in the private market when the core features of the program come into effect, he or she will be required to purchase insurance. This insurance would have to meet certain minimum standards so that citizens would then have substantial coverage for medical expenses. This provision is very similar to the program initiated in the state of Massachusetts when Mitt Romney was governor, although almost all Republicans opposed the program when it was adopted in Congress and also attacked the program vigorously in the 2012 presidential election.

The second significant component of the ACA is the creation of state level exchanges for medical insurance policies. These exchanges are designed as online resources for citizens and small businesses attempting to find insurance coverage to fulfill the requirements of their mandates. The assumption behind these exchanges is that their open and accessible nature will create more of a market in insurance that might otherwise exist, and therefore the citizens should be able to find lower cost policies. If a state chooses not to create its own exchanges the citizens of that state will be able to utilize an exchange at the federal level to find affordable policies.

The insurance to be provided in these exchanges, be they at the state or federal level, are required under the ACA to provide certain levels of coverage. This will not be the 'Cadillac' plans provided for the most fortunate private sector employees, and many public sector employees, but they will provide coverage for hospitalization, physician visits and diagnostic services. These insurance policies must also be 'community rated' so that, except for smokers, the premiums must be equal for subscribers in each policy option.

While these are equal rates, they may present some issues of adverse selection. For healthy people, especially young people, the penalty associated with the individual mandate may be less than the cost of the health insurance. If healthy individuals do not subscribe to the insurance policies then these insurance pools will over-represent people with health problems. And therefore the costs of this insurance will be higher than if the pool were defined more broadly.

Finally, as well as a mandate on individuals, the Act also contains a mandate on employers. Employers with 50 employees or more are mandated to provide health insurance for those employees or face an annual fine of $2,000 per employee over 30 employees. So, a firm with 50 employees who did not provide healthcare benefits would pay $40,000 per year. This part of the Act is analogous to the 'play or pay' provisions contained in previous attempts to reform healthcare, meaning that employers would have to 'play' (provide health insurance to their employees) or pay into a fund to provide that coverage. The ACA focuses more on fines than on mandatory contributions to an insurance fund as the 'stick' to induce participation by employers.

Smaller enterprises will not face the fine for non-participation in the program and there are subsidies for them to assist in providing insurance for their employers. Thus, the 'mom and pop' small store is protected against having to pay the full cost for insurance, although in general small businesses of all types have been most vehement in their opposition to the ACA. (To some extent, as was true of the Clinton health reform proposals, the ACA split the business community. Larger businesses that could perhaps reduce the costs of their policies, if total costs were reduced through the provisions of the Act, tended to be indifferent or even support the legislation, while smaller businesses were actively and vocally opposed.) The fear is that even modest involvement in providing health coverage will reduce their capacity to compete, even though all their competitors would be facing the same expenses for insuring their employees. And it has not been just small business that has expressed great concerns about the impacts of the mandate. One major national pizza chain has vowed to reduce nearly all employees to part-time hours to make them ineligible for mandated health insurance.

In addition to these basic operative elements in the ACA there are other provisions that also address significant issues within American healthcare. As noted above, the general style of American medical care has been to emphasize treatment over prevention and the ACA provides mandated coverage of screening and preventative procedures such as mammography. As well as making sense in terms of the health of the individuals involved, this emphasis on screening and prevention is projected also to save insurance companies and government significant amounts of money (Orszag and Emanuel, 2010).

In addition to addressing cost containment in medical care through encouraging prevention, the ACA also attempted to address costs through sponsoring the creation of Accountable Care Organizations (ACOs). These organizations are analogous to Health Maintenance Organizations (organizations which provide managed medical care) that had been promoted by the federal government during the 1970s (Baumann, 1976). Both the ACOs and HMOs attempt to control healthcare costs by replacing fee-for-service payments with a single annual payment from patients. The logic of the single payment is to remove the incentive for doctors and other providers within the ACOs to order additional services for patients. On the other hand, those doctors may have an incentive *not* to provide services because then the organization can retain the excess income from the annual contributions of the members.

Challenges to Obamacare

The first significant challenge to the ACA was to its constitutionality. Before the Supreme Court made its decision in 2012 some 28 states raised challenges to the legislation, and a number of other private organizations, mostly business ones, also challenged it. These direct constitutional challenges were supplemented by a steady stream of constitutional arguments from Republican Senators and a substantial mobilization by other political groups opposed to the legislation.

There were two major strands of constitutional argument against the ACA. The principal challenge was directed against the individual mandate provisions in the legislation. The question was whether Congress could compel individuals to purchase a privately provided product – health insurance. The argument was made that government could not compel citizens to buy broccoli and therefore could not compel people to purchase health insurance. It appeared clear that the states could make such legislation, for example requiring drivers to have liability insurance; but it was less clear that the federal government had such powers.

The second challenge was whether the federal government could compel the states to expand their Medicaid coverage. In *National Federation of Independent Businesses v Sebelius* the Supreme Court upheld the individual mandate provision of the ACA as an acceptable use of the taxing powers of Congress. The opinion reached was that the penalty imposed if individuals do not purchase private health insurance could be deemed to be a tax for not participating in the program. Chief Justice Roberts, an appointee of George W. Bush, wrote the majority opinion, with other conservative justices dissenting. The Court, however, did not uphold the capacity of Congress to mandate that the states had to expand Medicare to cover a larger portion of the population or risk losing their Medicaid funding in total. This decision therefore essentially defended the rights of the states against the federal government, although it did allow the federal government expanded controls over individual citizens.

Although it has become the law of the land, and has been upheld for the most part by the Supreme Court, the ACA still faces numerous challenges as it goes forward and is implemented. Perhaps the most important of these is the dependence on the states, and on state exchanges, to put the program into action. For both ideological and practical reasons most states had not developed the plans for their exchanges by mid-November 2012, as required by law (Goodnough and Cooper, 2012). Somewhat paradoxically, those states that had most stressed state control in opposing the federal legislation were the ones most likely not to have taken the opportunity to impose their own controls over the implementation of the program. However, as the date for implementation approached closer in late 2012, and it was clear that with President Obama's reelection the Act would not be repealed, some of the reluctant states began to scramble to develop their own programs (Kaiser Family Foundation, 2012).

Likewise, the states have shown little willingness to expand Medicaid as was envisioned in the legislation. As already noted, this health program already constitutes a major and rapidly increasing part of state budgets, and, particularly in the constrained financial situation in which most states now find themselves (see Chapter 10), there is little interest in expanding the program. Without this expansion a greater portion of the financial burden will fall directly on citizens or onto the federal government.

This reluctance on the part of the states to support the expansion of health insurance through the ACA is indicative of the underlying political conflicts over the program and some general skepticism on the part of the American public about a program which was designed to benefit many of them. Since the time the bill was adopted and signed, there has always been a majority of respondents in public opinion polls in favor of repealing the legislation, and at one point almost two-thirds of the public favored repeal. As the time for implementation nears, there appears to be some grudging acceptance of the legislation, and in the last polling before the presidential election a bare 50 percent favored repeal. The public appears to have remained deeply divided on the ACA even after the political debate over the legislation in the presidential campaign was over (Kaiser Family Foundation, 2012).

Much of the opposition to the ACA is ideological, and phrases such as 'socialized medicine' and 'government take over of healthcare' have been prominent in the negative discussion of the legislation, as they were also prominent in the 2012 presidential campaign. Some of the opposition also comes from concerns of businesses, and especially small businesses, that they will be coerced into paying for healthcare for their employees, even though the major mandates are on individuals and on the states. The individual mandate, however, produced its own opposition as being a major reduction of individual freedom.

Some portion of the opposition to Obamacare comes from misunderstanding of the nature of the program and from some purposive misinformation directed towards it by the opposition. For example, one of the major misunderstandings that spread rapidly during the debate over adoption of the legislation was that there would be 'death panels' that would decide whether individuals would get treatment or not, a canard advanced by Sarah Palin. Although this was perhaps to some extent pure scare tactics by the opponents of the legislation, the possible reference was to the Independent Payment Advisory Panels named in the legislation as means of addressing cost containment. Also, under the Act doctors will be reimbursed for advising patients on living wills and end of life decisions.

Options for further reform

Although the ACA represents a major political accomplishment for President Obama, and a significant policy advance in creating access to healthcare for all Americans, it is far from an optimal solution to the underlying issues in healthcare. The Act is extremely complex and convoluted, and therefore difficult for many citizens to understand and to use effectively. In addition, the Act depends heavily upon private sector insurers and the states for implementation. The states were already demonstrating themselves to be unreliable partners in 2012, so relying upon this pattern of implementation poses some dangers for creating an effective program nationwide.

Given the problems in the existing programs there are several possible options for change. One would be the type of plan favored by conservatives, such as Paul Ryan during the campaign, that would depend upon vouchers. This approach would simply subsidize citizens going into the private market and would therefore depend heavily on their capacity to make informed choices about purchasing insurance. Although many conservatives would prefer government simply to be out of the healthcare area entirely, the use of market instruments such as vouchers would meet some of their desires to utilize the market rather than having government as the principal source of care and insurance.

The alternative to the ACA that would be favored more by the political left would be to move toward a single-payer plan, with the federal government acting as the source of health insurance for all citizens. This insurance program would be, in essence, an extension of the existing Medicare system, or would be an analogous type of insurance program. This option could reduce the complexity and the administrative costs associated with Obamacare and with the private insurance system that continues for most Americans after the adoption of the Act. That said, however, the political opposition generated by the ACA might be intensified by a single-payer system that would appear to many citizens to be 'socialized medicine'.

Neither of these potential reforms, from the right or from the left, address effectively what is perhaps the central issue in American healthcare – the high and rapidly increasing costs. The market option assumes that competition will work and that consumers can place sufficient pressure on medical providers to reduce costs, although the experiences of the health system prior to the reforms seem to offer little support for that assumption. Likewise the single-payer plan favored by the political left could reduce administrative costs, as well as some of the redundancies that exist, but if fee-for-service medicine remains the primary form of provision then there will be little opportunity for reducing the underlying costs.

It is almost certainly too soon to begin advocating any more significant changes in the healthcare system, especially with President Obama winning a second term, which will ensure that the ACA will continue to be implemented. There are now four years for this to happen and for citizens and providers to become accustomed to the program. As of 2013 the program remains unpopular with many citizens, although the few proposals that have been implemented (for example coverage of pre-existing conditions) have been popular. The history of healthcare reform politics has had similar ambiguities among the public at a number of points and Americans remain divided about existing healthcare policies and the possibilities for continued reforms.

Chapter 14

Foreign and Security Policy

John Dumbrell

During his first term in office, President Barack Obama tried simultaneously to resolve aspects of the difficult foreign and security policy that he had inherited from President George W. Bush and to signal areas of departure from the previous regime. Academic and journalistic commentary on post-2008 US foreign and security policy has tended to focus on questions of change and continuity. How far could Obama and his team escape from the problems, structures and policy assumptions inherited from the controversial Bush years? To what extent was the War on Terror now ceasing to be the defining conceptual framework for American international engagement? Key developments of the Obama first term inevitably related to the major military commitments which had been made in the shadow of the terror attacks of 2001. Obama engineered an American exit from Iraq. He expanded the American force commitment to Afghanistan, while also setting a timetable for withdrawal by 2014. The rhetorical commitment to militarized and globalized anti-terrorism as the central international concern of the United States was toned down. Obama sought new strategic relationships and priorities. He achieved Senate ratification of an arms control agreement with Russia in 2010. He sought to prioritize relations with China, 'pivoting' towards East Asia in the context of a revised defense posture announced in late 2011. However, the first Obama term also involved a greatly accelerated reliance on unmanned 'drone' aircraft to kill terrorist suspects from the Sahara to Pakistan. The White House remained preoccupied with Iran's apparent dash to nuclear weapons capability, achieving a new multilateral sanctions regime targeted at Tehran. Even as it reached out in new directions, the Obama Administration seemed to find itself continually pulled back into the fraught international conflicts and controversies of the years 2001–09. Indeed in some areas – the frozen diplomacy of the Israel–Palestine peace process and policy towards North Korea come to mind – time, despite all Obama's promises of 'change', appeared almost to stand still.

Despite all these conflicts, I will argue that Obama has to a significant extent succeeded in pointing the United States in a new international direction. Post-2008 American foreign policy – the foreign policy of what may now be called the 'post-War on Terror era' – was profoundly influenced by the perception that the United States had become dangerously over-exposed internationally since (at least) 2001. The early Obama years saw new emphases on cost-sharing multilateralism, on a more modest internationalism, and on the need for a foreign and security policy suited to lean economic times. The shape of American global engagement after 2008 was only partly explicable in terms of the need to refocus, resolve and redirect the inheritance from Bush. As ever, American foreign policy between 2009 and 2013 was to an important degree simply reactive – responding to unpredicted global events and crises. The post-2010 'Arab Spring' uprisings against dictatorial regimes in North Africa and the Middle East constituted merely the most obvious of such developments. Obama's international policies were also the product of conflict and debate *within* the Administration: notably tensions between proponents of liberal, democracy-promoting interventionism on the one hand, and a more cautious, interests-oriented realism on the other.

By 2013, as Obama began his second term, the world had become familiar with a number of concepts, many of which pointed to an international order in which the United States would neither be seen as, nor would always be prepared to act as, the automatic and default provider of global security. Such concepts – some articulated by members of the Obama administration, some coined by outside commentators – included: the turn to East Asia; 'low cost' or 'soft power' American international leadership; 'leading from behind'; and America as 'indispensable catalyst' rather than undisputed global leader. The purpose of my chapter is to interrogate the Obama record in foreign and security policy, offering judgments on his achievements, on this putative new foreign policy direction, and on prospects for the second term. In order to set the stage for such a discussion, I will begin with a series of threshold or 'framing' issues.

Understanding Obama's foreign policy

At least four overarching considerations affect, and are likely to continue to affect, judgment and understanding of Obama's foreign and security policy. The most fundamental consideration relates to the question of how exactly we should evaluate presidential performance in these policy areas. The relevant literature is vast and complex. It embraces numerous approaches, from cognitive and psychological to managerialist and bureaucracy-oriented. The literature, however, does yield some significant general arguments, which illuminate the search for ways to judge and understand post-2008 policy. In very broad terms, evaluation here involves close understanding both of one president's inheritance from his predecessor and of the formidable problems of structure and agency which shape any leader's attempt to recast the direction of American international policy. Good leaders are generally held to be able clearly to recognize limits imposed by history and inheritance, by the complexities of international power relations, by the constraints of domestic politics, and by the dynamics and rivalries within and across the foreign and security policy bureaucracy. Successful leaders, however, are not paralyzed into nervous inaction by such recognition of limits and complexity. They aspire to procedural rationality, while retaining a keen awareness of the obstacles to optimal rationality. Successful presidents encourage multiple advocacy among advisers, yet are able clearly to adjudicate intra-administration disputes. They will have an integrating purpose, a central coherence, beyond a generalized commitment to advancing American interests and security. They will be able to 'sell' this purpose to appropriate domestic and international constituencies. The purpose itself, and its associated policies, must be suited to shifting international conditions (Renshon and Larsen, 2003; Dumbrell, 2009).

Secondly, given the defining theme of the 2008 presidential election campaign against Republican John McCain – and especially against the background of the exceptionally controversial nature of the foreign policy pursued by the administration of George W. Bush – the theme of 'change' and of the limits of change are bound to dog perceptions of the Obama Administration's performance. On both right and left, critics of Obama have tended to preface their remarks with *faux naïf* references to the hopes and heightened expectations of 2008. Sarah Palin, McCain's running mate from 2008, was soon making fun of 'that hopey-changey stuff'; while Paul Krugman introduced his liberal critique of Obama's economic strategy thus: 'what happened to the inspirational figure his supporters thought they elected? Who is this bland guy who doesn't seem to stand for anything in particular?' (Maddox, 2011).

A third framing point relates to the reappearance of the discourse of American international decline. By 2006, academic and journalistic perceptions of American global power as overweening, and even predatory, had been replaced by images of over-extension. President George W. Bush now appeared, in the midst of the post-invasion chaos in Iraq, almost as a post-imperial American Ozymandias – a leader laid low by militarized overstretch, as depicted in Shelley's poem. In some respects, this 'new' sense of decline recalled arguments from the 1970s and early 1980s about the supposed eclipse of American international power following the defeat in Vietnam and in the context of a poorly performing American economy. Some contemporary commentators do raise the specter of global chaos resulting from a possible abdication of US global leadership (Kupchan, 2012). However, in general, the post-2005 decline debate has been rather less apocalyptic than its post-Vietnam War predecessor. The current debate centers on the dramatic international rise of China. Yet it also invokes the 'rise of the rest' – the increased economic clout of countries like Brazil and India – and the possibility of a new era of complex global multipolarity (Zakaria, 2008; Dumbrell, 2010; Mandelbaum, 2010; Niblett, 2010; LSE, 2011). An important strand in the contemporary 'discourse of decline' involves the extent to which American-sponsored ideas and ideals (from free trade to political democracy) may remain embedded in international institutions even if US economic and military power is fading (Quinn, 2011b; Ikenberry, 2012). To many Americans, however, the 'new' decline actually does seem quite apocalyptic, especially in relation to China's rise and to America's post-2007 economic woes. Pew Center polling in 2010 indicated that a plurality of Americans considered China, not America, to be the world's leading economic power (Drezner, 2011).

Our final framing point concerns what Senator Evan Bayh (D: Indiana) called 'brain-dead partisanship' in Washington (Bayh, 2010; Mann and Ornstein, 2012). Extreme partisanship, polarization and personalized attack-oriented politics are hardly new phenomena in American political history, yet they do set the context for Obama's efforts to construct a 'post-partisan', consensual order in foreign and security policy. Attacks on his foreign policy leadership have frequently reflected the fevered politics of budgetary clashes on Capitol Hill, not to mention the emotional intensity associated with Republican Tea Party conservative radicalism. Nevertheless, it is worth emphasizing that this partisan intensity is more apparent in domestic than in foreign and security policy. As will be seen below, foreign policy positions on Capitol Hill have involved significant intra-party cleavages. In that respect, leading foreign policy (especially after the Republican gains in the 2010 midterm elections) has proved a little easier than taking initiatives in domestic policy. Observers of the televised foreign policy debate between Obama and Republican candidate Mitt Romney, ahead of the 2012 election, could have been forgiven for concluding that there was actually an awful lot on which the candidates agreed. Jeffrey Bader, East Asian officer on Obama's national security council between 2009 and 2011, went so far as to recall in 2012 that 'the extreme polarization that marked domestic politics in the Obama years was absent from foreign policy' (Bader, 2012; Pletka, 2013).

Lines of criticism

By turns, the Obama foreign and security policy has been attacked from various quarters as timid, apologetic, imperialist, dismissive of international law and unmindful of traditional allies. Following on from the previous section, I will now consider various charges levied at Obama from both right and left, noting the complex and cross-cutting nature of both rightist and leftist critiques.

Some attacks from the right – typically on Obama as the ideological friend of appeasement, national apology and American decline – have been unreflective and almost absurdly partisan (D'Souza, 2010). For some critics, Obama has been the president who accepted the inevitability of American decline and sought merely to manage it (Bolton, 2009; see also Kagan, 2012). Many American conservatives argue that Obama's 'return' to multilateralism was part a betrayal of national purpose, part a failure to pay respect to valued allies, notably Israel. An influential and thoughtful conservative analysis was provided by Colin Dueck in his depiction of Obama as 'the accommodator'. According to Dueck, Obama is a domestic-oriented leader, believing 'that genuine and overarching international cooperation is possible, if apparent adversaries can learn to listen to and accommodate one another'. Adopting a style learned in his days as a community organizer in Chicago, Obama thus is seen as trying to lead by example – something which Dueck sees as 'essentially taking the lead in making concessions'. In the case of North Korea, Cuba and Iran – governments defined 'at a fundamental level by violent hostility to America' – Obama's approach was, according to Dueck, 'simply naive' (Dueck, 2011).

Yet there were other, somewhat contradictory, Republican perspectives on Obama. Some influential neo-conservative commentators credited Obama with keeping America globally engaged in difficult economic times when siren calls for a neo-isolationist foreign policy were making themselves heard. Robert Kagan in June 2010 applauded Obama's commitment to Afghanistan and his strengthening of the US–Japanese alliance (Kagan, 2010). In the case of Congresswoman Michele Bachmann, sometime candidate for the 2012 Republican nomination, contradiction followed contradiction. Thus, Obama was both the soft, ineffectual leader who made the despised Jimmy Carter 'look like a Rambo tough guy' *and* the president who led America into the dangerous 2011 air-based intervention in Libya where: 'we were not threatened with attack. There was no vital interest' (Lindsay, 2011a, 2011b). Neo-isolationist forces on the Republican right were to some degree crystallized in Congressman Ron Paul's campaign for the 2012 nomination. The Tea Party movement became divided between a neo-isolationism, which harked back to the pre-Cold War era, and the kind of assertive militarism with which Mitt Romney briefly flirted before retreating to the political center during the final stages of the 2012 election campaign (Mead, 2011).

Elements of Republican neo-isolationism were echoed by those Democrats who saw foreign military commitments, especially in the Arab world, as almost inevitably leading to the kind of intractable miseries associated with the 2003 invasion of Iraq. Thus Dianne Feinstein, Democratic Senator from California, opposed action in Libya as she surveyed the Administration response to the Arab Spring in March 2011: 'these are essentially civil wars. If you get involved in Libya, you get involved in Bahrain, you get involved in Saudi Arabia, then it's big trouble' (Feinstein, 2011). For Bob Casey, Democratic chair of the Senate Foreign Relations subcommittee on the Near East, Obama's 2011 commitment to Libya was neither a belated rediscovery of 'principle' nor an imperialist adventure too far. Rather, it was a betrayal of Obama's commitment to what might be called cost-conscious realism: 'we can't afford a war in Libya, it's as simple as that' (Broder, 2011). On the other hand, liberal interventionist Democrats joined democracy-promoting Republicans in criticizing Obama's muted support in 2009 for 'green movement' oppositionists in Iran and his apparent reluctance to raise concerns about China's human rights record (Feller and Pace, 2011). Obama has been chided from several points on the political spectrum for his apparent reluctance to involve himself energetically in the Middle East peace process. From the left more generally, he was attacked for not breaking more decisively with the Bush approach, especially in failing to close the Guantanamo detention camp in Cuba and in pursuing the drone attacks. Perceptions of Bush–Obama continuity were to some degree reinforced by the massive leaks of confidential State Department cables in 2010–11 (the so-called 'wikileaks' material). As communications definitely not intended for public airing, the leaked material appeared to strengthen the case for seeing Obama's Administration as more cynically pragmatic than crusading and idealistic: for example, in respect of Chinese human rights and Saudi support for terror groups. The point is often made that Washington changed Obama more than Obama changed Washington (Brenner, 2010; Parmar, 2011; Gerges, 2012).

Like moderate Democratic leaders before him, Obama has been assaulted from many points of the political compass. The sheer variety and cross-cutting nature of the criticisms, as we have noted, made it somewhat easier for the Administration in its pursuit of coherent international engagement to dodge the super-partisan context in which Obama had to develop his domestic initiatives. To what extent, however, do these complex attacks on Obama point to a foreign and security policy which is itself confused and contradictory? I will devote the remainder of this chapter to answering that question. I will focus on policy coherence and purpose: initially, in relation to the dialectic of principles and pragmatism, and then regarding the integrity and efficiency of Obama's foreign policy process. I then consider the theme of 'change', before offering an academically informed evaluation of Obama's first term.

Coherence, principle and pragmatism

According to Martin Indyk, Kenneth Lieberthal and Michael O'Hanlon, Obama is a 'progressive pragmatist': 'there was inevitable tension between his soaring rhetoric and desire to depart fundamentally from the policies of the Bush Administration on the one hand, and his instinct for governing pragmatically on the other'. During the 2008 campaign, Obama announced that 'the lesson of the Bush years is that not talking does not work' (Indyk et al., 2012). The resulting policy of 'pragmatic engagement' or 'principled pragmatism' was encapsulated by Hillary Clinton before her first visit to China as Secretary of State in 2009. Asked about the US attitude to human rights issues, Secretary Clinton indicated that 'we know what they're going to say' on issues such as Tibetan autonomy 'and they know what we're going to say': 'we don't know yet how we're going to engage on the global economic crisis, the global climate change crisis, and the security crisis ... So if we talk more about those, it's in large measure because that's where the opportunity for engagement is' (Clinton, 2009).

The foreign policy of Obama's first term can indeed be interpreted in terms of attempting to hold a balance between opposing approaches. Thus cost-conscious realism and the careful weighing of options in terms of national interest calculation tended constantly to rub up against concerns for human rights and even democracy-promotion: all in the context of an underpinning commitment, rooted in a reaction to the perceived over-extensions of the Bush years, to leaving a light international footprint. As we have seen, this balancing act continually ran the risk of appearing simultaneously timid, inconsistent and even cynical. Where Obama was criticized for his naivety in offering to open a dialogue with Tehran in 2009, he was subsequently attacked in some quarters for withdrawing the olive branch to Iran too quickly when Brazil and Turkey entered the diplomacy of nuclear proliferation (Parsi, 2012). Obama, the one-time champion of the 'audacity of change', is generally seen as favoring cautious realist analysis. He famously proclaimed himself an admirer of the pragmatic realist approach of President George H. W. Bush and his national security adviser, Brent Scowcroft (Lizza, 2011). He arguably learned from the Bush–Scowcroft handling of the diplomacy surrounding the end of the Cold War that cautious realism is often the best path, even if its exponents do sometimes risk ending up on the wrong side of history. In the case of the Arab Spring, Obama did switch quite quickly to supporting regime change in Egypt in 2011, even as he remained very cautious about revolutionary change in countries like Bahrain and Syria. Reasons for such caution – from Saudi pressure to the sheer intrinsic difficulty of any credible intervention against the Syrian regime – are not difficult to find. However, my main point is that Obama has tended to lean towards pragmatism and that such a stance is not without its problems. According to an anonymous Obama adviser interviewed by James Mann, the president 'wants to be buddies with Brent Scowcroft, and he also wants to go out and give speeches about democracy. He thinks he can do both at the same time'. The job of 'selling' Obama's foreign and security policy in the language of idealism often fell to Ben Rhodes, the White House speechwriter whom commentators came to identify as a guardian of the 'change we can believe in' themes of 2008 (Mann, 2012).

Despite Obama's retention of 'idealist' rhetorical themes, it is striking how often both Administration insiders and outside commentators on his foreign policy have invoked memories of the Republican pragmatic tradition. Robert Singh, for example, notes the deliberate echoing of President Eisenhower's 'calls for budgetary prudence and balance between competing national priorities' in Obama's December 2009 West Point address on policy in Afghanistan (Singh, 2012). Obama was understandably less willing to acknowledge parallels between his strategy for leaving Afghanistan and Richard Nixon's efforts to use 'Vietnamization' – the handing over of security responsibilities to South Vietnam itself – as cover for the American retreat from Southeast Asia in the early 1970s. The parallels with Eisenhower, nonetheless, are interesting, particularly in regard to Eisenhower's concern with economic constraints on American power-projection. Obama's own willingness to invoke links with Republican presidents also underlined his desire to appear 'non-ideological'. Here, so it appeared, was a leader returning to bipartisan ways of international cooperation and strategic restraint.

Ignoring charges that the Administration has somehow compromised the hopes of 2008, some defenders of Obama have concentrated precisely upon his pragmatism. For Fareed Zakaria, for example, the central Obama doctrine is that of strategic restraint, 'operationalised by a careful calculation of costs and benefits' (Zakaria, 2011). Admirers of the Obama Administration's deft reactiveness can point to his frequently quick witted and effective handling of difficult and unanticipated problems, as in the case of the 2010 Russian spy exchanges. Nevertheless, a credible and successful presidential foreign policy (at least in the terms outlined earlier in this chapter) needs to embrace more than deft particularized calculation. It needs to *unite* particularized pragmatism with general principle in a coherent and 'sellable' way. Denial of the need for a foreign policy compass is no more good politics than it is good policy. Obama is sometimes seen as a president who tries to substitute soaring rhetoric for coherent policy, attempting to reconcile impossibly contradictory aspirations in speech when they cannot be reconciled in actual policy. For Zbigniew Brzezinski, national security adviser to President Carter and sometime adviser to the 2008 Obama campaign, Obama 'doesn't strategise, he sermonizes' (Lizza, 2011). In fact, a reasonable case *can* be made for seeing the Obama foreign policy as coherent, even cynical, pragmatism bolstered by empty rhetoric. Such a case would proceed as follows.

The Obama priorities – exiting as swiftly as possible from Iraq, achieving some kind of 'good enough' solution in Afghanistan, containing nuclear proliferation – became clear in 2009. There may have been a degree of cheap rhetoric in the 2008 campaign, but the Obama White House has consciously seen and cleverly exploited the contribution which the presidential eloquence can make to inexpensive, and at least sometimes effective, American 'soft power'. The Obama 'answer' to the over-extension of the Bush years was the policy of pragmatic engagement, both in terms of the 'outstretched hand' to the Muslim world and policy towards China. The policy of pragmatic engagement was broadly in line with the demands of cost-conscious realism, while not being entirely neglectful of human rights. The Obama approach involved the sensible realization that success abroad must stem from economic recovery at home. The failure of Muslim 'outreach', especially towards Iran, led logically to new policy emphases, including the toughening of sanctions. Obama, whether in Libya or in the case of anti-terror action, showed that he was prepared to take military action, though not to the extent of compromising his own understanding of the claims of principled pragmatism. The 'pivot' to the Pacific in the later months of 2011 and in early 2012 caused a degree of consternation in Europe, but was announced with an unusual degree of clarity (Clinton, 2011; Bader, 2012; Heisbourg et al., 2012). In further pleading the case for attributing coherence to Obama's foreign policy, it can be argued that policy development was not mere random reaction, but the product of a conscious and measured debate within the Obama team. The debate, in very schematic terms, saw post-Bush cost-conscious realist approaches to world order (exemplified by figures as diverse as Robert Gates, Obama's first Secretary of Defense, and Tom Donilon, his second national security adviser) ranged against idealist/liberal interventionist positions, associated with White House personnel such as Samantha Power and Michael McFaul, United Nations Ambassador Susan Rice and (until her resignation from the State Department in February 2010) Anne-Marie Slaughter. Obama himself tended to lean towards 'cost-conscious realism', though he appears in 2011 to have been converted to support for Libyan intervention by 'idealist' arguments put by Power and Rice (Mann, 2012; Dowd, 2011).

Process

The operation of 'bureaucratic politics' – the cooperation and collision between agencies such as the State Department, the specialized foreign policy staff in the White House (headed by the National Security Advisor), and the Defense Department (or Pentagon) – forms vital evidence for judging and understanding leadership in foreign and security policy. A degree of conflict between the various departments and agencies engaged in forming US foreign and security policy is inevitable. Each body sees international problems from different perspectives and competes for the ear and approval of the president. I turn now directly to consider Obama's key appointments, bureaucratic leadership and adjudication of conflict within his own Administration.

The nomination of Hillary Clinton as Secretary of State and the retention of Robert Gates at the Pentagon were high-risk gambles that succeeded. Far from seeking to undermine her former rival for the Democratic presidential nomination in 2008, Hillary Clinton developed into an effective, loyal and extraordinarily energetic Secretary of State, even if her commitment to American global leadership sometimes seemed to out-run that of her boss (*The Economist*, 2012b; Mann, 2012). Not the least of Clinton's achievements was a complex reorganization of the State Department, designed to make the organization more geared to long-term policy development and more attuned to global economic and human rights agendas. Secretary Clinton's championing of 'economic statecraft' and women's rights (as stated, for example, in the 2010 first Quadrennial Diplomacy and Development Review) represented a conscious reorientation of the national diplomatic outlook. Secretaries Clinton and Gates cooperated in the Administration's first two years, in vivid contrast with the Pentagon–State Department tensions of the early years of George W. Bush. Especially as he neared retirement, Gates became very outspoken on imbalances in US defense budgeting, as well as on divisions within NATO. However, Gates represented effective Republican asbestos for Obama's potentially tricky relationship with the US military. Hillary Clinton sided with Robert Gates over the Afghan 'surge and drawdown' decision of 2009, just as Gates sided with Clinton over the Administration's commitment to 'soft power' diplomacy. The two parted company over Libya, with Secretary Gates urging greater caution, including, to some extent, over the Afghan drawbacks announced in mid-2011. Yet, tensions between major foreign policy principals within the Obama 'team of' (potential) 'rivals' were kept in check. Vice President Joe Biden emerged as an effective leader of diplomacy designed to extricate the US from Iraq. He did not succeed in obtaining Baghdad's support for a residual American presence beyond 2011, but led a concerted Administration effort to achieve a negotiated exit. Biden and Clinton found themselves on opposite sides in the Afghan 'surge' debate, with the former favoring a much swifter US drawdown. However, there was arguably less personal tension between Biden and Clinton in this period than there had been between Hillary, in her role as First Lady, and Vice President Al Gore in the 1990s.

Early Obama intra-administration policy debates tended to be much more open than their equivalents under George W. Bush. However, as time elapsed and with a certain sense of inevitability, control of policy-making tended to flow to Obama's foreign policy inner circle and away from the 'team of rivals' comprising Cabinet officers. According to James Mann (2012), this inner circle embraced Tom Donilon, Dennis McDonough, John Brennan and Ben Rhodes from the national security council staff; while White House chiefs Rahm Emanuel, Peter Rouse and Bill Daley were also included as political contributors to key foreign and security policy decisions. Key intra-administration rifts identified by Bob Woodward (2010) included those between Donilon and Gates and between the White House staff, particularly Emanuel, and Director of National Intelligence Dennis Blair. Blair, who was effectively sacked in May 2010, also clashed with John Brennan, intelligence adviser within the White House, and with Obama's second Defense Secretary, Leon Panetta (Mann, 2012). Obama's White House-centric policy process, however, was certainly not a return to the model of decision-making under President Nixon, where the State Department had been subjected to extreme marginalization. Differences of approach among key personnel were clear and indeed often openly acknowledged. At times, Richard Holbrooke ('special representative' for 'Afpak', the embodiment of the Administration's commitment to bring together policy for Afghanistan and Pakistan), Robert Gates, Hillary Clinton, Tom Donilon and Karl Eikenberry (US Ambassador to Afghanistan) were clearly at odds with one another. With Holbrooke's relationship with the Kabul government at the point of almost complete breakdown, his dismissal was averted only by the direct intervention of Secretary Clinton. The role of 'special representative' – not just Holbrooke, but also 'special envoy' George Mitchell in the Middle East – was not adequately defined within the Administration's power structure. The unhappy White House career of James Jones, the Marine General whose appointment as Obama's first national security adviser was designed to reassure the military, should also be acknowledged as a major policy process failure. Apparently unable to connect with the White House inner circle, even with his own chief of staff Dennis McDonough, Jones was an early casualty of the Administration's procedural dynamics.

There were some significant procedural lapses during Obama's first term. Policy towards Israel, especially in relation to Israeli settlements on the West Bank, was often confused. Efforts to blame Frank Wisner (former Ambassador to Egypt and the Administration's main conduit to the Cairo government in February 2011) could not disguise the policy contradictions which attended the outbreak of revolution in Egypt. The assassination of US diplomatic personnel in Libya during the 2012 reelection campaign raised difficult problems for Obama – problems which were exacerbated by clumsy and contradictory Administration press statements. The subsequent resignation of David Petraeus as head of the Central Intelligence Agency added to a degree of procedural confusion in the immediate post-reelection period. The perception of Obama as a decisional ditherer was also not always entirely wide of the mark. The Afghan 'surge and drawdown' decision of late 2009 was the product of a peculiarly public and protracted contest between rival views (broadly Secretary Gates and General David Petraeus – then acting as US military chief in Afghanistan – versus Richard Holbrooke and Vice President Biden). The emergence of the decision can be interpreted as indicating Obama's sensible concern for rational calculation of options, consensus-building and collegial due process (Pfiffner, 2011). However, it can just as easily be seen as illustrating Obama's tendency to plump for 'middle way' solutions – in this case, sending smaller numbers than requested by Petraeus, while also setting the exit-door clock ticking. It is not reassuring to reflect that the previous American president most identified with 'middle way' foreign policy solutions was Lyndon B. Johnson. Against the image of Obama as a ditherer, however, it is important to record his clear-sighted direction of the hunt for Osama bin Laden, culminating in the terrorist leader's dramatic killing in Pakistan (Bowden, 2012).

Despite some procedural inconsistencies and even occasional periods when Obama seemed to be paralyzed by foreign policy complexity, the first-term policy process did bear positive comparison with the record of most recent presidents. Only George H. W. Bush may plausibly be seen as having an undeniably superior record in terms of procedural coherence. Obama was scarcely the favored choice for the US military in the 2008 contest against Senator John McCain. At the time of Obama's inauguration it was predicted that the new president would follow his Democratic predecessor, Bill Clinton, as a president who risked having his authority undermined by the hostility of senior figures in his own military. Yet Obama proved himself more than able to stand up to military criticism. His 2010 sacking of General Stanley McChrystal was well handled, decisive and generally respected by the military community (Mann, 2012).

In terms of policy process, what was less defensible than the general working together of the top personnel was Obama's sidelining of congressional war powers. Here Obama was able to exploit the cross-cutting legislative positions on controversial military action indicated above. The presidential opinion of July 2011 regarding the inapplicability of the 1973 War Powers Resolution to the Libyan engagement involved the White House Counsel (Robert F. Bauer) effectively preempting the judgment of the Justice Department's Office of Legal Counsel (Ackerman, 2011; see also Congressional Research Service, 2011). It rested on a controversial, though not unprecedented, definition of 'hostilities' under war powers legislation. Defenders of the Administration could point, of course, to the marginalization of the War Powers Resolution in recent history, as well as to doubts concerning both its precise intent and its constitutionality. The presidential attitude towards legislative war powers did, however, give ammunition to those critics who saw Obama as simply 'Bush lite'.

Change and Obama's record

While aspects of the Obama record, such as the cavalier presidential attitude towards legislative war powers, proclaimed a measure of continuity with the preceding administration – the conservative notion of a timid appeaser in January 2009 replacing a defender of freedom is unconvincing. Such a view severely underplays the extent to which the second George W. Bush Administration (2005–09) had already moved in a more multilateralist, less confrontational direction. Perceptions of Obama as apologist-in-chief also distort the record of the 44th president's willingness to use force, not least in Pakistan. By early 2012, there had been over 200 drone strikes in Pakistan under Obama, compared to about 50 in the Bush years (Indyk et al., 2012). The drone strikes were the most prominent and controversial aspect of the redefined 'Afpak' strategy for Pakistan, as well as of wider anti-terror commitments in Somalia and Yemen. Especially controversial were the so-called 'signature strikes' – attacks aimed at unknown 'combatants', identified as such by their behavior rather than by any specific intelligence trail (Zenko, 2013).

Issues of change and continuity in foreign policy raise complex questions of structure and agency in international relations, as well as the simple fact (revealed graphically in the 'wikileaked' State Department material) of bureaucratic continuity. Perception of 'change' is, in fact, largely a matter of perspective. Viewed from remote enough a distance, American foreign policy since 1945 (if not before) is a story of continuity with only a few, usually externally generated, breaks. More realistically, change is constant and continuous, as presidential leadership and domestic debates over foreign policy interact with shifting international dynamics. Naturally, there were significant layers of Bush–Obama continuity. Withdrawal from Iraq proceeded along the track laid by Bush. Jeffrey Bader's account of East Asian policy under Obama stressed the continuity of pragmatically conceived national interest under both presidents, though Bader also argued that prioritization of the region rose significantly under Obama (Bader, 2012). The 2010 Nuclear Posture Review included invitations to other countries to work with the US on strategic issues and declared that strategic deterrence was not assisted by excessive reliance on nuclear weapons. Obama formally committed himself to nuclear 'global zero' and hosted a vast Washington conference later in 2010 on nuclear weapons reduction. However, the substance of the posture review effectively continued the Bush line on nuclear strategy, including the development of advanced conventional weapons as a replacement for nuclear ones. The New Start Treaty ratification (December 2010) was a major administration success, but nevertheless followed the approach embodied in the 2002 strategic offence reductions, with little in the way of formal verification. Partly as the price for some Republican support for the ratification, New Start pledged some \$80 billion for nuclear modernization. Obama's decision to halt Eastern European ballistic missile installations appeared on the surface to be a significant part of his 'change' agenda. However, it did not amount to anything approaching cancellation of ballistic missile defense. Such defense, technically now conceived in terms of 'phased adaptation', remained at the center of the new NATO security concept (promulgated in late 2010), which also embraced nuclear weapons and tactical deterrence (*The Economist*, 2012a; Blank and Jordan, 2012).

Despite important elements of continuity with his predecessor, Barack Obama, especially in his first two years in office, unquestionably uttered many thousands of words, notably in terms of outreach to Muslim countries, which hardly anyone could ever imagine coming from the mouth of a George W. Bush or indeed a putative President John McCain. This is not merely a matter of public diplomacy, of style and rhetoric – 'sermonizing' over 'strategizing'. Presidential words matter: they constitute interventions, often with unpredictable and long-term consequences, in the politics of nations. Much American foreign policy is declaratory. Moreover, Obama's stated and actualized commitment to multilateralism greatly outweighed that of even second-term George W. Bush (Slaughter, 2012). Examples included the restoration of American funding to the United Nations Population Fund and new initiatives designed partly to respond to, partly to deflect, criticisms of US domination of global financial institutions such as the World Bank.

The 2010 National Security Strategy made it clear that terrorism should not be allowed to define America's role in the world. Obama transformed policy in Afghanistan and Pakistan – not necessarily in line with the hopes of some of his supporters in 2008, but transformed it none the less. His defense budgets saw significant shifts. Major defense cuts – some \$10 billion over ten years – were the product both of economic stringency and of the winding down of inherited wars. Military spending – as 'discretionary' spending (rather than part of the 'entitlement' budget represented by programs such as Social Security) – was vulnerable in the political and economic conditions prevailing under Obama. Indeed, the possibility of further major 'automatic' cuts emerged from the failure in 2011 of congressional Republicans and Democrats to agree a prioritized schedule of budget deficit reduction. Such cuts raised the question of balance between capability and commitment, and certainly pointed to a less grandiose role for the US in terms of global security provision. Key features of Obama's security posture included commitments to unmanned attack aircraft and to balancing (alongside other regional powers) China's perceived long-term strategy of 'anti-access/area denial' in the Pacific. In 2012, the Administration undertook to shift 60 percent of naval assets to the Asia–Pacific region within eight years (Quinn, 2011a).

Looking briefly at the geographical range of Obama's foreign policy, the early 'resetting' of relations with Russia may be judged a success, not least in terms of gaining a degree of cooperation from Moscow in regard to US policy in Afghanistan. The resurgence of authoritarianism in Russia, along with differing perspectives on the Arab Spring (and especially with regard to Syria), pose problems for the second term. Despite the initial outreach, policy towards Iran became trapped between the stick of sanctions and the carrot of incentives, with American hopes being increasingly pinned on the former. Computer-based sabotage – the 'stuxnet' virus – seemed by 2011 at least to have delayed Iran's nuclear program. Yet, as the second term began, Washington found itself boxed in-between a nuclear-weaponizing Iran, an unpredictable Israel and the unattractiveness of a US military option, especially in view of the latter's likely impact on oil prices (Hurst, 2012). Rather than recalcitrant 'rogues', both Iran and North Korea were publicly described by the Obama Administration as 'out-liers' who might one day come to comply with international norms (Litwak, 2012). By the beginning of the second term, little progress had been made in either case. The Administration, though it failed to revive the multilateral regional talks last held in 2008, recognized that any solution to a resolution of the North Korean nuclear proliferation crisis involved some kind of joint pressure via Beijing. In the case of Iran and North Korea, Washington had little choice but to embrace a kind of 'strategic patience'.

Prospects in Afghanistan veered during the first term between the hopeful and the desperately pessimistic, with little prospect of more than what Richard Haass called in May 2011 'a messy stalemate' following America's exit. For Haass, president of the Council on Foreign Relations, Afghanistan had become under Obama's direction 'a strategic distraction, pure and simple' (Haass, 2011; see also O'Hanlon and Sherjan, 2010). The security outlook for Pakistan remained dire. Two or so years into his administration, Obama appeared to have concluded that any serious drive for an Israel–Palestine peace process would have to await a second term. While remaining feared and hated on the Arab street, the Administration had also succeeded in alienating Israeli public opinion (Indyk et al., 2012). Policy towards Latin America broadly continued in the mold inherited from Bush, with Obama signing a free trade deal with Colombia and becoming preoccupied with Mexican drug-related security. Tensions within NATO over European defense spending levels, as well as over the Europeans' military performance in Afghanistan, became intense (Michta, 2011). Rather than sponsoring grand initiatives, Obama vainly urged eurozone countries to act decisively to stem their economic crisis. By 2013, some progress had been made on the 'visionary' themes of 2008. US support was forthcoming for the G-20 group of countries (which by now had largely superseded the narrower G-8) not only as a forum which reflected international change, but also as a body capable of tackling humanitarian agendas. A carbon emissions deal of sorts was achieved at Copenhagen in 2009, though it lacked binding force. In late 2012, Obama announced that ratification of the Comprehensive Test Ban Treaty and multilateral action on climate change would be prominent second-term concerns. By this time, in regard to one of most common predictions from 2008, it was being argued that George W. Bush had been as good, if not a better, president for Africa than Obama had thus far been.

The first term record was patchy. In October 2010, David Ignatius offered something which might be seen as coming close to a consensual verdict on the whole first term: 'Obama's achievement is that he has reconnected America to the world. But even though the US is less hated, it may also be taken less seriously by other nations' (Ignatius, 2010).

'Change we can believe in' and the second term agenda

As Obama began his second term, two opposing narratives of the first term foreign policy approach and sense of direction presented themselves. From one perspective, the Obama foreign policy grew rather naturally from the second George W. Bush Administration. Proponents of this interpretation could point to the retention of Robert Gates at the Pentagon and to the generally cautious choice of Obama's senior foreign policy 'team of rivals'. The proliferation of drone attacks can be seen as constituting a new stage in what was still a strategy-defining War on Terror, designed to eradicate senior terrorist personnel even as it cut the ground from under some Republican critics of the Administration's putative timidity. In this perspective, the Afghan 'surge' decision revealed the Administration's unwillingness clearly to break with its inheritance from Bush. Obama, it might be argued, remained excessively unwilling to accept the governmental legitimacy of political Islam. At home, Obama quietly dropped his objections to the Foreign Intelligence Surveillance and Patriot Acts, while retaining a high-handed attitude towards legislative war powers. From a rather different perspective, it might be argued that the Obama approach was in some measure to recognize the blindingly obvious fact of China's rise, while essentially missing the chance to redraw priorities as the US withdrew from Iraq and planned to withdraw from Afghanistan. Thus, even as economic constraints on Pentagon spending became increasingly evident, the US (in this line of argument) remained globally over-committed (Mearsheimer, 2011; Singh, 2012). It can also be argued that the new prioritization of East Asia was less a realistic adjustment to global change than a more potentially dangerous raising of tension. Cold War 'security dilemmas' – cycles of mutual worry and constant remilitarization – might thus (arguably) reappear in the context of Sino-American relations as a result of America's much-signaled turn to the Pacific.

A second interpretation would take the announced shifts of the Obama first term much more seriously. In this perspective, Obama had a clear purpose: to adapt US foreign policy to a post-unipolar (indeed, if the term is not too loaded, to a 'post-American') world of economic constraint and continued strategic uncertainty. In his first term he had no reason to feel embarrassed about the need to step back a little from foreign engagement in order to make space for domestic renewal. Real progress (it might be argued) was made in degrading terrorist capabilities, without the War on Terror being allowed to determine America's strategic outlook. By late 2012, Administration officials were able explicitly to look forward to an era when direction of the battle against global terrorism could be handed over to international agencies. The US under Obama thus sought to return to strategic restraint and multi-lateral cooperative liberalism. In a sense, the strategic post-Cold War debates about the appropriate international posture for the United States had properly resumed, following their hyper-violent interruption on September 11, 2001. Under Obama, pragmatic engagement superseded the 'freedom agenda', even if his Administration (like the Bill Clinton Administration) remained torn between the perceived need to assert 'values' and the need to engage enemies in dialogue. Obama's cost-conscious realism – so a sympathetic account of recent presidential diplomacy might proceed – often trumped, but did not entirely extinguish, the visionary themes of the 2008 campaign. Obama managed to thread a route around extreme domestic partisanship, securing both the ratification of the New Start Treaty and workable legislative support for the Libyan air intervention of 2011. He succeeded in finding a way out of both Iraq and Afghanistan, even if the exit from the latter was excessively delayed by the retention of unrealistic hopes. Above all (in this interpretation of the Obama record) the turn towards Asia represented a deliberate and defensible strategic choice, to be understood as much in economic as in security terms: not an abandonment of other regions, but a sensible adjustment to international change.

Some elements of the first line of interpretation are persuasive; however, in this chapter I incline to the second more positive evaluation of Obama's foreign policy. Recalling my earlier points about how to evaluate presidential foreign policy, it may convincingly be argued that Obama managed to convert a potentially disastrous legacy from Bush into a foreign policy which pointed away from the over-extensions of the War on Terror. Obama's decisional processes demonstrated commitments to procedural rationality. His preference for the 'middle way' was not always reassuring. His first term decision-making (it must be admitted) was sometimes slow and seemed occasionally to be in danger of becoming paralyzed by the recognition of complexity. Yet policy direction was at least situated firmly in the White House, while preserving both a considerable degree of multiple advocacy and a constructive role for big foreign policy players outside the White House. Like President Franklin Roosevelt in 1933, Obama appreciated in 2009 that domestic reform must be given priority. On the international stage, the first term Obama Administration did not always maintain a viable balance between retreating from over-extension and recognizing that the alternative to American global leadership is often no leadership at all. Yet it is misleading to portray the Administration as over-fixated by American 'decline'. Obama, during his first term, at least began the necessary process of making strategic choices.

The second Obama term began with a clear indication in the President's State of the Union address (February 2013) that American forces would indeed leave Afghanistan by 2014; that the 'Arab Spring' rebels in Syria could not expect much in the way of direct American help; that the US would do what was necessary to ensure that Iran did not acquire a nuclear weapons capability; and that somehow the nuclear threat from North Korea would be contained. Obama indicated his desire to move ahead with a new bilateral free trade deal with the European Union. Such a development seemed at one level designed to deflect criticism about American insouciance over economic disorder in Europe in the context of evident American preoccupation with East Asia. The new move towards a European free trade deal, however, also reflected the failure of global trade diplomacy (the so-called 'Doha round'). Obama's second term appointments – John Kerry at the State Department, (former Republican Senator) Chuck Hagel at the

Pentagon, and John Brennan at the CIA – were widely interpreted as evidencing presidential caution about 'idealist' intervention, though also indicating continued commitment to anti-terror 'drone' strategy.

Looking at the second term agenda more broadly, it seems certain that the enhanced preoccupation with East Asia will continue. It is tempting to argue that Obama, a second term president facing the prospect of intense and efficacious Republican opposition on Capitol Hill, may (like many of his predecessors) move increasingly to favor foreign policy activism over domestic reform. Obama's preference may, however, be for so-called 'intermestic' initiatives – policy areas which straddle foreign/domestic divisions – such as climate change and immigration reform. In reality, second term foreign and security policy will to a major extent be driven by external constraints and surprises. The prospects for the success of some dramatic presidential diplomatic initiative in respect of the Israel–Palestine peace process are so poor that Obama may not be inclined to offer any such initiative. Major defense spending cuts, possibly bringing down the size of the US Army from 500,000 to 400,000, are likely to result from a combination of budgetary austerity and the failure in Congress to agree a taxing and spending strategy (*The Economist*, 2013). The second term seems likely to confirm the shift to a more modest and regionally differentiated American internationalism.

Chapter 15

America's Civil Rights State: Amelioration, Stagnation or Failure?

Desmond King

Racial divisions dominate modern American elections. In the presidential election in November 2012, the following voting patterns confirm this influence: 94 percent of African Americans voted for Democrat Obama and 6 percent for Republican Romney; 59 percent of whites voted for Romney and 39 percent for Obama; 73 percent of Asian Americans supported Obama compared with 27 percent for Romney; and 71 percent of Latinos voted for Obama compared with 29 percent supporting Romney. This dichotomy shows the challenge facing Republican Party candidates in the coming years as their core racial support group is a declining percentage of the electorate.

One reason for this powerful racial polarization – which mirrors polarization more generally in the electorate – is the historical role of the American State. State policy fostered racial inequality by supporting segregated race relations; but since the 1960s the State has acted as the agent of race equality. The American State in other words has had a fundamental though changing relationship with African Americans since 1776 (see Table 15.1). The country democratized and reformed its anti-racial laws in the 1960s, establishing equal rights of citizenship for African Americans. Although it is often treated as a purely historical subject, a racial crisis is looming for American civil rights. This crisis consists in the paradox of the enduring material racial inequality in the context of a national government which has been transformed from a suppressor into a rights enforcer. Furthermore, the attempted progression toward greater racial equality has resulted in the pattern of the last two decades that is one of failed policy and greater inequality. Why did the momentum of the 1965–75 years dissipate and even, in some ways, start to go backwards after the 1990s?

The American State is unquestionably now a civil rights State. And in many ways its transformation in the 1960s toward African Americans'

Table 15.1   *Periodization of the American state and African Americans*

Eras	Role of the Federal Government
A. 1776–1861: the era of slavery. [1860s–1870s: the transition from abortive Reconstruction.]	Accepted and upheld slavery.
B. 1880s–1964: the era of segregation. [1965–1978: the transition from comprehensive intervention.]	Fostered racial segregation.
C. 1978–2008: the era of civil rights. [2008+: the racial crisis of America's civil rights state.]	Enforcer of equal rights.

Source: King and Smith (2011: chs 1–3).

rights of citizenship was complete and dramatic (King and Lieberman, 2009, 2011). As the threefold periodization in Table 15.1 shows, the state's position was transformed in respect of this historically discriminated against and unequally treated group. Measured in the eras of segregation an civil rights, the state has been the most fundamental institution for the historical, political, economic and legal development of African Americans. It assumed multiple roles over time, including as: an oppressor failing to uphold federal civil rights laws such as anti-lynching legislation; an instrument of segregation through partial employment patterns and stunted advancement prospects; an agent of rights, via the courts; an enforcer of voting rights; and a source of economic uplift, in a mixture of affirmative action policy and disproportionately high public sector employment.

The Civil Rights Act in 1964 and the Voting Rights Act in 1965 (accompanied with enforcement powers in the Department of Justice), and the ambitious effort under the Great Society to instigate a comprehensive program of historical redress and future economic advancement, all placed the state in an active and leading role as a defender of African Americans as citizens. The voting laws and rights set the trajectory without which Barack Obama could not have been elected President. The state's role in these changes, galvanized by a civil rights movement, was crucial as the two eminent scholars of political transition, Acemoglu and Robinson, recently acknowledge in their book *Why Nations Fail*: from the 1940s and 1950s 'the US Supreme Court and the federal government finally began to intervene systematically to reform the extractive institutions in the South' (2012). What they term the 'inclusive federal institutions of the US' worked, in their view, in coalition with African American civil rights reformers. It marked a reversal of pre-1960s policy when the segregationist order was accommodated and fostered in federal government: in this setting of political transformation and reform it was bureaucratic autonomy at work, defining the contours of the state. For instance, federal bureaucrats in housing agencies engaged in systematic racial structuring of mortgage applications, using the instrument of 'redlining' – a negative assessment of those properties occupied by African Americans – to prevent African Americans becoming home owners, a strategy consistent with many white northerners' preferences (King, 2007; Jackson, 1985; Massey and Denton, 1993; Katz et al., 2005; Dreier et al., 2001; Pattillo-McCoy, 1999; Anderson, 2010).

Yet 50 years after this apparent transformation of the American state the material position of African Americans remains highly unequal. The scale of the material racial inequality crisis now facing the United States must reflect in some way on how this transformation occurred and ultimately failed. In 2007 and 2011 the average unemployment rates for African Americans were 7.9 and 15.8 percent compared with 4.2 and 7.9 percent for whites. Comparable disparities are manifest even when the level of education is controlled for (US Department of Labor, 2012). In adumbrating the importance of state employment activity to African Americans in the civil rights era, the analysis also exposes African Americans' vulnerability to American fiscal crises and public employment patterns. This is one dimension of the racial crisis.

The new state activities established in the 1960s and 1970s transformation proved limited and inadequate. Many of the measures designed to enforce anti-discrimination in schools, housing and labor markets lacked teeth, and above all the ambition, first aired in the controversial Moynihan Report, to initiate a comprehensive work scheme to ameliorate African American economic circumstances after the passage of the 1964 Civil Rights Act quickly lost momentum and depth (Patterson, 2010).

Dimensions of American state activity and African Americans

I distinguish several strands to the state's role in African Americans' lives and circumstances. These strands reveal aspects of the unfolding racial crisis, as changes in national state policy do not just fail adequately to facilitate inclusive institutions but preside over regressive effects.

Public employment and wage inequality

The state has been a crucially important employer for African Americans since the end of the 19th century (Krislov, 1967; King,

2007). Between the collapse of Reconstruction in 1877 and the 1960s this public employment relationship was segregationist: that is, workers were segregated by race and senior posts were held by whites. The framework of segregated race relations in public sector hiring changed from the 1960s, though the number of African Americans working in the sector remained high. Three trends stand out.

First, the enactment of civil and voting rights legislation in the 1960s marked a new phase in how the state related to African Americans. Public sector departments became *employers committed to equality including equal opportunity*. The state's agencies – notably the EEOC and some administrative courts – became enforcers of non-discrimination in the public sector.

Second, the number of African Americans working in the public sector steadily grew until it came to employ a disproportionately high number of them – that is disproportionately high compared to their number in the labor force. For African Americans the public sector, from federal to local government, is the 'single most important source of employment'. According to Pitts, 'during 2008–2010, 21.2 percent of all Black workers are public employees, compared with 16.3 percent of non-Black workers. Both before and after the onset of the Great Recession, African Americans were 30 percent more likely than other workers to be employed in the public sector' (2011: 1).

Third, public sector employment has benefited the economic circumstances of many African American employees by having a positive effect on wage inequality and through associated benefits and entitlements. Public sector employment translates into a higher number of decent-paying jobs gained by African Americans compared with private sector jobs: 'the median wage earned by Black employees is significantly higher in the public sector than in other industries' (ibid.: 2).

Along these three dimensions – equal employer, disproportionately high employer and source of reduced wage inequality – as an employer the state has been crucial for African Americans and proved to be an important aspect of the transformative process.

However, African American employees are under-represented in the industries experiencing the most job growth since the slow recovery commenced in 2009. As the US Department of Labor (2011: 2) reports:

> once unemployed, Blacks are less likely to find jobs and tend to stay unemployed for longer periods of time. Blacks remained unemployed longer than Whites or Hispanics in 2011, with a medium duration of unemployment of 27.0 weeks (compared to 19.7 weeks for Whites and 18.5 for Hispanics). Nearly half (49.5 per cent) of all unemployed Blacks were unemployed for 27 weeks or longer in 2011, compared to 41.7 per cent of unemployed Whites and 39.9 per cent of unemployed Hispanics.

Because African Americans are given fewer senior positions in the private sector, redundancies there tend to affect them more adversely as they are seen as more expendable employees. As labor market economists have shown, the longer a person is unemployed the harder finding a job becomes; and a characteristic of the Great Recession is that the numbers unemployed for six months or longer has been much higher than in previous recessions, thereby deepening the reemployment crisis (Elsby et al., 2010). The growth in the private healthcare sector has helped improve the outlook for African American job seekers since 2011, and Department of Labor statistics report the unemployment rate for Blacks moving to 13.6 percent in 2012.

Debt and assets

The subprime mortgage crisis has affected African American households more severely than other groups, in many cases devastating their nominal household wealth. A generation of black homeowners has been set back hugely by the meltdown, damaged by the racialization of residential housing patterns. As two scholars observe: 'discriminatory subprime lending is simply the latest in a long line of illegal practices that have been foisted on minorities in the United States. It is all the more shocking because these practices were well-known and documented long before the housing bubble burst' (Rugh and Massey, 2010). This housing debt is a powerful instance of the American state's dramatic failure to enforce regulatory standards necessary for denting material racial inequality.

The Pew Research Center's (2012) data (taken from an analysis of the government generated Survey of Income and Program Participation about patterns of household wealth by race) find historically high levels of inequality. In 2005 the median net worth of white households was $134,992; by 2009 this figure had dropped to $113,149. For African American households the 2005 median net worth of households was $18,359, a figure which plummets to $6,325 in 2009. And for Latino households the figures are $12,124 in 2005 and $5,677 in 2009. Of white households, 15 percent had zero or negative wealth in 2009. This figure compares with 35 percent of African Americans and 31 percent of Latino households. Pew's analysis shows the divergence in household wealth by race. Latinos who make up 16 percent of the US population and African Americans who compose 12 percent are now on very different levels of household equity compared with white Americans. The achievements of recent years toward reducing material race inequality have been squandered. This trend affects the notion of inclusion and equal rights of citizenship.

Non-random and systematic sources of discrimination or bias confront African Americans' dealings with the state in numerous ways. In respect to bankruptcy for instance – a key dimension of debt – researchers find, regarding homeownership, assets and education, even when adjusted for income, that 'blacks are about twice as likely as whites to wind up in the more onerous and costly form of consumer bankruptcy as they try to dig out from their debts' (Bernard, 2012).

Enforcer of rights

The state's record as an enforcer of equal rights and anti-discrimination measures is mixed (Pager and Shepherd, 2008). Upholding voting rights has been the shining example of strong enforcement. With rigorous Justice Department monitoring and enforcement of the 1965 act in recalcitrant states, the Supreme Court has supported minority-majority districting and the end of literacy tests or poll taxes. But recently the rise of photo ID tests as a prerequisite for registration and voting in numerous Republican controlled states, the inaccurate purging of electoral rolls, and the shortening of the period for early voting has eroded some of the gains from the 1960s and 1970s (Perez, 2008; Weiser and Norden, 2011; Aguilar, 2011).

Enforcement of anti-discrimination laws in the housing and labor markets is inadequate. Passage of the Fair Housing Act in 1968 resulted only because of the assassination of Martin Luther King Jr, and even then the agreed legislation watered down tougher measures by putting primary onus on the plaintiff to demonstrate intentional racism (King and Smith, 2011). It took 20 years for a more robust set of amendments to be added in 1988 to restrict real estate agents directing or 'steering' African American or white prospective buyers or renters to particular neighborhoods. But the strengthened measures passed in 1988 have had limited impact as the persistence of intense residential segregation shows – the two sociologists Joseph Rugh and Douglas Massey observe that 'in 2000 a majority of black urban dwellers continued to live under conditions of hyper-segregation. At the same time, levels of Hispanic segregation have been rising' (2010; Massey, 2007). This effect was intentional since the legislation still placed the onus on those discriminated against to make a case. The evidence is overwhelming that black homeowners were much more likely than comparable white buyers – measured in credit ratings, size of down-payment required, personal characteristics and residential location – to receive subprime rather than prime mortgages and to have unfavorable terms such as high prepayment penalties built into their contracts (Rugh and Massey, 2010). These are non-random enduring inequalities, racially based, tolerated by the State's inadequate housing regulatory and anti-discrimination regime.

In labor markets there is strong scholarly evidence about the persistence of discrimination. As in housing markets, audit studies and tests find that some employers respond differently to African Americans compared with white job seekers, and there are profound difficulties for former African American prisoners seeking employment (Pager, 2007; King and Smith, 2011). The last law passed to help excise discrimination in the labor market was the Civil Rights Act 1991 which banned hiring practices with racially disparate impacts, though when signing the law (having vetoed a previous version) President George W. H. Bush declared it did not include this element. The leading scholar of labor market discrimination, Devah Pager, writes that 'experimental audit studies focusing on hiring decisions have consistently found strong evidence of racial discrimination, with estimates of white preferences ranging from 50 percent to 24 percent', a study she cites from Boston and Chicago in which employers were mailed CVs for jobs using racially identifiable names for the job seekers, and which found that 'white names triggered a call back rate that was 50 percent higher than that of equally qualified black applicants' (Pager and Shepherd, 2008: 6, 7). These findings are consistent with the large scale Urban Poverty and Family Life Study undertaken by William Julius Wilson among Chicago employers: 'the available research does suggest that African Americans, more than any other major racial or ethnic group, face negative employer perceptions about their qualifications and their work ethic' (Wilson, 1996: 111). Employment outcomes clearly vary by race.

On the other hand the positive effects of active State anti-discrimination enforcement have been demonstrated empirically. One influential study found a marked improvement in the economic position of African Americans between 1940 and 1980, following the implementation of federal law, when race became a less significant issue in determining wages (Heckman and Payner, 1989). The kind of tests used by potential employers make a difference to hiring decisions. Thus the scope for enforcement and regulation to tackle discrimination is compelling.

Incarceration

For every 100,000 of the population the US has 751 people incarcerated compared with 63 in Japan or 151 in England (which is one of the highest amongst Western democracies) or 88 in Germany. That this increase in American lock-up rates is dramatic comes from the country's own history where between 1925 and 1975 only 110 per 100,000 Americans faced imprisonment (Western, 2006).

African Americans and increasingly Latinos disproportionately number amongst those Americans experiencing the federal and state correctional systems. Despite the growth of a prosperous, middle-class, African American community, the experience of many low income and poor African Americans is incarceration at rates above that predictable from income status alone. In 2012 one in seven black males between

16 and 35 were in prison or had had experience of incarceration. The numbers may have peaked, however, due to recent fiscal pressures on federal and state government.

Historically felon disenfranchisement has been a distinctive feature of the United States. One reliable scholarly estimate concludes that more than 16 million Americans carry a felony record which disenfranchises them from voting in elections, from the very local to the national, in their states. Because the prison population is not a random profile of Americans in terms of race or class or gender so this large disenfranchised population is not a random cross-section of Americans. Thus I would argue that high incarceration feeds non-randomly into levels of political participation. The negative effects of incarceration for American politics are wide and deep (Goffman, 2009; Weaver, and Lerman 2010; Desmond and Valdez, 2012).

As sociologist Bruce Western (2007) explains, one of the striking aspects of contemporary incarceration patterns is 'their concentration among young African American men with little schooling'. While 13.5 percent of young black men aged 22 to 30 were in prison in 2004, among similarly aged young white men the rate was below 2 percent. For young black men without any college experience '21.1 percent were locked up on an average day in 2004'. Western's calculations show that 'for men born in the late 1940s who reached their mid-thirties in 1979, blacks were 9 percent likely to go to prison. For black men born in the late 1960s, the lifetime chances of imprisonment had grown to 22.8 percent'. Therefore, 'for young black male dropouts, prison time has become a normal life event, affecting 60 percent of those born since the late 1960s'.

The civil rights lawyer, Michelle Alexander (2010), calls the modern pattern the 'new Jim Crow' (a reference to the system of segregated race relations practiced throughout the United States between the 1880s and 1954, especially in the South). She writes that 'the fact that more than half of the young black men in any large American city are currently under the control of the criminal justice system (or saddled with criminal records) is not – as many argue – just a symptom of poverty or poor choices, but rather evidence of a new racial caste system at work' (ibid.; and see Goffman, 2009). It is also the case that, in some states, the expansion of prison capacity under a segregated framework in the first half of the 20th century created the conditions for accommodating the post-1980s prison population growth (Schoenfeld, 2012).

Affirmative action

The American state has engaged in affirmative action since it began expanding into public policy. The system of civil war pensions created in the 1860s was racially distorted. Affirmative action was a policy tool used to protect white Americans' interests in the century before civil rights reform in the 1960s. Ira Katznelson's book *When Affirmative Action Was White* (2007) shows how a white affirmative action program functioned under state tutelage during the 1930s and 1940s. The post-war GI Bill providing college access to veterans has been seen as a program benefiting whites by several scholars (Mettler, 2005). The state's affirmative action policy played a huge role in bringing positive change in the labor market position of tens of thousands of African Americans. For both those white and African American beneficiaries affirmative action has one key effect: it transfers positive benefits and prospects to the next generation, thereby providing a pattern of intergenerational mobility and household asset advancement; this trend is underlined in recent Pew Center findings about the declining social mobility of African Americans because of the housing crisis compared with white middle-class children. But affirmative action is deeply under challenge, facing another Court test in the 2012–13 term (*Fisher v Texas*) after being significantly weakened in the *Ricci* case in 2009. In Fisher the Court decided by a 7–1 majority to return the case to the lower court and directed it (and other appeals courts) to apply more rigorous 'strict scrutiny' criteria to university admissions policy using the principle of 'diversity'.

Varying participation rates and levels of employment/unemployment among African Americans is a continuing problem in the United States labor market. Variation cannot be explained solely by such standard factors as lower education qualifications. For instance, as noted above, at every level of educational achievement (or non-achievement) African American unemployment rates are higher than those for whites, though the gap narrows the higher the level of education attainment. Labor market discrimination has been identified as a key factor. In the financial year 2011 the Office of Federal Contract Compliance Programs (in DOL) resolved 134 cases of discrimination (totaling $12 million compensation) arising from employees' complaints of those employed on federal contractors' or subcontractors' schemes. The Office monitors and enforces affirmative action and non-discrimination obligations amongst holders of federal contracts. Of those 134, 'twenty-three cases specifically involved African Americans (up 44 percent from the previous year) resulting in over $2 million in back pay (an increase of 33 percent over last years)' (Pager and Shepherd, 2008).

African Americans do live in more economically depressed areas with concentrated unemployment rates. For instance in 2008–10, 62.9 percent of African Americans were more likely to live in areas with double-digit unemployment compared with 39 percent of whites (Pager and Shepherd, 2008). But the jobs crisis for significant parts of the African American community is not merely an income or class based problem but one with a specific racial dimension that determines life chances. This proposition sets a challenge for the American State and, if accurate, marks a regression from the progressive trajectory observed in the 1970s and even the 1980s, when researchers started to find evidence of meaningful intergenerational mobility in class terms comparable to that of whites – many of these studies found public sector employment to be a key determinant of occupational improvement. But discrimination persisted. One study using panel data from 1976 and 1985 compared young African American men for wage differences with whites and 'found that the effect of race, after controlling for other variables, increased during their period, and that the proportion of the racial gap in hourly wages due to discrimination (that is, after racial differences measured qualifications were taken into account) also increased during this time span'. This means that 'the government's retreat from anti-discrimination initiatives in the 1980s resulted in organizational discrimination against blacks and contributed to the reversal in the postwar trend toward racial parity in earnings' (Cancio et al., 1996, quoted in Wilson, 2011). Wilson's analysis of CPS data confirms this reversal: 'despite some improvements during the 1990s, by 2007, the income ratio of young black college-educated males was significantly below the ratio of 1977' (Wilson, 2011). Furthermore, income disparities within the African American community itself have increased as its middle class has gained public employment.

Official calculations about the jobs crisis, grim though the data mostly appear, are substantially rosier than the reality because they exclude many of those who have stopped seeking work and those young males who are in prison. The employment-to-population ratio – based on monthly Census Bureau household surveys – exaggerates employment levels as a consequence. Bruce Western argues that prisoners should be included in the calculation of the number of jobless or job seekers, which would then show that there were no gains for young non-college African American men in the 1990s. Examining the period 1980–2000, Western concludes that 'improvements in black relative wages are not substantially because of improvements in the market position of black workers'. Rather he argues that 'jobless rates increased among black low-wage workers, and incarceration rates increased among young black workers, removing those with little earnings power from standard labor market accounts'. In other words, the high incarceration rates affecting young African American men 'conceal inequality by removing low-wage men from the labor market' (Western and Pettit 2005). Historian Michael Katz reports that 'among 26 to 30 year old black men, labor force nonparticipation leaped from about 9 percent in 1940 to 30 percent in 2000' (Katz et al., 2005).

Three pathways: amelioration, stagnation or failure

This pattern of enduring, material, race inequalities reflects the limited transformation in the American State's evolution as not just an upholder of a *de jure* civil rights state but as an effective promoter of the material race equality necessary for genuine egalitarianism. The puzzle is why, in Acemoglu and Robinson's (2012) terms, having democratized and embedded inclusive political institutions, not only have these arrangements failed to deliver sharp ameliorations in inequality but have in numerous ways regressed. And a conflict theorist might well ask why there has not been more disorder and public instability. In response to historian Michael Katz's question 'why don't American cities burn?' (2012) we may note that American cities *have* been centers of intense violence and riots, notably in 1992 in Los Angeles after the Rodney King incident and throughout the 1960s, so it could happen again. But identifying thresholds for public disorder is notoriously complex. It is more profitable to focus on the mechanisms that help explain the trajectory from 1960s democratization to contemporary stubbornly inadequate state measures for remedying enduring inequality. Persisting, material, racial inequality after a half century of legal equality implies that the structural barriers to amelioration are overarching and that without a populist social movement or widespread social protest of the sort preceding the 1960s reforms some sort of civil rights crisis is building in America. The 2012 racially polarized election results certainly demonstrate how divided by race voters are and how they side with quite different approaches to government's role in society. Table 15.2 summarizes three possible pathways from the reforms of the 1960s.

So what happened to the state's changing relationship with African Americans and to the policies which seemed to signal progressive improvement rather than a trajectory of unraveling integration and change? Three sorts of factors are germane: short-term influences rooted in economic crisis; institutional aspects of the American polity, notably the weak capacity of the executive-centralized State; and structural constraints such as embedded political divisions about whether to address material race inequality and weak pluralistic institutions.

Short-term factors

Some of the current racial crisis can be explained through immediate and short-term factors not necessarily related to embedded racism or discrimination. The economic crisis including the subprime mortgage implosion helps account for the prolonged absence of jobs and the steep indebtedness and impoverishment of many African American households. The effort to broaden home ownership was an official

Table 15.2   *Pathways of transformation from civil rights democratization*

Path A	Path B	Path C
New laws (1964 and 1965) which result in:		
(i) Enforcement of rights and regulations	(i) Indifferent enforcement and weak regulation	(i) Backlash against civil rights and pro-incarceration
[which leads to]	[which leads to]	[which leads to]
(ii) Political inclusion through affirmative action and material advances	(ii) Status quo regarding jobs and wages	(ii) Political exclusion within democratic polity and structural rigidity
Outcome for economic crisis:		
Changes able to withstand crises	Vulnerable and reversion to pre-crisis inequalities	Reassertion of enduring marginality and inequalities in labor markets
Systemic outcome:		
State transformation enhancing legitimacy through inclusion and democratization	Arrested transformation deepening material inequality	State reversal, with new segregation, new inequalities and episodic protests

state policy exploited by inadequately regulated private actors, revealing the failure of market based solutions to enduring problems. But the short-term factors point to a deeper issue – the inadequacy of the material bases of life for many individuals, including African Americans, knocked sideways by recessionary pressures.

Short-term effects are exaggerated because of the disproportionately high level of African American employment in the public sector. The crisis in this type of employment has been deleterious for African Americans, close to a fifth of whom (if in work) are in the public sector (Williams, 2011). Teaching, firefighting and policing jobs have been crucial to the development of the black middle class since the 1970s, and it is these positions which have suffered losses since 2011. America's black communities are thus disproportionately damaged by public sector layoffs, just as they have been ravaged by another part of the American state: prisons.

Although shaped by the post-2007 economic crisis (Lodge and Hood, 2012), the reduction in public sector employment is not a random process. It is part of a Republican Party agenda to reduce the size of the public employment budget and to weaken or abolish collective bargaining in the public sector. The most salient example is Wisconsin. The GOP is increasingly a white party with negligable support from African Americans and support from less than a third of Hispanic voters (Trende, 2012). In states such as Wisconsin, Michigan and Indiana GOP governors and legislatures have targeted public employees to reduce government spending. In 2011 250,000 state and local government employees lost their jobs. Many were public school teachers. Since 2008 a total of 650,000 have been laid off by state and local governments alone (Hicks, 2012). The Obama 2009 stimulus package provided money to keep many public sector workers in post at state and local level for another two years but once it expired in 2011 the number of public employment lay-offs has grown. So ironically from being initially more protected, public employees, especially in jobs such as teachers, firefighters, police and other public workers, have lost posts at a higher rate since the official end of the recession.

Data from the 2006, 2008 and 2010 Displaced Worker Surveys (a part of the Current Population Surveys), document a negative increase in the different employment prospects between whites and African Americans. As one researcher writes, despite the presence of 'more formal rules of public sector displacement' instituted to 'generate race neutral displacement outcomes', the force of discriminatory practices prevailed during the crisis (Rodgers, 2012). The importance of these trends is the damage it does to the role of the state's public sector as a mechanism to erode wage and asset inequalities between African Americans and whites.

The evidence about this historically positive effect of public sector employment on African American mobility is now more appreciated by scholars. African American public sector employment grew from the 1960s and 1970s as government programs expanded under the Great Society, and affirmative action measures required employers to hire African Americans (Dobbin, 2010). And writing recently in a reflection on his classic book *The Declining Significance of Race* the Harvard sociologist William Julius Wilson notes that he would 'underline the role and importance of affirmative action programs. In the process, I would discuss the impact of a possible contraction in government employment as well as waning public support for affirmative action on the occupational mobility of the more advantaged and educated African Americans'. A few pages later he reiterates the need to place 'greater emphasis not only on the role of the public sector in accounting for black occupational mobility, but also on the importance of sustained public support for anti-discrimination action, to ensure that the gains continue or, at the least, are not reversed' (Wilson, 2011). Since Wilson's scholarship is renowned, especially for his analysis of how post-1970s de-industrialization removed the industrial and manufacturing jobs that had helped a black middle class develop after civil rights reform, his new emphasis is noteworthy. What Wilson does not develop is an explanation for the way in which the State's transformation in the 1960s and 1970s led to its becoming the contemporary racially partial state, a state in which policy-making continues to have significant positive and negative effects for African Americans. Understanding this pattern requires understanding how transformation takes distinct but parallel forms and the limits of inactive state policy.

Institutional failures/obstacles

Enforcement and disparate impact

The Equal Employment Opportunity Commission (EEOC) distinguishes between differential treatment and disparate impact, following the *Griggs v Duke Power Co* (1971) US Supreme Court ruling. Differential treatment is straightforward unequal treatment – applying a prejudice or bias against a member of a group because of that membership. This is proscribed under Title VII of the 1964 Civil Rights Act. Also proscribed is the use of apparently routine procedures and rules to make hiring decisions where the resulting patterns of employment empirically under-represent certain groups. The EEOC explains that Title VII 'prohibits employers from using neutral tests or selection procedures that have the effect of disproportionately excluding persons based on race, color, religion, sex, or national origin, where the tests or selection procedures are not "job-related and consistent with business necessity"'. Such patterns induce 'disparate impact' discrimination. In a later ruling, *Wards Cove Packing Co. v Antonio* (1989), the Court held that plaintiffs cannot merely collect statistics demonstrating disparities in a workforce but must demonstrate a causal connection between the employer practice and any harmful, particularly racial, effect. This rule helps the Court claim judicial decision-making is race or color blind.

The notion of disparate impact needs broadening so as to be part of a more general analysis of American state policy outcomes: for example, the explosion in prison numbers incorporates a non-random cross-section of the population and this makes its effect non-random on communities, individuals and racial or ethnic groups. The trend is especially alarming in part because it reverses the pattern of the preceding decades. Such a broadening resonates with more thoughtful accounts of affirmative action policy and its value. Affirmative action comes in four types according to Elizabeth Anderson: (1) the compensatory model, whereby individuals discriminated against win remedy; (2) the diversity model, which is the commitment to ensuring proportionate representation from previously under-represented groups in public programs and institutions; (3) the discrimination-blocking model, designed to overcome existing discriminatory mechanisms facing some groups and individuals; and (4) the integrative model, aimed at ending the existing levels of racial segregation (Anderson, 2010: 135–53). To end material racial inequality state policy must focus on types 1 and 2 urgently, foster type 3 and decide where Americans stand on type 4. Without explicit policy efforts, amelioration will be partial and limited.

Executive weakness

Acemoglu and Robinson accord a decisive role to the state in achieving democratic reform. Reformers' efforts to emphasize the unsustainable conflict between principles of civil rights embodied in the Constitution and widespread discrimination imploded in the 1960s: 'existing institutions shaped the path to change. In this case, it was pivotal that southern institutions were situated within the inclusive federal institutions of the United States, and this allowed southern blacks finally to mobilize the federal government and institutions for their cause' (2012). But they overestimate centralization, one of their key variables for political inclusivity, and this overestimation helps explain the current policy failure.

The powers of the executive-centered State are misunderstood in this process of State transformation. The American State is primarily a resource of the executive, that is, the president. It is the president who endeavors to mobilize resources on concentrated policy goals – for example, the Great Society, or the Civil Rights Act of 1964 itself, or Obama's emergency jobs initiative promulgated in December 2011 but rejected by Congress. It is the executive which has grown most dramatically and significantly as an institution which employs state power. The presidency has expanded its power through such strategies as increased use of executive orders and signing statements to augment often-elusive statutory instruments (Edwards and Howell, 2009). Like post-1950 court decisions, executive orders were an important component of the state's expansion into civil rights protection; they were key elements of the development of federal affirmative action in the 1960s (Graham, 1990; Mayer, 2001; Howell, 2003). Two legal scholars have pushed an executive-centered analysis of the American state furthest, concluding that 'in the administrative state, it is not the case that legislatures govern, even subject to constraints and the need for cooperation with other branches. Rather the executive governs, in the sense that it drives the policy agenda even where the cooperation of other branches is needed for political reasons.

Moreover, in many domains the executive can proceed through unilateral action' (Posner and Vermeule, 2010). There is now on this view little political difference at the center between the Republicans and Democrats about wanting to control the state – though they each wish to use it for different ends.

Nonetheless, while it is correct to emphasize the leadership capacities of the executive and the authority that its office has to articulate and pursue concentrated policy initiatives, the presidency is a constrained institution, squeezed by competing national institutions in Congress and Court. Furthermore the federal bureaucracy upon which the president relies is characterized both by highly autonomous agencies (despite the upper layer in each being appointed politically) and by significant interagency conflicts about policy development and protection of each agency's remit. Delivering policy change in this institutional context is politically hard.

Federalism

The American state is multilayered. Federalism is an inherently conservative institutional force. For example, 49 of the 50 states are required by their constitutions to produce balanced budgets each year, permitting them to lay off workers casually, though different regions have resisted federal laws. In American federalism, decisive enforcement is rare – the Voting Rights Act stands out for this reason; yet it is the case that an effective democratization requires such state-led enforcements and initiatives.

Structural factors

The American state arguably confronts a deeper and structural layer of challenges in its relationship with African Americans in at least two senses: comprehensive affirmative action and the national racial division.

Comprehensive affirmative action

The failure to develop a comprehensive jobs and family income program consolidating the mid-1960s democratization has intensified rather than receded as an issue in the last two decades, in part because the market has proved incapable of sufficient high wage job generation, and dependence on the public sector as a means to economic advancement has been underestimated. No level playing field was established after civil rights democratization in the 1960s. This was the singular failure of the ambitious Moynihan Report, officially *The Negro Family: The Case for National Action*, written in March 1965 by Daniel Patrick Moynihan in the Department of Labor (US Department of Labor, 1965). A report intended by its author and the President, Lyndon

Johnson, to formulate a comprehensive strategy for helping African Americans became mired in controversy about the Report's critical portrayal of African American family structures. This overshadowed its policy recommendations which rapidly receded from being acted upon. In understanding the challenge facing the US after civil rights reform, Moynihan emphasized how the sudden granting of equal rights of citizenship could not be taken as the equivalent to providing equal material income or future opportunity. But the sociological evidence he received and compiled while writing the report shifted his focus to African American family structure and what he unhelpfully came to term the 'tangle of pathology': 'the Negro community has been forced into a matriarchical structure which, because it is so out of line with the rest of American society, seriously retards the progress of the group as a whole, and imposes a crushing burden on the Negro male and, in consequence, on a great many Negro women as well' (ibid.). Despite including copious data about low wage rates, limited employment opportunities, poor educational attainment and numerous other factors contributing to the searing economic inequality facing African Americans and demonstrating a knowledge of major African American research findings such as Du Bois's work on Philadelphia and the writings of Kenneth Clark and Franklin Frazier (Patterson, 2010), Moynihan's conclusions focused primarily on the family crisis: 'in a word, a national effort toward the problems of Negro Americans must be directed towards the question of family structure' (US Department of Labor, 1965). The failure to attend to the overpowering significance of structural factors such as housing, schools and proper jobs became an easy target for African Americans, about whom this writing was being done externally – and for whom racism was not an academic issue. Moynihan was not presenting a simplistic cultural account of the issues but his focus on the structure of African American families was curiously disconnected from the economic context of that structure. He did support a rigorous national program – 'national action' in the Report's title – consistent with what came to be understood as affirmative action combined with family allowances and job schemes, but this aspiration got drowned out in the negative response to his main report (Patterson, 2010).

The national racial division

The problem of material race inequality has been written out of national politics and solidified in a bipartisan silence about the issue (King and Smith, 2011). Since the late 1970s and particularly the 1980s (Carmines and Stimson, 1989), a color-blind policy, devaluing targeted race conscious measures, has come to dominate the national political center and policy view about race inequality. One explanatory factor identified by scholars is the backlash to civil rights, often linked to the expansion of the criminal justice system (Murakawa, 2007).

The color-blind policy has a public opinion basis (Tesler, 2013). Polls find that divisions between whites and African Americans on racial policy matters remain wide and that racial issues polarize voters. Using American National Election Studies (ANES) data, Vincent Hutchings (2009) examines attitudes to the question of whether the American State or federal government should enforce fair treatment in labor markets for African Americans: 'the 1988 results reveal a deep racial divide on this issue with 93 percent of Blacks endorsing government action in this area but only 48 percent of Whites holding a similar view'. The division is entrenched: in 2008 '90 percent of Blacks still favour governmental efforts to ensure fair treatment in the job market, while less than half of Whites share this position' (2009). Racial issues and preferences have intensified since Barack Obama's election. Political scientist Michael Tesler finds that once Obama engages with and becomes identified with a public policy issue, such engagement polarizes 'issue opinions by racial attitudes and race'. Tesler concludes that 'health care policies were significantly more racialized when attributed to President Obama than they were when these same proposals were framed as President Clinton's 1993 reform efforts'. Pooling a range of opinion sources, Tesler finds that the 'racial divide in health care opinions was 20 percentage points greater than it was over President Clinton's plan back in 1993–94' (2012). Healthcare opinions have become more divided by race since 2009 when Obama pursued his reform – African Americans are highly supportive but white opponents have become more opposed to healthcare reform since the issue was picked up by Obama. Tesler finds that 'President Obama possesses a unique potential to polarize public opinion by race ... the 26-point racial division in 1993–94 expanded into a 45-point gulf in 2009–10, with 83 percent of blacks supporting President Obama's health care proposals and only 38 percent of whites doing the same' (ibid.). White Americans' partisan preferences evince 'old fashioned racism' in a new version (Tesler, 2013).

These findings are consistent with the two racial policy alliances identified by this author and Rogers M. Smith – those promoting *color-blind* approaches to racial inequality, which treat material inequality as an individual issue; and those promoting a *race-conscious* approach requiring remedial targeted programs addressing enduring material inequalities. In contrast to previous periods, these two alliances now overlap with the Republican and Democrat parties making division about racial policy a core element of contemporary partisan polarization (King and Smith, 2011).

Structural power

The accumulated knowledge about the American political system confirms a non-pluralist, special interests and money dominated system in

which the famous heavenly chorus sings with a distinctly unrepresentative tone (Jacobs and Skocpol, 2005; Schozman et al., 2012). Such
biases shape the way in which elected officials solicit campaign contributions and explain the rise of legislative strategies to deliver fiscal
rewards to donors such as earmarks (Rocca and Gordon, 2013).
Political scientist Larry Bartels (2008) argues that elected office holders
disproportionately promote policies favorable to the affluent at the
expense of the less well off. There is nothing very surprising here other
than to observe how the scale of money has grown since the January
2011 Supreme Court decision in *Citizens United v the FEC*, and how
that expansion structures both the intensified ideological polarization
and the privileging of certain voices in the process. The result is a profoundly unequal and polarized system that is remote from the pluralism celebrated by Acemoglu and Robinson.

Conclusion

An instrument of oppression and active agent of racial segregation
from the post-Civil War years until the 1960s, the American state then
transmogrified into an enforcer of civil and legal rights. This dramatic
volte-face is comparatively exceptional. *The American State is a civil
rights state and both prejudice and racism have declined dramatically
in American society.* But the contemporary material profile of African
Americans is uneven and politically dangerous for politics and society
in the United States (Desmond and Valdez, 2012; Tesler, 2013). Despite
the historically significant election of Barack Obama to the White
House in November 2008 (and his reelection in 2012), the position of
many African Americans has worsened under the impact of the 2007–
08 recession, measured in terms of household wealth, education participation, labor market participation, exposure to the criminal justice
system, health and debt.

The scale of state failure to ameliorate the material racial inequalities
inherited by post-democratization America constitutes a failure in state
regulation and enforcement of meaningful equal opportunity.
Influenced by fiscal, identity, ideological and nationalist sources of
pressure on government policy, this failure is best characterized as *the
structural and material crisis of America's Civil Rights State.* It alludes
to the singular and unrelenting failure of state policy to deliver the
basis for equal rights of citizenship, to the feedback effects of that
failure in generating further racial inequalities, and to the bipartisan
silence about the issue and about possible remedies. State policy
broadly conceived – employment, affirmative action, anti-discrimination enforcement, education investment, purposeful public sector
employment – is necessary to build genuinely inclusive political institu-

tions. As Wilson remarks, 'in black inner cities, where the number of very low skilled individuals vastly exceeds the number of low-skill jobs, a healthy dose of public-sector job creation is needed' (2011).

Two points are worth underlining in conclusion. Firstly, the notion of the United States as a political system with fully inclusive political institutions and a matching set of inclusive economic institutions, as proposed by Acemoglu and Robinson, is too schematic and simplistic – it can only be deemed to be empirically accurate if the historical relationship between the American State and African Americans is ignored. Part of the explanation for this error is simply analytical – the United States is a patchily centralized state, with the executive able to galvanize new legislation under certain circumstances; but it is more often thwarted or succumbs to short-term crisis management which merely postpones the problem (see for example the responses to debt ceiling and budget crises since the summer of 2011). It fails these two scholars' criterion of centralization. The notion that the United States national political system is a genuinely pluralist political environment open equally to all voters is wrong. Rather it is a competitive political environment in which competition for campaign finance has stimulated deep partisan and ideological polarization and in which as a result many issues including those of material race inequality get structurally excluded from politics.

Secondly, scholars of State transformation assume linear improvement. But the absence of change or even a reversal (Tuck, 2009) of progress towards the reduction of material race inequalities is more integral to American political development than is commonly recognized by scholars. Progress toward greater material racial equality in the 1970s and 1980s has reversed since the late 1990s and accelerated in the 2000s. Given the presence of such non-linear change it is notable that the data presented earlier in this chapter documenting the contemporary expression of these material inequalities mirror in different form, but with alarming similarities of scale and endurance, the data on racial inequality compiled for Moynihan's report in 1965 – that is, relative to core standards enjoyed by white Americans, the relative gap between them and African Americans contains alarming ratios.

How might this key issue in American political development end? The most likely short-term pattern is more of the same: stagnation or racial inequality and falling standards for African Americans compared with white Americans. Such a trend is politically unsustainable however, with a two-party system divided fundamentally about racial issues and electorally supported by distinct racial groups. Persistent racial inequality will therefore either explode with episodic incidents of public disorder or generate a powerful social protest movement. Historically these two elements have grown together to force political change and an effective policy response. It is hard to contemplate another decade of material racial inequality proceeding without such popular and political responses.

An illustration of this tension and its pervasiveness came in July 2013 with the acquittal of George Zimmerman on the charge of murder for killing a 17-year-old African American youth, Trayvon Martin, in Sanford, Florida in the previous year. This verdict not only prompted responses of protest from such groups as the National Association for the Advancement of Colored People and the National Urban League and of nationwide protest meetings, but a promise from the US Attorney General, Eric Holder, to revisit the case through the Department of Justice. But most dramatically the verdict provoked an impromptu statement from President Barack Obama at a White House press conference. The President has largely avoided speaking about race since his election in 2008 but on this occasion he personalized the experience of African American men in the United States, remarking that 'Trayvon Martin could have been me 35 years ago.' Obama described the experience of racial profiling faced daily by African Americans, especially men, as they are followed by guards in department stores or observe white people locking their cars when they see them. He noted how commonly women would nervously hold their bag if riding in an elevator with an African American man. The President explained that 'those sets of experiences inform how the African-American community interprets what happened one night in Florida. And its inescapable for people to bring those experiences to bear.' A majority of whites think the verdict was fair while all African Americans polled consider it an unjust decision. This racial division and the legacies of segregation and inequality upon which it rests continues fundamentally to shape American politics and to show how far America is from being a post-racial polity.

Guide to Further Reading

Chapter 1   Introduction: Obama's Second Term

There are a number of insightful studies of the United States in the Obama years. Of particular interest are Grunwald (2012) and Gilens (2012) which both look at the social and economic problems and the efforts to address them. Jacobs and King (2009) provides a stimulating analysis of the problems of governance and Dowdle et al. (2012) provides an overview of the Obama presidency. Woodward (2010) and Mann (2012) offer insights into Obama's foreign policy and the staff surrounding him, while Edwards (2012) provides a critical look at Obama's leadership style. Biographical insight into Obama can be gleaned from Maraniss (2012) and Remnick (2010).

Chapter 2   An Emerging Constitutional Debate

Excellent discussion of the constitution can be found in Amar (2005, 2012) as well as in Balkin (2011) and Ackerman (1991, 2006, 2010) Levinson (2006, 2011) provides a distinctive critical analysis. Balkin and Segal (2009) suggest what the Constitution might look like in 2020.

On the weaknesses of Congress, see Mann and Ornstein (2006) and Kaiser (2013). The constitutional powers of the presidency are covered in Rudalevige (2005), Howell (2003) and Pfiffner (2008). Fisher (2008) provides recent reflections on the modern constitutional balance. Klarman (2013) offers an insightful account of the role of the courts and politics in the gay marriage debate. Lessig (2011) and Kaiser (2009) offer lively commentary on the role of money and special interests in American politics as does Lessig (2011). Dionne (2013) looks at values in the United States. Fiorina and Abrams (2009) and Abramowitz (2010) provide different views on the polarization debate. Overviews of Congress can be found in scholarly work by Man and Ornstein (2006). Kaiser (2013) offers more journalistic insights into the way Congress works.

Chapter 3 The 2012 Elections

There are many excellent studies of the 2012 elections. A good insider account can be found in Alter (2013) while Balz (2013) offers a pertinent analysis of the election and its likely impact on future contests. Sides and Vavreck (forthcoming) provide a political science perspective on the factors affecting strategy in the 2012 elections and Simon (2013) explores the implications of the contest for American identity and values.

Chapter 4 Political Parties

For a manageable review of the current literature on parties and polarization see Fiorina and Abrams (2008). Hetherington (2009) provides a more comprehensive account of both elite and popular polarization, as do Layman et al. (2010), though the latter's focus is principally on the role of activists in contributing to the phenomenon. McCarty et al. (2006) provide a book length treatment of the role of inequality in contributing to polarization. Fiorina's (2006) book makes the case that sorting, rather than polarization, is occurring amongst the electorate. For an up-to-date discussion of the effects of polarization on Congress and policy-making, see Mann and Ornstein (2012). See Herrnson (2009) for an overview of the elements of the party organization and patterns of spending by party affiliated groups in elections.

Up-to-date information on spending in elections can be found at www.opensecrets.org; data on spending by Super PACs and other outside groups is gathered by the Sunlight Foundation; see http://reporting.sunlightfoundation.com/outside-spending/overview/. Current roll call vote data and graphical representations of polarization in Congress are available at Howard Rosenthal and Keith Poole's website at http://polarizedamerica.com/political_polarization.asp (the site also includes a list of their published and working papers on the topic).

Chapter 5 Interest Groups

Baumgartner and Leech (1998) provide a good overview of recent scholarship on lobbying, and Baumgartner et al. (2009) provide the most comprehensive study of lobbying influence. McFarland (2004) offers a more historical interpretation on the ways in which scholars have evolved theories of influence over time. Berry and Wilcox (2008), Nownes (2006), Goldwin and Ainsworth (2012) and Andres (2008) offer book-length explanations of the facets of modern lobbying.

Those looking for a how-to guide to modern lobbying may find value in Levine (2008).

The Sunlight Foundation is a nonprofit, nonpartisan organization that uses the power of the internet to catalyze greater government openness and transparency, and provides new tools and resources for media and citizens, alike.

Chapter 6　Media and Politics

The latest editions of Graber's many contributions (2009, 2010, 2011) are always worthwhile, as is Graber et al. (2007). West (2013) takes a particularly close look at campaign advertising, and Iyengar (2011) at the general endeavors in the media of campaigns and campaigners. Bennett (2011) has been following the news closely through many editions. Gainous and Wagner (2011) and Tewksbury and Rittenberg (2012) consider especially the changes that the internet has brought to US politics. Ladd (2011) examines the relationship between the public and the mass media – a relationship that has interacted with the new technological opportunities in creating the current media landscape. The Pew Research Centre (www.pewresearch.org), especially the Pew Research Center for the People and the Press (www.people-press.org) provide extensive and up-to-date research findings.

Chapter 7　The Presidency

Pfiffner (2010) is a very good introduction to the US presidency. Edwards and Wayne (2009) and Pika and Maltese (2012) are excellent, more extensive undertakings. Nelson (2009) and Pfiffner and Davidson (2012) each gather work from interesting scholars.

Neustadt (1960, 1991) is still key in the field, but Edwards (2009) offers a much more constrained view of the office. For presidential–congressional relations, Thurber (2005) offers good analyses. On presidential communication, Kernell (2006) is still crucial, but Edwards (2003) challenges his approach, while Canes-Wrone (2006), Cohen (2008, 2009) and Eshbaugh-Soha and Peake (2011) have much to add. Scholarship on executive power is developing rapidly. Schlesinger (2004) and Rudalevige (2005) consider the 'Imperial Presidency' concept, while Howell (2003) and Howell and Pevehouse (2007) propose a more qualified understanding of executive power.

Online, the Center for the Study of the Presidency and Congress maintains a website (www.thepresidency.org/) as do the Miller Center of Public Affairs (www.millercenter.org/) and CB Presidential Research Services (www.presidentsusa.net/). For searchable versions of presidential rhetoric, the American Presidency Project (www.presidency.ucsb.edu/) is very useful.

Chapter 8 Congress: The Causes and Consequences of Partisanship Deadlock

The 10th edition of *Congress Reconsidered*, edited by Dodd and Oppenheimer (2012), includes a number of relevant articles on partisanship, elections, committees and policy formation in congress. *It's Even Worse Than It Looks* (Mann and Ornstein, 2012) updates the authors' previous work on congressional dysfunction, focusing on party polarization and barriers to compromise. For more on the links between redistricting and polarization, see McCarty et al. (2009) and Carson et al. (2007). Theriault and Rohde (2011) examine the role of legislative succession on polarization in the Senate. Bailey et al. (2012) provide an analysis of the rise of the Tea Party in American Politics. For additional information about potential congressional reforms, see *What's Wrong with Congress and What Should Be Done About It?* (Thurber, 2012).

Chapter 9 The Supreme Court

For further reading about the Supreme Court the updated editions of O'Brien (2011) and Abraham (2008) are excellent introductions to the history of the Court and the politics surrounding the appointment of justices. For a recent discussion of the relationship between the Robert's Court and the Obama Administration see Toobin (2012). Whittington (2007), Crowe (2012) and Engel (2011) provide the best historical and empirical accounts of how electoral politics have shaped the Court's power over time. Rosenberg (2008) and Hall (2011) similarly discuss judicial power, but within the context of analyzing when the Court can have an impact on social policy. There are many good works examining the various factors influencing Supreme Court decision-making: Segal and Spaeth (2002) and the edited volume by Clayton and Gillman (1999) remain essential. Epstein et al. (2013), Pacelle et al. (2011), Bailey and Maltzman (2011), Clark (2011) and Keck (2004) all provide more recent accounts of Supreme Court behavior and influences on the justices' decisions. Gillman et al. (2012) provide the best historical overview of American constitutional law. Balkin (2011) and Bennett and Solum (2011) offer contrasting views on the recent debate over constitutional originalism.

Published research on the Supreme Court can also be found in the *Journal of Law and Courts, Judicature* and the *Journal of Supreme Court History*. In addition to these scholarly journals, the Oyez Project (www.oyez.org) is a useful resource devoted to the Supreme Court that contains a multimedia archive and detailed information of past and future cases, as well as information about past and current justices.

Chapter 10   American Federalism at a Crossroads

American federalism has been assessed in a wide ranging literature in recent years. Its relevance to today's challenges is contested by several authors. Martha Derthick (2001) provides an important treatment of the values that federalism lends to governance. Malcolm Feeley and Edward Rubin (2011) on the other hand suggest that federalism no longer deserves to be valued as a first principle in governance owing to the nationalization of American society and politics.

Much of the literature is critical of the fragmented and overly centralized nature of the American federal intergovernmental grants and mandate system and many authors offer proposals for reform. Posner (1998) offers a review of the centralizing effects of federal regulation on the federal system. A comprehensive assessment of the politics and promise of perennial federalism reform initiatives is presented by Conlan (1998).

Important readings address how federalism issues play out in particular policy arenas, often drawing out not only issues in policy formulation but also the critical implementation process. For healthcare, an excellent recent overview of intergovernmental tensions in health policy that are now playing out in the implementation of President Obama's health reform is the review of the federal Medicaid program by Frank Thompson (2012). An authoritative study of intergovernmental conflict in the recent federal application of standards for the nation's schools is Paul Manna's (2011), while conflicts between federal and state governments in implementing the nation's environmental laws are well portrayed by Denise Scheberle (2004).

The critical backdrop for the relationship between governments in the American system will increasingly be driven by the realities of fiscal retrenchment playing out at all levels of government. An authoritative presentation of future fiscal forces bearing down on the state and local sector can be found in the report by the US Government Accountability Office (2012b). Rivlin (1992) is now a classic which offers a vision of how fiscal pressures can ultimately lead to a healthy rationalization of roles and responsibilities between federal and state governments.

Chapter 11   The Troubled Economy

The financial crisis of 2007–08, and the Great Recession that followed, have generated a considerable literature. A good introduction which contains contributions from leading economists of different theoretical persuasions is Friedman (2011). Cassidy (2010) and Buckley (2011) also offer an accessible introduction to the crisis and its consequences. Leading accounts of the crisis by liberal economists include the works by Nobel Laureates Joseph Stiglitz (2010) and Paul Krugman (2008). Taylor (2009) offers a conservative counterpoint to these works. The expanded role of the Federal Reserve in making economic policy is detailed in Wessel (2010). Provocative studies of what the crisis means for America's place in the world include Moran and Roubini (2012) and Fouskas and Gokay (2012).

Chapter 12   American Social Policy

For a detailed historical account of the development of US social welfare programs, see Trattner (1999) and Noble (1997). Pierson (1994) and Hacker (2004) highlight the more recent era of retrenchment. The central role of US race relations in the evolution of American welfare programs is detailed by Quadagno (1994) and more recently by Gilens (1999) and Soss et al. (2011).

Charles Murray (1984) provided one of the most important, yet controversial, critiques of US public assistance programs and their expansion during the War on Poverty. Wilson (1987) provides an alternative perspective. Together, these two works are representative of the US conservative critique of social welfare (Murray) and the left-wing rebuttal to Murray's argument that social welfare programs are ineffective at alleviating poverty (Wilson).

For detailed, comprehensive statistics on individual and family income, including poverty rates, see the most recent report from the Census Bureau (DeNavas-Walt et al., 2012).

Chapter 13   Health Policy in the United States: 'Obamacare' and After

Gibson and Singh (2013) address the political battles that have raged over health care both before and after the Affordable Care Act. Jacobs and Skocpol (2010) provide excellent background for understanding the healthcare reforms and possible changes in the system. Kronfield et al. (2012) provide a wide–ranging set of analyses of the politics and economics of healthcare in the US. Marmor (2007) puts the analysis of American health policy into some comparative perspective. Hwang (2009) provides a physician's insights into how technological innovation might solve some of the problems of cost and quality in the field of healthcare.

Chapter 14   Foreign and Security Policy

Contrasting assessments of President Obama's first term foreign and security policy may be found in Indyk et al. (2012) and in Singh (2012). James Mann (2012) provides a riveting and very well informed account of foreign and security policy decision-making processes under Obama. Bader (2012) offers an 'insider' account of Obama's foreign policy towards China. Nasr (2013) presents a critical analysis of Obama's foreign policy, written from the point of view of a former senior adviser to Richard Holbrooke (Obama's special representative for Afghanistan and Pakistan). Various positions on the global context for contemporary American foreign and security policy are outlined in Mandelbaum (2010), Ikenberry (2011), Brzezinski (2012), Kupchan (2012) and Kagan (2012). Students of contemporary American foreign and security policy should consult issues of the following journals: *Foreign Affairs*, *Foreign Policy* and *International Affairs*. The Council on Foreign Policy website (www.cfr.org) also provides a superb gateway into masses of information and debate concerning contemporary US foreign and security policy.

Chapter 15   America's Civil Rights State: Amelioration, Stagnation or Failure?

On racial divisions in American elections see Carmines and Stimson (1989), Hutchings (2009), King and Smith (2011), Tesler (2012) and Trende (2012). On the development of civil rights including issues of affirmative action see Anderson (2010), Dobbin (2010), Graham (1990), Katznelson (2007), King and Smith (2011) and Weaver and Lerman (2010). On enduring, material, racial inequalities in America including incarceration and labor markets, see Harris (2012), Katz (2012), King (2007), King and Smith (2011), Massey and Denton (1993), Murakawa (2007), Pager (2007), Pattillo-McCoy (1999), Rugh and Massey (2010), Tesler (2012), Western (2006) and Wilson (2011). On the role of the American state in racial politics see King and Lieberman (2009), King (2007), Posner and Vermeule (2010) and Western and Pettit (2005). For updates on law changes and restrictions to voting rights consult the website of the Brennan Center for Justice at the New York University School of Law; and for African American politics more generally see the websites of the Congressional Black Caucus and the NAACP.

Bibliography

Aberbach, J. and G. Peele (2011) *Crisis of Conservatism? The Republican Party, The Conservative Movement and American Politics After Bush*, New York: Oxford University Press.

Abraham, H. J. (2008) *Justices, Presidents, and Senators: A History of the U.S. Supreme Court Appointments from Washington to Bush II*, Lanham, MD: Rowman & Littlefield.

Abramowitz, A. (1994) 'Issue Evolution Reconsidered: Racial Attitudes and Partisanship in the American Electorate', *American Journal of Political Science*, 38(1), 1–24.

Abromowitz, A. and K. Saunders (1998) 'Is Polarization a Myth?', *Journal of Politics*, 70: 634–652.

Abramowitz, A. and K. Saunders, (2010) 'Ideological Realignment and US Congressional Elections', in B. Norrander and C. Wilcox (eds.), *Understanding Public Opinion*, Washington, DC: CQ Press.

Acemoglu, D. and J. A. Robinson (2012) *Why Nations Fail: The Origin of Power, Prosperity and Poverty*, New York: Crown.

Ackerman, B. (1991) *We The People, Volume 1: Foundations*, Cambridge, MA: Harvard University Press.

Ackerman, B. (1998) *We The People, Volume 2: Transformations*, Cambridge, MA: Harvard University Press.

Ackerman, B. (2010) *Decline and Fall of the American Republic*, Cambridge, MA: Belknap Press.

Ackerman, B. (2011) 'Legal Acrobatics, Illegal War', *New York Times*, June 20.

Agency for Healthcare Quality and Research (2013) *Health Care Expenses in the United States*. Washington, DC: AHQR.

Aguilar, J. (2011) 'AG Eric Holder: We Must Uphold the Voting Rights Act', *Texas Tribune*, December 13, www.texastribune.org/texas-politics/voter-id/holder-we-must-uphold-voting-rights-act/.

Ainsworth, S. (1993) 'Regulating Lobbyists and Interest Group Influence', *The Journal of Politics*, 55(1): 41–56.

Aldrich, J. and D. Rohde (2001) 'The Logic of Conditional Party Government: Revisiting the Electoral Connection', in C. Dodd and B. Oppenheimer (eds), *Congress Reconsidered*, Washington, DC: CQ Press.

Alexander, M. (2010) *The New Jim Crow*, New York: New Press.

Allard, N. W. (2008) 'Lobbying is an Honorable Profession: The Right to Petition and the Competition to be Right', *Stanford Law and Policy Review*, 19(1).

Alliance for Audited Media (2012) 'Average Circulation at the Top 25 US Daily Newspapers', September, www.auditedmedia.com/news/research-and-data/top-25–us-newspapers-for-september-2012.aspx.

Alter, J. (2013) *The Center Holds: Obama and his Enemies*, New York: Simon & Schuster.

Amar, A. (2005) *America's Constitution: A Biography*, New York, Random House.

Amar, A. (2012) *America's Unwritten Constitution: The Principles and Precedents We Live By*, New York: Basic Books.

Anderson, E. (2010) *The Imperative of Integration*, Princeton, NJ: Princeton University Press.

Andrews, E. L. (2009) 'Ailing Banks Need $75 billion, US Says', *New York Times*, May 7.

Ansolabehere, S., J. M. de Figueiredo and J. M. Snyder (2003) 'Why Is There so Little Money in US Politics?', *Journal of Economic Perspectives*, 17(1): 105–130.

Appelbaum, B. (2012) 'Family Net Worth Drops to Level of Early '90s, Fed Says', *New York Times*, June 11.

APSA (American Political Science Association) (1950) 'Towards a More Responsible Two Party System', *American Political Science Review*, 44(3).

Arnold, R. D. (1990) *The Logic of Congressional Action*, New Haven: Yale University Press.

Associated Press (2012) 'Study: Voter ID Law would Exclude up to 700,000 Young Minorities', September 12, www.cbsnews.com/8301-250_162-57511312/study-voter-id-law-would-exclude-up-to-700000–young-minorities/.

Bader, J. A. (2012) *Obama and China's Rise: An Insider's Account of America's Asia Strategy*, Washington, DC: Brookings Institution.

Bai, M. (2012) 'Obama vs Boehner: Who Killed the Debt Deal?', *The New York Times*, March 28.

Bailey, M. and F. Maltzman (2011) *The Constrained Court: Law, Politics, and the Decisions Justices Make*, Princeton, NJ: Princeton University Press.

Bailey, M., J. Mummolo, and H. Noel (2012) 'Tea Party Influence: A Story of Activists and Elites', *American Politics Research*, 40: 769.

Baker, L. and S. Dinkin (1997) 'The Senate: An Institution Whose Time has Gone?', *Journal of Law and Politics* 21: 69–70.

Baker, P. (2013) 'Obama's First Term: A Romantic Oral History', *The New York Times*, January 16.

Baker, W. (2005) *America's Crisis of Values Reality and Perception*, Princeton, NJ: Princeton University Press.

Balkin, J. M. (2011) *Living Originalism*, Cambridge, MA: The Belknap Press..

Balkin, J. and S. Levinson (2001) 'Understanding the Constitutional Revolution', *University of Virginia Law Review*, 87(6): 1045–1109.

Balkin, J. and R. Segal (2009) *The Constitution in 2020*, New York: Oxford University Press.

Balz, D. (2013) *Collision 2012: Obama v Romney and the Future of Elections in America*, London: Viking.

Balz, D. and J. Cohen (2012) 'Big Gulf between Political Parties, Divisions Within', *The Washington Post*, August 18, http://articles.washingtonpost.com/2012–08–18/politics/35492941_1_democratic-party-fractious-coalitions-gop-coalition.

Barbaro, M., J. Zeleny and M. Davey (2011) 'Democrats Fret Aloud Over Obama's Chances', *The New York Times*, September 11, www.nytimes.com/2011/09/11/us/politics/11obama.html?pagewanted=all&_r=0.

Barnes, R. (2012) 'Pennsylvania Voter ID Law shouldn't be Enforced this Time, Judge Rules', *Washington Post*, October 2, www.washingtonpost.com/politics/decision2012/pennsylvania-voter-id-law-enforcement-halted-by-judge/2012/10/02/bf240ffc-0c9d-11e2–bb5e-492c0d30bff6_story.html .

Barone, M. (2010) 'The Depth & Breadth of GOP Victories', *Real Clear Politics*, November 8, www.realclearpolitics.com/articles/2010/11/08/gop_poised_to_reap_redistricting_rewards_107871.html.

Barrett et al. (2011) '"Super Committee" fails to reach agreement", *CNN.com*, November 21.

Bartels, L. (2000) 'Partisanship and Voting Behavior, 1952–1996', *American Journal of Political Science*, 44: 35–50.

Bartels, L. (2006) 'What's the Matter with Kansas?', *Quarterly Journal of Political Science*, 1(2): 201–226.

Bartels, L. (2008) *Unequal Democracy: The Political Economy of the New Gilded Age*, Princeton, NJ: Princeton University Press.

Baumann, P. (1976) 'The Formulation and Evolution of Health Maintenance Organization Policy, 1970–73', *Social Science and Medicine*, 10: 129–142.

Baumgartner, F. R. and B. L. Leech (1998) *Basic Interests: The Importance of Groups in Politics and in Political Science*, Princeton, NJ: Princeton University Press.

Baumgartner, F. R., J. M. Berry, M. Hojnacki, D. C. Kimball and B. L. Leech (2009) *Lobbying and Policy Change: Who Wins, Who Loses, and Why*, Chicago: University of Chicago Press.

Bayh, E. (2010) 'Why I'm Leaving the Senate', *New York Times*, February 21.

Beck, P. (1977) 'Partisan dealignment in the Postwar South', *American Political Science Review*, 71: 477–496.

Beer, S. H. (1973) 'The Modernization of American Federalism', *Publius*, 3: 49–96.

Bennett, R. W. and L. B. Solum (2011) *Constitutional Originalism: A Debate*, Ithaca, NY: Cornell University Press.

Bergan, D. E. (2009) 'Does Grassroots Lobbying Work? A Field Experiment Measuring the Effects of an e-mail Lobbying Campaign on Legislative Behavior', *American Politics Research*, 37(2): 327–352.

Bernard, T. S. (2012) 'Blacks Face Bias in Bankruptcy, Study Suggests', *New York Times*, January 20.

Berry, J. M. and C. Wilcox (2008) *The Interest Group Society*, New York: Pearson.

Bertrand, M., M. Bombardini and F. Trebbi (2011) 'Is It Whom You Know or What You Know? An Empirical Assessment of the Lobbying Process', *National Bureau of Economic Research*, Working Paper 16765, February.

Bimber, B. A. (1996) *The Politics of Expertise in Congress: The Rise and Fall of the Office of Technology Assessment*, Albany, NY: State University of New York Press.

Binder, S. (2003) *Stalemate: Causes and Consequences of Legislative Gridlock*, Washington, DC: Brookings Institution.

Binder, S. and S. Smith (1997) *Politics or Principle? Filibustering in the United States Senate*, Washington, DC: Brookings Institution.

Bishop, B. (2004) 'The Cost of Political Uniformity', *Austin American Statesman* , April 8.

Blanes i Vidal, J., M. Draca and C. Fons-Rosen (2010) *Revolving Door Lobbyists*, SSRN eLibrary.

Blank, R. and B. Kovak (2008) 'The Growing Problem of Disconnected Single Mothers', *National Poverty Centre*, Working Paper Series #07–28.

Blank, S. J. and L. H. Jordan (eds) (2012) *Arms Control and European Security*, Carlisle, PA: Security Studies Institute.

Blumenthal, S. (2006) *How Bush Rules: Chronicles of a Radical Regime*, Princeton, NJ: Princeton University Press.

Boerma, L. (2012) 'Obama reflects on his biggest mistake as president', *CBSNews.com*, July 12.

Bolton, J. (2009) 'The Post-American Presidency', *Prospect*, July/August: 42–5.

Bond, J. and R. Fleischer (2000) *Polarised Politics: Congress and the President in a Partisan Era*, Washington, DC: CQ Press.

Bowden, M. (2012) *The Finish: The Killing of Osama bin Laden*, New York: Atlantic Monthly Press.

Break, G. (1980) *Financing Government in a Federal System*, Washington, DC: Brookings Institution.

Brenner, M. (2010) 'America's World', *Huffington Post*, September 20, www.huffingtonpost.com/michael-brenner/americasworld_b_731794.html.

Broder, J. (2011) 'The Limits of Intervention', *CQ Weekly-In Focus*, March 28.

Brokaw, T. (2012) 'Meet The Press', *NBC*, December 30, www.nbcnews.com/id/50314590/ns/meet_the_press-transcripts/#.UQ5We2fLyMv.

Bronner, E. (2012) 'Legal Battles Erupt Over Tough Voter ID Laws', *The New York Times*, July 19, www.nytimes.com/2012/07/20/us/politics/tougher-voter-id-laws-set-off-court-battles.html.

Brooks, D. (2012a) 'Meet the Press', *NBC*, December 30, www.nbcnews.com/id/50314590/ns/meet_the_press-transcripts/#.UQ5We2fLyMv.

Brooks, D. (2012b) 'The Two Economies', *New York Times*, April 9.

Brooks, D. (2013) 'Op-Ed: The Collective Turn', *New York Times*, January 21.

Brownstein, R. (2012) 'Romney is Now Trapped Demographically', *National Journal, The Next America*, September 21, www.nationaljournal.com/thenextamerica/politics/romney-is-now-trapped-demographically-20120921.

Bruhl, A. (2011) 'The Senate Out of Order?', *Connecticut Law Review*, 43(4): 1041–1058.

Bryce, J. (1995 [1910]) *The American Commonwealth*, Indianapolis, IN: Liberty Fund.

Brzezinski, Z. (2012) *Strategic Vision: America and the Crisis of Global Power*, New York: Perseus.

Bullock III, C., D. Hoffman and R. Gaddie (2005) 'The Consolidation of the White Southern Congressional Vote' *Political Research Quarterly*, 58: 231–243.

Burrelles Luce (2005) 'Top 100 Daily Newspapers in US by Circulation, 2005', www.burrellesluce.com/top100/2005_Top_100List.pdf.

Cain, B. (Forthcoming) *Regulating Politics: Election Law and Democratic Theory*, Cambridge: Cambridge University Press.

Campbell, J., P. Converse, W. Miller and D. Stokes (1960) *The American Voter*, Chicago: University of Chicago Press.

Cancio, A. S., T. D. Evans and D. J. Maume Jr. (1996) 'Reconsidering the Declining Significance of Race: Racial Differences in Early Career Wages', *American Sociological Review*, 61.

Canes-Wrone, B. (2001) 'The President's Legislative Influence from Public Appeals', *American Journal of Political Science*, 45(2): 313–329.

Canes-Wrone, B. (2006) *Who Leads Whom? Presidents, Policy, and the Public*, Chicago: University of Chicago Press.

Caraley, D. J. (2009) 'Three Trends Over Eight Presidential Elections, 1980–2008: Toward the Emergence of a Democratic Majority Realignment?', *Political Science Quarterly*, 124(3): 423–442.

Carey, B. (2012) 'Academic "Dream Team" Helped Obama's Effort', *New York Times*, November 12, www.nytimes.com/2012/11/13/health/dream-team-of-behavioral-scientists-advised-obama-campaign.html?pagewanted=all&_r=0.

Carmines, E. and J. Stimson (1989) *Issue Evolution: Race and the Transformation of American Politics*, Princeton, NJ: Princeton University Press.

Carson, J. and M. Crespin (2004) 'The Effect of State Redistricting Methods on Electoral Competition in United States House Races', *State Politics and Policy Quarterly*, 4(4): 455–569.

Carson, J. L. and B. A. Kleinerman (2002) 'A Switch in time saves nine: Institutions, Strategic Actors, and FDR's Court-Packing Plan', *Public Choice*, 113: 301–24.

Carson, J. L., M. H. Crespin, C. J. Finocchiaro and D. W. Rhode (2007) 'Redistricting and Party Polarization in the US House of Representatives', *American Politics Research*, 35(6): 878–904.

Carter, B. (2012) 'As Obama Accepts Offers, Late-Night Television Longs for Romney', *New York Times*, October 28, www.rollcall.com/issues/58_30/Binders-Full-of-Women-Illustrates-Memes-Power-218295–1.html.

Carter, B. (2013) 'Cable News Networks See Big Falloff From 2009 in Inauguration Ratings', *New York Times*, January 22, http://mediadecoder.blogs.nytimes.com/2013/01/22/cable-news-networks-see-big-falloff-from-2009–in-inauguration-ratings/?smid=tw-mediadecodernyt&seid=auto.

Cassidy, J. (2012) 'Is the United States Moving to the Left?', *New Yorker*, December 11.

Center for Responsive Politics (2013) '2012 Presidential Race', *Center for Responsive Politics*, www.opensecrets.org/pres12/#out.

Center on Congress (2012) 'December 2011 Political Scientists Survey', *Center on Congress*, www.centeroncongress.org/december-2011–political-scientists-survey-0.

Cernetich, K. (2012) 'Turzai: Voter ID Law Means Romney Can Win PA', *Politics PA*, June 25, www.politicspa.com/turzai-voter-id-law-means-romney-can-win-pa/37153/.

Cha, A. E. and J. Cohen (2010) 'Most Americans Worry about Ability to Pay Mmortgage or Rent, Poll Finds', *The Washington Post*, October 28, www.washingtonpost.com/wp-dyn/content/article/2010/10/27/AR2010102703683.html.

Cigler, A. and B. Loomis (eds) (2006) *Interest Group Politics*, Washington, DC: CQ Press.

Clark, T. S. (2011) *The Limits of Judicial Independence*, New York: Cambridge University Press.

Clawson, D., A. Neustadtl and D. Scott (1992) *Money Talks: Corporate PACs and Political Influence*, New York: Basic Books.

Clawson, D., A. Neustadl and M. Weller (1998) *Dollars and Votes: How Business Campaign Contributions Subvert Democracy*, Philadelphia: Temple University Press.

Clayton, C. W. (1992) *The Politics of Justice: The Attorney General and the Making of Legal Policy*, New York: M.E. Sharpe.

Clayton, C. W. (2011) 'Review of *Making Democracy Work: A Judge's View* by Justice Stephen Breyer', *The Forum*, 9(1): 1–9.

Clayton, C. W. and H. Gillman (eds) (1999) *Supreme Court Decision-Making: New Institutionalist Perspectives*, Chicago: University of Chicago Press.

Clayton, C. W. and L. K. McMillan (2012) 'The Roberts Court in an Era of Polarized Politics', *The Forum*, 10(4): 132–146.

Clayton, C. W. and J. M. Pickerill (2004) 'The Supreme Court's Federalism Decisions: Guess What Happened on the Way to the Revolution? Precursors to the Supreme Court's Federalism Revolution', *Publius*, 34(3): 85–114.

Clement, S., J. Cohen and P. Craighill (2012) 'Exit Polls 2012: How the Vote has Shifted', *Washington Post*, November 6, www.washingtonpost.com/wp-srv/special/politics/2012–exit-polls/.

Clinton, H. (2009) 'Remarks', February 20, www.state.gov/secretary/rm/2009a/02/119430.htm.

Clinton, H. (2011) 'America's Pacific Century', *Foreign Policy*, November.

CNN Wire Staff (2012) 'Judge Blocks Pennsylvania Voter ID Law for November Election', *CNN Politics*, October 2, www.cnn.com/2012/10/02/politics/pennsylvania-voter-id.

Coffin, M. (2003) 'The Latino Vote: Shaping America's Electoral Future', *Political Quarterly* 94(2): 214–222.

Cohen, A. (2012) 'No one in America should have to wait 7 hours to vote', *The Atlantic*, November 5, www.theatlantic.com/politics/archive/2012/11/no-one-in-america-should-have-to-wait-7–hours-to-vote/264506/#.

Cohn, J. (2010) 'How They Did It', *New Republic*, May 21.

Cohn, J. (2012) 'Affordable Care Act is Constitutional', *New Republic*, June 28.

Cohen, J., S. Clement and P. Craighill (2012) 'Exit Polls 2012: How the Vote has Shifted', *Washington Post*, November 6, www.washingtonpost.com/wp-srv/special/politics/2012–exit-polls/.

Congressional Management Foundation (2009) *2009 House of Representatives Compensation Study*. Washington, DC: Congressional Management Foundation.

Congressional Management Foundation (2010) *Communicating with Congress: Perception of Citizen Advocacy on Capitol Hill*. Washington, DC: Congressional Management Foundation.

Congressional Research Service (2011) *Report: No Fly Zones: Strategic, Operational and Legal Considerations for Congress*, March 18. Washington, DC: Congressional Research Service.

Conlan, T. (1998) *From New Federalism to Devolution: Twenty Five Years of Intergovernmental Reform*, Washington, DC: Brookings Institution.

Conlan, T. J. and J. Dinan (2007) 'Federalism, the Bush Administration and the Transformation of American Conservatism', *Publius*, 37(3): 270–303.

Conlan, T. J. and P. L. Posner (2011) 'Inflection Point? Federalism and the Obama Administration', *Publius: The Journal of Federalism*, 41: 421–446.

Conlan, T. J. and P. L. Posner (2012) 'Federalism Trends, Tensions and Outlook', in R. D. Ebel and J. E. Peterson (eds), *The Oxford Handbook on State and Local Finance*, New York: Oxford University Press.

Connecticut Law Review Symposium (2010) 'Is Our Constitutional System Broken?', *Connecticut Law Review*, 43(10).

Converse, P. (2006) 'The Nature of Belief Systems in Mass Publics (1964)', reprinted in *Critical Review: A Journal of Politics and Society*, 18(1): 1–74.

Converse, P. and G. Markus (1979) 'Plus ça Change ... The New CPS Election Study Panel', *American Political Science Review*, 73: 32–49.

Cook, C. (2013) 'Next Fiscal Fight Shifts Focus to Spending Cuts', *National Journal*, January 15.

Cooper, M. (2011) 'Public Split on Parties' Super Committee Ideas', *National Journal*, November 9.

Cooper, P. J. (2002) *By Order of the President: The Use and Abuse of Executive Direct Action*, Lawrence, KS: University Press of Kansas.

Copeland, C. W. and M. P. Carey (2011) *REINS Act: Number and Types of 'Major Rules' in Recent Years*. Washington, DC: Congressional Research Service.

Corwin, E. S. (1950) 'The Passing of Dual Federalism', *Virginia Law Review*, 36: 1–22.

Crawford, J. (2012) 'Roberts Switched views to Uphold Health Care Law', *CBS News*, July 1, www.cbsnews.com/8301–3460_162–57464549/roberts-switched-views-to-uphold-health-care-law/.

Crotty, W. (2001) 'Policy Coherence in Political Parties :The Elections of 1984, 1988 and 1992', in J. Cohen, R. Fleischer and P. Kantor (eds), *American Political Parties: Decline or Resurgence?* Washington, DC: CQ Press.

Crowe, J. (2012) *Building Judicial Supremacy: Law, Courts, and the Politics of Institutional Development*, Princeton, NJ: Princeton University Press.

Currinder, M. (2005) 'Campaign Finance: Funding the Presidential and Congressional Elections', in M. Nelson (ed.), *The Election of 2004*, Washington, DC: CQ Press.

Cutler, L. (1980) 'To Form a Government', *Foreign Affairs* 59(1): 126–143.

Dahl, R. A. (1957) 'Decision-making in a Democracy: The Supreme Court as a National Policy-maker', *Journal of Public Law*, 6: 279–295.

Dahl, R. A. (1990) 'Myth of the Presidential Mandate', *Political Science Quarterly*, 105(3): 355–372.

Dash, E. (2009) 'Failure of Small Banks Grows, Straining FDIC', *New York Times*, October 10.

Dash, E. (2010) 'A Big Surprise: Troubled Assets Garner Rewards', *New York Times*, August 26.

de Moraes, L. (2013) 'CNN Wins Inauguration Day Ratings', *Washington Post*, January 23, www.washingtonpost.com/lifestyle/style/tv-column-cnn-wins-inauguration-day-ratings/2013/01/22/f48ce79a-64ea-11e2–85f5–a8 a9228e55e7_story.html?hpid=z11.

DeNavas-Walt, Carmen, Bernadette D. Proctor and Jessica C. Smith (2012) *Income, Poverty, and Health Insurance Coverage in the United States: 2011*,

US Census Bureau, Current Population Reports, P60–243. Washington, DC: US Government Printing Office.

Department of Health and Human Services, Administration for Children and Families (2010) http://www.acf.hhs.gov/programs/ofa/data/2010fin/table_a2.pdf

Derthick, M. (1970) *The Influence of Federal Grants*, Cambridge, MA: Harvard University Press.

Derthick, M. (2001) *Keeping the Compound Republic: Essays on American Federalism*, Washington, DC: Brookings Institution.

Desmond, M. and N. Valdez (2012) 'Unpolicing the Urban Poor: Consequences of Third-Party Policing for Inner City Women', *American Sociological Review*, 78(1): 117–141.

Dilger, R. J. (2009) *Federal Grants in Aid: An Historical Perspective on Contemporary Issues*, Washington, DC: Congressional Research Service.

DiMaggio, P., J. Evans and B. Bryson (1996) 'Have Americans Social Attitudes Become More Polarized?', *American Journal of Sociology*, 102: 690–755.

Dionne, E. J. (2013) *Our Divided Political Heart: The Battle for the American Idea in an Age of Discontent*, London: Bloomsbury.

Dobbin, F. (2010) *Inventing Equal Opportunity*, Princeton, NJ: Princeton University Press.

Dodd, L. and B. Oppenheimer (eds) (2012) *Congress Reconsidered*, Washington, DC: CQ Press.

Dowd, M. (2011) 'Flight of the Valkyries', *New York Times*, March 22.

Dowdle, A., D. van Raemdonck and R. Maranto (eds) (2012) *The Obama Presidency: Change and Continuity*, London: Routledge.

Draper, R. (2012) *Do Not Ask What Good We Do*, New York: Free Press.

Dreier, P., J. Mollenkopf and T. Swanstrom (2011) *Place Matters: Metropolitics for the Twenty-first Century*, Lawrence, KS: University Press of Kansas.

Drezner, D. (2011) 'Does Obama Have a Grand Strategy? Why We Need Doctrines in Uncertain Times', *Foreign Affairs*, 90(4): 57–69.

Driver, J. (2011) 'The Significance of the Frontier in American Constitutional Law', *The Supreme Court Review*, 1: 345–398.

Drutman, L. (2011) *The Political One Percent of the One Percent*, Washington, DC: The Sunlight Foundation.

Drutman, L. (2012a) *Big Banks Dominate Dodd-Frank Meetings with Regulators*, Washington, DC: The Sunlight Foundation.

Drutman, L. (2012b) *Federal Candidates Depend on Financial Sector more than any other for Campaign Money*, Washington, DC: The Sunlight Foundation.

Drutman, L. and B. E. Cain (2013) 'Congressional Staff and the Revolving Door: The Impact of Regulatory Change', *Midwest Political Science Association Conference*.

D'Souza, D. (2010) *The Roots of Obama's Rage*, New York: Regnery.

Dueck, C. (2011) 'The Accommodator: Obama's Foreign Policy', *Policy Review*, 169: 1–5.

Dumbrell, J. (2009) *Clinton's Foreign Policy: Between the Bushes*, London and New York: Routledge.

Dumbrell, J. (2010) 'American Power: Crisis or Renewal?', *Politics*, 30: 15–23.

Dunne, P. F. (1899) *Mr. Dooley in Peace and War*, Boston: Small, Maynard & Co.

Duverger, M. (1951) *Political Parties: Their Organization and Activity in the Modern State*, New York: Wiley.

Economic Policy Institute (2012) 'The China Toll', Economic Policy Institute Briefing Paper 345, August 23.

Edgecliffe-Johnson, A. (2012) 'Bleak Outlook for US Newspapers', March 16, www.ft.com/cms/s/0/3eef0bc4–6f73–11e1–9c57–00144feab49a.html#axzz2JS vDwl7n.

Edmond, R., E. Guskin, T. Rosenstiel and A. Mitchell (2012) 'The State of the News Media 2012: An Annual Report on American Journalism', The Pew Research Centre's Project for Excellence in Journalism, http://stateofthe-media.org/2012/newspapers-building-digital-revenues-proves-painfully-slow/.

Edwards, G. III (1990) *At the Margins: Presidential Leadership of Congress*, New Haven, CT: Yale University Press.

Edwards, G. C. III (2003) *On Deaf Ears: The Limits of the Bully Pulpit*, New Haven, CT: Yale University Press.

Edwards, G. C. III (2009) *The Strategic President: Persuasion and Opportunity in Presidential Leadership*, Princeton, NJ: Princeton University Press.

Edwards, G. C. III (2012) *Overreach: Leadership in the Obama Presidency*, Princeton, NJ: Princeton University Press.

Edwards, G. C. III and W. Howell (eds) (2009) *The Oxford Handbook of the American Presidency*, Oxford: Oxford University Press.

Edwards, G. C. III and S. J. Wayne (2009) *Presidential Leadership: Politics and Policy Making*, Stamford, CT: Wadsworth/Cengage Learning.

Elazar, D. J. (1962) *The American Partnership: Intergovernmental Cooperation in the United States*, Chicago: University of Chicago Press.

Elsby, M., B. Hobijn and A. Sahin (2010) *The Labor Market in the Great Depression*, Federal Reserve Bank of San Francisco Working Paper, March 7.

Ely, J. H. (1980) *Democracy and Distrust: A Theory of Judicial Review*, Cambridge, MA: Harvard University Press.

Engel, S. (2011) *American Politicians Confront the Court*, Cambridge, NY: Cambridge University Press.

Epstein, L. (1986) *Political Parties in the American Mold*, Madison, WI: University of Wisconsin Press.

Epstein, L., W. M. Landes and R. A. Posner (2013) *The Behavior of Federal Judges: A Theoretical and Empirical Study of Rational Choice*, Cambridge, MA: Harvard University Press.

Eshbaugh-Soha, M. and T. Miles (2011) 'Presidential Speeches and the Stages of the Legislative Process', *Congress and the Presidency*, 38(3): 301–321.

Eshbaugh-Soha, M. and J. S. Peake (2011) *Breaking Through the Noise: Presidential Leadership, Public Opinion, and the News Media*, Stanford, CA: Stanford University Press.

Esterling, K. M. (2004) *The Political Economy of Expertise: Information and Efficiency in American National Politics*, Ann Arbor, MI: University of Michigan Press.

Executive Office of the President, Office of Management and Budget (2010) *Fiscal Year 2012: Historical Tables, Budget of the US Government*, Washington, DC: US Government Printing Office.

Fantone, D. M. (2011) *Federal Mandates: Few Rules Trigger the Unfunded Mandate Reform Act*, Washington, DC: GAO-11–385T.

Federal Reserve (2012) 'Household Sector Liabilities: Household Credit Market Debt Outstanding', *FRED Economic Research*, Federal Reserve Bank of St. Louis, www.research.stlouisfed.org.

Federman, M. (2004) *What is the Meaning of the Medium is the Message?*, July 23, http://individual.utoronto.ca/markfederman/article_mediumisthemessage.htm.

Feeley, M. and E. Rubin (2011) *Federalism, Political Identity and Tragic Compromise*, Ann Arbor, MI: University of Michigan Press.

Feinstein, D. (2011) 'Issue Statements', http://feinstein.senate.gov (accessed April 7, 2011).

Feldman, S. and J. Zaino (2012) 'Election Confirms Deep Ideological Divide', *CBS News*, November 7, www.cbsnews.com/8301-250_162-57546153/election-confirms-deep-ideological-divide/.

Feller, B. and J. Pace (2011) 'Both Democrats and Republicans Criticize Obama's Afghanistan Plan', *CNS News*, June 23, www.cnsnews.com/news/article/obamas-afghanistan-plan-criticized-dems.

Finche, I. and L. Schott (2011) 'TANF Benefits Fell Further in 2011 and Are Worth Much Less than in 1996 in Most States', Center for Budget and Policy Priorities, November 21, www.cbpp.org/cms/?fa=view&id=3625.

Finer, H. (1949) *Theory and Practice of Modern Government*, New York: H. Holt.

Fiorina, M. and S. Abrams (2008) 'Political Polarisation in the American Public', *Annual Review of Political Science*, 11: 563–588.

Fiorina, M. and S. Abrams (2009) *Disconnect: The Breakdown of Representation in American Politics,* Norman, OK: University of Oklahoma Press.

Fiorina, M., S. Abrams and J. Pope (2006) *Culture War? The Myth of a Polarized America*, New York: Pearson Longman.

Fisher, L. (2008) *The Constitution and 9/11: Recurring Threats to America's Freedoms*, Lawrence, KS: Kansas University Press.

Fisher, L. (2011) *Defending Congress and the Constitution*, Lawrence, KS: Kansas University Press.

Fleisher, R. and J. Bond (2001) 'Evidence of Increasing Polarization Among Ordinary Citizens', in J.R. Cohen, R. Fleisher and P. Kantor (eds), *American Political Parties: Decline or Resurgence?*, Washington, DC: CQ Press.

Fleming, J. (2007) 'The Balkanization of Originalism', *Maryland Law Review*, 67: 10–13.

Fleming, J. (2009) 'Towards a More Democratic Congress?', *Boston Law Review*, 89: 629–640.

Fletcher, M. A. and Z. A. Goldfarb (2012) 'US Economic Fears Shift from Europe Toward "Fiscal Cliff"', *Washington Post*, July 17.

Fording, R. C. and J. Smith (2012) 'Barack Obama's "Fight" to End Poverty: Rhetoric and Reality', *Social Science Quarterly*, 93(5): 1161–1184.

Forsakes, V. K. and B. Gokay (2012) *The Fall of the US Empire*, London: Pluto Press.

Fowler, G. A. (2012) 'Facebook: One Billion and Counting', *Wall Street Journal*, October 4, http://online.wsj.com/article/SB1000087239639044363540457803616402738611 2.html.

Frank, T. (2004) *What's the Matter with Kansas? How Conservatives Won the Heart of America*, New York: Metropolitan Books.

Frates, C. (2010) 'Big banks hire DC heavyweights', *Politico*, May 11.

Frendreis, J. and A. Gitelson (1999) 'Local Parties in the 1990s: Spokes in a Candidate-Centered Wheel', in J. Green and D. Shea (eds), *The State of the Parties: The Changing Role of Contemporary American Parties*, Landham, MD: Rowman & Littlefield.

Furlong, S. R. (1997) 'Interest Group Influence on Rule Making', *Administration & Society*, 29(3): 325–347.

Furlong, S. R. and C. M. Kerwin (2005) 'Interest Group Participation in Rule Making: A Decade of Change', *Journal of Public Administration Research and Theory*, 15(3): 353–370.

Gallagher, L. J. (1999) *A Shrinking Portion of the Safety Net: General Assistance from 1989 to 1998*, Washington, DC: Urban Institute, www.ins. usdoj.gov/ *graphics/aboutins/statistics/legishist/act141.htm*.

Gallup (2012a) 'Majority in US Still Say Government Doing Too Much', September 17.

Gallup (2012b) 'Congressional Job Approval', Gallup, www.gallup.com/poll/ 1600/Congress-Public.aspx.

Garrett, M. (2010) 'After the Wave', *National Journal*, 42(43): 60–61.

Geoghegan, T. (2012) 'Who, What, Why: Who First Called it a "Fiscal Cliff"?', BBC News, November 15, www.bbc.co.uk/news/magazine-20318324.

Gerges, F. (2012) *Obama and the Middle East: The End of America's Moment?*, London: Palgrave Macmillan.

Gerring, J. (1998) *Party Ideologies in America, 1928–1996*, New York: Cambridge University Press.

Gibson, R. and J. P. Singh (2013) *The Battle Over Health Care*, Lanham, MD: Rowman & Littlefield.

Gilens, M. (1999) *Why Americans Hate Welfare: Race, Media, and the Politics of Antipoverty Policy*, Chicago: University of Chicago Press.

Gilens, M. (2012) *Affluence and Influence: Economic Inequality and Political Power in America*, Princeton, NJ: Princeton University Press.

Gillman, J., M. A. Graber and K. E. Whittington (2012) *American Constitutionalism*, New York: Oxford University Press.

Gillman, H. (2008) 'Courts and the Politics of Partisan Coalitions', in K. E. Whittington, R. D. Keleman and G. A. Caldeira (eds), *Oxford Handbook of Law and Politics*, Oxford: Oxford University Press.

Gilmour, J. B. (1995) *Strategic Disagreement: Stalemate in American Politics*, Pittsburgh: University of Pittsburgh Press.

Giroux, G. (2012) 'Senate Democrats: Best Defensive Record Since 1964 – Held 22 of 23', *Bloomberg*, November 10, http://go.bloomberg.com/ political-capital/2012–11–10/senate-democrats-best-defensive-record-since-1964–held-22–of-23/.

Goffman, A. (2009) 'On the Run: Wanted Men in a Philadelphia Ghetto', *American Sociological Review*, 74(3): 339–357.

Golden, M. M. (1998) 'Interest Groups in the Rule-Making Process: Who Participates? Whose Voices Get Heard?', *Journal of Public Administration Research and Theory*, 8(2): 245–270.

Goldfarb, Z. A. (2012a) 'Under Ben Bernanke, a more open and forceful Federal Reserve' *Washington Post*, September 24.

Goldfarb, Z. A. (2012b) 'Fed Ties Stimulus to Jobs, Inflation in Unprecedented Steps to Bolster Economy', *Washington Post*, December 12.

Goldfarb, Z. A. (2013) 'As Obama Signs Ssequestration Cuts, his Economic Goals are at Risk', *Washington Post*, March 25.

Goldfarb, Z. A. and P. Wallsten (2011) 'Economic News is Bad for Obama's Reelection Bid', *Washington Post*, June 3, http://articles.washingtonpost.com/2011–06–03/business/35234663_1_jobs-report-obama-job-market/.

Goldstein, K. M. (1999) *Interest Groups, Lobbying, and Participation in America*, New York: Cambridge University Press.

Goldstein, T. (2012) 'The Court in a Second Obama Term', *SCOTUSblog*, February 14, www.scotusblog.com/2012/02/the-court-in-a-second-obama-term/.

Goodnough, A. and M. Cooper (2012) 'Health Law has States Feeling Tense Over Deadline', *New York Times*, November 15.

Goren, P. (2002) 'Character Weakness, Partisan Bias and Presidential Evaluation' *American Journal of Political Science*, 46: 627–641.

Gorman, B. (2010) 'Where Did the Primetime Broadcast TV Audience Go?', April 12, http://tvbythenumbers.zap2it.com/2010/04/12/where-did-the-primetime-broadcast-tv-audience-go/47976/.

Government Technology News (2009) 'Real ID Postponed by the Department of Homeland Security', December 18.

Graber, D. A. (2009) *Mass Media and American Politics*, Washington, DC: CQ Press.

Graber, D. A. (2010) *Media Power in Politics*, Washington, DC: CQ Press.

Graber, D. A. (2011) *On Media: Making Sense of Politics*, Boulder, CO: Paradigm.

Graham, H. D. (1990) *The Civil Rights Era: Origins and Development of National Policy, 1960–1972*, New York: Oxford University Press.

Grainger, C. (2010) 'Redistricting and Polarization: Who Draws the Lines in California?', *Journal of Law and Economics*, 53(3): 545–567.

Green, D., B. Palmquist and E. Schickler (2002) *Partisan Hearts and Minds: Political Parties and the Social Identities of Voters*, New Haven, CT: Yale University Press.

Green, J., J. Guth, C. Smidt and L. Kellstedt (1996) *Religion and Culture Wars: Dispatches from the Front*, Lanham, MD: Rowman & Littlefield.

Greenstein, F. I. (2009) *The Presidential Difference: Leadership Style from FDR to Barack Obama*, Princeton, NJ: Princeton University Press.

Greenstein, F. I. (2011) 'Barack Obama: The Man and His Presidency at the Midterm', *PS: Political Science & Politics*, 44(1): 7–11.

Grodzins, M. (1969) 'The American System', in D. Elazar (ed.), *The Politics of American Federalism*, Chicago: Rand McNally.

Grossman, G. M. and E. Helpman (1994) 'Protection for Sale', *American Economic Review*, 84(4): 833–850.

Grossman, G. M. and E. Helpman (2001) *Special Interest Politics*, Cambridge, MA: MIT Press.

Gruber, J. (2008) 'Incremental Universalism in the United States: The States Move Fast', *Journal of Economic Perspectives*, 22: 51–68.

Grunwald, M. (2012) *The New New Deal: The Hidden story of Change in the Obama Era*, New York: Simon & Schuster.

Haass, R. N. (2011) 'Prepared Statement before the Senate Committee on Foreign Relations Hearing on Afghanistan, "What Is an Acceptable End-State, and How Do We Get There?"', May 3.

Hacker, Jacob S. (2004) 'Privatizing Risk without Privatizing the Welfare State: The Hidden Politics of Social Policy Retrenchment in the United States', *American Political Science Review*, 98: 243–260.

Hacker, J. S. (2010) 'The Road to Somewhere: Why Health Reform Happened Or Why Political Scientists Who Write about Public Policy Shouldn't Assume They Know How to Shape It', *Perspectives on Politics*, 8(3): 861–876.

Hacker, J. and P. Pierson (2005) *Off Center: The Republican Revolution and the Erosion of American Democracy*, New Haven, CT: Yale University Press.

Hacker, J. and P. Pierson (2011) *Winner Take All Politics: How Washington Made the Rich Richer – and Turned its Back on the Middle Class*, New York: Simon and Schuster.

Hall, M. E. K. (2011) *The Nature of Supreme Court Power*, Cambridge: Cambridge University Press.

Hall, R. L. and A. V. Deardorff (2006) 'Lobbying as Legislative Subsidy', *American Political Science Review*, 100(1): 69–84.

Hall, R. L. and F. W. Wayman (1990) 'Buying Time: Moneyed Interests and the Mobilization of Bias in Congressional Committees', *American Political Science Review*, 84(3): 797–820.

Hamilton, L. (2010) 'There is No Substitute for Robust Oversight', Center for Congressional Studies at Indiana University, June 9.

Harris, F. C. (2012) 'The Price of a Black President', *Washington Post*, October 27.

Harris, P. (2013) 'CNN Loses Way as Americans Switch to Partisan Hosts and Celebrity Chat', *Observer*, February 3.

Hart, D. M. (2004) 'Business is not an Interest Group: On the Study of Companies in American National Politics', *Annual Review of Political Science*, 7: 47–69.

Heberling, E. and B. Larson (2005) 'Redistributing Campaign Funds by US House Members: The Spiralling Costs of the Permanent Campaign', *Legislative Studies Quarterly*, 30: 597–624.

Heberling, E., M. Hetherington and B. Larson (2006) 'The Price of Leadership: Campaign Money and the Polarization of Political Parties', *Journal of Politics*, 68: 989–1002.

Heckman, J. and B. Payner (1989) 'Determining the Impact of Federal Anti-discrimination Policy on the Economic Progress of Black Americans', *American Economic Review*, 79: 138–176.

Heinz, J. P. (1993) *The Hollow Core: Private Interests in National Policy Making*, Cambridge, MA: Harvard University Press.

Heisbourg, F., W. Ischinger, G. Robertson, K. Schake and T. Valasek (2012) 'All Alone? What US Retrenchment Means for Europe and NATO', Centre For European Reform, March 1, www.cer.org.uk/publications/archive/report/2012/all-alone-what-us-retrenchment-means-europe-and-nato.

Herbert, J. (2013) 'The Problem of Presidential Strategy', in J. Dumbrell (ed.), *Issues in American Politics: Polarized Politics in the Age of Obama*, New York: Routledge.

Herrnson, P. S. (1988) *Party Campaigning in the 1980s*, Cambridge, MA: Harvard University Press.

Herrnson, P. S. (2008) *Congressional Elections: Campaigning at Home and in Washington*, Washington, DC: CQ Press.

Herrnson, P. S. (2009) 'The Roles of Party Organizations, Party-Connected Committees, and Party Allies in Elections', *Journal of Politics*, 71(4): 1207–1224.

Herszenhorn, D. M. (2010) 'The GOP Takes On Itself', *New York Times*, January 10, http://query.nytimes.com/gst/fullpage.html?res=9B06EFD9113 FF933A25752C0A9669D8B63&ref=teapartymovement.

Hetherington, M. J. (2001) 'Resurgent Mass Partisanship: The Role of Elite Polarization', *American Political Science Review*, 95: 619–631.

Hetherington, M. J. (2009) 'Review Article: Putting Polarization into Perspective', *British Journal of Political Science*, 39(2): 413–448.

Hibbing, J. and C. Larimer (2008) *The American Public's View of Congress*, Faculty Publications Political Science paper 27, http:digitalcommons. unl.edu/polisfacpub/27.

Hicks, J. P. (2012) 'Commentary: Unemployment Declines, But Why Not for Black America?', *Black Entertainment Television*, January 6.

Hinckley, B. (1990) *The Symbolic Presidency: How President Portray Themselves*, New York: Routledge.

Hirschman, A. O. (1971) *Exit, Voice and Loyalty*, Cambridge, MA: Harvard University Press.

Holohan, J., M. Beuggets, C. Carroll and S. Dorn (2012) *The Cost and Coverage Implications of the ACA Medicaid Expansion*, Washington, DC: Kaiser Family Foundation.

Hopkins, D. A. (2009) 'The 2008 Election and the Political Geography of the New Democratic Majority', *Polity*, 41: 368–387.

Howell, W. (2003) *Power Without Persuasion: The Politics of Direct Presidential Action*, Oxford: Princeton University Press.

Howell, W. G. and J. G. Pevehouse (2007) *While Dangers Gather: Congressional Checks on Presidential War Powers*, Oxford: Princeton University Press.

Hunter, J. (1991) *Culture Wars: The Struggle to Define America*, New York: Basic Books.

Hunter, J. (2003) 'Partisan Polarisation in Presidential Support: The Electoral Connection', *Congress and the Presidency*, 30: 1–36.

Hunter, J. (2005) 'Polarized Politics and the 2004 Congressional and Presidential Elections', *Political Science Quarterly*, 120: 199–218.

Hurst, S. (2012) 'Obama and Iran', *International Politics*, 49: 545–67.

Hutchings, V. L. (2009) 'Change or More of the Same? Evaluating Racial Attitudes in the Obama Era', *Public Opinion Quarterly*, 73.

Hwang, J. (2009) *The Innovators Prescription*, New York: McGraw-Hill.

Ignatius, D. (2010) 'Obama's Foreign Policy: Big Ideas, Little Implementation', *Washington Post*, October 17.

Ikenberry, G. (2011) *Liberal Leviathan: The Origins, Crisis, and Transformation of the American World Order*, Princeton, NJ: Princeton University Press.

Indyk, M. S., K. G. Lieberthal and M. E. O'Hanlon (2012) *Bending History: Barack Obama's Foreign Policy*, Washington, DC: The Brookings Institution.

Ingram, H. (1977) 'Policy Implementation through Bargaining: The Case of Federal Grants-in-Aid', *Public Policy*, 25: 499–526.

Issenberg, S. (2012) *The Victory Lab: The Secret Science of Winning Campaigns*, New York: Crown Publishers.

Jackson, K. T. (1985) *Crabgrass Frontier: The Suburbanization of the United States*, New York: Oxford University Press.

Jacobs, L. and D. King (2009) *The Unsustainable American State*, Oxford: Oxford University Press.

Jacobs, L. and R. Shapiro (2000) *Politicians Don't Pander: Political Manipulation and the Loss of Democratic Responsiveness*, Chicago: University of Chicago Press.

Jacobs, L. and T. Skocpol (2005) *Inequality and American Democracy*, New York: Oxford University Press.

Jacobs, L. and T. Skocpol (2010) *Health Care Reform and American Politics: What Everyone Needs to Know*, New York: Oxford University Press.

Jacobson, G. (1985) 'Party Organization and Campaign Resources in 1982', *Political Science Quarterly*, 100: 604–625.

Jacobson, G. (2003) 'Partisan Polarization in Presidential Support: The Electoral Connection', *Congress and the Presidency*, 30: 1–36.

Jacobson, G. (2005) 'Polarized Politics and the 2004 Congressional and Presidential Elections', *Political Science Quarterly*, 120: 199–218.

Jacobson G. (2007) *A Divider Not a United: George W. Bush and the American People: The 2006 Election and Beyond*, New York: Pearson Longman.

Jensen, J. M. (2011) 'Explaining Congressional Staff Members' Decisions to Leave the Hill', *Congress & the Presidency*, 38(1): 39–59.

Johnson, D. (2003) 'Ronald Reagan and the Rehnquist Court on Congressional Power: Presidential Influences on Constitutional Change', *Indiana Law Journal*, 78.

Johnson, K. (2006) *Governing the American State: Congress and the New Federalism*, Princeton, NJ: Princeton University Press.

Jones, C. (1998) *Passages to the Presidency: From Campaigning to Governing*, Washington, DC: Brookings Institution Press.

Jones, D. (2001) 'Party Polarization and Legislative Gridlock', *Political Research Quarterly* 54: 125–141.

Kagan, R. (2010) 'Obama's Five Foreign Policy Victories', *Washington Post*, June 29.

Kagan, R. (2012) *The World America Made*, New York: Knopf.

Kaiser, R. (2009) *So Much Damn Money: The Triumph of Lobbying and the Corrosion of American Government*, New York: Vintage.

Kaiser, R. (2013) *Act of Congress: How America's Essential Institution Works and Doesn't Work*, New York: Knopf.

Kaiser Family Foundation (2010) *A Primer on Health Care Costs.* Washington, DC: KFF.

Kaiser Family Foundation (2012) *Establishing Health Insurance Exchanges: An Overview of State Efforts.* Washington, DC: Kaiser Family Foundation.

Kamen, A. (2012) 'Mitt Romney's aide's "Etch a Sketch Moment"', *Washington Post*, March 21, www.washingtonpost.com/blogs/in-the-loop/post/mitt-romney- aides-etcha-sketch-moment/2012/03/21/gIQAKoRuRS_blog.html.

Kammen, M. (1986) *A Machine That Would Go of Itself: The Constitution in American Culture*, New York: Knopf.

Katz, M. B. (2012) *Why Don't American Cities Burn?*, Philadelphia: University of Pennsylvania Press.

Katz, M. B., M. J. Stern and J. J. Fader (2005) 'The New African American Inequality', *Journal of American History*, 92: 75–108.

Katznelson, I. (2007) *When Affirmative Action Was White*, New York: Basic Books.

Keck, T. M. (2004) *The Most Activist Supreme Court in History: The Road to Modern Judicial Conservatism*, Chicago: University of Chicago Press.

Keeter, S., J. Horowitz and A.Tyson (2008) 'Young Voters in the 2008 Election', *Pew Research Center*, November 13.

Kernell, S. (2006) *Going Public: New Strategies of Presidential Leadership*, Washington, DC: CQ Press.

Kessler, G. (2012) 'When Did McConnell Say He Wanted to Make Obama a "One-Term President"?', *WashingtonPost.com*, September 25.

Kiel, P. (2009) 'Show Me the TARP Money', *ProPublia*, February 9.

Kimball, D. C., F. R. Baumgartner, J. M. Berry, M. Hojnacki, B. L. Leech and B. Summary (2012) 'Who Cares about the Lobbying Agenda?', *Interest Groups & Advocacy*, 1(1): 5–25.

Kincaid, J. (1990) 'From Cooperative to Coercive Federalism', *Annals of the American Academy of Political and Social Science*, 509: 139–152.

King, D. (2007) *Separate and Unequal: African Americans and the US Federal Government*, New York: Oxford University Press.

King, D. and R. Lieberman (2009) 'Ironies of the American State', *World Politics*, 61: 547–588.

King, D. and R. Lieberman (2011) 'The Civil Rights State: How the American State Develops Itself', paper presented at the annual meeting of the American Political Science Association, Seattle.

King, D. and R. Smith (2011) *Still a House Divided: Race and Politics in Obama's America*, Princeton, NJ: Princeton University Press.

Klarman, M. (2013) *From the Closet to the Altar: Courts, Backlash and the Struggle for Same Sex Marriage*, New York: Oxford University Press.

Koger, G. (2010) *Filibustering: A Political History of Obstructionism in the House and the Senate*, Chicago, IL: University of Chicago Press.

Kohut, A., J. Green, S. Keeter and R. Toth (2000) *The Diminishing Divide: Religion's Changing Role in American Politics*, Washington, DC: Brookings Institution.

Kollman, K. (1998) *Outside Lobbying*, Princeton, NJ: Princeton University Press.

Kraushaar, J. (2010) 'Democrats' Losses Could Grow in 2012', *National Journal*, November 10, www.nationaljournal.com/columns/against-the-grain/democrats-losses-could-grow-in-2012–20101110.

Krislov, S. (1967) *The Negro in Federal Employment*, Minneapolis: University of Minnesota.

Kronfield, J. J., W. E. Parmet and M. A. Zezza (2012) *Debates on American Health Care*, Thousand Oaks, CA: Sage.

Krugman, P. (2010) 'Block Those Metaphors', *New York Times*, December 12.

Krugman, P. (2012) *End This Depression Now*, New York: W. W. Norton.

Krutz, G. (2001) *Hitching a Ride: Omnibus Legislating in Congress*, Washington, DC: Brookings Institution.

Kupchan, C. A. (2012) *The West, the Rising Rest, and the Coming Global Turn*, New York: Oxford University Press.

Kurz, K. (2012) 'A Significant Decline in Divided Government', *The Thicket at State Legislatures*, November 7.

LaFountain, M. and K. Shea (2011) 'Is Our Constitutional System Broken?' *Connecticut Law Review* 43(4).

Landler, M. (2012) 'Budget Author, a Romney Ally, Turns Into a Campaign Focus', *New York Times*, April 4.

Langbein, L. I. (1986) 'Money and Access: Some Empirical Evidence', *Journal of Politics*, 48(4): 1052–1062.

LaPira, T. and H. F. T. Thomas (2012) *Revolving Doors: Lobbyists' Government Experience, Expertise, and Access in Political Context*, SSRN eLibrary.

Layman, G. (2001) *The Great Divide: Religion and Cultural Conflict in American Party Politics*, New York: Columbia University Press.

Layman, G. and T. Carsey (2002) 'Party Polarization and "Conflict Extension" in the American Electorate', *American Journal of Political Science*, 46: 786–802.

Layman, G., T. Carsey and J. Horowitz (2006) 'Party Polarization in American Politics: Characteristics, Causes, and Consequences', *Annual Review of Political Science*, 9: 83–110.

Layman, G., T. Carsey, J. Green, R. Herrera and R. Cooperman (2010) 'Activists and Conflict Extension in American Party Politics', *American Political Science Review*, 104(2): 324–346.

Lazear, E. P. (2012) 'The Worst Economic Recovery in History', *Wall Street Journal*, April 2.

Leibovich, M. (2010) 'Message Maven Finds Fingers Pointing At Him', *New York Times*, March 6.

Leonhardt, D. (2009) 'Jobless Rate Hits 10.2%, with More Underemployed', *New York Times*, November 7.

Lessig, L. (2011) *Republic, Lost: How Money Corrupts Congress – and a Plan to Stop It*, New York: Twelve.

Leuchtenburg, W. E. (1963) *Franklin D. Roosevelt and the New Deal, 1932–1940*, New York: Harper & Row.

Levinson, S. (1988) *Constitutional Faith*, Princeton, NJ: Princeton University Press.

Levinson, S. (2006) *Our UnDemocratic Constitution*, New York: Oxford University Press.

Levinson, S. (2012) *Framed: America's Fifty One Constitutions and the Crisis of Governance*, New York: Oxford University Press.

Lindsay, J. M. (2011a) 'Foreign Policy and the 2012 Elections', June 10, www.cfr.org/.

Lindsay, J. M. (2011b) 'Michelle Bachmann's Foreign Policy', Global Public Square blogs, July 15.

Litwak, R. S. (2012) *Outlier States: American Strategies to Change, Contain, or Engage Regimes*, Washington, DC: Woodrow Wilson Center and Johns Hopkins University Press.

Lizza, R. (2011) 'The Consequentialist', *New Yorker*, May 2.

Lodge, M. and C. Hood (2012) 'Into an Age of Multiple Austerities? Public Management and Public Service Bargains across OECD Countries', *Governance*, 25: 19–101.

Lohr, S. (2012) 'The Obama Campaign's Technology Is a Force Multiplier', *New York Times*, November 8, http://bits.blogs.nytimes.com/2012/11/08/the-obama-campaigns-technology-the-force-multiplier/.

Lorber, J. (2012) '"Binders Full of Women" Illustrates Memes' Power', *Roll Call*, October 18, www.rollcall.com/issues/58_30/Binders-Full-of-Women-Illustrates-Memes-Power-218295–1.html.

Lowi, T. J. (1964) 'Review: American Business, Public Policy, Case-Studies, and Political Theory', *World Politics*, 16(4): 677–715.

Lowi, T. J. (1979) *The End of Liberalism: The Second Republic of the United States*, New York: W. W. Norton.

LSE (London School of Economics) (2011) 'The United States After Unipolarity', London School of Economics IDEAS: Special Report, December.

Maddox, B. (2011) 'The \$14.3 Trillion Question: Is America Broken?', *The Times*, April 22.

Madrigal, A. C. (2012) 'When the Nerds Go Marching In', *The Atlantic*, November 16, www.theatlantic.com/technology/archive/2012/11/when-the-nerds-go-marching-in/265325/.

Mandelbaum, M. (2010) *The Frugal Superpower: America's Global Leadership in a Cash-Strapped Era*, New York: PublicAffairs.

Mann, J. (2012) *The Obamians: The Struggle Inside the White House to Redefine American Power*, London: Viking.

Mann, T. (2010) 'Congress', in G. Peele, C. J. Bailey, B. Cain and B. G. Peters (eds), *Developments in American Politics 6*, Basingstoke: Palgrave Macmillan.

Mann, T. and N. Ornstein (2006) *The Broken Branch: How Congress is Failing America and How to Get it Back on Track*, New York: Oxford University Press.

Mann, T. and N. Ornstein (2012) *It's Even Worse Than It Looks: How the American Constitutional System Collided With the New Politics of Extremism*, New York: Basic Books.

Manna, P. (2011) *Collision Course: Federal Education Policy meets State and Local Realities*, Washington, DC: CQ Press.

Maraniss, D. (2012) *Barack Obama: The Story*, New York: Simon & Schuster.

Marcus, R. (2012) 'Obama's unsettling attack on the Supreme Court', *Washington Post*, April 2, www.washingtonpost.com/blogs/post-partisan/post/obamas-unsettling-attack-on-the-supreme-court/2012/04/02/gIQA4BXYrS_blog.html.

Markoff, J. (2012) 'Social Networks Can Affect Voter Turnout, Study Says', *New York Times*, September 12, www.nytimes.com/2012/09/13/us/politics/social-networks-affect-voter-turnout-study-finds.html.

Marmor, T. R. (2007) *Fads, Fallacies and Foolishness in Medical Care Management and Policy*, Hackensack, NJ: World Scientific.

Martin, A. K. and K. M. Quinn (2002) 'Dynamic Ideal Point Estimation via Markov Chain Monte Carlo for the US Supreme Court, 1953–1999', *Political Analysis*, 10: 134–153.

Massey, D. S. (2007) *Categorically Unequal*, New York: Russell Sage Foundation.

Massey, D. S. and N. A. Denton (1993) *American Apartheid: Segregation and the Making of the Underclass*, Cambridge, MA: Harvard University Press.

Mayer, J. (2012) 'The Voter-Fraud Myth: The Man Who Stoked Fears about Imposters at the Polls', *New Yorker*, October 29.

Mayer, K. R. (2001) *With the Stroke of a Pen: Executive Orders and Presidential Power*, Princeton, NJ: Princeton University Press.

Mayhew, D. (2009) 'Is Congress "The Broken Branch"?', *Boston Law Review*, 89: 357–369.

McCann, J. A. (1995) 'Nomination Politics and Ideological Polarization: Assessing the Attitudinal Effects of Campaign Involvement', *Journal of Politics*, 57: 101–120.

McCarty, N., K. Poole and H. Rosenthal (1997) *Income Redistribution and the Realignment of American Politics*, Washington, DC: American Enterprise Institute Press.

McCarty, N., K. Poole and H. Rosenthal (2006) *Polarized America: The Dance of Ideology and Unequal Riches*, Cambridge, MA: MIT Press.

McCarty, N., K. Poole and H. Rosenthal (2009) 'Does Gerrymandering Cause Polarization?', *American Journal of Political Science*, 53(3): 666–680.

McConnell, G. (1966) *Private Power and American Democracy*, New York: Knopf.

McDonald, M. and B. Grofman (1999) 'Redistricting and the Polarization of the House of Representatives', paper presented at the annual meeting of the Midwest Political Science Association, Chicago.

McGrane, V. (2012) 'Comments Flood in on Volcker Rule', *Wall Street Journal*, February 15.

McKay, A. and S. Yackee (2007) 'Interest Group Competition on Federal Agency Rules', *American Politics Research*, 35(3): 336–357.

McLuhan, M. (1964) *Understanding Media: The Extensions of Man*, New York: McGraw Hill.

McMahon, K. J. (2007) 'Presidents, Political Regimes, and Contentious Supreme Court Nominations: A Historical Institutional Model', *Law and Social Inquiry*, 32(4): 919–954.

Mead, W. R. (2011) 'The Tea Party and American Foreign Policy', *Foreign Affairs*, 90(2): 28–44.

Mearsheimer, J. (2011) 'Imperial by Design', *The National Interest*, 111: 16–34.

Meltzer, C. C. (2011) 'Summary of the Affordable Care Act', *American Journal of Neuroradiology*, 32(7): 1165–1166.

Mettler, S. (2005) *From Soldiers to Citizens*, New York: Oxford University Press.

Michta, A. A. (2011) 'NATO's Last Chance', *The American Interest*, May–June: 56–60.

Milyo, J., D. Primo and T. Groseclose (2000) 'Corporate PAC Campaign Contributions in Perspective', *Business and Politics*, 2(1): 75–88.

Moe, T. M. (1993) 'Presidents, Institutions and theory' in G. C. Edwards III, J. H. Hessel and B. A. Rockman (eds), *Researching the Presidency*, Pittsburgh, University of Pittsburgh Press.

Montgomery, L. (2012) 'Obama Budget: National Debt Will be $1 Trillion Higher in a Decade than Forecast', *Washington Post*, February 13.

Morales, L. (2012) 'Americans See Best Job Climate Since the Financial Crisis', *Gallup*, November 28, www.gallup.com.

Moran, M. and N. Roubini (2012) *The Reckoning: Debt, Democracy, and the Future of American Power*, New York: Palgrave Macmillan.

Mui, Y. Q. (2012) 'Americans saw Wealth Plummet 40 percent from 2007 to 2010, Federal Reserve says', *Washington Post*, June 11.

Murakawa, N. (2007) 'The Origin of the Carceral Crisis: Racial Order as "Law and Order" in Postwar American Racial Politics', in Lowndes, J., J. Novkov and D. Warren (eds), *Race and American Political Development*, New York: Routledge.

Murray, C. (1984) *Losing Ground*, New York: Basic Books.

Nasr, V. (2013) *The Dispensable Nation: American Foreign Policy in Retreat*, New York: Doubleday.

Nathan, R. (2008) 'Updating Theories of Federalism', in T. J. Conlan and P. L. Posner (eds), *Intergovernmental Management in the 21st Century*, Washington, DC: Brookings Institution.

National Conference of State Legislatures (2009) 'Update on State Budget Gap: FY2009 and FY2010', *National Conference of State Legislatures*, February 20, www.ncsl.org.

National Research Council (2013) *U.S. Health in International Perspective: Shorter Lives, Poorer Health*, Washington, DC: National Academy of Sciences.

Neuman, T., J. Cubanski, D. Waldo, F. Eppig and J. Mays (2011) 'Raising the Age of Medicare Eligibility: A Fresh Look Following Implementation of Health Reform', The Henry J. Kaiser Family Foundation, July, www.kff.org/medicare/upload/8169.pdf.

Neustadt, R. (1960) *Presidential Power: The Politics of Leadership*, New York: Wiley.

Neustadt, R. (1991) *Presidential Power and the Modern Presidents: The Politics of Leadership from Roosevelt to Reagan*, New York: Free Press.

New York Times (2008) 'National Exit Polls Table', *nytimes.com*, http://elections.nytimes.com/2008/results/president/national-exit-polls.html.

Niblett, R. (ed.) (2010) *America and a Changed World: A Question of Leadership*, London: Wiley/Blackwell.

Nicholson, S. (2012) 'LinkedIn Industry Trends: Winners and Losers During the Great Recession', March 8, http://blog.linkedin.com/2012/03/08/economic-report/.

Nicholson-Crotty, S. (2012) 'Leaving Money on the Table: Learning From Recent Refusals of Federal Grants in the American States', *Publius*, 42:3: 449–466.

Nivola, P. and D. Brady (2006–08) *Red and Blue Nation? Consequences and Correction of America's Polarized Politics*, Washington, DC: Brookings Institution.

Noah, T. (2012) 'How President Romney Would Crush the Recovery', *The New Republic*, September 14.

Noble, Charles (1997) *Welfare as We Knew It: A Political History of the American Welfare State*, New York: Oxford University Press.

Nunn, L. and J. Evans (2006) 'Geographic Polarization in Social Attitudes', paper presented at annual meeting of the American Sociological Association, Montreal, Quebec.

O'Brien, D. M. (2011) *Storm Center: The Supreme Court in American Politics*, New York: W.W. Norton.

O'Hanlon, M. and H. Sherjan (2010) *Toughing It Out in Afghanistan*, Washington, DC: Brookings Institution.

Obama, B. (2011) 'Remarks in Las Vegas, Nevada', online by Peters and Woolley, The American Presidency Project, October 24, www.presidency. ucsb.edu/ws/?pid=96941.

Obama, B. (2013) 'Remarks on Gun Violence', online by Peters and Woolley, The American Presidency Project, January 16, www.presidency.ucsb. edu/ws/?pid=103152.

Oleszek, W. (2004) *Congressional Procedures and the Policy Process*, Washington, DC: CQ Press.

Olson, M. (1965) *The Logic of Collective Action: Public Goods and the Theory of Groups*, Cambridge, MA: Harvard University Press.

Orszag, P. R. and E. J. Emanuel (2010) 'Health Care Reform and Cost Control', *New England Journal of Medicine*, 363: 601–603.

Pacelle, R. L., B. W. Curry and B. W. Marshall (2011) *Decision Making by the Modern Supreme Court*, Cambridge: University of Cambridge Press.

Page, B. and L. Jacobs (2010) 'Understanding Public Opinion On Deficits and Social Security', Roosevelt Institute Working Paper No. 2, June 27.

Pager, D. (2007) *Marked: Race, Crime and Finding Work in an Era of Mass Incarceration*, Chicago: University of Chicago Press.

Pager, D. and H. Shepherd (2008) 'The Sociology of Discrimination: Racial Discrimination in Employment, Housing, Credit and Consumer Markets', *Annual Review of Sociology*, 34: 181–209.

Parmar, I. (2011) 'American Power and Identities in the Age of Obama', *International Politics*, 48: 153–63.

Parsi, T. (2012) *A Single Roll of the Dice: Obama's Diplomacy with Iran*, New Haven, CT: Yale University Press.

Passell J. and D'Vera Cohn (2008) *US Populations Projections 2005–2050*, Pew Research Hispanic Center, February 11, www.pewhispanic.org/ 2008/02/11/us-population-projections-2005–2050/.

Patashnik, E. M. (2008) *Reforms at Risk: What Happens After Major Policy Changes Are Enacted*, Princeton, NJ: Princeton University Press.

Patterson, J. T. (1981) *The New Deal and the States: Federalism in Transition*, San Francisco: Greenwood Press.

Patterson, J. T. (2010) *Freedom Is Not Enough*, New York: Basic Books.

Patterson, K. D. and M. M. Singer (2006) 'Targeting Success: The Enduring Power of the NRA', in A. J. Cigler and B. A. Loomis (eds), *Interest Group Politics*, 7th edn, Washington, DC: CQ Press.

Pattillo-McCoy, M. (1999) *Black Picket Fences: Privilege and Peril among the Black Middle Classes*, Chicago: University of Chicago Press.

Pell, M. B. (2010) 'K Street cashes in on bill', *Politico*, May 21.

Perez, M. (2008) *Voter Purges*, New York: Brennan Center for Justice NYU School of Law, http://brennan.3cdn.net/5de1bb5cbe2c40cb0c_s0m6bqskv. pdf.

Peters, J. W. (2013) 'Waiting Times at Ballot Boxes Draw Scrutiny', *New York Times*, February 4, www.nytimes.com/2013/02/05/us/politics/waiting-times-to-vote-at-polls-draw-scrutiny.html.

Peterson, P. E. and M. C. Rom (1990) *Welfare Magnets: A New Case for a National Standard*, Washington, DC: Brookings Institution.

Peterson, P. E., B. Rabe and K. Wong, (1986) *Making Federalism Work*, Washington, DC: Brookings Institution.

Pethokoukis, J. (2012a) 'The 5 Economic Stats that Will Decide the Election . . . are all Pointing Down for Obama', AEIdeas (American Enterprise Institute), July 20, www.aei-ideas.org/2012/07/the-5–economic-stats-that-will-determine-the-next-president-are-all-pointing-down-for-obama/.

Pethokoukis, J. (2012b) 'Economic Forecasting Model Predicts Obama will Lose in Near-landslide', AEIdeas (American Enterprise Institute), August 2, www.aei-ideas.org/2012/08/economic-forecasting-model-predicts-obama-will-lose-in-near-landslide/.

Pethokoukis, J. (2012c) 'Welcome to the Recovery: 2012 may be the Worst Non-recession, Non-depression Year in the History of the United States', American Enterprise Institute, September 27, www.aei-ideas.org.

Pew Research Center (2011) 'Obama Job Approval Rating Improves, GOP Contest Remains Fluid', November 17, www.Pewresearch.org.

Pew Research Center (2012a) 'Trends in American Values 1987–2012', www.people-press.org/files/legacy-pdf/06–04–12 Values Release.pdf.

Pew Research Center (2012b) 'Trends in Party Identification 1939–2012', www.people-press.org/2012/06/01/trend-in-party-identification-1939–2012/.

Pew Research Center's Project for Excellence in Journalism (2008) 'The Color of News', October 29, www.journalism.org/node/13437.

Pew Research Center's Project for Excellence in Journalism (2012) 'Winning the Media Campaign 2012: Coverage of the Candidates by Media Sector and Cable Outlet', November 2, www.journalism.org/analysis_report/coverage_candidates_media_sector_and_cable_outlet.

Pew Research Center for People and the Press (2008) 'Internet Now Major Source of Campaign News', October 31, http://Pewresearch.org/pubs/1017/internet-now-major-source-of-campaign-news.

Pew Research Center for the People and the Press (2010a) 'Pessimistic Public Doubts Effectiveness of Stimulus, TARP', April 28, www.Pewresearch.org.

Pew Research Center for the People and the Press (2010b) 'Americans Spending More Time Following the News', September 10, www.people-press.org/2010/09/12/americans-spending-more-time-following-the-news/.

Pew Research Center for the People and the Press (2011) 'Internet Gains on Television as Public's Main News Source', January 4, www.people-press.org/2011/01/04/internet-gains-on-television-as-publics-main-news-source/.

Pew Research Center for People and the Press (2012) 'Low Marks for the 2012 Election', November 15, www.people-press.org/2012/11/15/section-4-news-sources-election-night-and-views-of-press-coverage/.

Pew Research Center on the States (2012) 'The Widening Gap Update', June 19, www.Pewstates.org.

Pfiffner, J. (2008) *Power Play: The Bush Presidency and the Constitution*, Washington, DC : Brookings Institution.

Pfiffner, J. (2011) 'Decision Making in the Obama White House', *Presidential Studies Quarterly*, 41: 244–262.

Pickerill, M. (2009) 'Something Old, Something New, Something Borrowed, Something Blue', *Santa Clara Law Review*, 49: 1063–1101.

Pierson, Paul (1994) *Dismantling the Welfare State? Reagan, Thatcher, and the Politics of Retrenchment*. New York, NY: Cambridge University Press.

Pitts, S. (2011) 'Black Workers and the Public Sector', Center for Labor Research and Education, University of California, Berkeley, April 4.

Pletka, D. (2013) 'Think Again: The Republican Party', *Foreign Policy*, January/February: 42–7.

Policy Council (2007) *The Changing of the Guard: 2007 State of the Industry for Lobbying and Advocacy*, Washington, DC.

Pomper, G. M. (2003) 'Parliamentary Government in the United States: A New Regime for a New Century?', in J. Green and R. Farmer (eds), *The State of the Parties*, Lanham, MD: Rowman & Littlefield.

Poole, K. and H. Rosenthal (2012) *The Polarization of the Congressional Parties*; data and graphs available at http://polarizedamerica.com/political_polarization.asp.

Poole, K. and H. Rosenthal (2013) 'Party Unity Scores', http://voteview.com/Party_Unity.html.

Posner, E. A. and A. Vermeule (2010) *The Executive Unbound*, New York: Oxford University Press.

Posner, P. L. (1998) *The Politics of Federal Mandates: Whither Federalism?*, Washington, DC: Georgetown University Press.

Posner, P. L. (2010) 'The Politics of Vertical Diffusion: States and Climate Change', in B. G. Rabe (ed.), *Greenhouse Governance: Addressing Climate Change in America*, Washington, DC: Brookings Institution.

President's Advisory Panel on Federal Taxation (2005) *Simple, Fair, and Pro-Growth: Proposals to Fix America's Tax System*.

Price, T. (2012) 'Social Media and Politics', *CQ Researcher*, 22(36): 865–888.

Prior, M. (2007) *Post-Broadcast Democracy: How Media Choice Increases Inequality in Political Involvement and Polarized Elections*, New York: Cambridge University Press.

Quadagno, J. (1994) *The Color of Welfare: How Racism Undermined the War on Poverty*, New York: Oxford University Press.

Quinn, A. (2011a) 'Hard Power in Hard Times: Relative Military Power in an Era of Budgetary Constraint', London School of Economics IDEAS: Special Report: 'The United States After Unipolarity', December.

Quinn, A. (2011b) 'The Art of Declining Politely: Obama's Prudent Presidency and the Waning of American Power', *International Affairs*, 87: 803–824.

Rampell, C. (2009) '"Great Recession": A Brief Etymology', *New York Times*, March 11.

Ranney, A. (1954) *The Doctrine of Responsible Party Government: Its Origins and Present State*, Urbana, IL: University of Illinois Press.

Rauch, J. (2007) 'Social Studies: On Foreign Policy, Shades of Agreement', *National Journal*, February 16.

Reeves, J. (2010) 'John Roberts: Scene at State of the Union was "Very Troubling"', *Huffington Post*, March 9, www.huffingtonpost.com/2010/03/09/john- roberts-scene-at-oba_n_492444.html.

Reinhart, C. M. and K. Rogoff (2009) *This Time Is Different: Eight Centuries of Financial Folly*, Princeton, NJ: Princeton University Press.

Remnick, D. (2010) *The Bridge: The Life and Rise of Barack Obama*, New York: Knopf.

Renshon, S. A. and D. W. Larson (eds) (2003) *Good Judgement in Foreign Policy: Theory and Application*, Lanham, MD: Rowman & Littlefield.

Riley, C. (2012) 'Romney Campaign spent $18.50 per Vote', *CNN Money*, April 25, http://money.cnn.com/2012/04/25/news/economy/Romney-campiagn-spending-vote/index.htm.

Rivlin, A. (1992) *Reviving the American Dream: The Economy, the States and the Federal Government*, Washington, DC: Brookings Institution.

Robinson, E. (2010) 'For President Obama, A Progressive Blitz Was Not An Option', *Washington Post*, October 26.

Rocca, M. S. and S. B. Gordon (2013) 'Earmarks as a Means *and* an End: The Link between Earmarks and Campaign Contributions in the US House of Representatives', *Journal of Politics*, 75(1): 241–257.

Rodgers III, W. M. (2012) 'The Great Recession's Impact on African American Public Sector Employment', National Poverty Center Working Paper Series, January.

Rohde, D. (2006) 'Committees and Policy Formation', in P. Quirk and S. Binder (eds), *The Legislative Branch*, New York: Oxford University Press.

Roper, J. (2010) 'The Presidency' in G. Peele, C. J. Bailey, B. Cain and B. G. Peters (eds), *Developments in American Politics* 6, Basingstoke: Palgrave Macmillan.

Roscoe, D. and S. Jenkins (2010) 'State and Local Parties in the 21st Century', paper presented at the 2010 Annual Meeting of the American Political Science Association, Washington, DC.

Rosenberg, G. N. (2008) *The Hollow Hope: Can Courts Bring About Social Change?*, Chicago: University of Chicago Press.

Rosenberg, P. (2009) 'Two Party Fail', *Open Left*, August 16, www.openleft.com/diary/14648/twoparty-fail.

Rudalevige, A. (2005) *The New Imperial Presidency: Renewing Presidential Power after Watergate*, Ann Arbor, MI: University of Michigan Press.

Rugh, J. S. and D. S. Massey (2010) 'Racial Segregation and the American Foreclosure Crisis', *American Sociological Review*, 75.

Sachs, J. (2009) 'The Failing US Government – The Crisis of Public Management', *Scientific American*, October 13.

Salisbury, R. H. (1984) 'Interest Representation: The Dominance of Institutions', *The American Political Science Review*, 78(1): 64–76.

Salisbury, R. H. and A. King (1990) *The Paradox of Interest Groups in Washington, DC: More Groups and Less Clout*, Washington, DC: American Enterprise Institute.

Savage, C. (2012) 'Shift on Executive Power Lets Obama Bypass Rivals', *New York Times*, April 22.

Schattschneider, E. E. (1960) *The Semi-Sovereign People: A Realist's View of Democracy in America*, New York: Holt, Rinehart & Winston.

Schatz, J. (2010) 'Looking for Room to Maneuver', *CQ Weekly*, April 19.

Scheberle, D. (2004) *Federalism and Environmental Policy: Trust and the Politics of Implementation*, Washington, DC: Georgetown University Press.

Scheiber, N. (2012) *The Escape Artists: How Obama's Team Fumbled the Recovery*, New York: Simon & Schuster.

Schlesinger, A. M. Jr. (2004) *The Imperial Presidency*, Boston: Houghton Mifflin.

Schlozman, K. L. and J. T. Tierney (1986) *Organized Interests and American Democracy*, New York: Harper & Row.

Schlozman, K. L., S. Verba and H. E. Brady (2012) *The Unheavenly Chorus: Unequal Political Voice and the Broken Promise of American Democracy*, Princeton, NJ: Princeton University Press.

Schoen, C., S. R. Collins, J. L. Kriss and M. M. Doty (2008) 'How Many are Insured: Trends Among US Adults 2003 and 2007', *Health Affairs*, 27: 289–307.

Schoenfeld, H. (2012) 'The Long term Consequences of Segregated Prisons in the American South', paper presented to the annual meeting of the Social Science History Meeting, Vancouver, November 1–4.

Schuman, D. (2010) 'Keeping Congress Competent: Staff Pay, Turnover, and What it Means for Democracy', The Sunlight Foundation Blog, December 21.

Segal, J. A. and H. J. Spaeth (2002) *The Supreme Court and the Attitudinal Model Revisited*, Cambridge: Cambridge University Press.

Shaefer, H. L. and K. Edin (2012) 'Extreme Poverty in the United States, 1996 to 2011' *Policy Brief no. 28, National Poverty Center*, University of Michigan, Ann Arbor.

Shanker, T. (2012) 'US Forecast as No. 2 Economy but Energy Independent', *New York Times*, December 10.

Sharp, D. (2012) 'In Farewell Speech, Snowe Pleads for Less Polarization', *The Boston Globe*, December 14.

Shepard, S. B. (2013) *Deadlines and Disruption: My Turbulent Path from Print to Digital*, New York: McGraw-Hill.

Sherman, A. (2011) 'Poverty and Financial Distress Would Have Been Substantially Worse in 2010 Without Government Action, New Census Data Show', Center for Budget and Policy Priorities, November 7, www.cbpp.org/cms/index.cfm?fa=view&id=3610.

Sides J. and L. Vavrek (forthcoming) *The Gamble: Choice and Chance in the 2012 Presidential Election*.

Silver, N. (2012) 'As Swing Districts Dwindle, Can a Divided House Stand?', *Five Thirty Eight Blog, New York Times,* December 27, http://five thirtyeight.blogs.nytimes.com/2012/12/27/as-swing-districts-dwindle-can-a-divided-house-stand/.

Silverleib, A. (2010) 'Gloves come off after Obama rips Supreme Court Ruling', CNN.com, January 28, www.cnn.com/2010/POLITICS/01/28/alito.obama.sotu/index.html?hpt=Sbin.

Simon, R. (2013) *Reckoning: Campaign 2012 and the Battle for the Soul of America*, Hermosa Beach, CA: Sumner Books.

Sinclair, B. (2002) 'The Dream Fulfilled? Party Development in Congress 1950–2000' in J. Green and P. Herrnson (eds), *Responsible Partisanship*, Lawrence: University of Kansas Press.

Sinclair, B. (2008) 'Orchestrators of Unorthodox Lawmaking: Pelosi and McConnell in the 100th Congress', *The Forum*, 6(3).

Sinclair, B. (2009) 'Partisan Polarization, Rules and Legislative Productivity', delivered at the Annual Meeting of the American Political Science Association, Toronto, September 3–6.

Sinclair, B. (2011a) *Unorthodox Lawmaking: New Legislative Processes in the US Congress*, Washington, DC: CQ Press.

Sinclair, B. (2011b) 'Doing Big Things: Obama and the 111th Congress', in B. A. Rockman, A. Rudalevige and C. Campbell (eds), *The Obama Presidency: Appraisals and Prospects*, Washington, DC: CQ Press.

Singh, R. (2012) *Barack Obama's Post-American Foreign Policy*, London: Bloomsbury Academic.

Sitkoff, H. and E. Foner (1992) *The Struggle for Black Equality, 1954–1992*, New York: Hill & Wang.

Skowronek, S. (1993) *The Politics Presidents Make: Leadership from John Adams to George Bush*, Cambridge, MA: The Belknap Press of Harvard University Press.

Slack, D. (2012) 'It's the Ground Game, Stupid . . .', *Politico*, November 10, www.politico.com/politico44/2012/11/its-the-ground-game-stupid-149204. html.

Slaughter, A. (2012) 'Grading America's Foreign Policy', *Foreign Policy*, January 23.

Smith, A. (2009) 'The Internet's Role in Campaign 2008', Pew Internet, April 15, www.Pewinternet.org/Reports/2009/6—The-Internets-Role-in-Campaign-2008.aspx.

Smith, M. A. (2000) *American Business and Political Power: Public Opinion, Elections, and Democracy*, Chicago: University of Chicago Press.

Smith, R. A. (1995) 'Interest Group Influence in the U. S. Congress', *Legislative Studies Quarterly*, 20(1): 89–139.

Social Security Administration (2011) 'Social Security Bulletin, Annual Statistical Supplement 2011', at www.ssa.gov/policy/docs/statcomps/supplement/2011/index.html.

Sonmez, F. and D. A. Fahrenthold (2012) 'Groups vow to push 'right to work' in other states', *Washington Post*, December 13.

Soss, J., R. C. Fording and S. F. Schram (2011) *Disciplining the Poor: Neoliberal Paternalism and the Persistent Power of Race*, Chicago: University of Chicago Press.

Spaeth, H. (2011) *The Supreme Court Database*. http://scdb.wustl.edu/index. php.

Spero, R. (1980) *The Duping of the American Voter: Dishonesty and Deception in Presidential Television Advertising*, New York: Lippincott & Crowell.

Standard & Poor's (2011) 'United States of America Long-Term Rating Lowered To "AA+" Due To Political Risks, Rising Debt Burden; Outlook Negative', www.standardandpoors.com/ratings/articles/en/us/?assetID=1245 316529563.

Stanley, M. (2013) Private conversation, January 15 (Marcus Stanley is head of Americans for Financial Reform).

Stein, S. and P. Blumenthal (2012) 'Obama 2012 Campaign Spending Buried Romney on Airwaves and with Staff', *Huffington Post*, December 12, www.huffingtonpost.com/2012/12/12/obama-2012–campaign-spending_n_ 2287978.html.

Steinbauer, J. (2011) 'Some Democrats Are Baulking at Obama's Jobs Bill', *New York Times*, September 27.

Stewart, J. B. (2011) 'Volcker Rule, Once Simple, Now Boggles', *New York Times*, October 21.

Stiglitz, J. E. (2010) *Freefall*, Harmondsworth: Penguin Books.

Stiglitz, J. E. (2013) 'Inequality Is Holding Back the Recovery', *New York Times*, January 19, http://opinionator.blogs.nytimes.com/2013/01/19/ inequality-is-holding-back-the-recovery/.

Stoker, R. P. (1991) *Reluctant Partners: Implementing Federal Policy*, Pittsburgh: University of Pittsburgh Press.

Sundquist, J. (1968) *Politics and Policy:The Eisenhower, Kennedy and Johnson Years*, Washington, DC: Brookings Institution.

Tanner, J. (2008) 'Gerrymandering', *Congressional Record* 154:12 (July 29) p. 16909.

Taylor, J. B. (2009) *Getting Off Track: How Government Actions and Interventions Caused, Prolonged, and Worsened the Financial Crisis*, Palo Alto: Hoover Institution Press.

Taylor, P. and M. Lopez (2013) 'Six Take-Aways from the Census Bureau's Voting Report', Pew Research Center, May 8, www.pewresearch.org/fact-tank/2013/05/08/six-take-aways-from-the-census-bureau.

Tesler, M. (2012) 'The Spillover of Racialization into Health Care: How President Obama Polarized Public Opinion by Racial Attitudes and Race', *American Journal Political Science*, 56: 690–704.

Tesler, M. (2013) 'The Return of Old-Fashioned Racism in White Americans' Partisan Preferences in the Early Obama Era', *Journal of Politics*, 75(1): 110–123.

The Associated Press (2012) 'Study: Voter ID Law would Exclude up to 700,000 Young Minorities', CBS News, September 12, www.cbsnews.com/8301-250_162-57511312/study-voter-id-law-would-exclude-up-to-700000-young-minorities/.

The Economist (2012a) 'The China Syndrome', June 9.

The Economist (2012b) 'What Hillary Did Next', March 24.

The Economist (2012c) 'America's Economy: Points of Light', July 14.

The Economist (2013) 'Deficit-reduction Disorder', February 9.

Theriault, S. and D. Rohde (2011) 'The Gingrich Senators and Party Polarization in the US Senate', *Journal of Politics*, 73(4): 1011–1024.

Thompson, F. (2012) *Medicaid Politics: Federalism, Policy Durability and Health Reform*, Washington, DC: Georgetown University Press.

Thrush, G. (2012) 'The Not-So-Great Communicator', *Politico*.com, September 6.

Thurber, J. A. (1996) 'Twenty Years of Congressional Budget Reform', *The Public Manager*, Summer: 6–10.

Thurber, J. A. (1997) 'Congressional Budget Reform: Impact on the Appropriations Committees', *Public Budgeting and Finance*, December: 66–73.

Thurber, J. A. (2006) 'Lobbying, Ethics, and Procedural Reforms: The Do-Nothing Congress; 109th Congress Does Nothing About Reforming Itself', *Extensions: A Journal of the Carl Albert Congressional Research and Studies Centre*, Fall: 10–15.

Thurber, J. A. (ed.) (2009) *Rivals for Power: Presidential-Congressional Relations*, Lanham, MD: Rowman & Littlefield.

Thurber, J. A. (2012a) 'What is Wrong with Congress and What Should Be Done About It. Can Government Be Repaired?: Lessons from America', in I. Morgan and P. Davies (eds), *Broken Government: American Politics in the Obama Era*. Washington, DC: Brookings Institution and London: University of London/Institute for the Study of the Americas Press.

Thurber, J. A. (2012b) 'Agony, Angst, and the Failure of the Supercommittee', *Extensions, Summer 2012, Carl Albert Congressional Research and Studies Center*, University of Oklahoma.

Thurber, J. A. (2012c) 'The Dynamics and Dysfunction of the Congressional Budget Process: From Inception to Deadlock', in B. I. Oppenheimer and L. C. Dodd (eds), *Congress Reconsidered*, Washington, DC: CQ Press.

Toobin, J. (2012) *The Oath: The Obama White House and the Supreme Court*, New York: Doubleday Press.

Trattner, Walter I. (1999) *From Poor Law to Welfare State: A History of Social Welfare in America*, 6th edn. New York: Simon & Schuster.

Trende, S. (2012) *The Lost Majority*, New York: Palgrave Macmillan.

Tribe, L. H. (2012) 'Chief Justice Roberts Comes into his Own and Saves the Court while Preventing a Constitutional Debacle', SCOTUSblog, June 28, www.scotusblog.com/2012/06/chief-justice-roberts-comes-into-his-own-and-saves-the-court-while-preventing-a-constitutional-debacle/.

Trygstad, K., J. Miller and S. Toeplitz (2011) 'Tough Terrain for Senate Democrats', *Roll Call*, July 21, www.rollcall.com/issues/57_11/senate-2012-landscape-207507-1.html.

Tuck, S. (2009) 'The Reversal of Black Voting Rights after Reconstruction', in D. King, R. Lieberman, G. Ritter and L. Whitehead (eds), *Democratization in America: A Comparative-Historical Analysis*, Baltimore: Johns Hopkins University Press.

Tushnet, M. (2003) *The New Constitutional Order*, Princeton, NJ: Princeton University Press.

US Advisory Commission on Intergovernmental Relations (1984) *Regulatory Federalism: Policy, Process, Impact and Reform*, A-95, Washington, DC: US ACIR.

US Advisory Commission on Intergovernmental Relations (1994) *Federally Induced Costs Affecting State and Local Governments*, M-193, Washington DC: US ACIR.

US Census Bureau (2012a) 'US Trade in Goods and Services: Balance of Payments (BOP) Basis', www.census.gov.

US Census Bureau (2012b) '2012 National Population Projections', www.census.gov.population/projections/data/national/2012.html.

US Census Bureau (2013) 'The Diversifying Electorate-Voting Rates by Race and Hispanic Origin in 2012 (and Other Recent Elections)', May 2013, P20–568, www.census.gov/prod/2013pubs/p20–568.pdf.

US Congress, Congressional Budget Office (2012) *Estimated Impact of the American Recovery and Reinvestment Act on Employment and Economic Output from October 2011 Through December 2011*, February, Washington, DC: Congressional Budget Office.

US Department of Agriculture, Food and Nutrition Service (2012) www.fns.usda.gov/pd/snapmain.htm.

US Department of Agriculture, Food and Nutrition Service (2013) http://www.fns.usda.gov/pd/snapmain.htm, accessed 2013

US Department of Labor (1965) *The Negro Family: The Case for National Action*, Washington, DC: US Department of Labor, March.

US Department of Labor, (2011) *The African American Labor Force in the Recovery*, Washington, DC: US Department of Labor, February.

US Department of Labor (2012) *The African American Labor Force in the Recovery*, Washington. DC: Department of Labor, February 29.

US Department of Labor, Employment and Training Administration (2012) http://ows.doleta.gov/unemploy/.

US Department of Labor, Employment and Training Administration (2013) http://ows.doleta.gov/unemploy, accessed 2013

US Government Accountability Office (2012a) *The Federal Government's Long Term Fiscal Outlook*, Washington, DC: GAO-13–148SP.

US Government Accountability Office (2012b) *State and Local Governments' Fiscal Outlook*, Washington, DC: GAO-12–523SP.

usgovernmentspending.com (2013) www.usgovernmentspending.com, accessed 2013

US Social Security Administration (2011) 'Social Security Bulletin', *Annual Statistical Supplement 2011*, www.ssa.gov/policy/docs/statcomps/supplement/2011/index.html.

Vestal, C. (2013) 'Future of Health Law is Largely in State Hands', *Stateline*, January 28.

Walker, D. B. (1998) *The Rebirth of Federalism: Slouching toward Washington*. Chatham, NJ: Chatham House.

Wallsten, P., L. Montgomery and S. Wilson (2012) 'Obama's Evolution: Behind the Failed "Grand Bargain" on the Debt', *Washington Post*, March 18.

Ward, A. (2003) *Deciding to Leave: The Politics of Retirement from the United States Supreme Court*, Albany, NY: State University of New York Press.

Warner, B. (2012) 'Voter ID Law may Affect more Pennsylvanians than Previously Estimated', *Philly.com The Inquirer*, July 5, http://articles.philly.com/2012–07–05/news/32537732_1_voter-id-new-voter-id-cards.

Washington Post (2004) 'A Polarized Nation?', November 14 2004, B06 http://www.washingtonpost.com/wp-dyn/articles/A48325–2004Nov13.html [accessed 08/06/2013].

Weaver, V. M. and A. E. Lerman (2010) 'Political Consequences of the Carceral State', *American Political Science Review*, 104.

Weiser, W. R. and L. Norden (2011) *Voting Law Changes in 2012*, New York: Brennan Center for Justice NYU School of Law, http://brennan.3cdn.net/92635ddafbc09e8d88_i3m6bjdeh.pdf.

Weprin, A. (2013) 'CNN Touts Inauguration Ratings Win in Ad', January 25, www.mediabistro.com/tvnewser/cnn-touts-inauguration-ratings-win-in-ad_b164247.

Wessel, D. (2010) *In FED We Trust: Ben Bernanke's War on the Great Panic*, New York: Crown Publishing.

West, P. and S. Mehta (2011) 'Tea Party Activists remain Wary of Romney', *Los Angeles Times*, November 17, http://articles.latimes.com/2011/nov/17/nation/la-na-romney-tea-party-20111118.

Westen, D. (2011) 'Decision 2013', *New York Times*, November 16, http://campaignstops.blogs.nytimes.com/2011/11/16/decision-2013/.

Western, B. (2006) *Punishment and Inequality in America*, New York: Russell Sage Foundation.

Western, B. (2007) Testimony before the Joint Economic Committee, US Congress, October 4, www.wjh.harvard.edu/soc/faculty/western/pdfs/western_jec_testimony.pdf.

Western, B. and B. Pettit (2005) 'Black-White Wage Inequality, Employment Rates, and Incarceration', *American Journal of Sociology*, 111.

Whatley, M. A.,J. M. Webster, R. H. Smith and A. Rhodes (1999) 'The Effect of a Favor on Public and Private Compliance: How Internalized is the Norm of Reciprocity?', *Basic and Applied Social Psychology*, 21(3): 251–259.

Whiteman, D. (1995) *Communication in Congress*, Lawrence, KS: University Press of Kansas.

Whittington, K. E. (2007) *The Political Foundations of Judicial Supremacy: The Presidency, The Supreme Court, and Constitutional Leadership in US History*, Princeton, NJ: Princeton University Press.

Whoriskey, P. (2012) 'Job recovery is scant for Americans in prime working years', *Washington Post*, May 30.

Williams, J. (2012) 'Opinion: GOP's Voter ID Campaign aimed at Suppressing Constitutional Rights', *The Hill*, October 15, http://thehill.com/opinion/columnists/juan-williams/261945–opinion-gops-voter-id-campaign-aimed-at-suppressing-constitutional-rights.

Williams, T. (2011) 'As Public Sector Sheds Jobs, Blacks Are Hit Hardest', *New York Times*, November 28.

Williamson, V., T. Skocpol and J. Coggin (2011) 'The Tea Party and the Remaking of Republican Conservatism', *Perspectives on Politics*, 9(1): 25–43.

Wilson, J. Q. (1980) *The Politics of Regulation*, New York: Basic Books.

Wilson, W. J. (1987) *The Truly Disadvantaged: The Inner City, the Underclass and Public Policy*, Chicago, IL: University of Chicago Press.

Wilson, W. J. (1996) *When Work Disappears*, New York: Random.

Wilson, W. J. (2011) 'The Declining Significance of Race: Revisited & Revised', *Daedalus*, Spring.

Wolfensberger, D. (2012) 'Getting Back to Legislating: Reflections of a Congressional Working Group', *Bipartisan Policy Center*, http://bipartisan-policy.org/sites/default/files/BPC%20Congress%20Report-5.pdf.

Woodward, B. (2010) *Obama's Wars: The Inside Story*, London: Simon and Schuster.

Wuthow, R. (1989) *The Struggle for America's Soul: Evangelicals, Liberals, and Secularism*, Grand Rapids, MI: Eerdmans.

Yackee, S. W. and A. McKay (2007) 'Interest Group Competition on Federal Agency Rules', *American Politics Research*, 35(3): 336–357.

Yackee, J. W. and S. W. Yackee (2006) 'A Bias Towards Business? Assessing Interest Group Influence on the US Bureaucracy', *Journal of Politics*, 68(1): 128–139.

Yeomans, W. (2013) 'GOP v. Voting Rights Act', Reuters, January 10, http://blogs.reuters.com/great-debate/2013/01/10/gop-v-voting-rights-act/.

Zakaria, F. (2008) *The Post-American World*, London: Allen Lane.

Zakaria, F. (2011) 'Stop Searching for the Obama Doctrine', *Washington Post*, July 7.

Zaller, J. (1992) *The Nature and Origins of Mass Opinion*, New York: Cambridge University Press.

Zelizer, J. (2004) *On Capitol Hill: The Struggle to Reform Congress and Its Consequences*, New York: Cambridge University Press.

Zenko, M. (2013) *Reforming US Drone Strike Policies*, Council on Foreign Relations (Center for Preventive Action), Council Special Report No. 65, available via Council on Foreign Relations website: www.cfr.org/.

Zernike, K. (2010) 'In Power Push, Movement Sees Base in GOP', *New York Times*, January 14, www.nytimes.com/2010/01/15/us/politics/15party.html?ref=teapartymovement.

Ziliak, J. P. (2009) 'Introduction', in J. P. Ziliak (ed.), *Welfare Reform and Its Long-Term Consequences for America's Poor*, New York: Cambridge University Press.

Zimmerman, J. F. (2005) *Congressional Preemption: Regulatory Federalism*, Albany , NY: State University of New York Press.

Index